With the Compliments of

The Korea
Foundation

C.P.O.BOX 2147 Seoul, KOREA Tel:(02)753-3462. Fax:757-2049

Structural Adjustment in a Newly Industrialized Country

The Korean Experience

A World Bank Book

Structural Adjustment in a Newly Industrialized Country

The Korean Experience

Edited by
Vittorio Corbo
Sang-Mok Suh

PUBLISHED FOR THE WORLD BANK
The Johns Hopkins University Press
Baltimore and London

The Johns Hopkins University Press
Baltimore, Maryland 21211–2190, U.S.A.

The findings, interpretations, and conclusions expressed in this publication are
those of the authors and do not necessarily represent the views and policies of the
World Bank or its Board of Executive Directors or the countries they represent.

The complete backlist of publications from the World Bank is shown in the annual
Index of Publications, which contains an alphabetical title list and indexes of subjects,
authors, and countries and regions. The latest edition is available free of charge
from the Distribution Unit, Office of the Publisher, The World Bank, 1818 H
Street, N.W., Washington, D.C. 20433, U.S.A., or from Publications, The World
Bank, 66 avenue d'Iéna, 75116 Paris, France.

Library of Congress Cataloging-in-Publication Data

Structural adjustment in a newly industrialized country : the Korean
   experience / edited by Vittorio Corbo, Sang-Mok Suh.
      p. cm.
   Includes bibliographical references and index.
   ISBN 0-8018-4328-6
   1. Structural adjustment (Economic policy)—Korea (South)
2. Korea (South)—Economic policy—1960–   I. Corbo, Vittorio.
II. Suh, Sang-Mok.
HC467.S78   1992
338.95195—dc20   91-43274
                                                     CIP

Contents

Preface

THE EXPERIENCE OF THE Republic of Korea has frequently been cited as an example of the advantages to be gained from an outward-oriented growth strategy. The success of Korea's strategies provides many valuable lessons for countries that are contemplating the integration of their economies into the world economy. Korea's recent experience is also of interest to the many countries that are struggling with inflation and high current account deficits.

In the late 1970s Korea faced a growing and unsustainable current account deficit, accelerated inflation, and a slowdown in growth. To deal with these problems, in the early 1980s the government introduced a comprehensive adjustment program that enabled the country to conquer inflation. A few years later, thanks in part to the program, Korea had large current account surpluses and was enjoying a dramatic rate of growth.

This book presents the results of a research project, sponsored jointly by the World Bank and the Korea Development Institute, that studied Korea's macroeconomic adjustment in the period following the oil shocks. As part of the project, two meetings of working groups were held: the first in Korea in October 1985 and the second in Washington, D.C., in June 1986. The latter meeting was devoted to a discussion of the first drafts of the chapters of this volume.

In preparing the final manuscript, we received valuable assistance from many individuals, in particular, Sang-Woo Nam. For their worthy contributions as discussants at the June meetings, sincere thanks are extended to Edgardo Barandiaran, Avi Braverman, Susan Collins, Mansoor Dailami, Dennis de Tray, James Hanson, Arturo Israel, Mohsin Khan, Ruth Klinov, Danny Leipziger, Mark Leiserson, Johannes Linn, Millard Long, Mohan Munasinghe, Miguel Urrutia, Alberto Valdés, Sweder van Wijnbergen, and John Williamson. Special thanks go to Whitney Watriss for important editorial assistance and to Myrian Bailey and Aludia Oropesa for word-processing assistance.

1   Introduction and Overview

VITTORIO CORBO, Catholic University of Chile
SANG-MOK SUH, Korea Development Institute

IN THE INTRODUCTION to any volume it is the duty of the author or editor to answer the question "why?" Why is this topic worth studying? Why is this particular volume worth reading?

Since the beginning of the 1980s the Republic of Korea has been successful both at stabilizing its economy and then at pursuing gradual structural adjustment with minimum inflationary or recessionary consequences. Although Korea's record of economic development and the outward-oriented strategy on which it is based have received a great deal of attention, the fact that the country achieved success with stabilization after experiencing substantial macroeconomic imbalances in the late 1970s and early 1980s has not been widely noted. The macroeconomic imbalances took the form of an acceleration of inflation, a sharp real appreciation, a slowdown in export growth, a large increase in the current account deficit, a large increase in foreign debt, and a reduction in the growth of output. In this regard, Korea's success is novel. Many other middle-income developing nations—often buffeted by high inflation and an unsustainable balance of payments—have floundered amid debt troubles, capital flight, and domestic resistance as they have tried to chart a course of adjustment.

The deterioration in Korea's fundamental macroeconomic indicators in the late 1970s and early 1980s followed a period in which monetary, fiscal, and exchange rate policies had been oriented toward the promotion of ambitious investment programs in the heavy and chemical industries. Import restrictions, credit rationing, and price controls were also utilized to support this industrialization effort. The second oil shock and two disastrous years for agriculture contributed further to the macroeconomic crisis that Korea faced in the early 1980s.

That crisis resembled the situation confronting many heavily indebted countries today. Although Korea's experience is in many ways unique, countries now struggling through adjustment can learn much from its success.

Korea's dramatic improvement in economic fortunes has placed many questions on the agenda for discussion. Why did the Korean economy grind so rapidly to a halt in 1980? How did the adjustment program revive the economy so quickly? How did the policies in individual areas of the economy contribute to successful adjustment? In this volume, authors from the Korea Development Institute (KDI), the World Bank, and the university community examine various facets of the Korean adjustment experience to identify the central elements of success, as well as the shortcomings. From the contributors' insights, lessons on policy design can be derived for other countries that are struggling to deal with the twin problems of stabilization and growth.

The chapters in this volume address these questions by providing a relatively comprehensive analysis of the performance of the Korean economy from the late 1970s through the first half of the 1980s. The primary objectives of this book are to offer some lessons in structural adjustment in a developing country and to provide a point of reference for policymakers and academics who will be formulating adjustment policies in the future. Another objective is to update past scholarship. Together with the Harvard Institute for International Development, in 1981 the KDI published a set of studies derived from a project on the modernization of Korea during the period 1945–75. The present volume picks up where these studies left off, in the mid-1970s. The differences in emphasis reflect changes in the Korean economy in recent years. When the KDI-Harvard study was initiated, Korea had emerged from basic modernization and was well on its way to sustainable growth. The structural and stabilization problems of the Korean economy emerged only after 1975, and they are the focus of the book.

The Analytic Approach

As used here, the term "structural adjustment" refers to two phenomena. In a narrow sense it stands for the short-term adjustment needed to stabilize the economy in the early 1980s. More broadly, it refers to an all-encompassing process in the long-term development of a nation. Once a country has achieved basic modernization, further advances require a restructuring of its economy, a rite of passage that both hastens and confirms a new level of economic maturity. As the following chapters show, during the period 1979–81 the need for long-term adjustment in many sectors of the economy was greater than the need to cushion the effects of the energy crunch.

The distinction between these two forms of adjustment explains much about the coverage of this volume. A broad, macroeconomic treatment of this topic is useful primarily in gauging the effects of the oil price rise and of responding policies. Because it is also important to analyze the long-term factors in economic growth, this volume pursues a more comprehensive treatment and examines the adjustment of specific sectors of the economy as well, including finance, trade, industrial organization, agriculture, energy, and labor. The focus, however, is on the macroeconomic adjustment and the sectoral policies that facilitated the process.

Tracing Korea's Success

Manifold aspects of Korea's adjustment efforts are analyzed in this volume. In chapter 2 Sang-Mok Suh sets the stage with a historical review of the Korean economy. The chapter provides a self-contained summary of Korean development during the past twenty-five years. In chapter 3 Vittorio Corbo and Sang-Woo Nam analyze Korea's recent macroeconomic history, concentrating on the buildup of the crisis in the late 1970s and early 1980s and on the role of domestic policies and external forces in the dramatic post-1982 turnaround. Once the macroeconomic crisis was controlled, large increases in productivity and capacity utilization led to high growth and large increases in real wages while inflation was kept in check. In chapter 4 Rudiger Dornbusch and Yung-Chul Park study the evolution of Korea's external balance. They put forward several hypotheses to explain how Korea was able to reduce its current account deficit while recovering growth and show that the main link between the success in stabilization and the capacity to generate high growth was the improvement in productivity. In chapter 5 Corbo and Nam examine the forces behind the acceleration of inflation in the late 1970s and the deceleration of the early 1980s.

Chapters 6 and 7 deal with the sectoral aspects of Korea's adjustment. In chapter 6 Yoon-Je Cho and David Cole analyze financial deregulation during the adjustment period and its role in the restructuring of the economy. In chapter 7 Dae-Hee Song and Byung-Seo Ryu examine agricultural policies during the years of adjustment. Agriculture was—and still is—a very important sector in Korea for both employment and output and thus has been subject to special treatment by government policies. In chapter 8 Soo-Gil Young looks at the import liberalization and industrial adjustment policies that were central to the restructuring of the economy in the early 1980s. In chapter 9 Kyu-Uck Lee, Shujiro Urata, and Inbom Choi consider changes in the competitiveness and concentration of the industrial sector and show how increased competitiveness facilitated the adjustment effort. Flexible labor markets were also essential to the success of both the stabilization and structural adjustment efforts, and in chapter 10 Tarsicio Castañeda and Funkoo Park discuss the role of the labor market in the adjustment process. Because of the importance of the second oil shock, the role of energy policies in the adjustment of the economy is reviewed in chapter 11 by Julio Rotemberg and Seok-Hyun Hong. Another objective of the adjustment effort was to improve the welfare of the population. The evolution of social welfare during the period of adjustment is analyzed in chapter 12 by Sang-Mok Suh and Ha-Cheong Yeon.

Today, as many countries are struggling to put in place and sustain comprehensive reforms, the political economy of the implementation of reforms is of interest. In chapter 13 In-Joung Whang describes how the economic decisions were made and implemented in Korea—in particular, how the stabilization program of 1979 moved through the government decisionmaking process and how the structural adjustment effort got its start under President Chun Doo Hwan. In chapter 14 Corbo and Suh discuss the lessons to be drawn from Korea's experience.

Conclusions and Lessons

The main purpose of this study, as noted, was to investigate how Korea adjusted successfully to the combination of low growth, high inflation, and unsustainable current account deficits. The following chapters show that the factors that contributed most to the successful adjustment were the restoration of the macroeconomic fundamentals (by reducing the fiscal deficit, expanding the money supply while keeping inflation low, and de-valuing the won to restore external competitiveness) and a favorable exter-nal environment. Financial reforms and measures to increase domestic competition facilitated the restructuring of the economy, and flexibility in the labor markets made adjustment possible without massive unemployment.

As for the cause of Korea's problems in the late 1970s, this volume assigns blame to both an aggressive import-substitution drive in the heavy and chemical industries and the complementary monetary and fiscal poli-cies. These strategies resulted in a large real appreciation, a crowding out of the traditional export-oriented sectors and a large current account defi-cit, unfavorable external shocks, and an uncompetitive and highly pro-tected domestic economy that limited further export expansion.

Important lessons emerge from this study of the structural adjustment of the Korean economy, although most relate to what to avoid rather than to what to do. The first lesson is to avoid major disequilibria in the macro-economic variables. In particular, inflation must not be allowed to get out of control. Real interest rates should be positive, but not too high; real wages should not be allowed to grow at a rate much above or below the rate of growth of labor productivity. The real exchange rate should not be allowed to move too far from the path compatible with the main fundamentals.

A second lesson is that if a drastic reduction in the current account is called for, it is important to avoid import controls. Instead, the macro-economics of the problem should be dealt with by introducing appropriate demand and switching policies and complementary export promotion poli-cies. A corollary to this lesson is that the economic costs of the distortions introduced through export promotion policies are explicit and much smaller than the costs of import compression policies.

Third, in an integrated and open system of world trade the only way to provide a sustainable and credible framework for export expansion is to avoid both the antiexport bias that results from indiscriminate protection of import-competing sectors and any artificial appreciation of the domestic currency.

Fourth, a competitive domestic economy and a flexible labor market facilitate the restructuring of the economy and reduce the potential adjustment costs of a structural adjustment program.

Fifth, a clear commitment by government authorities to a strategy of controlling inflation, improving competition in the domestic market, and improving the competitiveness of exports will facilitate the response of the economic agents to the structural adjustment measures and thus reduce the adjustment costs.

Note

This study ended in 1986. Since then, Korea's political situation and economic policies have undergone significant changes that have profound implications for the economy. Nevertheless, the analysis and conclusions contained in this volume concerning the structural adjustment of the 1970s and the first half of the 1980s remain valid. It is hoped that someone will undertake a follow-up study to cover the most recent period in Korea's economic history.

2 The Economy in Historical Perspective

SANG-MOK SUH, Korea Development Institute

THE MODERN ECONOMIC DEVELOPMENT of Korea has been among the most rapid and sustained in the world, despite the extreme turbulence caused by the end of the Japanese occupation in the 1940s and the Korean War in the early 1950s. It has taken place even though Korea is a small country with limited natural resources. Arable land, for example, accounts for only 22 percent of the total area. The marked population growth since 1953, currently running at 3 percent a year, has left Korea with the highest population density per acre of arable land of any country.

Table 2-1 presents statistics that show Korea's remarkable development. In 1986 per capita income reached $2,300,[1] while the country's total trade volume was estimated at over $68.4 billion,[2] the thirteenth highest among the noncommunist countries. The share of the manufacturing sector in the gross national product (GNP) reached 30.0 percent in 1986, and that of the agriculture, forestry, and fisheries sectors was 12.3 percent. The share of exports of primary products in total exports was 8 percent, that of manufactured goods 92 percent. Korea is now recognized as one of the most outstanding performers of the newly industrialized countries (NICS).

This chapter looks at economic development in Korea since the early 1950s to provide background for the analysis of recent structural adjustment. The process of industrialization between 1953 and 1986, which can be divided into four distinct phases, is analyzed to determine how Korea was able to adapt to changes in internal and external circumstances and overcome seemingly insurmountable obstacles to achieve sustained economic development. Each phase of Korea's development has been unique but complementary in its economic organization, public policies, and resources. At times the path of modernization has been neither smooth nor certain, but Korea has managed to move along it steadily and successfully.

Rebuilding Korea: 1953–62

With the end of World War II in 1945, Korea obtained independence after more than three decades of Japanese rule. The occupation remains controversial, not simply because of the repressive nature of the Japanese rule but also because of the strong economic growth between 1910 and 1940. Manufacturing grew at an average annual rate of over 10 percent. Industry witnessed spectacular growth and an expansion of exports during the 1930s, when Japan invested in Korea as a supply base for its military thrust into China. Agriculture grew at between 1.6 and 2 percent a year, depending on the estimates used. Slow population growth and large outmigration yielded per capita growth of about 2 percent. This rate seems slow compared with later growth rates, and the achievement was offset by a substantial worsening of income distribution as a result of the concentration of landholdings by the Japanese. Nonetheless, for the time, the economic performance was strong.

The importance of the Japanese period for subsequent development is unclear, however. Most firms were under Japanese management, and laws limited the opportunities for Korean businessmen. After the Japanese left, the number of manufacturing establishments fell by half and total output by 85 percent. Much of the physical plant left behind by the Japanese, including crucial industries such as power and chemicals, was located in the northern part of the country, which was cut off from the south when the peninsula was partitioned along the 38th parallel. In general, economic conditions in the late 1940s were extremely poor despite efforts by the U.S. military to revive the economy. Many of the remaining Japanese assets that fell into Korean hands were destroyed during the Korean War.

Nonetheless, the Japanese did contribute in various ways to Korea's long-term modernization. Many Korean firms originated under the Japanese, and there was substantial transfer of managerial technology. The urban workforce expanded dramatically, as did the education system. Despite discrimination against the Korean language, about a quarter of Korea's population had received some formal schooling by 1945. The Japanese also invested heavily in infrastructure, including roads, railroads, and port facilities. Although the Japanese emphasized extractive agriculture, and a number of peasant farmers were displaced as a result of this policy, the Japanese did help to modernize Korean agriculture through a highly developed extension system (Mason and others 1980, Sang-Chul Suh 1978).

The Korean War, which lasted from 1950 to 1953, worsened Korea's already poor economic conditions. A rebuilding effort was initiated during 1953–62 to end the economic stagnation that followed the war. This rebuilding was carried out during a period of political instability and in the face of what seemed to be the classic ingredients of perpetual underdevelopment—rampant inflation because of a rapid expansion in the supply of domestic currency, an extremely complex market system with a domestic market too small to support the building of social infrastructure or to attract investment, an inability to meet the basic needs of the rapidly growing and urbanizing population, and generally low income levels and high unemployment, all aggravated by the lack of natural resources and by poorly designed government policies. Many international observers, including those at the multilateral organizations, were pessimistic, seeing a

Table 2-1. Key Economic Indicators, 1963–86

| Year | Exports[a] (1) | GNP (2) | Wholesale price index (3) | Per capita GNP (dollars) (4) | Percentage of GNP | | Trade balance (billions of dollars) (7) | Terms of trade (1980 = 100) (8) | Real effective exchange rate[b] (1980 = 100) (9) | Nominal exchange rate[c] (won per dollar) (10) |
					Consolidated public sector deficit (5)	Current account balance (6)				
1963	9.0	9.1	19.4	100	—	-5.3	-0.41	111.3	75.3	130.00
1964	23.5	9.6	34.9	103	—	-0.9	-0.24	112.5	93.5	256.02
1965	35.9	5.8	10.3	105	—	0.3	-0.24	114.3	107.4	272.06
1966	42.4	12.7	8.6	125	—	-2.8	-0.43	127.7	103.7	271.46
1967	32.7	6.6	6.5	142	—	-4.5	-0.57	132.2	97.7	274.60
1968	39.5	11.3	8.1	169	—	-8.4	-0.84	137.7	93.0	281.50
1969	36.1	13.8	6.9	210	—	-8.3	-0.99	132.6	93.6	304.50
1970	19.6	7.6	9.4	252	—	-7.8	-0.92	133.8	96.4	316.70
1971	20.9	8.8	8.6	288	1.0	-9.0	-1.05	132.7	103.6	373.20
1972	36.6	5.7	13.8	318	4.6	-3.5	-0.57	132.1	112.6	398.90
1973	55.3	14.1	6.9	395	1.6	-2.3	-0.57	125.4	127.1	397.50
1974	-2.8	7.7	42.1	540	4.0	-10.9	-1.94	102.1	107.7	484.00
1975	15.9	6.9	26.5	590	4.6	-9.0	-1.67	92.1	110.3	484.00
1976	41.6	14.1	12.2	797	2.9	-1.1	-0.59	105.1	101.8	484.00
1977	22.6	12.7	9.0	1,008	2.6	0.0	-0.48	112.4	101.8	484.00
1978	19.9	9.7	11.6	1,392	2.5	-2.1	-1.78	117.8	104.4	484.00
1979	-3.8	6.5	18.8	1,640	1.4	-6.7	-4.40	115.3	97.1	484.00
1980	9.7	-5.2	38.9	1,589	3.2	-8.7	-4.38	100.0	100.0	659.90
1981	17.3	6.2	20.4	1,719	4.6	-6.8	-3.63	97.9	96.1	700.50
1982	6.2	5.6	4.7	1,773	4.3	-3.8	-2.59	102.2	95.5	748.80
1983	13.8	9.5	0.2	1,914	1.6	-2.1	-1.76	103.1	101.4	795.50
1984	8.1	7.5	0.7	2,044	1.4	-1.6	-1.04	105.3	104.1	827.40
1985	2.1	5.4	0.9	2,047	0.2	-1.1	-0.02	105.9	110.6	890.20
1986	26.6	12.5	-2.2	2,300	1.0	4.8	4.21	114.7	128.5	861.40

— Not available.

Note: For columns 1 and 2, the data up to 1970 are in 1965 constant prices, and the data from 1970 on are based on the new system of national accounts and are expressed in 1980 constant prices. Columns 1, 2, and 3 show the percentage change from the previous year. Columns 4 and 7 are in current U.S. dollars.

a. Total exports of goods and nonfactor services.

b. The real effective exchange rate is defined as foreign prices in domestic currency divided by domestic prices with trade weights.

c. At the end of the period.

Source: Bank of Korea and Economic Planning Board, except for column 10, which shows estimates from the Korea Development Institute.

Table 2-2. *Key Economic Indicators, 1950s*

Indicator	1953	1962	Average annual percentage change 1954–62
Per capita GNP			
Thousands of won	109	116	0.7
Dollars	67	87	2.9
GNP (billions of won)	2,205	3,071	3.7
U.S. aid (millions of dollars)	194.2	232.3	2.0
Investment rate (percent)[a]	15.4	12.8	n.a.
National savings rate (percent)[a]	8.8	3.2	n.a.

n.a. Not applicable.
Note: Won are in 1975 constant prices. Dollars are current U.S. dollars.
a. In current prices.
Source: Various issues of Korea, Economic Planning Board, *Statistical Yearbook.*

country with few natural resources and no potential for development in the foreseeable future.

The economic policy pursued during this period may be loosely characterized as the promotion of import substitution of nondurable consumer and intermediate goods through a protective wall of high tariffs and stringent quotas.[3] This development strategy soon reached its natural limits because the domestic market was small but the capital requirements were large. As a result, the average annual rate of growth of GNP during the nine-year period following the war (1954–62) was only 3.7 percent and that of per capita GNP a meager 0.7 percent (table 2-2). Commodity exports remained negligible throughout this period, usually amounting to less than 1 percent of GNP, because the persistently overvalued domestic currency and extreme anti-import bias of the trade regime thwarted exporting.

The inadequacy of the economic and administrative infrastructure made the formulation of long-term development plans difficult, and many projects proceeded on a trial-and-error basis.[4] Because industrial income was generally at subsistence levels and national savings were virtually nonexistent, funds for reconstruction projects could not be obtained except through foreign aid. Consequently, between 1954 and 1959, about 70 percent of all reconstruction projects were funded by aid from other countries, primarily the United States.[5]

A bright spot in this period was Korea's continued strengthening of its human capital, which was to be a very important element in its successful economic development in later years. Education received a great deal of emphasis. Considered a virtue under Confucianism, the state philosophy of Korea, education was seen as an important source of upward mobility as well as of new job options. At the same time, the Japanese occupation and the Korean War had leveled the traditional class system: at the beginning of the 1950s, all Koreans were more or less equal, and there was little ethnic or racial discrimination. Koreans were also united behind their common goal of reconstructing the nation. All these factors encouraged Korean parents to invest in their children's education.[6]

Enrollment in the formal education system increased rapidly at all levels: from 1945 to 1960, elementary school enrollment rose 265 percent, while enrollment in institutions of higher learning rose by a factor of 12. The number of college students rose from about 8,000 in 1945 to more than 100,000 by 1960. As a result of this expansion, the illiteracy rate fell from 78 percent to about 28 percent during the same period. A unique aspect of the Korean experience was how balanced the expansion in education was at all levels. In addition, educational development was achieved early in comparison with Korea's overall economic development. The dramatic increase in educational opportunities also created a serious problem, however—an unemployment rate among college graduates of approximately 20 percent during the 1950s. This underscored the need to develop the nation's industrial base as a source of jobs.

Another major development in the 1950s was land reform. As a first step toward a more equitable distribution of income, the government established a limit on the possession of farmland (a major source of the inequality of income) through the Land Reform Act of 1949.[7] Consequently the proportion of tenant farmers decreased from 42.1 percent in 1947 to 5.2 percent in 1964. Although land reform may temporarily have reduced productivity per acre, that loss was far outweighed by the political and social benefits. As a direct result of land reform and the reduction in tenant farming, the wealth of the minority upper-class landlords was reduced, and over time the earnings of small farmers and the general equitability of rural incomes increased substantially.

It appears that deliberate attempts by the Korean government to redistribute income in favor of small farmers, including the land reform of 1949, accounted for a substantial share of the improvement in rural living standards. It should also be noted that the Korean War had destroyed many sources of wealth, so that almost all Koreans were equally poor. An equitable income distribution structure prevailed in the midst of that poverty, setting the stage for the new development efforts.

Thus, during the period 1953–62, the Korean economy had generally experienced slow growth under a rather protectionist trade regime and import substitution strategy. At the same time, however, the rapid rise in the level of education and the relatively equitable distribution of both income and wealth paved the way for future development.

Development Strategy, 1963–71: Export Promotion

In 1961 the new government of the Third Republic, headed by President Park Chung Hee, came into power. Committed to economic development

and intent on playing an activist role in promoting growth, it transformed
Korea into one of the fastest-growing economies in the world, after years of
stagnation and rebuilding. The new regime succeeded in forging a consensus for a major shift in economic policies, then implemented its reforms
vigorously, beginning in 1963. The period from 1963 to 1971 was extremely important in the country's modern economic development because
of the significant progress made in strengthening the industrial base and
implementing fundamental changes in the nation's development strategies
through both policy reform and institutional change.

Economic Measures

Mindful of Korea's limited natural resources and small domestic market,
the new government adopted an outward-looking development strategy
that emphasized the growth of exports. In the 1960s the essence of this
strategy was the promotion of labor-intensive manufacturing exports in
which Korea had a comparative advantage. The government mobilized
both internal and external resources to this end. This approach proved
well-suited to Korea's resource endowment—an energetic, efficient, and
well-educated citizenry. Importing most of its raw materials and converting
them first into light consumption goods and later into consumer durables,
Korea enjoyed rapid growth through the end of the 1970s. By that time
Korea was being showcased, along with its East Asian NIC neighbors, as a
model for developing countries.

In keeping with the emphasis on exports, Korea's exchange rate and
trade policies were revamped during this period. In 1964 the government
devalued the national currency, the won, by almost 100 percent and introduced a unified floating exchange rate system to eliminate the bias against
the export sector.

To stimulate trade, especially exports, the government provided extensive direct export subsidies and other incentives, including a variety of tax
exemptions, lower rates for public utilities, tariff rebates for imports des-
tined for reexport, simpler customs procedures, accelerated depreciation
allowances, liberalization of credit restrictions (including numerous foreign
exchange loans, offshore procurement loans, and import-export credits for
overseas marketing), and easier financing regulations for new export companies. As for import policy, the government announced its intention to
liberalize trade. This policy never fully materialized, although in 1967 the
government did shift from a "positive list" to a "negative list" system of
import controls. The changes in the trade regime provided significant
incentives for export activities and lessened the differences in the incentives
across import-competing activities.

To mobilize domestic savings and resources, in 1965 the government
raised interest rates on deposits from 12 percent to as high as 26.4 percent.

As a result of this reform, for three years in a row after 1965, savings deposits in commercial banks nearly doubled, and the ratio of time and savings deposits to GNP rose from 3.8 percent in 1965 to 21.7 percent in 1969.[8]

The government also promoted industrial investment by increasing corporate tax incentives to mobilize new domestic resources for export and high-growth sectors. To encourage the inflow of foreign capital to make up for the insufficiency of domestic savings, the government enacted a comprehensive Foreign Capital Promotion Act in 1966, which stipulated that in selected situations the government would underwrite the risk borne by foreign investors.

Institutional Measures

The 1960s were a period of substantial institutional change. Measures taken included active government involvement in economic planning, a revamping of the tax administration, founding of an Export Promotion Council, and, most important, creation of five-year economic development plans, to be implemented by an Economic Planning Board (EPB) that was set up in 1961.

The EPB came to play, and continues to play, a critical role in Korea's economic development. It was the main force behind the government's orchestration of the nation's outward-looking development strategies. The decree in 1963 that the EPB's minister would also hold the position of deputy prime minister, along with the title of minister of economic planning, established the agency as a virtual superministry. The EPB not only created all long- and short-range development plans, a function not assigned to planning agencies in other developing nations, but also had far-reaching budgetary, regulatory, and statistical functions,[9] as well as responsibility for management of foreign capital. In this way, it was involved directly in implementing and controlling the measures to mobilize resources. As deputy prime minister, the head of the EPB coordinated the activities of all the ministries through the EPB's budgetary function, in addition to chairing the weekly meetings of the Economic Ministers' Council. Another responsibility of the EPB was to promote technical cooperation with industrialized countries to improve the level of technological advancement.

In line with the greater emphasis on economic planning, in 1961 an Office of Planning and Coordination was established under the prime minister.[10] It was responsible for assisting the prime minister in evaluating and monitoring the performance of major development projects and policies. In addition, a planning and management unit was organized at the assistant minister level within each ministry. The functions of these units included annual implementation planning, progress reviews, monitoring and evaluation of project performance, and collection and feedback of information for decisionmaking (Whang 1971).

The Export Promotion Council was another innovation. Chaired by the president of Korea, its purpose was to facilitate the implementation of export strategies, to develop and disseminate marketing information, and to promote communications between the government and the private sector. Beyond these tasks, the council served two primary functions: it provided motivation and economic incentives to businessmen, workers, and the general public for the promotion of the overall trade environment, and it provided a public forum and a shortcut for the resolution of grievances and complaints by businessmen about export and customs procedures.

The government revamped the domestic tax administration in an effort to eliminate the chronic budgetary deficits, minimize the price distortions caused by inflation, and increase government savings. The new National Tax Administration created under the Ministry of Finance in 1966 was given expanded powers in scheduling, auditing, and collecting taxes and in implementing penalties and fines. Although many other developing countries have had similarly well-planned tax reforms, few have been given the power to collect taxes directly or to impose substantial penalties on delinquent enterprises. As a result, this system helped to finance the ambitious development programs of the 1960s.[11]

A somewhat later measure, initiated in 1970, was the establishment of specialized policy research institutes. Designed to strengthen the policy planning function, these government-supported agencies included the Korea Development Institute (KDI); Korea Institute for Industrial Economics and Technology (KIET), under the Ministry of Trade and Industry; Korea Research Institute for Human Settlements (KRIHS), under the Ministry of Construction; Korea Rural Economic Institute (KREI), under the Ministry of Agriculture and Fisheries; Korea Institute of Population and Health (KIPH) and Korea Women's Development Institute (KWDI), under the Ministry of Health and Social Affairs; and Korea Education Development Institute (KEDI), under the Ministry of Education. The Korean government also sponsored many research institutes in the fields of science and technology.[12]

The Results

The results of the comprehensive changes in Korea's development strategy and institutional structure were exceptional. The share of total investment financed by national savings rose from less than 25 percent in 1962 to just under 61 percent in 1971, while the investment–gross domestic product (GDP) ratio in current prices rose from 13 percent to 25 percent (table 2-3). The share of total investment financed by foreign aid also declined sharply—to 50 percent in the early 1960s and 20 percent in the late 1960s,

Table 2-3. *Key Economic Indicators, 1960s*

Indicator	1962	1971	Average annual percentage change, 1963–71
Per capita GNP			
Thousands of won	116	212	6.9
Dollars	87	288	14.2
GNP (billions of won)	3,071	6,962	9.5
Exports			
Millions of dollars	55	1,068	39.0
Exports-GNP ratio (percent)[a]	2.40	11.7	
Imports			
Millions of dollars	422	2,394	21.3
Imports-GNP ratio (percent)[a]	18.2	26.5	
Investment rate (percent)[b]	12.8	25.1	n.a.
Domestic savings rate (percent)[b]	3.2	14.6	n.a.
Wholesale price index (1975 = 100)	16.1	45.7	12.3

n.a. Not applicable.
Note: Won are in 1975 constant prices. Dollars are current U.S. dollars.
a. In current U.S. dollars.
b. In current prices.
Source: Various issues of Korea, Economic Planning Board, *Statistical Yearbook.*

down from a level of 70 percent in the 1950s.[13] Average annual growth of real GNP for the 1963–71 period was more than double the 1954–62 average, with an average annual rate of 9.5 percent. On a per capita basis, real growth for the period was not less than 6.9 percent, compared with 0.7 percent for 1954–62.

Important structural changes took place in the economy. The mining and manufacturing sector increased its share of GNP from 16 percent in 1962 to 22.5 percent in 1971, while the share of the agricultural, forestry, and fisheries sector decreased from 37 percent to 26.6 percent. Reflecting these structural changes, employment in the latter declined from 63 percent to 48.4 percent of the total, while employment in mining and manufacturing increased from 9 percent to 14.2 percent.

Korea's rapid economic growth and structural change were largely the result of the surge in foreign trade (table 2-3). Total exports rose at an average annual rate of 39 percent, spurred by the incentives, the real devaluation, and a general expansion in world trade, which was growing at an average annual rate of 11.6 percent during 1963–71. The remarkable growth in trade was accompanied by a significant change in its composition. The share of primary products exported declined from 73 percent of the total in 1962 to only 14 percent in 1971, while that of industrial products increased dramatically from 27 percent to 86 percent. Commodity exports, which amounted to only about $55 million in 1962, grew at an average annual rate of 40 percent to a total of $1.07 billion in 1971 (based on exports cleared through customs). In the import sector, the share of capital goods increased dramatically from 17 percent in 1962 to 28.65

Table 2-4. *Changes in Income Distribution, 1965-70*

(percent)

Income group	1965	1970
Income shares of lowest 40 percent		
All households	19.3	19.6
Rural households	22.6	21.2
Urban households	14.1	18.9
Income shares of highest 20 percent		
All households	41.8	41.6
Rural households	38.0	38.6
Urban households	47.0	43.0

Source: Choo (1980).

percent by 1971. Commodity imports also expanded markedly, rising from $422 million in 1962 to $2.39 billion in 1971, an average annual increase of 21.3 percent.

Rationalization of the trade regime and the large devaluation in 1964 led to large increases in export and import values and in growth of GNP. The real exchange rate peaked in 1965. Then, with absorption growing at a rate higher than GNP, a continuous appreciation developed until 1968. Until 1966 there was a substantial improvement in the current account and high growth in exports.[14] Thereafter, the deterioration in the current account was a dominant factor. Following a year of a generally constant exchange rate (1968-69), there was a sharp real depreciation from 1969 to 1972. Overall, however, the movement in the exchange rate during the 1965-72 period was not a problem.

Domestic absorption moved slightly ahead of GNP, which rose at an average of more than 9 percent a year. Foreign transfers were insignificant. The deficit on the current account averaged about 5.0 for the period 1963-72, although it was 8.4 percent during 1968-71. Inflation ran above the one-digit level during 1963-71, reaching 16.8 percent based on the GNP deflator and 12.3 percent based on the wholesale price index (WPI).

Korea also had a fair degree of success in income distribution in the 1960s (table 2-4). Blessed with the relatively equitable distribution of income at the turn of the decade, a large number of citizens shared in the benefits of the rapid economic growth. The outward-looking strategy for growth expanded labor-intensive manufactured exports, which increased employment opportunities, thereby benefiting those at the lower end of the income scale.[15]

As seen in table 2-4, the trickle-down effect of the rapid expansion of labor-intensive export industries had a significant influence on the nation's social welfare. The main factor leading to the better overall distribution of income was the substantial improvement in income distribution among urban households during 1965-70. The income share of the lowest 40 percent of urban households increased from 14.1 percent in 1965 to 18.9

percent in 1970, and that of the highest 20 percent declined from 47 percent to 43 percent in the same period.

Korea's success in the 1960s should not be attributed entirely to the outward-looking development strategy. Korea had, as noted, a well-educated population, as well as dynamic entrepreneurs. The global economic environment was also favorable to Korea's export promotion in the 1960s: an international free trade philosophy and low rates of inflation resulted in a growing volume of world trade. Korea, however, used its resources and opportunities to the greatest advantage.

Economic Policy, 1972–79: Promotion of Heavy and Chemical Industries

The 1970s showed a number of similarities with the 1960s. Many of the promotional policies, such as those for exports, were continued, and the same group of policymakers was responsible for managing the economy. The development strategy of the 1970s was again characterized by continued government intervention. At the same time, the government made significant changes in policy in response to internal and external socioeconomic conditions. For example, there was a strong shift toward import substitution for investment goods and raw materials.

The two primary policy objectives in this period were the modernization of rural areas, which had begun to lag behind urban areas by the late 1960s, and, more important, the development of heavy and chemical industries. The first objective was necessitated by concern over the growing disparity in the standard of living between urban and rural populations. Productivity increases in the agricultural sector lagged behind those in the industrial sector; in addition agriculture faced unfavorable terms of trade, particularly for its principal crops, rice and barley. There was rapid migration of farm laborers to the cities, and the percentage of the population employed in agriculture dropped from 65.6 percent to 45.9 percent between 1960 and 1975.

Equity Measures

To deal with the rural-urban differential, as early as 1969 the government moved to boost the price supports for the major grain crops, particularly rice and barley. It also provided subsidies for fertilizer and farm machinery and sought to improve the rural credit system. In 1970 the government established the Grain Management Fund to provide farmers with adequate prices for their products while keeping the costs of foodstuffs to urban consumers low. In 1971 the government announced the Saemaul Undong (New Village Movement), a comprehensive rural community development program that was to include income-generating projects based on coopera-

Table 2-5. *Comparison of Rural Household Income and Urban Household Income*

(won)

Year	Urban (wage earner) household	Rural household	Rural household income as a percentage of urban household income
	Average monthly income		
1967	20,720	12,456	60.1
1970	31,770	21,317	67.1
1973	45,850	40,059	87.4
1976	95,980	96,355	100.0
1979	219,133	185,624	84.7

Source: Various issues of Korea, Economic Planning Board, *The Family Income and Expenditure Survey* and of Korea, Ministry of Agriculture and Fisheries, *The Farm Household Economy Survey.*

tive work, with the government providing technical and financial assistance to improve facilities in education, health, housing, roads, electrification, communications, and other services. The main objectives of the Saemaul Undong were to improve the farm village environment and increase agricultural production and income. It was not until 1973 that the government actually implemented the New Village Movement.

In the period from 1972 to 1975, total government investment in and loans to agriculture amounted to 1.46 trillion won[16] (in current prices), a 96 percent increase over the 1967–71 period. Under the Grain Management Fund price support program, the government purchased rice and barley at a price that gave farmers a sufficient rate of return and then sold those staples to urban consumers for less than the purchase price.[17] The sharp rise in grain import prices after the first oil shock stirred support for the proponents of self-sufficiency in major food grains. During 1975–78 the government upped its price support for rice. The resulting deficits in the Grain Management Fund and the Fertilizer Fund were jointly responsible for 37 percent of the total growth of the money supply during 1976–78.

The government's efforts, seconded by the farmers themselves, led to a significant increase in income in the agricultural sector. By 1974 average rural household income began to catch up to average urban working household income. It reached parity in 1976 (table 2-5). Between 1967 and 1976, rural household income went from 12,456 won to 96,355 won, approximately a 774 percent (eightfold) increase, compared with a 463 percent (fivefold) increase for urban household income during the same period. These gains in rural household income were the result of both greater agricultural productivity and the government's income transfer program. For example, the price support program for rice helped improve agriculture's terms of trade and simultaneously channeled inflationary pressures away from that sector, dispersing them more generally throughout the economy. A negative outcome of the price support program was its contribution to the chronic government budget deficit that lasted into the 1980s.[18]

Industrial Measures

Two main objectives underlay the government's drive for strong heavy and chemical industries: development of new strategic export industries and promotion of the import substitution of intermediate materials and capital goods. The government considered this drive essential to further industrial development. In addition, the nearly one-third reduction in the number of U.S. troops stationed in Korea in the early 1970s raised concern about the need for a strong defense industry to protect national security. There was also concern that Korea might lose its comparative advantage in light manufacturing exports.

In 1973 the government announced the Heavy and Chemical Industry Development Plan, which favored such industries as shipbuilding, automobiles, steel products, nonferrous metals, and petrochemicals. It encouraged large-scale investment projects in these industries through special tax incentives, preferential credit allocation, and negative real interest rates under a system of widespread credit rationing. The government also resorted to heavy foreign borrowing. To make economies of scale possible in a limited domestic market, monopolistic production was permitted in a few industries. A new National Investment Fund provided financial resources at lower interest rates to meet the large investment requirements of the new enterprises. The fund helped mobilize public employee pension resources and a substantial portion of private savings at regular banking institutions. These funds were channeled into heavy industry projects favored by the government. The administration also set up high protective barriers for these infant industries and maintained the protection until the industries became internationally competitive. Finally, the government provided many incentives for worker training and research and development.

This extensive investment in the heavy and chemical industries was sufficient to neutralize the recessionary effect of the drop in the terms of trade—30.3 percent between 1972 and 1975—that followed the first oil shock. At the same time an expansionary monetary policy resulted in a sharp increase in total real absorption and a current account deficit, financed by foreign debt, that reached 10.9 percent of GNP in 1974 (see table 2-1, column 6).

The first stage of import substitution (that involving "easy substitution") having been completed in the 1950s, in the 1970s the government inaugurated the second stage, with the aim of replacing imports of intermediate goods and consumer durables with domestic products. These commodities had different characteristics from those produced in the first stage. Like standard producer goods such as automobiles and machinery, inter-

Table 2-6. *Key Economic Indicators, 1970s*

Indicator	1971	1979	Average annual percentage change, 1972–79
Per capita GNP			
Thousands of won[a]	565	1,026	7.7
Dollars	288	1,640	24.3
GNP (billions of won)	18,564	38,503	9.6
Exports			
Billions of dollars	1.1	15.1	39.2
Exports-GNP ratio (percent)[b]	11.7	31.0	n.a.
Imports			
Billions of dollars	2.4	20.3	30.7
Imports-GNP ratio (percent)[b]	26.5	32.6	n.a.
Investment rate (percent)[c]	25.1	35.6	n.a.
National savings rate (percent)[c]	14.6	28.1	n.a.
Wholesale price index (1980 = 100)	20.3	72.0	17.1

n.a. Not applicable.
Note: Won are in 1980 constant prices. Dollars are current U.S. dollars.
a. Based on the new system of national accounts introduced in 1970.
b. In current U.S. dollars.
c. In current prices.
Source: Various issues of Korea, Economic Planning Board, *Statistical Yearbook.*

mediate goods (such as steel and petrochemicals) and durable consumer products were technology- and capital-intensive. They were also subject to important economies of scale, with plants larger than needed for domestic production and rapidly rising unit costs at lower output levels. At the same time, parts, components, and accessories had to be precision-made for consumer durables, particularly for machinery, and this could not be done without highly trained labor and sophisticated technology.

To finance the drive for heavy and chemical industrialization, the government had to scale down its support for exports from labor-intensive industries. The 50 percent reduction in corporate and income taxes on export earnings was abolished in 1972, and the system of tariff exemptions for capital equipment imported for the production of exports was changed to an installment payment system in January 1974. In July 1975 the tariff exemptions for imports of raw materials for export production were dropped in favor of a tariff drawback system, with a three-month grace period for actual payment. Nevertheless, until the late 1970s, exports as a whole continued to grow.

Hidden Problems

As can be seen in table 2-6, the active government intervention and aggressive policy measures led to remarkable growth. The economic expansion was manifested in three ways. First, between 1971 and 1979, the nation experienced rapidly increasing exports and strong GNP growth—

the average annual rates were 39.2 percent and 9.6 percent, respectively. As a result the exports-to-GNP ratio grew from 11.7 percent in 1971 to 31.0 percent in 1979. Second, the industrial structure shifted dramatically toward higher value added products. And third, as indicated earlier, the rural-urban income gap closed, almost reaching parity by the mid-1970s.

Below the surface, however, major problems were brewing. Excess capacity appeared in the heavy and chemical industries, and the financial sectors were accumulating nonperforming loans, primarily as a result of lending to those industries. Continuing incentives for these industries were producing a substantial increase in private investment. That phenomenon, along with the export of construction services to the Middle East, created an overheated labor market—unemployment fell to 3.2 percent in 1978, rising only slightly to 3.8 percent in 1979—that caused real wages in manufacturing and export activities to grow by 110.2 percent and 105.2 percent, respectively, between 1974–75 and 1979. Conditions in the labor market and an expansionary monetary policy—the growth of M2 averaged 31.3 percent a year during 1973–80—led to a high average annual inflation rate of 21.3 percent based on the GNP deflator, or 20.1 percent based on the WPI, despite controls on many wage goods.[19] A black market emerged and flourished. Moreover, the rate of increase in real wages was outstripping the rise in productivity. With domestic inflation higher than international levels, the real effective exchange rate appreciated 23.6 percent between 1973 and 1979 (table 2-1, column 9).[20] The rate of growth in output per unit of input slowed considerably, from 4.9 percentage points during 1963–72 to only 1.6 percentage points during 1972–82 (Kim and Park, 1985, p. 64).[21] External debt was burgeoning at an annual rate of 28.8 percent. By the late 1970s export performance was beginning to deteriorate: the rate of growth slowed to 8.4 percent a year and turned negative in 1979; meanwhile, export profitability declined continuously. The rise in wages and lack of access to bank credit hit the profitability of labor-intensive exports particularly hard, and they rapidly lost competitiveness in the face of lower unit labor costs in other NICs. Although Korea was exporting a growing volume of construction services to the Middle East, this activity entailed large government subsidies.

The results were threefold. First, as can be seen from table 2-7, Korean industries experienced a deterioration in their international competitiveness because of rising unit labor costs. Behind that deterioration were the expansionary policies of the 1970s that resulted in large increases in real wages and a sharp real appreciation.[22] The current account deficit as a share of GNP fell from 9.0 percent in 1975 to 1.1 percent in 1976, and to practically zero in 1977, before increasing steadily to 2.1 percent in 1978, 6.76 percent in 1979, and 8.7 percent in 1980.

Table 2-7. *International Comparison of Unit Labor Costs in Dollars*
(1975 = 100)

Economy	1976	1977	1978	1979	Average annual percentage change, 1976–79
Korea	131.8	161.6	194.8	273.3	27.5
Japan	104.6	123.2	166.3	155.7	14.2
Singapore	89.3	88.9	102.1	100.1	3.9
Taiwan	104.0	116.8	122.1	136.2	9.4

Source: Korea Development Institute estimates.

Second, the high rates of inflation and unbalanced regional and sectoral growth of the 1970s ultimately led to a slight worsening in the distribution of income. Although the outward-looking growth strategy that the government pursued throughout the 1960s had contributed to a more equitable distribution, Korea experienced some deterioration in this area during the 1970s (see table 2-8). There were several reasons: (a) with economic growth centered on large, capital-intensive projects, there were relatively fewer jobs for low-income workers, a pattern that resulted in a wider wage differential among workers; (b) the government's industrial policy fostered the rapid growth of large conglomerates, so that the distribution of business ownership worsened; and (c) given the high rate of inflation of the 1970s, Korean companies and households found it more profitable to invest in speculative domestic ventures, especially real estate.[23]

Third, the nation was left increasingly vulnerable to external shocks, and this vulnerability was intensified by the government's extensive financing and subsidy schemes for agriculture and heavy industry. The capital-intensive growth had required heavy borrowing, primarily from external financial markets, and throughout the 1970s Korea's external debt grew rapidly, reaching $20.3 billion in 1979, a 372 percent increase over the $4.3 billion

Table 2-8. *Changes in Income Distribution, 1970–80*
(percent)

Income group	1970	1976	1980
Income shares of lowest 40 percent			
All households	19.6	16.9	16.1
Rural households	21.2	19.5	17.5
Urban households	14.1	15.4	15.3
Income shares of highest 20 percent			
All households	41.8	45.3	45.4
Rural households	38.0	40.6	42.2
Urban households	47.0	48.7	46.9

Source: Choo (1980) for the 1970 and 1976 estimates; Korea, Bureau of Statistics (1981) for the 1980 estimates.

Table 2-9. *Korea's External Debt, 1973–86*

(billions of dollars)

Debt	1973	1975	1977	1979	1981	1983	1985	1986
Total debt	4.3	8.5	12.6	20.3	32.4	40.4	46.7	44.5
Net debt[a]	—	—	7.6	14.0	24.5	30.9	35.5	32.5

—Not available.

a. Net debt represents total external debt minus Korea's foreign assets.

Source: Ministry of Finance.

for 1973 (see table 2-9). The rapid growth in the heavy and chemical industries required large quantities of energy. Because Korea is lacking in natural energy resources, the nation's industrial structure required a vast amount of imported crude oil.[24]

Remedial Measures

In both 1977 and 1978 the government undertook partial measures to contain inflation. Some success was achieved in 1977 through sterilization of the monetary effects of the accumulation of foreign reserves by means of a reduction in the deficit of the government's Grain Management Fund and the removal of some import controls. In the spring of 1978 the EPB proposed, and the government carried out, further stabilization measures—cutting government expenditures, increasing the tariffs for public utilities, and raising interest rates—all to reduce the government deficit and control the expansion of credit.

The government introduced additional stabilization measures in the second half of 1978. These involved a tightening of fiscal and monetary policies and some supply-side actions in the agricultural and fisheries sector. Fiscal restraint meant further trimming of government expenditures and postponement of construction projects. Another stabilization measure was import liberalization. Concerned that the pressure from domestic demand was building too high, between 1978 and 1979 the government liberalized imports of a large number of commodities in several successive phases.

Nevertheless, in 1979, for the first time since Korea began its industrialization in the early 1960s, commodity exports declined in real terms by 4 percent, while the growth rate of GNP fell to 7.0 percent, the lowest level since 1975. The widespread price controls, imposed to curb inflation, and subsidized credit allocation schemes that led to negative real interest rates were encouraging rent-seeking activities, particularly in real estate. Corporate financial structures grew increasingly fragile. International interest rates increased after the second oil shock, and the wisdom of the heavy foreign borrowing of the 1970s was called into question.

A Radical Change in Course: Comprehensive Measures for Economic Stabilization

In late 1978, when the macroeconomic situation was deteriorating, President Park had asked the Economic and Scientific Council, the Bank of Korea, and the KDI each to propose measures to stabilize the economy. He entrusted the EPB with the task of preparing a comprehensive stabilization program based on their proposals. By early 1979 the overall role of the government in the economy was being questioned, and the EPB proposed a reorientation of economic policies toward increasing the efficiency of the manufacturing and agricultural sectors. It was clear a major shift was in order.

In April 1979 the government announced the Comprehensive Measures for Economic Stabilization (CMES) program, whose goal was nothing less than a restructuring of the entire economy so that Korea could make full use of its potential to achieve and sustain high levels of growth. The rapid growth of the Park years, however necessary, had created inefficiencies in the economy and high inflation that had decreased Korea's international competitiveness. Considerations of efficiency and price stability now had to move to the fore.

The CMES marked a striking change in both the philosophy and mode of national economic management: it required a redirection of government policy from simple growth maximization and heavy-handed public involvement in the economy toward more reliance on market forces and concern with stabilization. It was intended to bring about dramatic shifts in policy direction by reemphasizing stability as the basis for economic growth in the 1980s. Back in the 1970s, proposals for a gradual reduction of the fiscal and monetary incentives for export promotion and agricultural subsidies, decreases in rural housing loans, and a realignment of investment away from heavy and chemical industries could hardly be discussed because they were considered taboo.[25] Now there was a general consensus that stabilization was a precondition for resuming growth. The framers of the CMES believed that continuation of an expansionist approach would not ensure further growth and would lead to a breakdown in the economy.

It was also recognized that Korea's position in the world economy had changed. As a result of the ambitious heavy and chemical industry development program of the late 1970s, unit labor costs had risen and areas of comparative advantage shifted. Korea began to ascend the ladder of international trade, in some cases moving into direct competition with developed countries. This evolution, combined with the export sector's large and increasing shares of some world markets, required an increased emphasis on trade relations. It also limited policymakers' freedom of action, for many of their decisions would now significantly affect Korea's trading partners. These global ties became more of a problem as the world trade environment worsened in the late 1970s. Policymakers faced the unenviable task of trying to upgrade the industrial structure in an unfavorable trade environment; in its new industrial and trade strategies, Korea would have to pay far greater attention to trade relations.

The CMES was based on conservative fiscal and monetary policies and included a range of measures. One was restrictive budget management, with a targeted 5 percent cut in nominal current expenditures, the deferment, scaling down, or cancellation of some public investment projects, particularly in the heavy and chemical industries, a realignment of credit priorities in favor of light industries, and reduced investment in rural housing projects. A second was restrictive monetary policy to control excessive liquidity, with an emphasis on tightly controlling monetary expansion and fundamentally reforming the banking sector by denationalizing the commercial banks, reducing the subsidized credits, and maintaining a positive real interest rate. Finally, a major focus was stabilization of the prices of daily necessities, including, through the expansion of agricultural production complexes, increased stockpiles and imports, a streamlined system of commodity distribution, elimination of most price controls, and stepped-up import liberalization efforts (Kim 1984, pp. 17–18). (For details on the program, see Korea, Economic Planning Board 1979; and Nam 1984, pp. 18–25.)

Unfortunately, the stabilization efforts were undermined by unexpected, rapid changes in external and internal conditions. Along with the other NICS (except Mexico, which would later pay tenfold for its good fortune), Korea was hit hard by the second oil shock because of its overwhelming dependence on foreign energy, the resulting worldwide recession, and rising interest rates. Export-led growth became export-led recession. Short-term responses to the supply shock precluded implementation of the central elements of stabilization. In an already difficult time, the assassination of President Park produced profound political instability, which made it hard to formulate coherent long-term policies. An unusual drought caused a disastrous crop failure in 1980, which was followed by another crop failure the next year. Real agricultural GDP dropped in both 1978 and 1980, with the decline in 1980 an especially severe 21.7 percent. All these factors aggravated the mounting structural difficulties that had resulted from policies such as the drive for heavy and chemical industrialization, which had led to declining export performance, excess capacity, and unstable financial structures in many manufacturing industries. The banks were still plagued by accumulating nonperforming loans, real wages were increasing sharply, the real exchange rate was appreciating, and inflation as measured by the consumer price index (CPI) accelerated, reaching 34.6 percent in 1980 (December to December). The tight monetary policy magnified the recessionary effects of the oil shock. Unemployment reached 5.2 percent in

1980, the highest level in ten years. The current account deficit rose sharply to record levels as the price competitiveness of domestic industry continued to decline and the bill for energy imports soared. Exports were still weak. Inevitably, in 1980 the Korean economy experienced, for the first time in more than two decades, a negative growth rate: -4.8 percent.

These factors, and anticipation of a $3 billion increase in the oil import bill, forced the government to undertake a 20 percent devaluation of the won against the dollar in January 1980. At the same time, the government introduced a managed floating system to maintain export profitability and reduce the current account deficit. To engineer a real devaluation, supportive policies were implemented to reduce aggregate demand. In particular, the government pursued a strategy of monetary restraint and adjusted a wide range of interest rates upward by 5–6 percentage points.

These macroeconomic adjustment policies were supplemented with more specific switching and microeconomic policies. Financial support for public construction, small and medium-size firms, residential construction (especially for low-income families), and export of heavy industrial products on a deferred payment basis were augmented. Tax instruments were also actively utilized—a temporary investment tax credit, a reduction in personal and corporate income taxes, and capital gains and special excise taxes—on a selective basis.

The government anticipated that the second oil shock and the large 1980 devaluation would lead to a final increase in prices. As inflation rose, the government introduced income policies to prevent the price rise from becoming a new inflationary spiral. Mindful that nominal wages had risen more than 30 percent a year from 1974 to 1979, government officials believed that a slowdown was needed to minimize the output losses that lower inflation might incur. Thus moderate and well-publicized salary increases for the public sector were issued as informal guidelines for the private sector. The resultant wage restraint, coupled with some real exchange rate appreciation and declining international prices for imported raw materials, coincided with a substantial slowdown in inflation between 1981 and 1982. At the same time, monetary expansion was kept at a high level, while the tight fiscal policy of 1979 was relaxed in 1980. In short, the CMES could not be effectively implemented in 1979–80 and did not bring about the anticipated positive results.

Structural Adjustment: 1980–86

Despite its initial lack of success in 1979–80, the CMES program did establish the basis for the reform efforts of the government of President Chun Doo-Hwan, inaugurated in September of 1980.[26] The new government readopted the CMES immediately after assuming power. By early 1981 the Fifth Republic was firmly established, and Chun's government was ready to tackle the issue of stabilization and structural adjustment. Evidence of Chun's inclinations could be found in his early appointments: those who had advocated structural reform most forcefully during the later Park years became the principal architects of economic policy.

In 1981 the reformers launched a development strategy directed toward achieving three related goals: (a) price stability, particularly for daily necessities; (b) market liberalization; and (c) balanced economic growth. The most important manifesto of the reformers—as well as their primary instrument for achieving change—was the Fifth Five-Year Plan (1982–86), released to the public in 1981. Although the plan embodied the three areas of emphasis, price stabilization clearly took the highest priority. The plan was based on a package of restrictive monetary and fiscal measures that replaced the aggressive government spending of the late 1970s.

The economic planners pursued the new orthodoxy with great zeal. The EPB and other ministries simultaneously launched a massive publicity campaign to convert the public to stabilization, emphasizing the long-term benefits that short-term sacrifices would bring. Public support was crucial to the success of the program, because to break the inflationary cycle workers would have to moderate their wage demands and farmers and others would have to accept reductions in government subsidies.

Price Stabilization

In pursuit of price stability the government introduced a series of tight monetary and fiscal measures to eliminate the destructive cycle of inflation. In 1981 the government relaxed the fiscal and monetary policies to counter the severe economic recession. In response the public sector deficit rose from 3.2 percent of GNP in 1980 to 4.6 percent in 1981, and domestic credit expanded at an annual rate of 30 percent from May through September of 1982, in the face of financial scandal in the curb market in May of that year. In 1983, however, as the GNP growth rate recovered and turmoil in the financial markets subsided, the government took a very restrictive stance on financial policy.[27] Public sector expenditures, which throughout the 1970s had been growing, resulting in a public sector deficit, were cut back sharply. In 1984 the government went so far as to freeze nominal spending at 1983 levels. As a result the overall government budget deficit as a ratio of GNP dropped from 5.6 percent in 1981 to 1.5 percent in 1985. Aggregate demand was controlled through a restrictive monetary policy designed to limit the overall rate of expansion of the money supply, which slowed considerably after 1982.

Another important component of the stabilization program was income policy, which played an essential role in breaking the inflationary trend of the economy. By issuing suggested guidelines for wage increases and setting low scheduled raises for the salaries of its own employees, the government made a strenuous effort to keep nominal wage increases at reasonable levels. Although it is difficult to quantify the influence of the income policy on wage trends, the average increase in nominal wages dropped from 23.4 percent in 1980 to 9.2 percent in 1985. At the same time, real wages, after suffering declines in both 1980 and 1981, rebounded in 1982–85, with an average annual increase of 7.0 percent.

A further measure designed to stabilize prices was a steady reduction in the rice subsidy to farmers. Although the government had raised the purchase price of rice, Korea's staple crop, by 25 percent in 1980, it provided no increase in 1983 and only a slight boost of 3 percent in 1985.

Market Liberalization

In conjunction with the price stabilization program, the government pursued a wide-ranging policy of market liberalization. Through a variety of internal and external reforms it attempted to give more autonomy to the private sector and to allow market principles to play a larger role. In keeping with this policy, the government has shifted its style of economic management away from the direct intervention of the 1960s and 1970s and toward more reliance on indirect guidance and market forces. In many respects this approach is a radical departure from the previous forms of economic management, but it reflects the increased size and complexity of the Korean economy.

The first front in this campaign was the financial sector, where the government relinquished a degree of control by denationalizing the banks. In addition, the barriers to entry by foreign banks were lowered, a step that increased competition and thus allocative efficency. Foreign firms were also given greater access to the Korean securities market.[28]

The most significant aspect of the market liberalization program was import liberalization, designed to harness the market mechanism to improve the quality of Korean products. During the 1960s and 1970s imports had been tightly restricted and manufacturers faced little outside competition. Quality lagged behind the levels achieved in other countries, which threatened Korea's export-dependent economy. Import liberalization, by introducing foreign competition at a steadily increasing pace, was expected to pressure domestic producers into raising both productivity and quality.

The proportion of freely importable items among all commodities rose from 68.2 percent in 1979 to 74.7 percent in 1982 and 91.5 percent in 1986. Tariff rates were reduced from 38.7 percent in 1978 to 19.9 percent in 1986. Many industries, including pharmaceuticals, food processing, and services, were opened to foreign investors through liberalization of the restrictions on foreign ownership.[29]

Other elements of the liberalization program included partial deregulation of foreign investment—in most sectors, foreign firms could now enter without prior approval—and a strengthening of domestic antimonopoly regulations, which was intended to eliminate the market distortions caused by the huge domestic conglomerates.

The first step in the liberalization program was the enactment in 1981 of the Fair Trade and Anti-Monopoly Act. This legislation established a Fair Trade Administration under the EPB. Responsible for overseeing the activities of the nation's large business groups and for reducing unfair trade practices, the Fair Trade Administration helped eliminate cartel arrangements, price-fixing, and other monopolistic practices and thereby improved domestic competition and discouraged businesses from entering into monopolies.[30]

Korea's industrial policy also underwent a significant change as part of the liberalization effort. In the 1960s and 1970s targeted sectors had received preferential financing. Under the liberalization program all subsidized "policy" loans were eliminated, and the government no longer targeted areas of the economy for preferential treatment. Market forces increasingly dictated which sectors would prosper. This shift obviously signaled a large change from Korea's earlier growth strategy, but it reflected the reality that the subsidized loan policy had resulted in overinvestment in some industries, unbalanced industrial development, and an underdeveloped financial sector.

Balanced Growth

At the outset of the Fifth Plan, the administration placed strong emphasis on attaining balanced growth (growth with equity). Its early policy statements, for example, often contained references to the need to build a "welfare state" in Korea. In keeping with that priority, the third key policy objective was the promotion of balanced growth and social development. Limits on government resources, however, dictated that this goal receive even less rhetorical and legislative support than liberalization. Even that diminished level of priority was an improvement over the welfare policies of previous plans and it did attract attention to welfare concerns, lending them a greater degree of legitimacy than they had previously enjoyed.

This new acceptance and the overall resumption of economic growth did result in some progress. By 1985, 43.4 percent of the population was covered by the state's medical insurance program, up from 10.5 percent in 1978, and the percentage is expected to continue to rise rapidly. Expenditures under the Livelihood Protection Program, which provides various forms of assistance to the poorest members of society, nearly doubled between 1981 and 1985.

Another area of emphasis was the enhancement of off-farm employment opportunities and rural industrialization, which would extend the nation's spreading industrial estate to rural towns.[31] The government also promoted small-scale enterprises: in contrast to its policies in the 1970s, since 1981 the government has emphasized a balance between large- and small-scale industries by providing financial incentives for research and development, marketing, and industrial expansion of small and medium-size firms.

Although social welfare was a lower priority than other goals in the Fifth Plan, total government expenditures for social welfare have been rising steadily. As a percentage of overall government outlays, welfare expenditures rose from 21.4 percent in 1974 to almost 30 percent during 1982–86. The largest component went to education, which received 13.7 percent of total government expenditures in 1978 and 17.6 percent during 1982–86. Although this shift indicates an emphasis on indirect assistance, expenditures in other areas, notably housing, also registered an increase.[32]

The Results

How did the Korean economy respond to these reforms and policy directions? Although at the time this study was conducted it was too early to make a comprehensive evaluation, when Korea's economic performance through 1986, the cutoff year for this study, is considered, the results are good (see table 2-10).[33] In light of the international recession in 1980, the real growth rate of 6.6 percent in 1981 was quite acceptable, and continued momentum in 1983 produced 11.9 percent GNP growth and in 1984, 8.4 percent. Although growth slowed to 5.4 percent in 1985, it reached 12.5 percent in 1986. Given the reforms to eliminate the structural problems of the economy, this expansion represents a notable achievement.

The most significant recent achievement, however, was the success in curbing inflation. Compared with inflation rates of approximately 15 percent a year in the 1970s, wholesale prices in 1986 actually declined by 2.2 percent, while consumer prices rose at an annual rate of only 2.3 percent. Although a large factor in the successful stabilization of prices was the decline in the cost of oil and other imported raw materials, consistent efforts by the government to restrict wage and price increases helped the economy capitalize on these favorable external conditions.

The emphasis on improving the balance of payments and reducing the foreign debt also paid off. The current account deficit, which stood at $1.6 billion in 1983, was nearly halved to $0.9 billion in 1985, a drop that reduced Korea's foreign borrowing requirements. In 1986 the current account of the balance of payments registered a surplus of $4.6 billion, which helped to reduce the level of total outstanding external debt.

Moreover, the evidence suggests that Korea's structural adjustment efforts helped improve equity as well as efficiency. Income distribution improved somewhat, with the Gini coefficient dropping from 0.3891 in 1980 to 0.3567 in 1984. The improvement was significant for both farm and

Table 2-10. Key Economic Indicators, 1980s

Indicator	1979	1980	1981	1982	1983	1984	1985	1986
Economic growth rate (percent)[a]	7.0	−4.8	6.6	5.4	11.9	8.4	5.4	12.5
Per capita GNP (dollars)[b]	1,640	1,589	1,719	1,773	1,914	2,044	2,047	2,300
Prices (percentage change from previous year)								
Wholesale prices	18.8	38.9	20.4	4.7	0.2	0.7	0.9	−2.2
Consumer prices	18.3	28.7	21.3	7.2	3.4	2.3	2.5	2.3
Current account balance (100 millions of dollars)	−41.5	−53.2	−46.5	−26.5	−16.1	−13.7	−8.8	46.5
Trade balance (100 millions of dollars)	−44.0	−43.8	−36.3	−25.9	−17.6	−10.4	−0.2	42.5
Exports (100 millions of dollars)	147.0	172.1	206.7	208.8	232.0	263.3	264.4	338.8
Imports (100 millions of dollars)	191.0	215.0	243.0	234.7	249.7	273.7	264.6	296.3

a. Based on the new system of national accounts introduced in 1970; at 1980 prices.
b. In nominal terms.
Source: Various issues of Bank of Korea, *Economic Statistics Yearbook.*

Table 2-11. *A Comparison of Performance, 1980–84*
(average annual percentage rate)

Economy	Growth, 1980–84[a]	Inflation 1980–84	Inflation 1984	Debt/GNP 1983	Current account/GNP 1980–83[a]
Korea	5.4	13.0	2.0	54.0	5.3
Argentina	−1.0	269.0	627.0	65.0	3.6
Brazil	1.6	125.0	197.0	30.0	4.6
Israel	2.0	176.0	374.0	90.0	7.3
Mexico	1.3	70.0	66.0	61.0	2.6
Singapore	8.6[b]	5.0	3.0	68.5[c]	9.7
Thailand	5.6	9.0	1.0	32.0	5.8
Turkey	5.0	51.0	46.0	33.0	3.6

a. Period average.
b. 1980–83.
c. Public debt only.

nonfarm households. In addition, the incidence of poverty decreased markedly: in 1980 the percentage of the population at the absolute poverty level was 9.8 percent; in 1984 it was 4.5 percent. These improvements indicate the positive influence that the structural adjustment policies had on national welfare.

It is also interesting to look at how Korea did in coping with the crises of the late 1970s and early 1980s in comparison with other economies. As table 2-11 shows, with respect to growth and inflation, Korea outperformed its Latin American counterparts, as well as Israel and Turkey. The performance of Thailand was roughly the same, and that of Singapore was somewhat better.

Although Korean policy and its implementation were clearly dominant factors in the successful adjustment of the 1980s, it is also true that after 1982 Korea faced an increasingly favorable external environment. World trade picked up once again—particularly in the United States, Korea's most important export market—commodity prices declined significantly, oil prices dropped dramatically, and interest rates started coming down after 1983. The important point, however, is that Korea took full advantage of these opportunities.

Notes

1. All dollar amounts are in current U.S. dollars unless otherwise noted.
2. Billion is 1,000 million.
3. To restrict imports quantitatively, an import licensing system was administered on a semiannual basis. The average level of tariffs was about 40 percent. Although the government attempted to counteract the export disincentive effects of the currency overvaluation and high tariffs through a system linking exports and imports and by providing low-interest credit for exporters, industrial policy during the 1950s remained inward-looking.

4. In 1958 the government established an Economic Development Council within the Ministry of Reconstruction to prepare a three-year development plan for the period 1960–62. This plan was postponed for a year and came into effect only a few days before the fall of the Rhee regime in April 1960.

5. Mason and others (1980) estimate that, on the assumption of no substitution of domestic savings for foreign aid, GNP during 1953–62 would have been 3 percentage points lower, which implies that per capita income steadily declined during this period.

6. An unusually large share of the financial burden for education shifted to private households. The government's expenditures on education during the 1950s remained below 2 percent of GNP, considerably lower than the corresponding figures in other countries. McGinn and others (1980) estimate that private households paid about two-thirds of the direct cost of education, as opposed to perhaps one-third in a more typical developing country.

7. Land reform was implemented without much political resistance because about one-fifth of the land farmed by tenants was owned by Japanese landlords who left Korea in 1945. Korean landlords were politically weak because they carried the taint of collaboration with the Japanese.

8. Such rapid increases in the size of the financial system are almost unparalleled in recent world experience. Although some may argue that a large portion of the growth in bank deposits was merely a shift of funds away from the unorganized money markets, the 1965 reform seems to have resulted in a rise in the domestic savings rate. For example, the private savings rate rose from 5 percent of GNP in 1962–65 to 10 percent in 1966–70. See Chandavarkar (1971) and McKinnon (1973).

9. Later in the 1960s the EPB absorbed the Bureau of Budget from the Ministry of Finance and the Bureau of Statistics from the Ministry of Home Affairs.

10. In 1982 it would lose the programming function and become the Office of Administrative Coordination.

11. The tax most affected by the strengthening of tax administration was the income tax, the collection of which had suffered from widespread evasion. The income tax increased from 25 percent of nonagricultural personal income in 1964 to 53 percent in 1971, while taxable income under the corporate income tax rose from 2.26 percent of GNP in 1965 to 3.51 percent in 1970 (see Park 1977).

12. Chapter 13 discusses another important area of institutional operations, the effective channels of formal and informal communication within the government and between the government and the private sector, including the general public.

13. Although the foreign aid totals were much smaller in the 1960s than in the 1950s, their contribution to development per unit of aid increased as a result of the more sensible economic policies followed by the government. Aid agencies such as the U.S. Agency for International Development and the World Bank played an instrumental role in initiating the economic policy changes during the 1960s.

14. It has been claimed that in the initial years of the export promotion drive the real exchange rate was deliberately kept above its equilibrium level as a means of expanding exports.

15. The accelerating rate of growth in labor-intensive export industries provided a steadily expanding pool of job opportunities for the unemployed and under-employed and helped absorb the growing labor force. For example, the rates of

unemployment and underemployment (defined as those working less than eighteen hours a week) declined from 8.2 percent and 8.0 percent in 1963 to 4.5 percent and 4.7 percent in 1970, respectively.

16. Trillion is 1,000 billion.

17. For example, in 1968 the government selling price for rice was 24 percent higher than the purchase price, whereas in 1975 the purchase price was 16 percent higher than the selling price and, as a result, there was a substantial deficit.

18. The deficits in the grain and fertilizer accounts amounted, on average, to 110.5 percent of the total budget deficits during 1972–80.

19. M2 is currency plus demand deposits plus quasi-money.

20. Real appreciation was probably higher because price controls were quite extensive by 1979, and important premiums emerged in the black market.

21. On these points, see chapters 3, 5, 6, 7, and 9.

22. See chapters 3 and 5.

23. See chapter 12.

24. For example, in 1979 oil accounted for 63 percent of domestic energy consumption, and all the oil consumed in Korea was imported.

25. Interview with Kyung-sik Kang by In-Joung Wang.

26. See chapters 3 and 5. In addition, see chapter 12, where the author argues that the preparation that occurred under the CMES saved the economy from an even worse decline.

27. See chapters 3 and 5.

28. For an analysis of financial policies during the period, see chapter 6.

29. The import liberalization policy is analyzed in chapter 8.

30. See chapter 9.

31. See chapter 7 on agricultural policy.

32. On social welfare, see chapter 7.

33. For an overall assessment of Korea's adjustment program, see chapter 8.

References

Bank of Korea. Various issues. *Economic Statistics Yearbook*. In Korean. Seoul.

Chandavarkar, Anand G. 1971. "Some Aspects of Interest Rate Policies in Less Developed Economies: The Experience of Selected Asian Countries." *IMF Staff Papers* 18 (March): 48–112.

Choo, Hakchung. 1980. "Economic Growth and Income Distribution." In Chong Kee Park, ed., *Human Resources and Social Development in Korea*. Seoul: Korea Development Institute.

Kim, Kihwan. 1984. *The Korean Economy: Past Performance, Current Reforms and Future Prospects*. Seoul: Korea Development Institute.

Kim, K. S., and J. K. Park. 1985. *Sources of Economic Growth in South Korea: 1963– 82*. Seoul: Korea Development Institute.

Korea, Bureau of Statistics. 1981. *The 1981 Social Indicator Survey*. In Korean. Seoul.

Korea, Economic Planning Board. 1979. "Comprehensive Measures for Economic Stabilization." In Korean. Seoul.

———. Various issues. *Korea Statistical Yearbook*. In Korean. Seoul.

————. Various issues. *The Family Income and Expenditure Survey.* In Korean. Seoul.

Korea, Ministry of Agriculture and Fisheries. Various issues. *The Farm Household Economy Survey.* In Korean, Seoul.

Mason, Edward S., Mahn Je Kim, Dwight H. Perkins, Kwang Suk Kim, and David C. Cole. 1980. *The Economic and Social Modernization of the Republic of Korea.* Cambridge, Mass.: Council on East Asian Studies. Harvard University.

McGinn, Noel F., Donald R. Snodgrass, Yung Bong Kim, Shin Bok Kim, and Quee-Young Kim. 1980. *Education and Development in Korea.* Cambridge, Mass.: Council on East Asian Studies, Harvard University.

McKinnon, Ronald I. 1973. *Money and Capital in Economic Development.* Washington, D.C.: Brookings Institution.

Nam, Sang-Woo. 1984. "Korea's Stabilization Efforts since the Late 1970s." Working Paper 8405. Seoul: Korea Development Institute.

Park, Chong Kee. 1977. *Development and Modernization of Korea's Tax System.* Seoul: Korea Development Institute.

Suh, Sang-Chul. 1978. *Growth and Structural Changes in the Korean Economy, 1910–1940.* Cambridge, Mass.: Harvard University Press.

Whang, In-Joung. 1971. "Leadership and Organizational Development in Economic Ministries in Korea." *Asian Survey* 2 (October): 992–1004.

3 Recent Evolution of the Macroeconomy

VITTORIO CORBO, Catholic University of Chile
SANG-WOO NAM, World Bank

THIS CHAPTER PROVIDES an overview of the recent macroeconomic evolution of the Korean economy. Particular attention is given to the years 1977–86, which included a period of significant adjustment. The chapter is divided into five sections. The first reviews the evolution of the main macroeconomic variables over the past twenty-five years, especially the role of incentives in the evolution of exports and output and the effects of external shocks. The second section provides an accounting decomposition of gross national product (GNP) growth with regard to both demand and supply. The third considers the effect of external shocks on the Korean economy, an analysis that involved the building of a model of the current account, which was first estimated and then simulated for three counterfactual experiments. The first experiment assumed that the 1973–75 external environment—terms of trade, London interbank offered rate (LIBOR), and rate of growth in industrialized countries—corresponded to that in 1971–72 and took no account of the first oil shock and related economic dislocation. In the second experiment the external environment of 1979–82 was assumed to correspond to that of 1976–78 and not to encompass the second oil shock and the effects of the related world recession. In the final model it was assumed that the external environment of 1980–82 persisted in 1983–85. Korea's fiscal and monetary policy is examined in the fourth section: fiscal policy in 1971–84 is analyzed using methodology for measuring fiscal impulse developed by the International Monetary Fund (IMF) and the Organisation for Economic Co-operation and Development (OECD); monetary policy is evaluated for the years 1979–82 and 1983–84. The final section presents the main conclusions.

Twenty-five Years of Economic Development

For purposes of evaluating Korea's economic development in the past twenty-five years, it is useful to review briefly the major trends in three periods: 1963–72, 1973–80, and 1981–86.[1]

1963–72

During the years 1963 through 1972, a period in which exports were emphasized and incentives made more equal across import-competing activities, Korea achieved stunning successes. Real GNP growth averaged 9.1 percent a year, largely because of an explosion in exports, particularly manufactures. Annual inflation ran in the teens, while domestic absorption grew slightly faster than GNP. Foreign transfers were minimal. At its peak in 1968–71 the current account deficit was 8.4 percent of GNP. After an initial large real devaluation in 1963–64, the real exchange rate was relatively stable for the rest of the period, despite short-term variations.

Exports performed well because the large real devaluation of 1963–64 and the accompanying export promotion policies shifted incentives sharply in favor of export-oriented activities (Westphal 1978; Nam 1985) at a time of substantial expansion in world trade. In addition, the base value of commodity exports in 1962 was small.

1973–80

During 1973–80, Korea promoted import substitution for investment goods and raw materials. Encouraged by government policy, investment in the heavy and chemical industries was enormous. This investment neutralized the recessionary effect of the sharp drop in the terms of trade following the first oil shock, while an expansionary monetary policy boosted total real absorption. The government extended its price support program for rice, and the resulting deficits in the Grain Management Fund and Fertilizer Fund were responsible for 37 percent of the total growth of the money supply during 1976–78. The current account deficit financed by foreign debt reached the highest level in twenty-five years.

Expansionary aggregate demand policies and heavy foreign borrowing produced an average annual rate of GNP growth of 8.2 percent in the 1973–80 period, but at the cost of high inflation (21.3 percent based on the GNP deflator and 20.1 percent based on the world price index, or WPI), despite controls on many wage goods. They also produced a flourishing black market. The labor market, meanwhile, became very tight.

Appreciation of the real exchange rate was almost 24 percent, and perhaps higher, between 1973 and 1979. The rate of growth in output for a unit of input decelerated considerably. The expansion of exports also slowed, with negative figures reported in 1974 and 1979. As a consequence of the overheated labor market and rapidly rising real wages in manufacturing and exporting (see table 3-1, columns 2 and 4), Korea quickly lost its competitiveness in labor-intensive activities. The large increase in the export of construction services to the Middle East, although positive, was based on heavy government subsidies. The current account deficit as a share of GNP fell to near zero in 1977 before increasing to 8.7 percent in 1980.

At the end of the 1970s, Korea was at a crossroads: rent-seeking activities, especially those related to real estate, were commonplace; exports, the main engine of growth, had slowed considerably; and the heavy and chemi-

Table 3-1. *Relative Prices and Financial Variables, 1965–86*

Item	1965–73 (1)	1974–75 (2)	1976–78 (3)	1979 (4)	1980–81 (5)	1982–86 (6)
Relative prices (index: 1980 = 100)						
Real wages, deflated by						
Export prices	37.9	52.0	82.6	106.7	101.9	129.0
Manufacturing prices	41.5	54.8	86.6	115.2	100.8	136.6
Consumer price index	38.4	57.5	82.1	104.9	99.5	122.4
Real effective exchange rate	102.2	109.1	100.4	95.2	97.4	108.0
External terms of trade	129.8	97.1	111.8	115.3	99.0	106.2
Financial variables (percent)						
Interest rate[a]						
Bank deposit	11.6	−14.2	4.6	−0.1	−6.3	8.7
Curb market	38.0	5.4	26.2	19.9	8.4	27.0
Public sector deficit/GNP	2.4[b]	4.3	2.7	1.4	3.9	2.0
M2[c]	44.8	26.6	35.2	26.8	26.6	17.4
Bank credit[c]	45.8	43.2	30.4	35.6	36.6	17.3

a. Real rates, computed as $i - \pi / 1 + \pi$, where i is the nominal rate and π is the average annual inflation as measured by the wholesale price index.

b. Average for 1971–73.

c. Percentage rate of change.

Source: Bank of Korea and the Ministry of Finance.

cal industries showed excess capacity. The second oil shock threatened a further deterioration in the terms of trade. The related increase in international interest rates called into question the high level of borrowing of the late 1970s. To make matters worse, two consecutive bad harvests resulted in a severe drop in real agricultural GNP in 1978 and 1980. Unemployment, while still low, reached the highest level in ten years. As business firms borrowed as much as possible at negative real interest rates to invest in real assets, their corporate financial structures grew increasingly fragile. Predictably, the government's price controls led to supply shortages, black markets, and deteriorating product quality. In the late 1970s the public became increasingly concerned about the efficiency of widespread government control in an increasingly complex and highly open economy (Park 1985b).

In the spring of 1979 the government adopted the Comprehensive Measures for Economic Stabilization (CMES) program, which included economic liberalization actions. The second oil shock and rejection of the risky alternative of financing a large current account deficit lent urgency to the stabilization effort. Finally, in early 1980 the government instituted a large devaluation, which was followed by a managed float and restrictions on aggregate demand.

1981–86

The years 1981 through 1986 were a time of adjustment, following the CMES and other reforms.[2] Recovery took much longer than expected because of external shocks—the second oil shock, the slowdown in economic activity in the OECD countries, and the increase in international interest rates.

During this period the government used a variety of measures to promote stabilization and economic growth, including flexible fiscal and monetary policies. In 1981, for example, the government relaxed monetary policy to spur what appeared to be an unduly slow recovery. To encourage growth, it also instituted changes in tax policy, such as temporary tax credits for investment. After 1982, given new conditions, it slowed the monetary expansion and tightened fiscal policy. In the area of income policy, it provided only moderate wage increases to the public sector and successfully encouraged the private sector to exercise similar moderation. It also reduced interest rates and lowered its purchase price for rice. Exchange rate management was flexible.

Economic growth resumed strongly in 1983, led by private consumption, construction, and, in the second half of the year, growing exports. Once the macroeconomic crisis was brought under control, increases in productivity and capacity utilization made possible the return to high growth with low inflation (see also chapter 4). In 1985 less favorable external conditions and sluggishness in the construction industry led to a 2 percentage point drop in GNP growth. In response the government initiated stimulatory measures, such as a depreciation of the won and a looser monetary policy. Growth picked up again in 1986, and there was a big turnaround in the external balance, domestic savings increased, and inflation stayed low. Korea also benefited from an improvement in the terms of trade and more favorable external conditions. The current account moved into a surplus, while gross foreign debt declined by around $2 billion.

These results were possible because the government pursued macroeconomic policies that allowed the economy to take advantage of the positive external environment. A significant characteristic of this period was the considerable flexibility the government maintained in adapting economic policy to both domestic and foreign economic circumstances.

Exchange Rate Policy and Recovery

One point that emerges clearly from this review is the role of exchange rate policy. Overall, the government has kept the real effective exchange rate of the Korean won at a fairly constant level since the mid-1960s. Because inflation was generally much higher in Korea than in its major trading partners, this approach meant a steady depreciation of the nominal exchange rate, although with some deviations. Following a 100 percent nominal devaluation of the won in relation to the U.S. dollar, triggered by a foreign exchange crisis in 1964, the nominal exchange rate adjustment fell short of the difference in inflation rates. The result was a 13 percent appreciation in the real effective exchange rate during 1968–69 over the 1965

Table 3-2. *Sources of Growth by Demand Sector, 1961–86*
(percentage contribution)

Item	1961–70	1971–73	1974–75	1976–78	1979–82	1983–86[a]
Private consumption	5.5	5.7	4.6	5.6	2.5	3.8
Government consumption	0.7	0.5	0.8	1.1	0.3	0.6
Fixed investment	3.3	2.3	2.3	7.1	0.5	3.8
Private construction	1.3	1.2	1.0	2.9	0.5	—
Government construction	0.6	0.0	0.4	0.6	0.2	—
Producers' durable equipment	1.3	1.2	0.9	3.5	−0.3	1.8
Inventory change	0.4	0.2	1.5	−0.9	−0.6	0.0
External trade (net)	−1.4	0.6	−1.4	−0.8	0.6	1.5
Exports	2.1	5.4	1.4	7.0	2.4	5.3
Imports	−3.6	−4.5	−2.3	−8.8	−0.8	−3.7
Net factor income	0.0	−0.3	−0.5	0.9	−1.0	0.0
GNP growth rate (percent)	8.4	9.5	7.3	12.2	3.2	9.5

— Not available.

Note: The sectoral contributions were obtained by allocating the compound GNP growth rate to each sector in proportion to the accumulated changes in its value added. Because of statistical discrepancies and rounding errors, the sectoral contributions may not add up to the total.

a. Based on a new system of national accounts.

Source: Authors' estimates based on primary data from the Bank of Korea.

level. During 1970–72 the nominal depreciation of the Korean won was somewhat accelerated, while the value of the U.S. dollar fell against other major currencies during 1972–73. These developments led to a substantial depreciation in Korea's real effective exchange rate during 1970–73. High domestic inflation under the fixed exchange rate regime following the first oil price shock quickly eliminated most of the real effective depreciation, in spite of the two major nominal devaluations in late 1974 and early 1980.

Some additional real effective appreciation of the won took place during the first phase of the stabilization program in 1981–82, an indication that exchange rate management was biased toward curbing inflation. After 1983, when the deceleration of inflation was evident, exchange rate management was free of that stabilization bias and tilted toward stimulating exports and growth. As mentioned, the real effective exchange rate of the won showed substantial depreciation during 1985–86 in connection with the sharp slide of the U.S. dollar that began in mid-1985.

Sources of Economic Growth

A demand decomposition of the sources of growth (table 3-2) shows that the external sector contributed 0.6 percentage point to GNP growth in 1971–73, a big turnaround from the −1.4 percentage points achieved in 1961–70. A large and sustained expansion in exports provided the foreign exchange needed to buy the imports that made possible a large and sustained expansion in output.

The worldwide recession after the first oil price shock had such a severe effect on exports of Korean goods and nonfactor services that their contribution to GNP growth dropped from 5.4 percentage points during 1971–73 to 1.4 percentage points during 1974–75. Nevertheless, Korea managed to maintain a relatively high rate of GNP growth—7.3 percent—in 1974–75, when many non-oil-producing countries registered negative growth. The change in the relative price of energy products and the countercyclical aggregate demand policies seem to have been the main contributing factors.

During 1976–78 the economy was characterized by an overheated investment boom and rapid expansion of both exports and imports. With increased bank credit at subsidized interest rates and a large inflow of foreign capital, facilitated by the government's efforts to promote the heavy and chemical industries, fixed investment expanded at an annual rate of 27.0 percent and contributed 7.1 percentage points (58 percent) to the GNP growth of 12.2 percent. A substantial portion of this investment involved imported capital goods. Thus, despite fairly rapid export growth and overseas construction in the Middle East, on a demand-accounting basis the external sector was a net negative contributor to GNP growth during this period. Given that total consumption did not increase markedly to match GNP growth, the domestic savings ratio rose from 19.1 percent of GNP in 1975 to 28.5 percent of GNP in 1978.

By 1978 the appreciation of the real exchange rate (17.9 percent between 1973 and 1978) that had developed as a consequence of the expansionary demand policies of 1974–78 was having negative effects on export growth. Then came the second oil price shock. As a result of both factors the real growth of exports of goods and nonfactor services slowed from an annual rate of 27.7 percent during 1976–78 to 7.1 percent during 1979–82, despite the large depreciation in the exchange rate since early 1980.

A more dramatic development was the weakening of investment and import demand: fixed investment and imports of goods and nonfactor services rose at average annual rates of only 1.5 percent and 2.1 percent, respectively, during 1979–82, and investment in producers' durable equipment declined. Because of the slow growth of imports, the external sector made a positive contribution to real GNP in spite of the sharp deterioration in the balance of factor income that resulted from the high international interest rates. Fiscal policy at this time was generally restrictive, in line with the government's strong anti-inflationary efforts, and contributed to the weak demand. As consumption adjusted slowly and partially to the low growth in incomes, the domestic savings ratio dropped considerably to a level of 20 percent during 1980–82.

The real devaluation of the early 1980s and the post-1982 recovery of the world economy, particularly that of the United States, pulled Korea back to more normal growth rates after 1982. Korea's exports were constrained,

Table 3-3. *Sources of Growth by Industry, 1961–86*
(percentage contribution)

Industry	1961–70	1971–73	1974–75	1976–78	1979–82	1983–86[a]
Agriculture, forestry, and fishing	1.6	1.1	1.5	0.1	0.3	0.6
Other	6.8	8.4	5.8	12.0	2.8	8.8
Mining and manufacturing	2.3	3.4	2.9	4.9	1.4	3.6
Construction, electricity, gas, and water	0.8	0.8	0.6	1.7	0.5	1.3
Services	3.7	4.2	2.3	5.5	1.0	3.8
Wholesale and retail trade, restaurants, and hotels	1.6	2.5	1.2	1.9	0.5	1.3
GNP growth rate (percent)	8.4	9.5	7.3	12.2	3.2	9.5

Note: The sectoral contributions were obtained by allocating the compound GNP growth rate to each sector in proportion to the accumulated changes in its value added. Because of statistical discrepancies and rounding errors, the sectoral contributions may not add up to the total.

a. Based on a new system of national accounts. Import duties and net factor income from abroad are not included in the value added by industry, and accumulated changes in imputed bank service charges by industry are assumed to be proportional to the accumulated changes in the value added of the industries.

Source: Authors' estimates based on primary data from the Bank of Korea.

however, by growing protectionism in the industrialized world against exports from newly industrialized countries such as Korea and by the weakening incentives for exporters. Declining international interest rates slowed the deterioration in the factor income balance, and in 1986 the balance improved. The sharp expansion of exports in 1986 resulting from the appreciation of the Japanese yen also helped the external sector contribute a net 1.5 percentage points to GNP growth during 1983–86. The contribution of private fixed investment and fiscal expenditures held at normal levels, but consumption was slow to adjust to rising incomes, a phenomenon that could have been linked to consumers' lowered expectations about future income growth. The result was a rise in the domestic savings ratio to 32.8 percent in 1986.

The supply-side trend was toward increasing the contribution from the manufacturing sector and reducing the share of agriculture (table 3-3). The agricultural sector also suffered from sporadic crop failures, and unfavorable weather in the summer of 1980 reduced agricultural value added by more than 20 percent. In that year the agriculture, forestry, and fishing sector was responsible for 73 percent of the −4.8 percent growth in GNP.

Despite fluctuations in the expansion of the mining and manufacturing sectors, mainly a reflection of export performance, their relative contributions to GNP growth increased steadily from 27 percent in 1961–70, to 36 percent in 1971–73, and to a 40 percent level thereafter. As Korea's export structure moved toward heavy industry and chemical products, this sub-sector's share in manufacturing value added at current market prices rose from 37 percent in 1971–73 to over 50 percent in the early 1980s.

Following the expansionary demand policies of the second half of the 1970s, there was a boom in land values and construction. Reflecting the rapid expansion in housing construction during 1976–78, the construction sector's contribution to GNP growth rose substantially, although it returned to a normal level thereafter. The services sector showed some procyclical movement, and its relative contribution to growth declined when the econ-omy was weak. The most rapidly growing service areas during 1976–78 included finance, insurance, transport, and communications; the leaders in 1983–84 were wholesale and retail trade, finance, and insurance.

Further insights into Korea's economic performance can be found in a recent study by Kim and Park (1985) of the sources of growth in the economy. Using Denison's approach, Kim and Park found that the largest contributor to growth during 1963–82, accounting for a little more than one-third of the growth rate, was the expansion of labor input (excluding education), followed by capital accumulation and scale economies. Ad-vances in knowledge contributed 18.3 percent of the standardized growth rate. When the authors divided their period of study into two subperiods (1963–72 and 1973–82), they found that total labor input (excluding educa-tion) was the largest contributor to growth in both cases. They also found that the technological improvements residual, which made the second high-est contribution to growth in the first subperiod, made the lowest contribu-tion in the second. The contribution of capital accumulation increased from 13.9 percent of the standardized rate of growth to 26.2 percent in 1973–82.

Kim and Park attribute the slowdown in technical progress and the higher contribution of capital largely to the completion of the gains from the opening-up of the economy in the 1960s and the change in development strategy to the second import-substitution effort in the second half of the 1970s. In particular, they suggest that the capital-intensive, import-sub-stituting projects of that decade did not conform with Korea's comparative advantage (Kim and Park 1985, pp. 173–74).

Effects of the External Shocks on the Economy: A Model of the Current Account

The Korean economy[3] was hit hard by the unfavorable international eco-nomic environment during the decade from 1973 to 1982. For a relatively small, open economy that was heavily dependent on exports for growth and on imports for raw materials and capital goods, the impact of the two oil price shocks and the ensuing worldwide recession was profound.

Table 3-4. *Major Changes in Korea's External Environment,*
1971–85

Period	Terms of trade (1980 = 100)	International interest rate[a] (percent)	GDP growth of OECD countries (percent)	Percentage share of exports to the Middle East
Before the first shock				
1971	132.7	6.58	3.5	0.8
1972	132.1	5.37	5.2	3.3
After the first shock				
1973	125.4	9.42	5.5	1.3
1974	102.1	10.90	0.2	2.6
1975	92.1	6.95	−0.8	6.2
Before the second shock				
1976	105.1	5.57	5.2	9.1
1977	112.4	6.05	3.9	10.8
1978	117.8	8.85	4.0	9.0
After the second shock				
1979	115.3	12.09	3.0	7.7
1980	100.0	14.19	0.6	8.8
1981	97.9	16.87	1.5	8.1
1982	102.2	13.29	−0.2	7.9
Post-1982				
1983	103.1	9.72	3.0	9.9
1984	105.3	10.94	5.0	5.4
1985	105.9	8.40	3.0	4.8

a. Three-month Eurodollar rate.
Source: Bank of Korea and various issues of IMF, *International Financial Statistics.*

Table 3-4 shows the magnitude of the impact of the external shocks. The first produced a worldwide recession: gross domestic product (GDP) in the industrialized countries, which had grown by an average of more than 5 percent a year during 1971–73, stagnated during 1974–75. In addition, the short-term Eurodollar rate jumped from around 6 percent in 1971–72 to an average of 10.2 percent in 1973–74. For Korea, as the unit value of imports rose 113 percent during 1973–75, the external terms of trade deteriorated by 30 percent.

The second oil price shock was every bit as traumatic, and during 1979–81 Korea's terms of trade worsened by 28 percent. The industrialized countries adopted monetary policies that were more restrictive than those they had adopted after the first one. As a result, international interest rates rose dramatically. For example, the short-term Eurodollar rate more than doubled from an average of 6.8 percent during 1976–78 to an average of 14.1 percent during 1979–82. During 1980–82 average annual GDP growth in the industrialized countries was only 0.6 percent, a significant drop from the 4.0 percent average of 1976–79. Only in 1983 did the industrialized countries start to recover from the recession.

Two positive consequences of the oil price shocks were the rapid growth of imports in the oil-exporting countries and the active participation of Korean construction companies in ambitious development projects in the Middle East. Korean exports of products to that region expanded rapidly: their share in total exports jumped from 2.0 percent in 1971-74 to 10.8 percent in 1977. After the second oil price shock, however, there was no further increase in this component of Korea's exports.

The effect of the two shocks on the Korean economy was obvious. The external current account deficit jumped from an annual average of $340 million during 1972-73 to almost $2 billion during 1974-75. The weakening of the balance of payments after the second oil price shock was even more dramatic: the current account balance, which had recorded a small surplus in 1977 and a deficit of $1.1 billion in 1978, registered an annual average deficit of $4.7 billion during 1979-81.

A more accurate evaluation of the full impact of the external shocks on Korea requires a disaggregated econometric model of the economy. Because the remainder of this section is concerned mainly with the impact of these shocks on the current account balance in terms of trade and service flows, a small model that evaluates only the effect of the external shocks on the balance of payments was applied (the model is presented in the appendix to this chapter). The model was used to determine what would have happened to the balance of payments if there had been no external shocks.

The external situation that would have pertained in the absence of the oil price shocks is defined by the following:

- The unit value of imports during 1973-75 (during 1980-82) was such that the terms of trade would have remained the same as the average during 1971-72 (1976-79).
- The short-term Eurodollar rate during 1973-75 (1979-82) would have stayed the same as the average rate during 1971-72 (1976-78).
- The annual GDP growth rates of the industrialized countries during 1974-75 (1980-82) would have held the same as their average growth rates during 1971-73 (1976-79).
- The export share to the Middle East would have held at the 1974 level. (During the period of the second oil price shock, this share did not increase. Thus, this impact was excluded in the analysis of the second shock.)

Three dynamic simulations were run with three alternative sets of data for those external conditions: a base simulation using actual data and two counterfactual simulations in which the external conditions were as specified above. The results of the counterfactual simulations—one in which there was no first and one in which there was no second oil price shock—were then compared with the base simulation to evaluate the impact of the external shocks on commodity exports and imports, the current account, external debt, and real GDP.

Table 3-5 summarizes the results. Had the first oil price shock not taken place, the current account in 1975 might have been $2.6 billion (12.4 percent of GNP) better than the actual deficit of $1.9 billion. The net external debt in that year might have been about $4.5 billion less than the actual outstanding amount of $7.0 billion. The shock reduced nominal commodity exports by $2.3 billion; imports remained almost unchanged in 1975. Finally, real GDP was 4.4 percent lower in 1975 because of the shock.

The impact of the second oil price shock turned out to be more serious than that of the first. Without the second shock, Korea's current account balance might have been as much as $10.2 billion (14.7 percent of GNP) better in 1982. In that case, instead of the actual deficit of $2.7 billion there would have been a sizable surplus. Korea might have been able to limit its net debt outstanding to about $7 billion in 1982, given that the shock may have led to a growing external indebtedness of more than $21 billion (the actual net debt outstanding was $28.3 billion in 1982). The negative impact of the second shock on nominal exports of commodities was equivalent to 60 percent of the actual amounts in 1982, whereas the favorable impact on nominal imports was 21 percent of the actual amount.[4] The effect of the second shock on Korea's real GDP, estimated to have been 14.5 percent in 1982, was much more severe than that of the first shock.

Decomposition of the impact of the oil price shocks into four separate effects (table 3-6) indicates that for the first oil shock, the slowdown in exports attributable to the recession in the industrialized countries, on the one hand, and the deterioration in the terms of trade, on the other, accounted for 57 and 49 percent, respectively, of the total cumulative impact on the current account during 1973–75. These effects were responsible for an increase in Korea's net external debt of $2.6 billion and $2.2 billion, respectively, by the end of 1975. The negative interest rate effect and the positive Middle East construction effect were relatively insignificant during the period of the first oil shock.

The recession in the industrialized countries dominated the overall effects of the second oil price shock. It was responsible for 68 percent of the cumulative effect and caused a $14.5 billion increase in net external debt during 1979–82. The terms of trade and interest rate effects accounted, respectively, for 21 percent and 13 percent of the impact; they contributed $4.5 billion and $2.9 billion to net external debt, respectively, during 1979–82. During the initial period of both shocks the terms of trade effect proved to be important, while the effect of the recession in the industrialized countries dominated in the later stages of the shocks. International comparisons show that Korea was one of the developing countries hardest hit by the external shocks (Balassa 1985; Sachs 1985), which makes Korea's successful adjustment look even more impressive.

Table 3-5. Effect of the Oil Price Shocks on the External Balance and Real GDP
(billions of dollars, unless otherwise noted)

Year	Commodity exports		Commodity imports		Current account balance			Net external debt		Real GDP (trillions of 1980 won)	
						Impact					
	Actual	Impact	Actual	Impact	Actual	Amount	As a percentage of GNP	Actual	Impact	Actual	Impact
Effect of first oil price shock											
1973	3.28	..	3.85	0.13	-0.30	-0.16	1.2	3.02	0.16	22.75	0.11
1974	4.52	-1.20	6.45	0.40	-2.02	-1.75	9.5	5.02	1.91	24.55	-0.55
1975	5.00	-2.33	6.67	-0.03	-1.89	-2.60	12.4	7.03	4.51	26.41	-1.16
Effect of second oil price shock											
1979	14.71	..	19.10	..	-4.15	-0.15	0.2	14.0	0.15	38.98	..
1980	17.21	-3.13	21.60	0.46	-5.32	-4.29	7.1	19.6	4.44	37.91	-1.18
1981	20.67	-6.66	24.30	-1.55	-4.65	-6.75	10.2	24.5	11.19	40.72	-2.52
1982	20.88	-12.49	23.47	-4.99	-2.65	-10.17	14.7	28.3	21.36	43.04	-6.22

.. Negligible.

46

Table 3-6. *Decomposition of the Effects of the Oil Price Shocks*

(billions of dollars)

Item	Terms of trade	Interest rate	OECD recession	Middle East construction[a]	Total
Effect of first oil shock					
Commodity exports					
1973	n.a.	n.a.	n.a.	n.a.	n.a.
1974	n.a.	n.a.	−1.20	n.a.	−1.20
1975	n.a.	n.a.	−3.40	0.63	−2.33
Commodity imports					
1973	0.13	n.a.	n.a.	n.a.	0.13
1974	0.88	n.a.	−0.55	n.a.	0.40
1975	1.02	n.a.	−1.64	0.35	−0.03
Current account balance					
1973	−0.13	−0.03	n.a.	n.a.	−0.16
1974	−0.93	−0.09	−0.68	n.a.	−1.75
1975	−1.14	−0.10	−1.88	0.29	−2.60
Net external debt					
1973	0.13	0.03	n.a.	n.a.	0.16
1974	1.05	0.11	0.68	n.a.	1.91
1975	2.20	0.21	2.56	−0.30	4.51
Effect of second oil shock					
Commodity exports					
1979	n.a.	n.a.	n.a.	n.a.	n.a.
1980	n.a.	n.a.	−3.13	n.a.	−3.13
1981	n.a.	n.a.	−6.66	n.a.	−6.66
1982	n.a.	n.a.	−12.49	n.a.	−12.49
Commodity imports					
1979	n.a.	n.a.	n.a.	n.a.	n.a.
1980	1.70	n.a.	−1.35	n.a.	0.45
1981	1.29	n.a.	−2.98	n.a.	−1.53
1982	0.45	n.a.	−5.50	n.a.	−4.95
Current account balance					
1979	n.a.	−0.15	n.a.	n.a.	−0.15
1980	−1.81	−0.50	−1.90	n.a.	−4.26
1981	−1.65	−0.96	−4.23	n.a.	−6.71
1982	−1.00	−1.25	−8.40	n.a.	−10.13
Net external debt					
1979	n.a.	0.15	n.a.	n.a.	0.15
1980	1.81	0.65	1.90	n.a.	4.40
1981	3.46	1.61	6.13	n.a.	11.12
1982	4.46	2.85	14.53	n.a.	21.25

n.a. Not applicable.

Note: Data may not add to totals because of the compounding of various effects in the total.

a. The simulation result also shows that the positive contribution of Middle East construction to the current account was $780 million (2.7 percent of GNP) and $1,010 million (2.7 percent of GNP) in 1976 and 1977, respectively.

Source: Authors' estimates.

In this regard, it was deemed useful to evaluate the contribution of the favorable international environment after 1982 to the improvement in the Korean balance of payments. To this end, a third counterfactual simulation was run. In this simulation it was assumed that the external conditions after 1983 were the same as those during the period of the second oil price

Table 3-7. *Effects of the Favorable External Environment since 1983*
(billions of dollars, unless otherwise noted)

Item	Actual	Total impact[a]	Terms of trade	Interest rate	OECD growth	Middle East construction
Commodity exports						
1983	23.20	2.49	n.a.	n.a.	2.49	n.a.
1984	26.34	5.59	n.a.	n.a.	7.40	−2.49
1985	26.44	7.27	n.a.	n.a.	9.29	−3.11
Commodity imports						
1983	24.97	0.52	−0.53	n.a.	1.03	n.a.
1984	27.37	1.83	−0.67	n.a.	3.24	−0.90
1985	26.46	2.99	−0.56	n.a.	4.53	−1.28
Current account balance						
1983	−1.61	2.44 (3.2)[b]	0.56	0.34	1.54	n.a.
1984	−1.37	4.96 (6.0)[b]	0.76	0.69	4.55	−1.68
1985	−0.89	6.36 (7.7)[b]	0.73	0.95	5.67	−2.11
Net external debt						
1983	30.9	−2.44	−0.56	−0.34	−1.54	n.a.
1984	32.9	−7.39	−1.33	−1.03	−6.10	1.68
1985	35.5	−13.75	−2.06	−1.98	−11.77	3.79
Real GDP (trillions of 1980 won)						
1983	46.73	1.27	−0.18	n.a.	1.44	n.a.
1984	50.45	2.93	−0.48	n.a.	4.40	−1.39
1985	53.04	4.41	−0.64	n.a.	6.37	−2.01

n.a. Not applicable.

a. The total impact may not equal the sum of the individual impacts because of the compounding of various effects in the total.

b. The numbers in parentheses indicate the total impact as a percentage of GNP.

Source: Authors' estimates.

shock. More specifically, the external situation during 1983–85 was assumed to be as follows.

- The unit value of imports was such that the terms of trade did not change from the average during 1980–82.

- The short-term Eurodollar rate was the same as the average rate during 1979–82.

- The annual rate of GDP growth of the OECD countries was the same as their average rate of growth during 1980–82.

- The share of exports to the Middle East during 1984–85 was the same as the average share during 1979–82.

The simulation results are presented in table 3-7. They show that, under the conditions stated above, the current account deficit in 1985 could have been as large as $7.3 billion, compared with the actual deficit of $0.9 billion. It would have made the net external debt almost $14 billion larger than the actual level of $35.5 billion at the end of 1985. At the same time, it was estimated that changes in the external environment after 1983 contributed 8.3 percent to the 1985 GDP. The large favorable impact of external conditions, especially the OECD growth, on Korea's improved current account balance was made possible by domestic policies that kept the economy open and avoided overheating it by applying fiscal restraint when exports started to recover. The analysis clearly shows that appropriate domestic policies allowed Korea to benefit from the favorable external conditions. Ultimately, the result was an improvement in the balance of payments and growth in the post-1982 period.

The simulation results also indicate that the favorable effects of the external situation during 1983–85 were not quite as large as the negative effects of the second oil price shock on the cumulative current balance or real GDP growth rate. The small current account deficit in 1985 suggests that Korea might have achieved a sizable surplus had the second oil shock not occurred.

The Role of Fiscal and Monetary Policies

In Korea, monetary and fiscal policies have been used to adjust domestic demand to developments in the export markets. In periods of slack demand for exports, fiscal and monetary policies have played a countercyclical role. In the early 1980s, however, the acceleration of inflation forced a clear anti-inflation bias in those policies.

Flexible Monetary and Fiscal Policies: 1981–86

During the period of adjustment, fiscal and monetary policies were used to keep the economy from overheating when inflation was accelerating and to provide stimulus when growth was slowing. In 1981, in response to the unduly slow recovery, the government relaxed its monetary policies somewhat, providing greater financial support for public construction, small and medium-size firms, residential construction (especially for low-income families), and exports of heavy industrial products on a deferred payment basis. It also used the tax system actively, with temporary investment tax credits, lower personal and corporate income taxes, and selective use of capital gains and special excise taxes.

These measures indicate that fiscal management in Korea did not suffer from serious institutional rigidities; instead, it was very flexible. Even after a budget was drawn up, the government, depending on economic circumstances, implemented across-the-board or selective budget cuts, maintained flexible excise tax rates, allowed special tax reductions, prepared a supplementary budget, and borrowed for speedy spending. The fiscal lags were thus not significant.

After 1982 the government slowed monetary expansion substantially compared with the high rates through 1982. After the public sector deficit reached 4.6 percent of GNP in 1981, fiscal operations were tightened. Exchange rate management remained relatively rigid during 1981–82 to minimize the inflationary pressure from rising import costs: the exchange rate appreciated 4–5 percent in real terms.

After 1981 Korea's stabilization efforts relied heavily on income policy, in the belief that reliance on demand management alone required too much time and an excessively large sacrifice of income growth for the sake of price stability. Wage restraint was encouraged by using the salary increases for public servants as informal guidelines for the private sector, interest rates were adjusted downward parallel with inflation, and the government purchase prices for rice decreased. Although the effectiveness of these measures may be questioned and there were side effects, these actions clearly signaled a strong government commitment to price stabilization.

The combination of these policies and falling unit import prices resulted in a sharp decline in the rate of inflation, from 25.6 percent in 1980 to only 7.1 percent in 1982 in terms of the GNP deflator. At the same time, the large devaluation in 1980 boosted exports. Nevertheless, real GNP growth in 1981 recovered to only 6.2 percent following the −5.2 percent of 1980 and was disappointing in 1982 because of the slowdown in the growth of exports.

Thanks to favorable external terms of trade, together with active overseas construction in the Middle East, the annual current account deficit fell from $5 billion during 1979–81 to $2.7 billion in 1982. Nevertheless, as the international financial market grew increasingly unstable and loan reschedulings became more frequent, Korea—then the fourth largest borrower among developing countries—decided to emphasize an improvement in the balance of payments and a reduction in the external debt.

In step with the economic recovery, in 1982 the focus of macroeconomic policies shifted toward consolidating price stability and eliminating the current account deficit as soon as possible. Both fiscal and monetary policies remained restrictive. On a zero-base budgeting principle, the general account budget was designed to produce a sizable surplus to finance the deficits in some funds managed by the government. Consequently the consolidated public sector deficit was reduced from 4.3 percent of GNP in 1982 to 1.6 percent and 1.4 percent in 1983 and 1984, respectively. The expansion of M2 was also slowed, to 19.5 percent in 1983 and 11–12 percent during 1984–85—fairly restrictive levels in view of the declining velocity of money that resulted from decelerating actual and anticipated inflation. Bank interest rates were adjusted slightly upward to make them attractive for depositors compared with nonbank rates. In line with renewed concern about the external balance, exchange rate management was flexible enough to allow the real effective rate to depreciate by about 9 percent during 1983–84.

1983–84. The economy regained strong growth momentum in 1983, with GNP rising at 9.5 percent, a rate that was maintained through the first half of 1984. Private consumption and construction led the recovery, but rising exports were the primary source of growth after the second half of 1983. Late in 1984, however, export growth began to falter, in line with the noticeable slowdown in the U.S. economy and rising protectionist barriers against Korean exports. Housing and other private construction activity was also sluggish, and GNP growth dropped to 5.4 percent for 1985, compared with 7.5 percent in the previous year.

1985–86. In response to the disappointing growth performance and deteriorating labor market situation, the government pursued a number of stimulatory measures in 1985. They included a further depreciation of the Korean won (by about 6 percent on a year-average basis); a relaxation of monetary policy, mainly to encourage investment in the export sector; a new investment tax credit; and a stimulatory supplementary budget. The evidence suggests that the economy started to pick up by late 1985. In 1986 real GNP growth reached 12.5 percent, thanks to an export expansion of over 26 percent, the recovery of residential construction, and fairly strong facility investment.

As export growth was recovering during 1983–84, the current account deficit fell steadily to $1.5 billion. In 1985, in the face of growing protectionism abroad, declining revenues from overseas construction, and stronger pressure to liberalize imports, the current account deficit narrowed further to $0.9 billion, mainly because of a fall in imports of almost $1.0 billion. Also noteworthy were the government's efforts to improve the maturity structure of external debt. It discouraged short-term borrowing, and total foreign debt of this kind declined steadily to 23 percent by the end of 1985 from 33.5 percent three years earlier. Nevertheless, it was not until 1986 that Korea registered a big turnaround in its external balance. The terms of trade improved by more than 8 percent, and export competitiveness gained substantially as the real effective exchange rate depreciated considerably with the weakening of the U.S. dollar after mid-1985. As the current account recorded a surplus of $4.6 billion (4.7 percent of GNP), gross foreign debt also declined to $44.5 billion from $46.8 billion in the previous year. This turnaround was the result of appropriate macroeconomic policies and a favorable external environment.

The other side of the improvement in the external balance was an increase in the domestic savings ratio from 22.4 percent of GNP in 1982 to 28.6 percent in 1985 and 32.8 percent in 1986. A sectoral savings analysis suggests that the major factors were high income growth, price stability, a lower corporate tax burden, and a slowdown in the expansion of government consumption.

Finally, despite the full-fledged economic recovery, inflation in terms of the GNP deflator remained at a low 2–4 percent. Moderate fiscal and monetary policies, stable import unit prices, a good harvest, and an income policy that continued to keep major factor costs in line with the decelerating inflation rate all contributed to price stability. In chapter 5 Corbo and Nam argue that the main factors accounting for the slowdown in inflation after it peaked in 1980 were the decline in the rate of growth of the dollar prices of imported inputs and the tight fiscal and monetary policies of 1984–85, which produced an improvement in the real effective exchange rate with only a moderate nominal devaluation.

The Fiscal Impulse of the Public Sector

To evaluate Korea's fiscal policy, fiscal impulse, a crude indicator of change in fiscal stance rather than a measure of the economic effects of the budget, was calculated.[5] The fiscal impulse is computed by comparing the growth in government expenditures and taxes with the growth in nominal potential output. The IMF measure starts by establishing a base year in which actual and potential real output are assumed to be the same. A more than proportionate increase is defined as expansionary, and a less than proportionate increase as contractionary. Thus, the neutral budget is defined under the assumption of unitary elasticity of expenditures and revenues with respect to potential and actual output (Heller, Haas, and Mansur 1986). In the OECD measure the elasticities are not constrained to unity, and the values of the previous period are used instead of a value for a common base period. As such, fiscal impulse suffers from the problem of the so-called balanced budget multiplier: it adjusts only for the deviation in output from its potential level and ignores other effects, such as those from inflation and interest rates.

The estimates of fiscal impulse derived by using the IMF and OECD procedures are almost the same (table 3-8), except in 1980, a year when GNP dropped by more than 5 percent. Although alternative estimates of potential GNP produce somewhat larger differences in fiscal impulse, the differences in dynamic trajectory are relatively minor.

A comparison between the change in the actual deficit and the estimated fiscal impulse shows that the cyclical factor (cyclically neutral balance) could swing substantially. In the exceptional case of 1980, when the actual deficit increased by 1.7 percent of GNP, the cyclically neutral deficit rose by 2.1 percent of GNP for IMF measure *A*. The implication is that the fiscal impulse was contractionary.

By examining the changes in fiscal impulse over the business cycle, it may be possible to evaluate the extent to which fiscal management was countercyclical. With notable exceptions in 1979–81, a rather close inverse relation between the change in the rate of GNP growth and the fiscal impulse was confirmed for the 1971–84 sample period. The exceptions are easily explained by the stabilization efforts, which delayed (until 1981) a fiscal

Table 3-8. *Fiscal Impulse of the Public Sector, 1971–84*
(percent)

Year	Real GNP growth	Actual deficit Percentage of GNP	Change	Fiscal impulse[a] IMF measure A	B	OECD measure A	B
1971	8.8	2.3	1.4	0.7	1.3	0.7	1.3
1972	5.7	4.6	2.4	1.6	1.7	1.6	1.7
1973	14.1	1.6	−3.0	−2.2	−2.2	−2.2	−2.3
1974	7.7	4.0	2.4	2.1	2.1	2.1	2.1
1975	6.9	4.6	0.6	0.4	0.2	0.4	0.2
1976	14.1	2.9	−1.8	−1.0	−1.2	−1.0	−1.3
1977	12.7	2.6	−0.2	0.1	−0.1	0.1	−0.1
1978	9.7	2.5	−0.1	−0.1	−0.0	−0.1	−0.0
1979	6.5	1.4	−1.1	−1.6	−1.1	−1.7	−1.1
1980	−5.2	3.2	1.7	−0.4	−0.1	−0.8	−0.4
1981	6.2	4.6	1.5	1.7	1.6	1.6	1.5
1982	5.6	4.3	−0.3	−0.3	−0.5	−0.4	−0.6
1983	9.5	1.6	−2.7	−1.9	−2.1	−1.8	−2.0
1984	7.6	1.4	−0.2	0.2	0.1	0.3	0.1

Note: The public sector includes the central government (general account, twelve special accounts, and twenty-one funds) and five public enterprise accounts (grain management, monopoly, railways, communications, and supply), together with two related funds (grain management and supply).

a. Fiscal impulse measure A uses potential GNP (Y^p) obtained from a regression equation, while measure B uses peak-through interpolated Y^p (see the appendix at the end of this chapter).

Source: Authors' estimates.

reaction to the sluggish economy of 1979–80. Under the CMES program in 1979, Korea's fiscal management was restrictive until the first half of 1980. In 1981 the fiscal stance shifted toward strong expansion, given that the economy was still in deep recession, even though it had recovered from the substantial negative growth of the previous year.

It is also clear that the fiscal impulse for a given change in the rate of GNP growth was generally stronger before the stabilization program was launched in 1979 (particularly in 1971, 1972, and 1974; see figure 3-1). After the stabilization program, the fiscal impulse became restrictive, particularly in 1983, just as it had been in the 1979–80 period. The accumulated fiscal impulse during 1971–78 was 1.6 percent of GNP, in contrast to −2.3 percent of GNP during 1979–84.

Finally, given that the estimate of fiscal impulse is not a good measure of the fiscal contribution to economic growth, it is interesting to look at the movement of real government expenditures in relation to general economic trends (the revenue side has been left out of this analysis). As figure 3-2 shows, although the trends for the growth rates of government expenditures and GNP were similar over the growth cycle, the year-to-year direction of their changes was opposite except in a few cases.

Figure 3-1. *Fiscal Impulse and Change in the Real GNP Growth Rate, 1971-84*

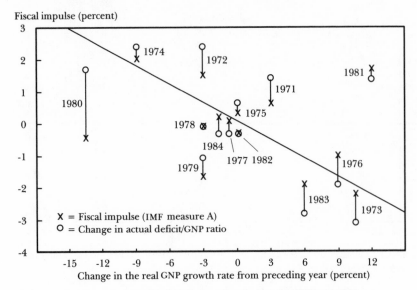

Note: The regression line was fitted excluding observations for 1980 and 1981.

$$FI = -0.162 - 0.210 \; \Delta \dot{Y}$$
$$(0.57) \quad (3.14)$$
$$R^2 = 0.496$$

Source: Table 3-8.

Thus, it can be concluded that fiscal policy played a central role in both the expansion in the second half of the 1970s and the macroadjustment effort in the 1980s.

The Role of Monetary Policy

To study the role of monetary policy, a standard transaction demand-for-money equation was estimated using quarterly data. The model was estimated first with data from the first quarter of 1972 to the last quarter of 1978. Forecasts for 1979 to 1981 were then generated with the estimated model and compared with the actual values of M2. Next the model was estimated with data for the period ending in the last quarter of 1982, with forecast values generated for 1983 and 1984. The forecasts were then compared with the actual values of M2 for these two years.

The stance of monetary policy was then measured using two demand-for-money models (estimated in the appendix at the end of this chapter). The difference between the two models is the variable used to measure the opportunity cost of holding money. In the first model the opportunity cost

Figure 3-2. *Real Growth Rates of Government Expenditures and GNP, 1971-84*

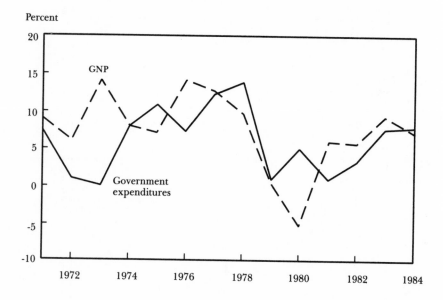

Percent

Source: Bank of Korea.

is measured by the curb market rate; in the second, by the expected rate of inflation. The results of the dynamic simulations with the shorter sample are presented in table 3-9.

In both specifications of the demand-for-money models, monetary policy emerged as mildly restrictive in 1979 and 1981. The results for 1980 were ambiguous: on the basis of the equation using the curb market rate, monetary policy was marginally expansionary, but the equation using the expected inflation measure suggests that monetary policy was restrictive.

To evaluate the stance of monetary policy in 1983–84, the equations for the larger sample were used and the demand for money for the 1983–84 period was simulated. The results of the simulations for both equations indicate that monetary policy was restrictive during this period (see part B of table 3-9).

Further insights into the stance of monetary policy can be obtained by observing the trajectory of real interest rates (table 3-1). In the present case, however, the sudden, unexpected drop in the rate of inflation could have resulted in a higher real interest rate than could be attributed directly to a restrictive monetary policy. The curb market rate reached 19.9 percent in 1979. It was reduced to 4.4 percent in 1980, but climbed to 18.3 percent

Table 3-9. The Stance of Monetary Policy, 1979–81 and 1983–84

(billions of won)

Year and quarter	Predicted M2		Actual M2	Percentage difference	
	Simulation 1	Simulation 2		Simulation 1	Simulation 2
A. First period					
1979:I	8,120.5	8,143.1	8,096.5	−0.3	−0.6
1979:II	8,579.9	8,617.4	8,232.3	−4.1	−4.5
1979:III	8,951.1	9,113.3	8,629.1	−3.6	−5.3
1979:IV	9,270.4	9,702.0	9,264.2	0.0	−4.5
1980:I	9,894.0	10,441.9	10,015.8	1.2	−4.1
1980:II	10,312.2	10,881.7	10,439.8	1.2	−4.1
1980:III	10,657.5	11,387.3	10,948.7	2.3	−3.9
1980:IV	11,552.6	12,154.3	11,652.1	0.9	−4.1
1981:I	12,668.1	13,002.8	12,682.8	0.1	−2.5
1981:II	13,331.3	13,752.9	13,212.7	−0.9	−3.9
1981:III	14,181.8	14,731.2	14,029.3	−1.1	−4.8
1981:IV	14,455.5	15,706.1	14,934.6	3.3	−4.9
B. Second period					
1983:I	20,976.8	20,652.2	19,993.6	−4.5	−3.4
1983:II	20,409.3	21,538.7	20,459.6	0.2	−5.0
1983:III	21,740.3	23,157.8	21,348.7	−1.8	−8.0
1983:IV	22,471.8	24,184.7	22,218.0	−1.1	−8.1
1984:I	23,660.5	25,458.8	22,800.2	−3.6	−10.4
1984:II	24,287.1	26,526.6	22,742.2	−6.4	−14.3
1984:III	25,019.6	27,567.3	23,349.2	−6.7	−15.3
1984:IV	25,249.2	28,512.3	24,152.9	−4.3	−15.3

Note: Simulation 1 is based on the equation using the curb market rate as the opportunity cost of holding money; simulation 2 is based on the equation using the expected rate of inflation (see the appendix at the end of this chapter for the equations).

Source: Authors' estimates.

in 1981 and 27.4 percent in 1982. It then declined somewhat to 26.7 percent in 1983, 22.6 percent in 1984, and 23.0 percent in 1985. The real bank deposit rate shows a similar trajectory: it was −0.1 percent in 1979 and −11.4 percent in 1980. It then began to rise, reaching 4.4 percent in 1981, 8.2 percent in 1982, and 8.8 percent in 1983, at which point it fell to 7.3 percent in 1984, only to reach 9 percent in 1985.

The picture that emerges from the movement of these rates is one of a monetary policy that was restrictive during 1983–84, but that had been, if anything, expansionary in 1979–80. In any event, the evidence for the restrictiveness of monetary policy in 1983–84 is clear. It therefore seems reasonable to conclude that a moderate fiscal policy and a moderately restrictive monetary policy contributed to the macroadjustment of the 1983–84 period and helped slow inflation (see chapter 5).

Conclusions

This chapter presents an overview of recent macroeconomic developments in Korea. It also presents a somewhat detailed evaluation of the effect of the external shocks on the Korean economy. Finally, it provides an analysis of the stance of monetary and fiscal policies.

It was found that the external shocks had strongly adverse effects on Korea's current account and external debt positions. Initially the adjustment to these shocks involved a slowdown in absorption and output growth, accompanied by a buildup of foreign debt. Since 1983 the recovery of the Korean economy has been helped significantly by improvements in the terms of trade, the recovery of the U.S. economy, and the general decline in interest rates. In 1980, and especially since 1983, the real exchange rate was one of the key macroeconomic policies used to encourage growth.

It was found that the government used both fiscal and monetary policies in a discretionary manner beginning in the early 1960s. Although a lot of fine tuning was involved, the key consideration was to keep the momentum of export growth. Thus, it is not surprising that the most enduring aspect of policy was the effort to maintain a stable real effective exchange rate, with due account taken of the size and sustainability of the current account deficit. It is indeed remarkable that an economy with such a high rate of technical progress in tradables kept its real effective exchange rate relatively constant.

The main lesson for other countries is the importance of maintaining the stability of incentives for tradable activities. In the early 1980s macroeconomic policies played a more important role, with both fiscal and monetary policies used to achieve a slowdown in the rate of inflation and a real devaluation.

Appendix

A Simple Model of the Current Account

The structure of the model is as follows:

$$\ln EX_r = f_1[\ln y^*, \ln (Px/\$ULC_k), \ln (\$ULC_k/\$ULC_o), D(1974, 79),$$
$$\ln (EX_{me}/EX)]$$
$$\ln IM_r^o = f_2[\ln V, \ln (P_m^o \cdot Rex/WPI)]$$
$$\ln IM_r^n = f_3[\ln V^a, \ln EX_r, \ln (P_m^n \cdot Rex/WPI)]$$
$$\ln V^a = f_4 (\ln EX_r, \ln V^a_{-1})$$
$$\Delta i_k = f_5(\Delta LIBO)$$
$$EX = EX_r \cdot Px$$
$$IM = IM_r^o \cdot P_m^o + IM_r^n \cdot P_m^n$$
$$NIP = (i_k/100) \cdot (ND + ND_{-1})/2$$
$$CA = EX - IM - NIP + CA_o$$
$$ND = ND_{-1} - CA + SD$$
$$V = V^a + (EX_r - IM_r^o - IM_r^n) \cdot (Rex[80]/1,000) + V^o$$

where

EX_r = Real commodity exports (millions of 1980 U.S. dollars)

IM_r^o, IM_r^n = Real imports of crude oil and non-oil products, respectively (millions of 1980 U.S. dollars)

Px = Unit value of exports in U.S. dollars (1980 = 1.0)

P_m^o, P_m^n = Unit value of crude oil and non-oil imports, respectively (1980 = 1.0)

y^* = Real GDP of the industrialized countries (1980 = 100.0)

$Rex, Rex[80]$ = Nominal exchange rate and the nominal exchange rate for 1980, respectively (won per U.S. dollar)

$\$ULC_k$ = Korea's unit labor cost in the manufacturing sector, measured as the value added per employee in U.S. dollars (1980 = 100.0)

$\$ULC_o$ = Average unit labor cost of the manufacturing sectors for competing economies (Taiwan, Singapore, and Hong Kong), measured as the value added per employee in U.S. dollars (1980 = 100.0)

$D(1974, 79)$ = Dummy variable for 1974 and 1979 that captures the speculation effect (leads and lags effect) before the exchange rate devaluation

EX, IM = Commodity exports and imports, respectively (millions of U.S. nominal dollars)

EX_{me} = Commodity exports to the Middle East (millions of U.S. nominal dollars)

V = Gross domestic product (billions of 1980 won)

V^a = Domestic absorption (billions of 1980 won)
V^o = Net exports of nonfactor services and statistical discrepancies in the national income accounts (billions of 1980 won)
WPI = Wholesale prices (1980 = 100.0)
i_k = Effective interest rate on external borrowing (percent)
$LIBO$ = Two-year moving average of short-term Eurodollar interest rate (percent)
NIP = Net interest payments on external borrowing (millions of U.S. dollars)
ND = Balance of net external borrowing (millions of U.S. dollars)
CA = Current account balance (millions of U.S. dollars)
CA_o = Residual items in the current account balance (millions of U.S. dollars)
SD = Statistical discrepancy and foreign exchange gain or loss from non-dollar-denominated external debt (millions of U.S. dollars).

The structural equations above were estimated by ordinary least squares using annual data. The results of the estimated equations are presented below.

Commodity exports

$$\ln EX_r = -15.30 + 5.376 \ln y^* - 0.518 \ln (\$ULC_k/\$ULC_o)$$
$$\qquad\qquad (19.7) \qquad\qquad (4.06)$$

$$-0.058\, D(1974, 79) + 0.162\, (EX_{me}/EX) - 0.226\, D(1985)$$
$$(1.09) \qquad\qquad (4.42) \qquad\qquad (2.39)$$

$$R^2 = 0.993; \text{ sample: } 1971\text{--}85$$

$$\ln EX_r = -13.10 + 4.887 \ln y^* - 0.301 \ln (\$ULC_k/\$ULC_o)$$
$$\qquad\qquad (32.7) \qquad\qquad (3.94)$$

$$-0.106\, D(1974, 79) + 0.197\, (EX_{me}/EX) - 0.127\, D(1985)$$
$$(3.25) \qquad\qquad (4.32) \qquad\qquad (3.00)$$

$$R^2 = 0.997; \text{ sample: } 1975\text{--}85$$

Commodity imports

$$\ln IM_r^o = 5.92 + 0.866 \ln V - 0.092\, (P_m^o \cdot Rex/WPI)$$
$$\qquad\qquad (6.07) \qquad\quad (1.30)$$

$$R^2 = 0.890; \text{ sample: } 1972\text{--}85$$

$$\ln IM_r^n = 9.29 + 0.944 \ln V^a + 0.240 \ln EX_r - 0.847 \ln (P_m^n \cdot Rex/WPI)$$
$$(4.62) \qquad (3.02) \qquad (6.24)$$

$$R^2 = 0.995; \text{ sample: } 1966-85$$

Alternatively, an aggregate import equation was estimated as follows (this equation was used for the simulation):

$$\ln IM_r = 7.77 + 1.054 \ln V^a + 0.259 \ln EX_r - 0.668 \ln (P_m \cdot Rex/WPI)$$
$$(6.33) \qquad (3.95) \qquad (5.00)$$

$$R^2 = 0.997; \text{ sample: } 1966-85$$

Domestic absorption

$$\ln V^a = 0.183 + 0.100 \ln EX_r + 0.697 \ln V^a_{-1}$$
$$(2.07) \qquad (5.78)$$

$$R^2 = 0.991; \text{ sample: } 1966-85$$

Interest rate on foreign debt

$$\Delta i_k = 0.38 + 0.337 \, \Delta LIBO$$
$$(1.30) \quad (2.38)$$

$$R^2 = 0.303; \text{ sample: } 1971-85$$

$$\Delta i_k = 0.33 + 0.492 \, \Delta LIBO$$
$$(1.00) \quad (3.09)$$

$$R^2 = 0.516; \text{ sample: } 1975-85$$

In the equations above, $D(1985)$ is the dummy variable for 1985; IM_r and Pm are total real commodity imports and the unit value of aggregate imports, respectively; R^2 is the coefficient of determination; and the numbers in parentheses are t-values.

In estimating the export equations, the two price variables could not be included simultaneously because of the multicollinearity between them. The equations incorporating Korea's unit labor cost compared with the three competing countries ($\$ULC_k/\$ULC_o$) proved to be superior to those using the ratio of the unit export price to the unit labor cost ($Px/\$ULC_k$). Because of data limitations, the export equations with ($\$ULC_k/\$ULC_o$) could be estimated for only the small sample starting in 1971.

The elasticity of Korean exports with respect to the GDP of industrialized countries is estimated to have been as high as 4.9–5.4. The relative unit labor cost is also very significant, with an estimated elasticity ranging from 0.30 to 0.52. The coefficient for $D(1974, 79)$ shows that the exchange rate speculation that occurred just before the large devaluations in late 1974 and early 1980 reduced exports by 6–11 percent in 1974 and 1979. The share of exports to the Middle East, introduced to reflect increased exports related to the new construction boom, also turned out to be significant. Finally, the coefficient of $D(1985)$ shows that Korea's export environment was aggravated substantially by the higher protectionist barriers in the industrialized countries.

The estimation of the equation for crude oil imports was also based on a small sample, 1972–85, because it was only in the early 1970s that Korea had adequate refinery capacity. In earlier years substantial quantities of processed oil products had been imported in the place of imports of crude oil. The elasticity of these imports with respect to GDP was 0.87, and the price elasticity was low and insignificant. In the equation for non-oil imports, both absorption and exports showed quite reasonable and significant coefficients. The absorption elasticities of import demand were estimated at 0.94 for non-oil imports and 1.05 for total imports. The elasticities of both non-oil and total imports with respect to exports were estimated at around 0.25, a result that is consistent with the information on the import intensity of exports. The price elasticity of imports relative to domestic wholesale prices was estimated at 0.85 for non-oil imports and 0.67 for total imports.

As expected, domestic absorption was influenced by exports. Finally, each 1 percentage point increase in the Eurodollar rate raised the effective interest rate on the external debt by 0.34–0.49 percentage points, depending on the sample periods. This effect was somewhat smaller than the share of debt at variable interest rates, which was more than 60 percent of the total in recent years. The positive but insignificant constant term in the Δi_k equation seems to reflect, in part, the increasing share of debt at variable interest rates at a time when interest rates were rising.

If some of the elasticities are believed to have a trend, an estimated elasticity would be most reasonable for the midsample years. In the model used here, the foreign income elasticity of exports and the impact of the Eurodollar rate on interest rates for foreign debt were found to be sensitive to the sample periods. In analyzing the effect of the first oil price shock, therefore, the export and interest rate equations fitted for the 1971–85 sample were utilized. For the analysis of the impact of the second oil price shock and subsequent improvement in the external environment, the equations based on the 1975–85 data were used.

The Stance of Fiscal Policy

The IMF measure of fiscal stance (FIS) is defined as

$$\begin{aligned} FIS &= -B + Bcn \\ &= -B + (t_o Y - g_o Y^P) \end{aligned}$$

where

B = Actual budget balance

Bcn = Cyclically neutral budget balance calculated under the assumption of unitary elasticities of expenditures and revenue with respect to potential and actual output, respectively

t_0, g_0 = The revenue and expenditure ratios to GNP, respectively, in the base year, when actual and potential GNP are judged to be the same

Y, Y^P = Actual and potential GNP (nominal), respectively.

Fiscal impulse (FI), which indicates any change in fiscal stance, is defined as $FI = \Delta(FIS/Y)$. This measure of fiscal impulse includes not only the effects of discretionary changes in fiscal policy, but also the contribution of the automatic stabilizers; it is intended to show whether the budget is moving toward expansion or restriction. The OECD measure of fiscal stance is calculated residually by subtracting the effect of the built-in stabilizers from the actual budget deficit:

$$FIS = -B - \tau(Y^P - Y)$$

where

τ = The marginal tax rate with respect to the divergence between the actual and potential levels of output.

Again, fiscal impulse is obtained by $\Delta(FIS/Y)$. In this measure of fiscal impulse, discretionary shifts in fiscal policy and fiscal drag arising from inflation are included, while the automatic stabilizer effects are excluded.

To derive τ, a revenue equation was estimated over the sample period, 1971–84:

$$R^* = -195.4 + 0.172\,Y + (0.646/10^6)\,Y^2$$
$$(2.36)(24.7)\qquad(6.13)$$

$$R^2 = 0.9993;\ DW = 1.54$$

where

R^* = Public sector revenue adjusted for discretionary changes in the tax system[6]

DW = Durbin-Watson test statistic.

Based on the above equation:

$$\tau = \partial R^*/\partial Y = 0.172 + 2\,(0.646/10^6)Y$$

τ increases continuously from 0.176 in 1971 to 0.256 in 1984.

Two alternative estimates of Y^P were tried. First, it was derived from the peak-through interpolation of GDP (real) in the logarithmic scale between the benchmark years (1970, 1978, and 1979) and by assuming that the GDP

Figure 3-3. *Capacity Utilization Ratio, 1970-84*

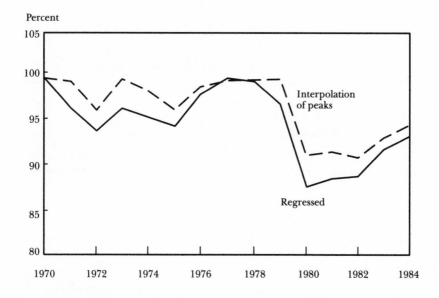

Percent

Source: Bank of Korea.

capacity utilization rate for 1984 was 95 percent (see figure 3-3) and adding net factor income from abroad and multiplying the actual GNP deflator.

In the second, possibly more refined alternative, the above peak-through GDP (*GDP**) was regressed with capital stock as given below. The fitted values, readjusted proportionally to make actual and fitted GDP the same for 1970 (the starting benchmark year), were then used as potential GDP (real). Net factor income from abroad was then added, and the result was multiplied by the actual GNP deflator to get Y^P:

$$GDP^* = -94.843 + 0.1734\,K^m + 11.184\ln K^m$$
$$(10.0) \quad (8.54) \quad\quad (11.4)$$

$$R^2 = 0.9984;\ DW = 0.76;\ \text{sample} = 1970\text{--}84\ \text{(annual)}$$

where

K^m = Midyear capital stock.[7]

Demand for Money

A demand-for-money model was estimated to investigate the stance of monetary policy. Following Goldfeld (1973, 1976), Corbo (1982), and Nam

(1984), a semilog demand-for-money equation of the form below was specified:

(3-1) $\ln M^*(t) = \alpha_o + \alpha_1 \ln Q^e(t) + \alpha_2 I^e(t) + \alpha_3 r(t) + u(t)$

where

$M^*(t)$ = Long-run demand for real money balances in period t

$Q^e(t)$ = Expected nonagricultural domestic product in period t, expressed in constant prices

$I^e(t)$ = Expected cost of holding money in period t

$r(t)$ = Curb market interest rate.

$M^*(t)$ was not, however, directly observable because of the presence of adjustment costs, restrictions on international trade, and unexpected money growth. As seen in Chow (1966), the adjustment of $\ln M(t)$ toward $\ln M^*(t)$ is represented by a logarithmic partial adjustment mechanism of the form:

(3-2) $\ln M(t) - \ln M(t - 1) = \gamma[\ln M^*(t) - \ln M(t - 1)]$

where

$M(t)$ = The short-run demand for real money balances in period t.

Introducing (3-1) into (3-2) gives a short-run demand-for-money equation:

Table 3-10. *Quarterly Demand-for-Money Equation: Alternative Definitions of Opportunity Cost*

| | Curb market rate | | Expected inflation[a] | |
Coefficient	$n = 29$	$n = 45$	$n = 29$	$n = 45$
α_o	−2.004	−2.059	−2.039	−1.757
	(−3.350)	(−4.364)	(−1.515)	(−2.155)
α_1	0.803	0.839	0.872	0.794
	(10.986)	(17.084)	(3.921)	(9.356)
α_2	0	0	−13.436	−11.857
			(−1.241)	(−3.066)
α_3	−4.755	−7.063	0	0
	(−2.134)	(−3.967)		
β	1	1	0.522	0.491
			(4.192)	(5.990)
γ	0.396	0.290	0.121	0.147
	(2.589)	(3.530)	(1.125)	(2.579)
δ	0.933	1.026	1.288	1.292
	(3.582)	(6.082)	(5.911)	(7.857)
R^2	0.975	0.989	0.993	0.997
DW	1.69	1.88	2.11	2.15

Note: $n = 29$ corresponds to the sample 1971:IV to 1978:IV; $n = 45$ corresponds to the sample 1971:IV to 1982: IV.

a. Expected inflation is measured as the percentage change in the nonagricultural GNP deflator.

Source: Authors' estimates.

(3-3) $\ln M(t) = \gamma\alpha_o + \gamma\alpha_1 \ln Q^e(t) + \gamma\alpha_2 I^e(t) + \gamma\alpha_3 r(t)$
             $+ (1 - \gamma)\ln M(t - 1) - \gamma u(t)$

There remains, however, the problem of expressing $I^e(t)$ and $Q^e(t)$ with directly observable variables. For $I^e(t)$, the best alternative to holding money in Korea was holding real assets. Thus, the expected cost of holding money can be measured as the expected rate of inflation. To arrive at the expected cost, a Cagan-Nerlove adaptive expectations model was assumed:

(3-4) $I^e(t) - I^e(t - 1) = \beta[I(t) - I^e(t - 1)]$

Similarly, as in most permanent income formulations, $Q^e(t)$ was expressed in terms of actual output by assuming that

(3-5) $\ln Q^e(t) - \ln Q^e(t - 1) = \delta[\ln Q(t) - \ln Q^e(t - 1)]$

Replacing $I^e(t)$ and $Q^e(t)$ using equations (3-4) and (3-5), the following equations were obtained in observable variables:

(3-6)
$$\begin{aligned}
\ln M(t) = {} & \gamma\delta\alpha_o\beta + \gamma\delta\alpha_1 [\ln Q(t) - (1 - \beta)\ln Q(t - 1)] \\
& + \gamma\alpha_2\beta[I(t) - (1-\delta)I(t - 1)] \\
& + \gamma\alpha_3[r(t) - (1 - \beta)\, r(t - 1)] \\
& - \gamma(1 - \delta)[r(t - 1) - (1 - \beta)\, r(t - 2)] \\
& + [(1 - \gamma) + (1 - \delta)] \cdot [\ln M(t - 1) \\
& - (1 - \beta)\ln M(t - 2)] \\
& - (1 - \gamma)(1 - \delta) \cdot [\ln M(t - 2) - (1 - \beta)\ln M(t - 3)] \\
& + (1 - \beta)\ln M(t - 1) + \epsilon(t)
\end{aligned}$$

Equation (3-6) was estimated using the maximum likelihood (*ML*) estimation procedure. The estimates arrived at by this method would be consistent and asymptotically efficient if the disturbances $\epsilon(t)$ were independent and identically normally distributed.

When both inflation and the curb market interest rates were introduced as regressors, neither was significant, but both variables were individually significant. The separate results for each measure are presented in table 3-10. The two different sample sizes for each definition of the opportunity cost of holding money are defined in the note to the table.

From the point of view of the magnitude of coefficients, the long-run elasticities are fairly stable across the specifications; the income elasticity ranges from 0.794 to 0.872. The partial adjustment coefficient is, however, substantially lower with the inflation measure of the opportunity cost of holding money. In the shorter sample, the adjustment coefficient takes a value of 0.121. This coefficient implies an average lag in the adjustment of actual real balances toward desired real balances of close to seven quarters. In contrast, the result with the curb market rate for the longer sample implies an average lag of 5.8 quarters. The semielasticity of the demand for money is estimated with more precision for the curb market rate. Finally, the coefficient of the adaptive expectations model for inflation expectations is around 0.5, which seems low for a country with a long period of intermediate inflation.

Notes

The authors are grateful to John Williamson for his comments and to Inbom Choi for his assistance with the research.

1. Greater detail on the first two periods can be found in chapter 2; table 2-1 provides the key economic indicators for the years 1963 to 1986.

2. For another evaluation of the adjustment program in these years, see Aghevli and Marquez-Ruarte (1985).

3. For an alternative model of the sources of Korean external debt, see Park (1985a). For a more detailed analysis of external sector policies in Korea's recent adjustment, see chapter 4.

4. Balassa (1985) estimated similar effects from the external shocks on the balance of payments in newly industrialized economies. For the effect of the worldwide recession on exports, he used the 1963–73 trend value of exports by major commodity and assumed constant market shares. His results show that the negative effect of the first oil price shock on Korea's balance of payments was 16.1 percent of GNP in 1975 (without the interest rate effect) and that of the second shock 20.9 percent of GNP (including the interest rate effect) in 1981.

5. For a recent evaluation of the economic measures of fiscal stance, see Buiter (1985). The IMF and OECD measures of fiscal stance are discussed in Heller, Haas, and Mansur (1986).

6. The Prest Adjustment Method was used to get R^*, with 1980 as the benchmark year. In other words, $R^* = (R - DIS/R_{-1})R^*_{-1}$, where R is actual public sector revenue and DIS is the effect on revenue of any new discretionary changes in the tax system (estimated by the Ministry of Finance).

7. The capital stock series (K) was obtained from the annual fixed investment data (I_i) and constant depreciation rates (δ_1) for each asset type: $K_i = \Sigma [K_{i-1} (1 - \sigma_i) + I_i]$. The annual depreciation rates estimated by Dr. Kwack Taiwon at the Korea Development Institute are 0.1282 for machinery, 0.1727 for transportation equipment, and 0.0272 for buildings and other structures. The initial stock $K_i(1952)$ was estimated under the assumption that, before 1953, I_i increased at the same annual rate as the average for the 1954–58 period, and that 25 percent of the stock was destroyed during the Korean War (1950–53). The resulting economywide annual depreciation rate ranged from 5.4 percent to 6.0 percent during the 1970–84 period.

References

Aghevli, B. B., and Jorge Marquez-Ruarte. 1985. *A Case of Successful Adjustment: South Korea's Experience during 1980–84.* IMF Occasional Paper no. 39. Washington, D.C.: International Monetary Fund.

Balassa, Bela. 1985. "Adjusting to External Shocks: The Newly Industrializing Developing Economies in 1974–1976 and 1976–1981." *Weltwirtschaftliches Archiv* 121(1):116–41.

Buiter, W. H. 1985. "A Guide to Public Sector Debt and Deficits." *Economic Policy* 1:13–79.

Chow, Gregory. 1966. "On the Long Run and Short Run Demand for Money." *Journal of Political Economy* 74 (April):111–31.

Corbo, Vittorio. 1982. "Monetary Policy with an Overrestricted Demand for Money Equation." *Journal of Development Economics* 10 (February):119–26.

Goldfeld, Stephen M. 1973. "The Demand for Money Revisited." *Brookings Papers on Economic Activity* (3):577–638.

———. 1976. "The Case of Missing Money." *Brookings Papers on Economic Activity* (3):683–730.

Heller, P. S., R. D. Haas, and A. S. Mansur. 1986. *A Review of the Fiscal Impulse Measure.* Occasional Paper no. 44. Washington, D.C.: International Monetary Fund.

IMF (International Monetary Fund). Various years. *International Financial Statistics.* Washington, D.C.

Kim, K. S., and J. K. Park. 1985. *Sources of Economic Growth in South Korea: 1963–82.* Seoul: Korea Development Institute.

Nam, C. H. 1985. "Trade Policy and Economic Development in Korea." Discussion Paper no. 9. Seoul: Korea University.

Nam, Sang-Woo. 1984. "Korea's Stabilization Efforts since the Late 1970s." Working Paper 8405. Seoul: Korea Development Institute.

Park, Y. C. 1985a. "Korea's Experience with External Debt Management." In Gordon W. Smith and John T. Cudington, eds., *International Debt and the Developing Countries.* Washington, D.C.: World Bank.

———. 1985b. "Economic Stabilization and Liberalization in Korea: 1980–84. In Bank of Korea, *Monetary Policy in a Changing Financial Environment.* Seoul.

Sachs, Jeffrey D. 1985. "External Debt and Macroeconomic Performance in Latin America and East Asia." *Brookings Papers on Economic Activity* (2):523–64.

Westphal, Larry. 1978. "Republic of Korea's Experience with Export-Led Industrial Development." *World Development* (March):347–82.

4 The External Balance

RUDIGER DORNBUSCH, Massachusetts Institute of
   Technology
YUNG-CHUL PARK, Korea University

KOREA IS AMONG the past decade's few examples of highly successful adjustment to repeated external shocks. It is the Korean experience, together with that of Turkey, that World Bank officials use in their discussions with Latin American governments of the feasibility and benefits of external balance adjustment. Creditor banks give the same favorable message:

> Korea's achievements in adapting its economy to the turbulent world of the 1980s exemplify the benefits that can flow from an outward-looking, market-oriented strategy for economic adjustment and development similar to that now being urged on many other developing countries. (Morgan Guaranty 1984, p. 1)

What were the strategic elements in Korea's successful performance? Why did growth not collapse, at least not for any extended period? Why did inflation not increase sharply? How did the need to adjust the external balance become a source of growth rather than an awful blow to real wages and the standard of living? These questions are relevant because Korea is an oil importer, a debtor, and an exporter of manufactures. It thus has, at least on the surface, all the structural characteristics of the problem countries, Brazil being one example.

This paper looks at the determinants of Korea's external balance and performance over the past ten years. Important factors were luck (a mark of any truly successful policy)—in the form of a favorable external environment—and appropriate strategic policy decisions. The assessment of Korea's record is followed by macroeconomic recommendations for the future conduct of policy in Korea and in other countries facing adjustment difficulty.

The conclusion reached here is that a confluence of sensible wage and exchange rate policies, exceptionally high productivity growth, and a favorable external environment explains Korea's adjustment. None of these factors by itself would have been enough. In a broader sense, it can be said that there are two ways to get ahead in life: switch off the light when leaving the room, or hit the jackpot. Korea's success is more nearly of the first kind. This conclusion is based on pieces of evidence, not on a constructive proof. The analysis is meant to serve as a counterfoil to the presumption that policy alone, in some magical way, was responsible for performance. Rather, it was the lack of major policy mistakes in conjunction with favorable factors that explained Korea's experience of adjustment with growth.

An Overview and Comparison

Figure 4-1 shows in summary fashion what is analyzed here—the trends for the current account as a fraction of gross domestic product (GDP) and the growth rate of real GDP.[1] Three episodes are of particular interest: the oil shocks of 1973–74 and 1978–79 and the debt shock of 1980–82. In the case of the two oil shocks there was an immediate, dramatic deterioration in the external balance, followed by sustained improvement. The adjustment in 1978–81 was bumpy: growth actually turned negative before resuming its usual high level in 1981. In this deterioration of performance, policy mistakes and uncertainties, and their impact on the external balance, played an important role. The focus here, however, is on identifying the main elements in the structure of the Korean economy and the major policy decisions that can plausibly explain why growth has continued to be strong and inflation low on average, in the face of some of the same shocks that have dislocated Latin American economies.[2]

Although no single-factor explanation of performance or specific quantitative evaluation of the links between explanatory factors and the success or failure of economic performance is attempted here, a framework for analysis is needed. Much of the literature on external balance focuses on the short-term macroeconomic setting. Based on potential output, the explanations of growth and the external balance emphasize the changes in capacity utilization. Aggregate demand could change as a result of autonomous disturbances or, more likely, in response to policies. Specifically, monetary and fiscal policies would receive primary attention. With respect to the world economy, the level of foreign demand, terms of trade (oil and real commodity prices in particular), and world interest rates would be of primary importance.

Although all these considerations apply in the case of Korea, they do not provide a sufficient framework for analysis. Because investment rates have been very significant and productivity growth has proceeded at high rates, potential output and related issues must be central to the analysis. Investment and productivity growth shift an economy's potential output and its composition at constant relative prices in a way that inevitably has a bearing on the external balance. The growth in real disposable income also affects demand, and hence employment and the current account. In most industrial countries a 10 percent increase in the real price of domestic goods would be treated as evidence of overvaluation. In the case of Korea, it is more likely a reflection of particularly strong productivity performance. To

Figure 4-1. Real GDP Growth and the Current Account Balance, 1971-86

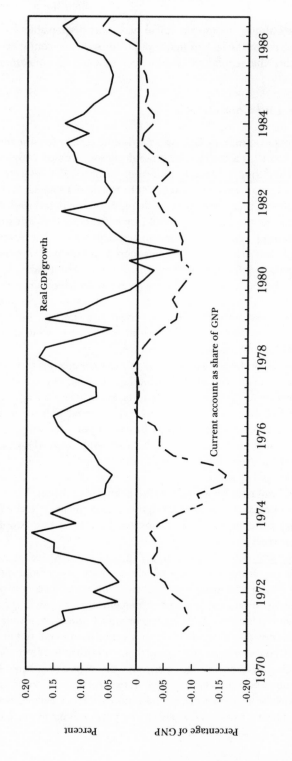

Note: Real GDP growth is shown as a four-quarter growth rate with respect to the quarter of the preceding year; the current account is shown as a three-quarter moving average.
Source: Bank of Korea.

give another example of important structural change, the opening of new export opportunities, as in construction projects in the Middle East, has immediate and large results not only on income and foreign exchange earnings, but also on labor absorption.

The interaction of macroeconomics and growth is also apparent in investment opportunities. Partly as a result of increased productivity and partly as a result of policy, a country experiences an opportunity to enter a new industry. For a few years there is a lot of investment that worsens the external balance. When the investment phase pays off, however, the external balance may improve in an unusually strong manner. Not only is investment with high import content reduced, but capacity in an export sector has been created. Where previously a particular good, for instance, in heavy industry, was imported, now it is exported. These structural or growth effects are at least as important as the macroeconomics of the demand side, even if they are less easily amenable to the standard examination based on growth and the external balance.

Structural Features of the Korean Economy

Several features of the Korean economy that help explain the effects of external shocks have also helped to account for the strong success in employment and growth that sound wage and exchange rate policies achieved. Analyzed below are export growth and the composition of trade, invisibles and the capital account, external debt and debt service, and savings and investment.

Export Growth and the Composition of Trade

Over a period of two decades—since it embarked on a strategy of outward-looking development—Korea has been successful in sustaining rapid growth through the promotion of exports. During the 1981–84 period exports of goods increased at an average annual rate of 14 percent, amounting to almost $30 billion in 1984. The share of exports in gross national product (GNP) rose to more than 40 percent by 1984.

As an economy poor in natural resources, Korea at first exported mostly labor-intensive manufactures. This pattern was natural at an early stage of export-led industrialization. Over time, however, as Korea's comparative advantage shifted to skill- and technology-intensive products, it has successfully restructured its industries. The share of chemicals and such heavy industrial products as machinery, transport equipment, and electronics has increased significantly. During the 1980–84 period more than 93 percent of total exports were manufactured goods, about half of which consisted of chemicals and heavy industrial products.

Table 4-1. *Import Content of Exports, Consumption, and Investment, Selected Years*
(percent)

Item	1970	1975	1980	1983
Consumption	13	19	23	22
Exports	26	36	38	36
Investment	39	48	42	35

Source: Bank of Korea.

The expansion of exports has brought about a dramatic change in the structure of the economy. The manufacturing sector grew to hold a 31 percent share of GNP in 1984. Employment in agriculture, forestry, and fisheries as a percentage of the total labor force dropped substantially, while that in manufacturing rose significantly.

The import content of exports in Korea has been very high, although in recent years it has declined somewhat (table 4-1). The bulk of imports has been used to produce exports as well as capital goods: since 1975 raw materials for export production, crude oil, and capital goods have represented an average of 70 percent of Korea's total imports. The remainder has included raw materials for domestic uses and other purposes. Imports of finished consumer goods have been less than 5 percent of total imports because of controls or high tariff rates. According to estimates by the Bank of Korea based on input-output tables, a one-unit increase in investment creates a 0.35-unit increase in imports, while a one-unit increase in exports leads to a 0.36-unit increase in imports.

One obvious reason for the high import content of exports is the poor resource base: Korea must secure practically all primary commodities, including oil, from foreign sources.[3] Another reason is that, in pursuing export-led industrialization, Korea's planners have not encouraged import-substitution activities because the domestic market was not thought large enough to realize the scale economies from investments in those industries. A third reason is that export incentives have been biased toward heavy use of imported capital and intermediate goods.[4]

Invisibles and the Capital Account

Prior to the oil price increases in 1979 and 1980, the invisible trade account consistently showed a surplus except during the first oil crisis (1974–75), when interest payments on foreign loans more than doubled. After 1979, however, the large accumulation of foreign debt with relatively high interest rates (compared with the rates prevailing in the early 1970s) led to a sharp deterioration in the service account. Between 1980 and 1984 interest payments ranged above 40 percent of total service payments.

Exports of construction services to the Middle East after the first oil crisis rose markedly, from $1.8 million in 1970 to more than $2 billion in 1978. This huge increase contributed to an improvement in the service account by offsetting the rising interest payments. Beginning in 1983 earnings from exports of construction services started to fall, largely because of the slowdown in construction activities in the Middle East. This slowdown was responsible for a sharp deterioration in the invisible account and complicated current account management. In 1985 the trade account deficit fell to $30.4 million, whereas the invisible account recorded a $1.4 billion deficit and emerged as the major source of the current account imbalances.

Capital account transactions have been strictly regulated, whether they have involved short-term borrowings or direct foreign investment. They are generally undertaken to accommodate current account transactions. Because the current account has been in deficit continuously, the capital account has financed the current account deficit. Long-term capital inflows have included, in order of importance, public and commercial loans that have been tied to imports of capital goods, trade credits with a maturity longer than a year, and direct and portfolio investment. Short-term capital flows have consisted primarily of trade credits and exports on credit that have all been trade-related.

Both long- and short-term borrowing has required prior government approval. Repayments of interest and principal have then been guaranteed by the banks, some of which are owned and all of which are strictly controlled by the government. The implication is that all foreign borrowing has been carried out by the government, because it has the final responsibility for ensuring repayment. Thus, there is no point in distinguishing private borrowing from government indebtedness.

External Debt and Debt Service

At the end of 1984, Korea's total foreign debt, including short-term obligations, stood at $43.1 billion. Total debt rose to 53.2 percent of GNP in 1984 from about 30 percent five years earlier. Between 1979 and 1984, Korea's external indebtedness more than doubled (table 4-2), with average growth of about 22 percent a year. Export earnings also rose, but at a much slower rate. As a consequence, debt service as a proportion of exports climbed. Much of the increase in external debt came from the short end of its maturity distribution: short-term obligations increased to almost 34 percent of the total in 1982.

Prior to the 1970s, foreign loans with variable interest rates constituted less than 5 percent of total external debt. Since 1973 a growing proportion of capital inflows has been contracted at floating interest rates: between 1977 and 1983 more than 60 percent of new loans carried variable rates.

Table 4-2. *External Debt and Debt Service, 1979–85*

Item	1979	1980	1981	1982	1983	1984	1985
Total foreign debt (billions of dollars)	20.3	27.2	32.4	37.1	40.4	43.1	46.8
Long-term (percentage of total foreign debt)	72.9	65.4	68.5	66.6	70.0	73.5	77.1
Short-term (percentage of total foreign debt)	27.1	34.6	31.5	33.4	30.0	26.5	22.9
Total foreign debt/GNP (percent)	32.7	44.6	48.3	52.4	53.7	53.2	56.3
Debt service/GNP (percent)	5.0	6.8	8.2	8.2	7.6	8.3	8.5
Debt service/export (percent)	16.0	18.5	20.1	20.6	18.8	20.1	21.4

Source: Ministry of Finance and Bank of Korea.

The persistence of high interest rates has raised the average interest rate on Korea's loans to over 10 percent in recent years from less than 5 percent in the early 1970s. Coupled with an increasingly large share of foreign debt with flexible interest rates, these high interest rates have added to the debt-servicing burden. As a proportion of GNP, debt service jumped to 6.8 percent in 1980 from 5.0 percent a year before; in 1985 it climbed to 8.5 percent.

The buildup in external debt has been closely associated with chronic current account deficits, the need to hold larger reserves to accommodate the growing volume of foreign transactions, and, recently, the expansion of exports on credit. As shown in table 4-3, throughout the 1970s the cumulative increases in the current account deficits and reserve holdings accounted for practically all the increase in debt. During the 1980–85 period there was a relative decline in the use of foreign funds for these purposes.

An important feature of the economic picture in Korea, at least in contrast with the situation in many Latin American countries, has been the complete absence of overt capital flight. The reason is not only prudent and timely adjustment policies, but also an uncompromising government policy

Table 4-3. *Uses of Foreign Borrowing, 1970–85*
(billions of dollars)

Years	Increase of total foreign debt (1+2+3)	Increase of foreign assets (1)	Current account deficit (2)	Discrepancy[a] (3)
1970–79	18.6	5.8	11.6	1.2
1980	6.9	1.2	5.3	0.1
1981	5.3	0.5	4.6	0.1
1982	4.6	0.8	2.6	1.2
1983	3.3	0.7	1.6	1.0
1984	2.7	0.6	1.4	0.7
1985	3.7	1.1	0.9	1.7
1980–85	26.5	4.9	16.4	5.2

a. Consists mostly of errors and omissions.
Source: Economic Planning Board.

Table 4-4. *Composition of Savings, 1978–85*
(percentage of GNP at current prices)

Year	National savings	Household savings	Business savings	Government savings
1978	28.5	12.4	9.6	6.3
1979	28.1	11.7	9.5	6.9
1980	20.8	6.6	8.8	5.4
1981	20.5	6.7	8.2	5.6
1982	20.9	6.8	8.0	6.1
1983	25.3	7.6	10.4	7.2
1984	27.9	9.9	11.0	7.1
1985	28.6	10.6	11.1	6.9

Note: The data for 1980–85 are not comparable with earlier data.
Source: Economic Planning Board.

that ruled out the very idea of capital flight. Capital flight has simply not been acceptable. At the same time, of course, there is a large statistical discrepancy (errors and omissions) that might actually reflect unrecorded capital account transactions.[5]

Savings and Investment

Domestic savings as a proportion of GNP showed a sustained increase between 1981 and 1985 (table 4-4). In 1980, when GNP in real terms declined by 5.6 percent because of the recession in Korea's major trading partners, along with a rice crop failure and domestic political unrest, the domestic savings–GNP ratio tumbled to about 21 percent from just over 28 percent a year earlier. It remained at that level for a year before starting to climb in 1982, reaching a level of 29 percent in 1985.

Broken down by sector, during 1980–85 the business sector accounted for the largest share of total national savings, followed by the household sector, which includes unincorporated firms, and then the government. The sharpest decline in sectoral savings occurred in the household sector in 1980; savings as a percentage of GNP plummeted to 6.6 percent from 11.7 percent in 1979. For the next three years the ratio remained below the 7 percent level, but it shot up to 10.6 percent in 1985. During the same period, business savings as a proportion of GNP fluctuated between 9.5 percent and 11.1 percent. The seemingly high variability in the behavior of household savings might be attributable to the instability in agricultural inventory holdings and the large fluctuations in the profit earnings of unincorporated firms. Smoothing of consumption in the face of a recession is also an important consideration.

In investments, two developments may have had a significant bearing on the movement of the current account in recent years. One was the substantial depletion of inventories in 1982–83, which amounted in each year to

Table 4-5. *Investment and External Balance, 1978–85*

(percentage of GNP at current prices)

Item	1978	1979	1980	1981	1982	1983	1984	1985
Overall investment	31.2	35.6	32.1	30.3	28.6	29.8	31.9	31.2
Fixed investment	30.8	32.8	32.2	28.7	30.5	31.3	31.3	30.7
Manufacturing	6.6	6.9	7.2	6.1	6.3	5.7	6.8	8.0
Inventory investment	0.4	2.9	−0.1	1.6	−1.9	−1.5	0.6	0.3
Imported raw material; finished and semifinished goods	1.4	1.1	1.1	−0.1	−0.7	−0.8	0.0	—
External balance[a]	−2.1	−6.7	−8.6	−6.8	−3.8	−2.1	−1.6	−1.1

—Not available.

Note: Data for 1980–84 are not comparable with earlier data.

a. Current account deficit as a percentage of GNP.

Source: Bank of Korea.

between 1.5 percent and 2 percent of GNP (table 4-5). There was a particularly significant reduction in the inventories of imported raw materials and oil.

The second development has been the significant shift in investment resources to service industries since 1980. Manufacturing's share in total investment declined an average of almost 5 percentage points during the 1980–84 period compared with its average in the preceding ten years. From 1970 to 1979 manufacturing investment accounted for 21 percent of the total, a share that had been stable. In 1980 this proportion fell to less than 15 percent of total investment; since then, it has been less than 15 percent on average. During the 1980–84 period sectors such as electricity, gas and water, wholesale and retail trade, ownership of dwellings, and public administration, which may be classified as nontradable industries, gained in shares.

The government's support for investment in heavy industries initiated in 1973 was being phased out by 1983. The tapering off of the investment bulge in these industries represented a decline in the level of investment and a shift in composition toward activities with less import content.

The 1978–82 Period of Crisis and Adjustment

By late 1977 the current account had reached zero (figure 4-1) and even a slight surplus. The adjustment to the first oil shock was largely complete. Moreover, that adjustment had taken place while the economy achieved a growth rate of real GNP averaging 10.4 percent between 1974 and 1977. Then came the crisis of 1979–81, the result of three main disturbances: two dramatic harvest failures, a real appreciation in the exchange rate, and an unfavorable external environment. Domestic policy mistakes and uncertainties also contributed to the poor performance. Figure 4-2 shows the

Figure 4-2. *Growth of Real GDP and Export Volume, 1971-86*

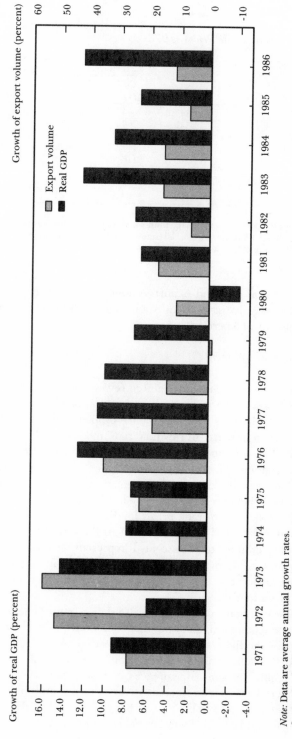

Note: Data are average annual growth rates.
Source: Bank of Korea, and Economic Planning Board, *Korean Economic Indicators* (1986), vol. IV.

Table 4-6. *Foreign Trade Prices, 1978–85*
(1980 = 100)

				World trade prices[a]		
Year	Imports (1)	Exports (2)	Trade (3)	Oil (4)	Manufacturing (5)	Commodities (6)
1978	62	81	117.8	44	76	79
1979	78	96	115.3	60	88	92
1980	100	100	100.0	100	100	100
1981	104	103	97.9	113	96	85
1982	99	99	102.2	116	93	74
1983	94	96	103.1	102	90	80
1984	94	98	105.3	98	87	82
1985	91	96	105.9	94	86	72

Note: All prices are in dollars.

a. IMF indexes for petroleum prices (column 4), export unit values of industrial countries (column 5), and index for dollar prices of all (non-oil) commodities (column 6).

Source: IMF and Bank of Korea.

growth rate of real GDP and export volume. The year 1979 stands out because of the negative growth in export volume; 1980 is notable for the decline in real GDP of 3 percent.

The External Environment

In analyzing the crisis years it is useful to review the external factors first. The large increase in the price of oil and of non-oil commodities was an important part of Korea's external balance problems in the late 1970s. As noted, Korea is an importer of raw materials and is entirely dependent on imported oil. The commodity shocks thus represented a dramatic disturbance to the economy. The problem of adjustment was made more difficult by the trend in world trade: the global economy went into a recession from which it did not begin to recover until 1983.

Table 4-6 shows foreign trade prices for Korea and the world economy for the period 1978–85. The deterioration in the terms of trade between 1977 and 1980 amounted to 20 percent. It represents primarily the increase in oil prices and, to a much smaller degree, the gain in external competitiveness that arose because Korea's export prices did not quite keep up with prices in world trade.

The adverse external environment is also shown in the behavior of world industrial production, real GDP, and the dollar value of world trade. Tables 4-6 and 4-7 list the figures for the 1978–85 period. After 1979 world production and the dollar value of trade came to a standstill. At the same time—and highly relevant to Korea as a debtor country—the London interbank offered rate (LIBOR) increased very sharply, and the cost of debt service escalated. The consolidation of Korea's external balance must be evaluated against this decidedly unfavorable background.

Table 4-7. World Activity (Production and GDP), Manufactured Exports, and Interest Rates, 1978–85

(1980 = 100)

Year	Production	GDP	Manufactured exports[a]	LIBOR[b] (percent)
1978	96	95	90	8.7
1979	101	98	95	11.9
1980	100	100	100	14.1
1981	100	102	105	16.8
1982	96	102	109	13.6
1983	99	105	107	9.7
1984	106	109	112	10.9
1985	110	112	125	8.4

a. Volume of world exports.
b. LIBOR for three-month dollar deposit.
Source: IMF and GATT.

The Current Account

Table 4-8 shows the evolution of the external balance in the 1978–85 period. In calibrating these data relative to the Korean economy, it may be observed that the 1980 current account deficit of $5.3 billion amounted to 8.7 percent of GNP.

Three points in table 4-8 are striking. The first is the sharp rise in import spending of $7 billion between 1978 and 1980. Of this increase, only half is explained by greater oil spending. The implication is that a significant part of the increase is attributable to larger outlays for non-oil items, including food.

The second point is the invisibles balance. Despite a steeply rising interest bill, attributable to debt accumulation and higher interest rates, the invisibles balance did not deteriorate correspondingly. The reason for this is the important offsets provided by invisible exports. The offset in this

Table 4-8. Korean Balance of Payments, 1978–85

(billions of dollars)

Year	Current account	Noninterest current account[a]	Trade balance Net	Trade balance Exports	Trade balance Imports	Invisibles Net	Invisibles Interest
1978	−1.1	−0.1	−1.8	12.7	14.5	0.2	1.0
1979	−4.2	−2.7	−4.4	14.7	19.1	−0.2	1.5
1980	−5.3	−2.7	−4.4	17.2	21.6	−1.4	2.6
1981	−4.6	−1.1	−3.6	20.7	24.3	−1.5	3.5
1982	−2.6	1.0	−2.6	20.9	23.5	−0.6	3.6
1983	−1.6	1.6	−1.8	23.2	25.0	−0.4	3.2
1984	−1.4	2.4	−1.0	26.3	27.4	−0.9	3.8
1985	−0.9	2.7	0.0	26.4	26.4	−1.4	3.6

a. Current account without interest payments.
Source: Bank of Korea.

period did not come from the contraction of construction in the oil-producing countries; the greatest contribution came from a turnaround in the balance for shipping and transportation. The third point is the very strong growth in export revenue. This is especially noteworthy in the context of stagnant world trade.

The shift in the external balance in 1980–82 is divided between improved merchandise trade and improved net invisibles. The invisibles balance improved further, although the interest bill increased by $1 billion. The major part of the improvement, however, came from merchandise exports, which realized a 22 percent increase in revenue over the period. The main sources of increased demand were the United States and the United Kingdom, which together accounted for two-thirds of the rise; exports to continental Europe declined.

Table 4-8 also shows the ongoing improvement in the external balance. That trend continued to stem from a broadly spread adjustment in the form of an improved trade balance and a reduction in the invisibles deficit. The improvement was not in any way the result of reduced interest payments or a sharp contraction in imports in any area. On the contrary, it stemmed from increased exports of goods and services.

Here is a striking difference between Korea and countries in Latin America—specifically, Brazil. In Korea, most of the adjustment was on the export side; in Latin America, the major part of the adjustment was the result of a decline in imports. In both regions the noninterest current account improved sharply but with very different adjustment patterns. Brazil has certainly been the most successful of the adjusting countries in Latin America, but even its export growth of 25 percent during 1980–85 compares poorly with Korea's more than 50 percent increase.

Hypotheses about Success with Adjustment

There are basically six hypotheses to explain Korea's successful external balance adjustment. The first centers on the favorable shift in the world environment after 1982. The second highlights investment behavior, the decumulation of inventory, and shifts in the composition of imports. The third hypothesis involves the very large increase in savings. The fourth singles out wage and exchange rate policies as the central factors. The fifth hypothesis considers the implications of the shift in the composition of spending toward domestic goods. The sixth focuses on monetary and fiscal policies, arguing that the return to positive real interest rates and the correction of the budget deficit were responsible for the improvement in the external balance.

It is important to recognize that these hypotheses are complementary and are quite unlikely to be independent. Expenditure shifts, for example, will occur, at least in part, as a response to changes in relative prices

brought about by government policy. Savings and investment behavior will
also depend on incentives, as well as on overall fiscal policy. Even so, it is
useful to consider each hypothesis by itself.

An Improved External Environment

Tables 4-6 and 4-7 show a significant improvement in the external environment. World growth picked up sharply, particularly in the United States,
Korea's most important export market. Commodity prices declined markedly as a result of the strong dollar and increased supply in developing
countries. Nominal and real oil prices have been declining ever since the
1978–79 hike. Finally, interest rates, although still very high, at least
started to come down after 1983.

Since 1982 Korea's terms of trade have been improving; by 1985 they
had improved significantly over the 1975 level. This experience is very
different from that of Brazil, for example (figure 4-3). Taking the 1978–84
period as a basis of comparison, while Korea showed a 25 percent cumulative worsening in its terms of trade, Brazil experienced a nearly 50 percent
decline.

Figure 4-3. *The Terms of Trade of Korea and Brazil, 1973-85*

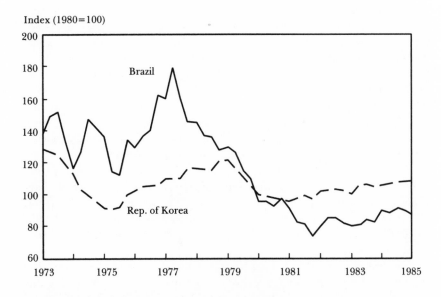

Index (1980=100)

Notes: Data are the unit value index of exports divided by the unit value index of imports
and calculated as a three-quarters-centered moving average.
Source: Various issues of IMF, *International Financial Statistics.*

Both countries experienced terms-of-trade deterioration because of the jump in real oil prices. The difference arises because a significant part of Brazil's exports, despite its status as a newly industrialized country, consisted of primary commodities or manufactures with very little value added beyond the material content, which in turn was domestic. As a result, Korea's terms of trade improved with the decline in real commodity prices, whereas Brazil's deteriorated.

An accounting equation for these differential effects finds that a 10 percent rise in the real price of oil (in terms of industrial countries' export unit values) will cause Brazil's terms of trade to deteriorate by 2.5 percent and Korea's by only 1 percent. A 10 percent rise in the real price of commodities will improve Brazil's terms of trade by 8 percent, while worsening Korea's by 2.2 percent (see Dornbusch 1985, table 7). This disparity leads to a dramatic difference in the impact of commodity prices. In 1985, when commodity prices were lower in dollar terms than they had been in 1978, Korea received an important offset to the oil shock. In the period since 1981 these prices have declined more than 10 percent at a time when oil prices have also fallen. The combined effects have given Korea an important advantage in the adjustment process. The need for external balance adjustment was lessened, and the real income cost of the external shocks was significantly less than in Latin America.

The view taken here is that the ability to adjust without sacrificing growth and without massive inflation depends to a significant extent on the size of the shock. Korea experienced both the oil shock and the interest rate shock. The effects were lessened, however, by the shift to favorable commodity prices. More of the adjustment could be achieved by a cut in wage growth relative to the growth in productivity than by recession.

The argument can be turned in another direction. The real income cost of the terms-of-trade shocks depends on the ratio of imports to income. Although Korea had a much smaller terms-of-trade loss than, for example, Brazil, its much greater openness—40 percent rather than only 10 percent—might have more than made up for the difference and left Korea with a much larger problem. That assumption is not altogether correct, however, because an adjustment must be made for the significant import content of exports. The reason is that terms-of-trade changes derived from unit trade values significantly overstate the terms-of-trade change relevant for welfare or real income calculations. All things considered, Korea had a smaller external shock and, since 1982, an outright favorable turn in external prices.

The second factor that helped Korea's adjustment in the period beginning in 1982 was the strong recovery of the world economy. Following the Kemp-Roth tax cuts, U.S. demand expanded strongly and helped pull in imports from everywhere, including Korea. Over the period from 1983 to 1985, U.S. demand increased at the annual rates of 5 percent, 8.7 percent, and 3.5 percent. Import volume in the United States grew at yearly rates of 7.6 percent, 27 percent, and 7 percent. Thus there was an unusually powerful locomotive pulling Korean exports, an immensely favorable factor in the adjustment period. This trend began only after 1982 and does little to explain the 1980–82 improvement, which Korea achieved under unfavorable international demand conditions.[6]

Investment Behavior

From the point of view of national accounting it is possible to look at the external balance in terms of the relationship between savings (S) and investment (I).

(4-1)   Current account $= S - I = S - I_{fm} - I_{fnm} - I_i$

where
    m = manufacturing
    nm = nonmanufacturing
    f = fixed investment
    i = inventory investment.

The current account surplus is equal to the difference between savings and investment. For the purpose of this discussion, however, it is convenient to work at a more disaggregated level, focusing on households, firms, and the government; separating fixed investment and inventories; and, on the side of fixed investment, distinguishing between manufacturing and nonmanufacturing.

Table 4-5 shows both investment as a fraction of GNP and the external balance. Fixed investment and changes in inventories are distinguished. Two points must be noted in interpreting the data. First, there was a substantial revision in the data for the 1980–84 period, and the data for prior years are not available on the new basis. The second point is the reclassification of the reporting for manufacturing investment from a user to an owner basis.[7] Nevertheless, even though the revision of the investment data was significant, there was virtually no change in the reported external balance because the reduced estimates of fixed investment in the new series were countered by a smaller decumulation of inventories.

Two points are apparent from table 4-5. The first is the pair of negative entries for inventory investment for 1982–83. This is important in the explanation of the improvement in the external balance: it helps reconcile why import growth was contained in the face of the strong domestic expansion in 1983. The explanation is simply that inventories of importables, especially oil, were run down.

The reason for the inventory decumulation is not apparent, but one argument can be offered readily. Domestic real interest rates were very high, certainly when nominal interest rates are compared with the rate of change (in won) of commodities held in inventory. Commodity prices in dollars were falling. When measured in won, they were barely constant, so that the won rate of interest—the alternative cost of carrying raw materials and intermediate goods in inventory—was very significant.

This is, of course, an adjustment of limited duration. It does not represent a sustainable improvement in import performance. Once inventories reach their equilibrium level with output, imports will grow more nearly in line with production, and the external balance will show some deterioration.

The other contribution of investment to the improvement of the external balance relates to a shift in composition. Investment moved from manufacturing to nonmanufacturing, and because manufacturing has a significant import content, there was a reduction in demand for imports and an increase in demand for domestic resources. An example of this shift is the decline in investment in heavy industry and the increase in construction activity. As noted, the subsidy program for heavy industry tapered off in the early 1980s, at the same time that the investment phase was completed. The natural result was a reduction in imports of investment goods by this industry.

With respect to the identity in equation (4-1), a pure shift in investment does not improve the external balance. A dollar of extra investment, with everything else constant, worsens the external balance just as much whether it goes for imports or for domestic resources. It thus cannot help explain the improvement in the external balance. It can only provide an understanding of why, in the face of other measures that saved external resources (for example, the budget correction and higher private saving, discussed below), adjustment could be achieved without slack and with significant growth.

Investment did increase in the service sector. The 1986 Asian and impending 1988 Olympic Games were an important impetus for increased construction. For example, investment in the wholesale and retail trade (including restaurants and hotels) rose from 6.5 percent to 12.6 percent of GNP over the 1978–84 period. There was also a more general shift in investment away from the export sector and toward the home economy. The growing prospect of protectionism abroad may have been one of the reasons manufacturing investment slowed and attention shifted to services.

The other reason is the rapid growth in real incomes, which increased the demand for services, and did so more than proportionately because of the high income elasticity of demand. Rapid real income growth thus called for an expansion in capacity in the services industry at a rate well in excess of real income growth. This point may well be the most important one.

As noted, withdrawal of government support of investment in heavy industry had a lot to do with the decline in investment. At least part of the decline represents a response to that policy. Once the support was ended in the early 1980s and specific investment programs were completed, investment naturally returned to its trend level.

Savings Behavior

The focus here is again on the net external balance identity in equation (4-1), this time from the point of view of the disaggregated savings balance:

$$(4\text{-}2) \qquad \text{Current account} = S - I = S_h + S_b + S_g - I$$

where

S = savings
I = investment
h = household
b = business
g = government.

From this perspective the improvement in net exports arose in response to the increase in national savings.

If table 4-4 is reviewed,[8] it is immediately apparent that, following the decline in the national savings rate in 1980–82, there was a large improvement in 1983–84. The major contributor to the improvement was a rise in household saving, although there was also some increase in government and business saving. With respect to household saving, the most interesting feature is the large decline—by a full 6 percentage points—between 1978 and 1980. This drop must be attributed to the impact of the adverse real income shock (recession and terms-of-trade deterioration).

Many would argue that the decline was attributable to the high rate of inflation in 1980–81 and the resulting negative real rates of return on assets. This argument is not persuasive. The compositional characteristics of saving cast some doubt on the positive effect of the increase in real interest rates on total saving. A higher real rate of interest may induce households to save more out of their incomes, but that increase can be offset by the possible negative effect of a higher real interest rate on corporate saving, which consists of capital consumption allowances and undistributed profits. To the extent that the high real interest rate squeezes corporate profits, it may lower corporate saving and hence may not increase domestic saving, even if households are sensitive to changes in real interest rates.

The fact that the household savings rate has not returned to its previous high level may, in part, be a reflection of the rise in government saving. Budget improvement reduces disposable income and, with it, saving, although increased business saving would tend to have offset reduced household saving somewhat. Table 4-9 shows the government's budget and an estimate of its cyclically adjusted level. A major part of the actual budget change was in expenditures; outlays were cut by more than 2 percent of

Table 4-9. *Budget of the Public Sector, 1979–84*

(percentage of GNP)

Item	1979	1980	1981	1982	1983	1984
Actual budget	1.4	3.2	4.6	4.3	1.6	1.4
Revenue	18.5	19.6	20.2	19.4	19.9	20.0
Expenditures	19.9	22.8	24.8	23.7	21.5	21.4
Cyclically adjusted budget	2.5	5.0	4.9	4.9	4.2	3.8

Source: Aghevli and Marquez-Ruarte (1985).

GNP. To the extent that these outlays represent a reduction in import spending, there would have been an immediate improvement in the external balance without further macroeconomic adjustment difficulties.

As in the case of investment, the contribution of savings to the external balance can be looked at in terms of the identity in equation (4-1), as well as from a broader macroeconomic perspective that takes into account the effect of changes in sectoral and aggregate savings on demand and the external balance. The effect of a budget improvement through cuts in spending and transfers and through increased taxation is to increase government savings while reducing real disposable income and aggregate demand. Unless the private sector finances the budget improvement by a matching reduction in savings, there will be an improvement in the external balance. At constant relative prices and in the absence of any other disturbance, there should also be an excess supply of domestic goods that reflects the decline in aggregate demand. That counterpart will exist unless reduced government spending is solely the result of less spending on importables or on exportables that can be sold at a given world price. Because that extreme is unreasonable, domestic counterpart slack should be expected.

At this point it is possible to link the discussions of saving and investment. The shift in investment was directed toward domestic resources, away from manufacturing with its high import content. This switch in expenditures offset the expenditure reduction provided by the increased savings rates and kept the use of resources close to their availability. There was no precise match between the expenditure switches and increased savings, so that relative prices may have had to move. This point is reinforced by the knowledge that in a strongly growing economy such as Korea's, potential output rises significantly even in the short run. Biases between traded and nontraded goods on the production side are thus a further complication in determining relative price movements.

Wages and the Real Exchange Rate

Wage and exchange rate policies probably have been the most visible and outstanding aspect of Korea's adjustment program. Table 4-10 provides

Table 4-10. *Nominal and Real Effective Exchange Rates, 1970–84*
(percent)

Year	Nominal exchange rate	Real effective exchange rate (1980 = 100)
1970	316.6	95
1971	373.2	102
1972	398.9	111
1973	397.5	127
1974	484.0	108
1975	484.0	109
1976	484.0	102
1977	484.0	102
1978	484.0	106
1979	484.0	97
1980	659.9	100
1981	700.5	97
1982	748.8	96
1983	795.5	103
1984	827.4	106

Note: The real exchange rate is defined as $R = eP^*/P$, where e is the nominal exchange rate and P and P^* are Korea's and its trading partners' wholesale price indexes.
Source: Park (1985).

data on the nominal and effective real exchange rates. Table 4-11 offers a comparison of different measures of real exchange rates, including the real wage and internal relative price. A comparison of 1980–82 and 1984 shows a clear gain in external competitiveness of about 8 percent. That gain was achieved even though unit labor costs in dollars remained roughly unchanged, while real wages increased sharply.

The striking fact in table 4-11 is the behavior of the real exchange rate and of the relative price, $V = P_{NT}/P_T$. The real effective exchange rate

Table 4-11. *Real Wages and Real Exchange Rate, 1975–84*
(1980 = 100)

Year	Real wage	Real effective exchange rate	Relative price[a]	Relative unit labor cost
1975–79	93	103	88	—
1979	105	97	100	—
1980	100	100	100	100
1981	99	97	102	97
1982	106	96	103	107
1983	115	103	105	106
1984	122	106	109	101

—Not available.
Note: The real exchange rate is defined as $R = eP^*/P$; the relative price is the ratio of the nonmanufacturing to the manufacturing deflator, $V = P_{NT}/P_T$. The relative unit labor cost uses the following weights: United States = 0.457, Japan = 0.428, Germany = 0.073, and United Kingdom = 0.042.
a. Nontradable/tradable.
Source: Park (1985) and U.S. Bureau of Labor Statistics.

measures price competitiveness by looking at relative wholesale prices in a common currency. The relative price (nontradables to tradables) includes the domestic price structure and a comparison of domestic and traded goods. That comparison is always difficult because indexes for nontraded goods are not readily available. The distinction between manufacturing and other sectors, however, has a long tradition (see the studies by Balassa 1964 and Kravis 1986). It can be observed that although the relative price of nontraded goods rose, the real effective exchange rate depreciated after 1980. Moreover, the discrepancy in only four years was substantial.

Two elements seem to go far in explaining this pattern. The rise in the relative price of domestic goods is largely attributable to the high rates of growth of productivity. If a country is a price-taker in world markets, high productivity growth translates into growth in product wages in the traded goods sector. This pushes up labor costs for other activities, but they do not share fully in the growth of productivity. As a result their relative prices increase. From this perspective a high real price for domestic goods reflects strong productivity performance, not overvaluation.

The other explanation involves the interaction of exchange rate and wage policies. The unit labor costs in dollars increased sharply in 1980–82, but then declined by about 7 percent. As a result the effective real unit labor costs showed a modest improvement by 1984, and they have improved even more since then. In any event, the gain in price competitiveness or the reduction in relative effective unit labor costs was so small that it is hard to disentangle the structural and policy effects from the imperfections in the correspondence of indexes.

It may also be observed that Korea did well, although its adjustment in external competitiveness was relatively small and the gain in real wages huge compared with Latin America. The consideration of competitiveness and relative costs suggests that Korea pursued an exchange rate policy that sustained international competitiveness, at least in comparison with the economies that purchased its products, although not necessarily with other suppliers in the developing world competing in the same markets. Argentina, Brazil, Chile, Colombia, Indonesia, Mexico, Peru, Singapore, Taiwan, Turkey, and Venezuela all showed depreciations compared with 1980–82 of approximately the same or even larger magnitudes than Korea's.[9]

When Korea is compared with its Asian competitors, using the Morgan Guaranty index of real exchange rates in manufacturing, steadiness is about equal (table 4-12). Korea and its competitors show real appreciation in 1981–82 and subsequent real depreciation. The movements were extremely small, however, both absolutely and between the two groups. The exception is 1985. With that qualification in mind, it is still the case that Korea showed a larger cumulative appreciation in 1978–82 and a larger subsequent correction. With real exchange rates applying to a large export

Table 4-12. *Real Exchange Rates for Korea and Its Asian Competitors, 1978–85*

(1980–82 = 100)

Year	Korea	Competitors[a]
1978	86.5	95.6
1979	95.3	92.8
1980	95.9	96.7
1981	101.2	100.8
1982	102.9	102.5
1983	97.3	99.8
1984	95.9	101.7
1985	88.7	97.8

Note: The real exchange rate is defined as $R^1 = eP^*/P$.

a. The index for competitors is the simple average of the real exchange rates for Hong Kong, Indonesia, Malaysia, Singapore, Taiwan, and Thailand.

Source: Morgan Guaranty.

base and with significant substitutability across alternative Asian suppliers, there is some room for real exchange rate movements as an explanation for the deterioration and subsequent improvement of trade performance.

Nevertheless, based on the comparison with other developing countries, Korea above all did not make major exchange rate mistakes. At the same time it is difficult to single out exchange rate policy as the only strategic factor promoting external balance adjustment. Korea's case provides further evidence for the proposition that exchange rate policy shows big results mostly when it goes wrong.

Expenditure Shifting

The fifth hypothesis considers the external balance implications of the structural shift in demand. Over the past five years demand has shifted from traded toward domestic goods. One important part of this structural change comes from the composition of investment: it has moved from capital goods toward construction. The import content of these two kinds of investment is very different, with that of construction much lower. Another significant factor is the improvement in the terms of trade.

The large decline in the real prices of materials meant that a won of spending by a Korean household had a much smaller import content and a larger domestic (or labor and capital services) content. This factor was reinforced by the expansion in services that went along with economic growth, because services had an even higher nontraded goods content. As a result, a high income elasticity for services implied expenditure shifts in the direction of nontraded goods over time.

The observed increase in the real price of domestic goods, already shown in table 4-11, thus reflects not only the impact of differential productivity growth but also the impact of a shift in demand. This point can be readily

Figure 4-4. *The Domestic Goods Market*

Price of domestic
goods (P)

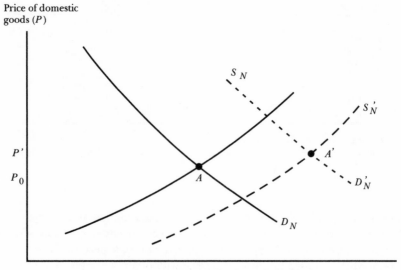

Quantity demanded and supplied (Q_{NT})

Note: P = price; D = demand; S = supply; A = equilibrium point at which supply
equals demand at a given price.
Source: Authors' calculations.

seen from the equilibrium in the domestic goods market in figure 4-4. The
vertical axis measures the relative price of domestic goods, $p = P_{NT}/P_T$; the
horizontal axis, the quantity demanded and supplied. Over time the supply
schedule shifts outward because of growth in productivity, the labor force,
and capital formation. If growth is neutral across sectors, the supply schedule will shift at a rate proportional to the growth rate of real GNP. By
assumption, the income elasticity of demand is larger than unity. The real
price of domestic goods must rise to equilibrate the domestic goods market.

This analysis helps explain why external balance adjustment took place
without a sharp contraction of demand. The reason is that the growth in
demand was biased toward the domestic goods sector so that the import
content of demand decreased. Korean growth was thus less prone to result
in a foreign exchange bottleneck.

The Monetary-Fiscal Mix

The last hypothesis concerns the monetary-fiscal mix. The 1980–82 period
was characterized by a large budget deficit and a reduction in real returns

Table 4-13. *Real Interest Rates in Korea, 1978–85*

(percent)

Year	Deposit rate	Inflation (CPI)	Private saving rate[a]
1978	—	14.5	—
1979	18.6	18.3	—
1980	14.8	28.7	15.4
1981	14.4	21.3	14.9
1982	7.6	7.3	14.8
1983	7.6	3.4	18.1
1984	6.0	2.3	20.9
1985	6.0	2.5	21.7

— Not available.

a. Percentage of GNP.

Source: IMF and Bank of Korea.

on savings. By 1984, however, the budget, actual or cyclically adjusted, showed a much reduced deficit, and real interest rates had become positive. Table 4-13, which shows measures of real interest rates in Korea, highlights the substantially negative real deposit rates in 1980–81 and the subsequent turn toward a positive return on savings. These policy developments certainly influenced aggregate demand in relation to potential output in a way that improved the current account and also helped sustain the higher real exchange rate.

Little is known about the savings response to real interest rates. Theory offers ambiguous advice, because the intertemporal substitution effect of increased real rates, which promotes saving, is potentially offset by the income effect, which raises consumption. In a world of target savings, or in a Modigliani-style life-cycle savings scheme, these income effects receive prominent attention. The review of empirical evidence by Giovannini (1983) does not encourage the belief that there is a significant positive savings response.

These remarks notwithstanding, Korea provides a case for the claim that real interest rates are a prime determinant of the aggregate savings rate. The distinction between the effects of sectoral distribution and the net savings, by sector and in the aggregate, remains a critical topic for research.

Lessons from the Korean Experience

What lessons can be derived from Korea's external balance adjustment? Are there obvious policy lessons with ready application in other developing countries?

It was argued that Korea's significant success in external balance adjustment, combined with growth and disinflation, relied on a conjunction of elements. The chief factor was an exceptionally favorable external environment: in 1980–84 real commodity prices plummeted, and after 1982 growth in the United States took off strongly. These external factors meant there was no foreign exchange crisis.

At the same time, Korean policy strongly capitalized on the favorable external environment in two ways. First, the government undertook an important fiscal correction that translated into an improved external balance. Second, wage and exchange rate policies combined to keep Korea competitive in its main markets, even if the gain in competitiveness was not particularly large. On the domestic side, wage restraint rather than over-valuation or recession was the chief instrument used to bring about adjustment and sustained competitiveness and, at the same time, a cut in inflation to approximately zero.

This account leads to the conclusion that Korea's achievement was not the result of a single, decisive action. On the contrary, it was made up of a lot of small pieces, each reinforcing the other. The good fortune of the external environment and the rapid growth in productivity allowed non-inflationary real wage gains. The increase in private demand, with a shift toward domestic goods, required resources that could be freed by a retrenchment of the public sector, so there was no problem of either excess demand or unemployment. Because demand growth was biased toward domestic goods, particularly construction, it generated employment without creating foreign exchange problems. Exchange rate policy was not locked in for the purpose of disinflation, nor directed toward bringing about a massive shift in the external balance, as occurred in Latin America. As a result, wage restraint—wages rising in line with productivity—was sufficient to ensure price stability. Borrowing for productive investment rather than consumption or capital flight was another feature of Korean policy.

Korea has demonstrated that with sound management of both wages and the exchange rate (not falling behind on the real exchange rate and not getting ahead on the real wage), high productivity growth associated with catching up on existing technology and a policy of import substitution can provide outstanding economic performance. Good domestic management often is not enough, however. When adverse external shocks create a major disruption and bring about a massive deterioration in the terms of trade, problems of distribution easily become macroeconomic and find their way into the budget and into inflation. That was the case in Korea in 1978–81, just as it was in Brazil in, for example, 1982–85.

The conclusions drawn here from Korea's experience differ from those of many other observers. Large weight is given to the favorable external factor that made possible the pursuit of reasonable policies. Domestic policies wisely capitalized on this external factor and constantly locked in the gains, benefiting from an economic regime that did not require many concessions. For Korea, the challenge will be to sustain that performance when oil price declines and lower interest rates remove the external constraints altogether. Will Korea then become like Mexico?

Notes

The authors are indebted to Susan Collins and Mohsin Khan for their helpful suggestions and are especially appreciative of Vittorio Corbo's many valuable criticisms and suggestions.

1. See also table 2-1 for the major macroeconomic trends over the past twenty-five years or so.

2. An ambitious explanation of the differences in performance among debtor developing countries has been offered by Sachs (1985).

3. Korea relies entirely on foreign supplies of crude oil, which amounted to an average of 23 percent of the total import bill during 1980–84.

4. The sharp decline in the import content of investment in 1983 shown in table 4-1 may be misleading because of two developments. One is the decumulation of inventories of imported raw materials. Another is the relative price change, in which the investment deflator rose by 23 percent, whereas import prices remained unchanged during 1980–83. Adjusted for these changes, it is unlikely that the import content of investment would show a decline in recent years. (Data in constant prices are not available.)

5. There is a question of how to classify the errors and omissions, which in 1982 took a sizable jump from a negative entry of less than $0.4 billion to a deficit of more than $1 billion. Military imports might be the reason for these errors and omissions, just as capital outflows might be. There is also a question of the valuation changes for official external assets.

6. Strong U.S. growth also favored the other developing countries and thus cannot by itself explain their different performances.

7. For comparison, figures from the old manufacturing investment series for the period 1980–84 are 4.8, 4.7, 4.1, 3.5, and 3.5. The difference shows that the manufacturing sector is investing outside manufacturing.

8. Once more, a very significant revision of the data for the 1980–84 period was made, with no data on the new basis available for prior years.

9. The relevant information for this statement is Morgan Guaranty's real effective exchange rate calculation for developing countries.

References

Aghevli, B. B., and Jorge Marquez-Ruarte. 1985. *A Case of Successful Adjustment: Korea's Experience during 1980–84.* IMF Occasional Paper no. 39. Washington, D.C.: International Monetary Fund.

Balassa, Bela. 1964. "The Purchasing-Power Parity Doctrine." *Journal of Political Economy* 72 (February):584–96.

Dornbusch, Rudiger. 1985. "Policy and Performance Links between LDC Debtors and Industrial Nations." *Brookings Papers on Economic Activity* (2):303–56.

Giersch, H. 1979. "Aspects of Growth, Structural Change and Employment." In H. Giersch, ed. *Macroeconomic Policies for Growth and Stability.* Tübingen, Germany; J.C.B. Mohr.

Giovannini, A. 1983. "The Interest Elasticity of Savings in Developing Countries: The Existing Evidence." *World Development* 11 (July): 601–07.

IMF (International Monetary Fund). Various years. *International Financial Statistics.* Washington, D.C.

Korea, Economic Planning Board. 1986. *Korean Economic Indicators.* Seoul.

Kravis, I. 1986. "The Three Faces of the National Income Comparison Project." *Research Reporter* 1.

Morgan Guaranty. 1984. "Korea: Adjustment Model for the 1980s?" *World Financial Markets* (March).

Park, Y. C. 1985. "Economic Stabilization and Liberalization in Korea: 1980–84." In Bank of Korea, *Monetary Policy in a Changing Financial Environment.* Seoul.

Sachs, Jeffrey D. 1985. "External Debt and Macroeconomic Performance in Latin America and East Asia." *Brookings Papers on Economic Activity* (2):523–64.

5 Recent Experience in Controlling Inflation

VITTORIO CORBO, Catholic University of Chile

SANG-WOO NAM, Korea Development Institute

ONE OF THE MOST IMPORTANT characteristics of Korea's economic performance in the first half of the 1980s was the dramatic reduction in inflation, which had become particularly severe in the late 1970s and early 1980s. As long as real gross national product (GNP) was growing at an average annual rate of close to 10 percent and the rate of inflation was in a range of 10–15 percent, inflation was not a major concern. In the late 1970s and in 1980, when the consumer price index (CPI) rose 34.6 percent (December to December) despite some price controls, fighting inflation became a priority.[1]

The Evolution of Inflation

As early as 1977 the Korean government had instituted stabilization measures to control inflation. As a result of the economic downturn in 1980, however, the focus of the comparatively restrictive stabilization program shifted toward promoting a resumption of economic growth and a slower rise in foreign debt and away from controlling inflation, although the latter followed from the effort to achieve the former. The results of the stabilization efforts were remarkable. By 1982 the annual rate of inflation was below 10 percent, and during 1983–84 it was only 2.3 percent. This slowdown was accomplished while the economy sustained a high rate of GNP growth.

The Outburst of Inflation

Inflation was not new to Korea. In 1963 and 1964, a time when the foundations for modern economic growth were being laid, it ran at over 20 percent a year. There ensued a period of strong economic growth that lasted until 1973 and was characterized by only modest inflation: as measured by the CPI it averaged 11.3 percent a year in the period 1965–73 (table 5-1). In 1974–75, following the first oil shock, inflation jumped to an average of 24.9 percent a year. Although it declined in 1976–77, it then again rose rapidly until 1980–81. In contrast, it fell consistently during 1982–86. When measured by the other price indexes—the wholesale price index (WPI) and the nonagricultural GNP deflator (PV1)—the pattern was similar.

Table 5-1. *Average Annual Rate of Change in Prices and Its Determinants, 1965–86*
(percent)

Item	1965–73	1974–75	1976–77	1978–79	1980–81	1982	1983	1984	1985	1986
Inflation										
CPI	11.3	24.9	12.7	16.4	25.0	7.3	3.4	2.3	2.5	2.3
WPI	8.8	34.3	10.6	15.2	21.3[a] 29.6	4.7	0.2	0.7	0.9	-2.2
PVI[b]	14.0	26.4	18.7	20.2	20.4[a] 21.8 16.9[a]	7.8	4.4	2.6	3.8	2.5
Determinants										
Manufacturing wages	18.7	31.2	34.3	31.5	21.4	14.7	12.2	8.1	9.9	9.1
Productivity	8.2	2.3	6.4	9.6	7.9	-1.8	4.2	12.0	-0.8	7.6
Agricultural prices	14.0	34.9	22.2	22.6	26.1	0.3	3.4	-0.1	6.0	-0.2
Price of imported materials[c]	12.0	27.9	1.6	16.4	37.6	1.3	1.2	4.0	3.0	-15.4
Price of imported oil	18.8	135.2	6.1	21.9	72.2	2.5	-6.6	0.4	7.5	-41.5
Price of non-oil materials	11.6	18.1	0.4	14.8	25.6	0.7	5.7	5.9	0.8	-2.0
M2	47.6	26.6	33.1	33.0	26.6	28.2	19.5	10.7	11.8	17.0
Bank credit	45.8	43.2	22.7	40.7	36.6	25.0	15.7	13.2	18.0	14.4

Note: The data are arithmetic averages.

a. The figure is for 1981 alone.

b. PVI denotes the nonagricultural GNP deflator.

c. Percentages are based on prices in won.

Source: Bank of Korea and Economic Planning Board.

The second half of table 5-1 shows the evolution of the main determinants of Korea's inflation: unit labor costs (growth in manufacturing wages minus the rate of growth of productivity), external prices, and monetary expansion (M2 and bank credit). Nominal wages in manufacturing rose faster than inflation through 1978-79; real wages thus grew substantially in the 1965-73 period and again in 1976-77. Moreover, the expansionary policies of 1976-77 resulted in a large real currency appreciation and a consequent loss in export competitiveness. A large expansion in overseas construction led to a small surplus in the current account of the balance of payments in 1977, but the currency appreciation was starting to hurt export and GNP growth. By 1979, for the first time in Korea's modern economic history, the volume of exports fell. This decline was hardly surprising, given that their dollar unit value had increased by 61.8 percent during 1975-79, while unit labor costs had risen by 137.3 percent (table 5-2), a situation that created a substantial profit squeeze on export activities.

The trend in the won price for imported materials reflected, among other things, the trends in the price of oil, the general fall in commodity prices from 1980 to 1982 (Beckerman and Jenkinson 1986), and adjustments in the nominal exchange rate. The jump in import prices in 1974-75 stemmed from the first oil shock and the large devaluation of 1974; the jump in 1978-79 was mostly attributable to the second oil shock and the boom in the international prices of raw materials. The large increase in 1980-81 reflected the large devaluation in 1980. Finally, the substantial

Table 5-2. *Export Profitability and Growth, 1976-79*

Item	1976	1977	1978	1979
Index (1975 = 100)				
I. Nominal wages (manufacturing)	134.7	180.2	242.1	311.4
II. Labor productivity[a] (manufacturing)	101.0	110.5	123.8	131.2
III. Unit labor cost (I/II)	133.4	163.1	195.6	237.3
IV. Unit value of exports[b] (in won)	111.7	122.3	135.4	161.8
V. Export profitability (IV/III)	83.7	75.0	69.2	68.2
Growth of exports (percent)				
Based on value measured in current U.S. dollars				
Korea	51.8	30.2	26.5	18.4
Taiwan	53.8	14.6	35.5	26.9
Singapore	22.5	25.1	23.0	40.4
Hong Kong	41.9	12.9	19.5	31.7
Based on value measured in constant U.S. dollars				
Korea	35.6	19.1	14.4	-1.4
Taiwan	50.2	7.7	27.9	9.3
Singapore	14.2	15.5	27.9	22.6
Hong Kong	28.5	10.7	11.2	13.0

a. Computed using national income data (value added per worker).

b. Because the exchange rate was fixed with respect to the dollar during the whole period, the indexes based on won and dollar values are equal.

Source: IMF (1982); for Taiwan, various issues of Taiwan, China, Directorate General of Budget, Accounting, and Statistics, *Monthly Bulletin of Statistics.*

drop in the post-1981 period was primarily the result of the collapse of international commodity prices.

During 1965-73, monetary expansion, measured by the rate of growth of M2, was quite high, but inflation remained low. Financial deregulation and positive real interest rates promoted the growth of the formal financial sector. Monetary growth slowed in the 1970s, except in 1976-77 and 1978-79, when it was about 33 percent a year. The rate of growth of M2 fell in 1980-81, recovered somewhat in 1982, and fell again in 1983-84.

The expansionary policies resulted in an average rate of inflation during 1976-79 of 14.6 percent in the CPI and 19.7 percent in the nonagricultural GNP deflator. Inflation might have been higher still had it not been for some price controls and an increasing real appreciation. As a result of the use of external financing to cover the current account deficits, net foreign debt rose from $7.6 billion at the end of 1977 to $14.0 billion at the end of 1979. The final result was an unsustainable real appreciation. Not surprisingly, Korea's East Asian neighbors were achieving much better export performance, as the bottom of table 5-2 shows.

Stabilization Policies

By 1978 it was clear to Korea's government that a more comprehensive stabilization was needed. In the spring of 1978 the government cut its expenditures and increased the tariffs for public utilities to reduce the deficit. It also controlled the expansion of credit by, among other things, adjusting interest rates upward. In the second half of 1978 it tightened fiscal and monetary policies and took some supply-side actions in the agricultural and fishery sectors. It trimmed government expenditures further and postponed construction projects. Import liberalization was also used. At the same time, however, government incentives encouraged the expansion of the heavy and chemical industries, and private investment rose substantially.

In April 1979 the government announced the Comprehensive Measures for Economic Stabilization (CMES) program. At the time, a consensus was developing in Korea that stabilization was a precondition for resuming growth. A restrictive fiscal management program called for a 5 percent cut in current expenditures and a restricted investment program. In the sphere of monetary policy, the government raised interest rates and emphasized a reduction in subsidized lending. Finally, a comprehensive price stabilization program for daily necessities was initiated. No immediate action was taken to restore the accumulated loss of profitability in export activities, and the volume of exports showed negative growth in 1979. Then, in the third month of the program came the second oil price shock and the assassination of President Park.

[In January 1980 the government devalued the won by 20 percent against the U.S. dollar and introduced a managed floating system. To engineer a real devaluation, it introduced supportive policies (monetary restraint and higher interest rates) to reduce aggregate demand. It supplemented these macroeconomic adjustment policies with more specific switching and microeconomic policies. [Financial support for public construction, small and medium-size firms, residential construction (especially for low-income families), and exports of heavy industrial products on a deferred payment basis was augmented. Tax instruments—a temporary investment tax credit and a reduction in personal and corporate income taxes, together with capital gains and special excise taxes—were also utilized.]

The second oil shock and the large nominal devaluation of early 1980 were supposed to result in a once-and-for-all increase in prices, and thus in a temporal increase in measured inflation. [When measured inflation rose in 1980, the government used income policies to avoid a new inflationary spiral.] It believed that a slowdown in nominal wage increases was needed to minimize the output losses that could result from a reduction in inflation. The government encouraged the private sector to follow its moderate and well-publicized public sector salary increases.] The resultant wage restraint, together with some real exchange rate appreciation and declining international prices for imported raw materials, coincided with a substantial slowdown in inflation between 1981 and 1982.] The average annual inflation in the nonagricultural GNP deflator decreased from 27.1 percent in 1980 to only 16.9 percent in 1981; in the WPI, from 38.9 percent in 1980 to 20.4 percent in 1981; and in the CPI, from 28.7 percent in 1980 to 21.3 percent in 1981.

With respect to external competitiveness, the real effective exchange rate dropped by 8.1 percent between the last quarter of 1980 and the last quarter of 1981. Thanks to favorable external terms of trade and active overseas construction business in the Middle East, however, the annual current account deficit fell from $5 billion during 1979–81 to only $2.7 billion in 1982.

Monetary expansion, although substantially reduced, was still high, and only when the public sector deficit reached 4.6 percent of GNP was fiscal policy tightened. With the dramatic slowdown in the rate of increase in the won price of imported raw materials and the moderation in nominal wage increases, inflation dropped sharply in 1982. A small appreciation (3.0 percent) in the real effective exchange rate in the last quarter of 1982 contributed to the slowdown. [Finally, in the post-1982 period, despite a strong economic recovery, inflation decelerated further. Tight fiscal and monetary policies, stable unit import prices, a good harvest, and a continued income policy that kept key factor costs in line with the deceleration of inflation seem to have contributed to the deceleration.]

The Sources of Inflation: An Aggregate Model

Although there is no good macroeconomic theory to explain the dynamics of price changes, much can be learned about the dynamics of inflation using small structural models. To establish the main determinants of the acceleration of inflation in Korea in the late 1970s and of its deceleration in the early 1980s, a small aggregate quarterly model that assesses the relationship among the various inflationary forces was formulated and tested. The model is geared toward providing an understanding of the dynamics of inflation. It consists of six endogenous variables—five endogenous prices (agriculture, manufacturing, wholesale, energy, and consumer) and manufacturing wages. In the model of a semiopen economy used here, manufacturing prices behave as sheltered sector prices do in the standard Scandinavian model (Aukrust 1977; Calmfors 1977; Lindbeck 1979; Corbo 1985).

The effects of the two oil shocks and of the 1980 devaluation on the price of imported raw materials played a central role in the acceleration of inflation, and the collapse of international commodity prices in the early 1980s was closely associated with its deceleration.

The Model

The model is given by the following equations:

$$(5\text{-}1) \quad \hat{P}_{W,t} \equiv a_1 \hat{P}_{A,t} \frac{P_{A,t-1}}{P_{W,t-1}} + a_2 \hat{P}_{M,t} \frac{P_{M,t-1}}{P_{W,t-1}} + (1 - a_1 - a_2) \hat{P}_{E,t} \frac{P_{E,t-1}}{P_{W,t-1}}$$

$$(5\text{-}2) \quad \hat{P}_{M,t} = b_1 + b_2 \, PDL \, (\hat{W}_{M,t} - \hat{q}_{M,t}) + b_3 \, PDL \, (\widehat{PMR}_t) + b_4 DM_t$$

$$(5\text{-}3) \quad \hat{W}_{M,t} = c_1 + c_2 \frac{1}{U_t} + c_3 \frac{1}{U_{t-1}} + c_4 \hat{P}_{C,t-1} + c_5 D_t + c_6 DS1_t$$

$$(5\text{-}4) \quad \hat{P}_{C,t} = d_1 + d_2 \hat{P}_{A,t} + d_3 \hat{P}_{M,t} + d_4 \hat{P}_{C,t-1}$$

$$(5\text{-}5) \quad \hat{P}_{A,t} = \widehat{RP}_{A,t} + \hat{P}_{C,t}$$

$$(5\text{-}6) \quad \hat{P}_{E,t} = e_1 + e_2 \, PDL \, (\widehat{PMR1}_t)$$

$$(5\text{-}7) \quad \widehat{PMR}_t \equiv f_1 \, PMR1_t \frac{\widehat{PMR1}_{t-1}}{PMR_{t-1}} + (1 - f_1) \, PMR2_t \frac{\widehat{PMR2}_{t-1}}{PMR_{t-1}}$$

where

$$(\hat{\ }) = \text{Quarterly rate of change}$$
$$P_W = \text{WPI}$$

P_A = agricultural prices (WPI)

P_M = manufacturing prices (WPI), excluding energy products

P_E = energy prices (WPI), a weighted average of petroleum and related products and of coal and electric power

q_M = four-quarter moving average of labor productivity in manufacturing

PMR = price of imported materials in domestic currency

DM = inventory-to-sales ratio in manufacturing (demand pressure)

W_M = wage rate in manufacturing

U = total unemployment rate

P_C = consumer price index

D = dummy variable that takes a value of one for the first quarter of 1980 onwards and zero otherwise

$DS1$ = seasonal dummy variable that takes a value of one for the first quarter of every year starting in 1978 and zero otherwise

RP_A = real price of agricultural products in terms of the CPI

$PMR1$ = price of imported petroleum and related products, in domestic currency

$PMR2$ = price of imported nonpetroleum materials, in domestic currency

PDL = indicates a polynomial distributed lag for the weights of the variable M in parentheses.

Equation (5-1) defines the WPI as the weighted average of its agricultural, manufacturing, and energy components. The weights are taken directly from the WPI index ($a_1 = 0.16$, $a_2 = 0.64$).

For equation (5-2) a model of a semiopen economy along the lines of those employed by Bruno (1979, 1980), Corbo (1974, 1985), Gordon (1975), and Nam (1984) was used. The rate of change in manufacturing prices ($\hat{P}_M$) is a function of a distributed lag in the rate of change in the unit labor cost in manufacturing ($\hat{W}_M - \hat{q}_M$), a distributed lag in the rate of change in the domestic currency price of imported materials ($\widehat{PMR}$), and a measure of demand pressures (DM).

For equation (5-3), the wage equation, a standard expectation augmented Phillips curve, extended to incorporate the income policies of the 1980s, was assumed. In the specification of equation (5-3) it was also assumed that expected inflation was equal to the previous quarter's inflation.

Equation (5-4) links the changes in the CPI to the evolution of the agricultural and manufacturing components of the WPI and the lagged value of the CPI. This value of the CPI was taken as the main determinant of the price of the service components of the CPI and of the trade and commerce margins for agricultural and manufacturing goods.

Equation (5-5) assumes that the real price of agricultural goods is an exogenous variable. This assumption reflects both government price support policies for rice and barley and the effects of supply shocks.

Equation (5-6) links the evolution of the energy component of the WPI (P_E) to the price in domestic currency of imported petroleum and related products ($\widehat{PMR}1$) through a polynomial distributed lag.

Finally, equation (5-7) defines PMR, the price of imported materials in domestic currency, as an arithmetic average of its two components, petroleum and related products ($PMR1$) and nonpetroleum materials ($PMR2$). The weights are taken from the WPI ($f_1 = 0.6688$).

Equations (5-2), (5-3), (5-4), and (5-5) were estimated simultaneously. Equation (5-5) is really an identity, and it was used as such in the estimation. The equations were estimated individually using quarterly data for the period between the first quarter of 1972 and the last quarter of 1984 and as a system of four equations in four endogenous variables: change in agricultural prices ($\hat{P}_{A,t}$); change in manufacturing prices ($\hat{P}_{M,t}$); change in the wage rate in manufacturing ($\hat{W}_{M,t}$); and change in the CPI ($\hat{P}_{C,t}$). The individual equations were estimated by least squares, and the system of equations was estimated using the full information maximum likelihood procedure. With the second method, the simultaneous nature of the model was explicitly taken into account. In both cases the equations were estimated including a first-order autoregressive process for the random errors of the individual equations.

When the full system was estimated, the changes in the four-quarter moving average of labor productivity in manufacturing ($\hat{q}_M$), the price of imported material in domestic currency ($\widehat{PMR}$), the inventory-to-sales ratio in manufacturing (DM), the total unemployment rate (U_t), the price of agricultural products in the CPI ($\widehat{RP}_A$), and the lagged value of the change in the CPI ($\hat{P}_C$) were taken as exogenous variables. The assumption that the rate of change in the real CPI price of agricultural products ($\widehat{RP}_A$) was exogenous is discussed above. That the rate of change in the price of imported materials in domestic currency, ($\widehat{PMR}$) was exogenous until early 1980 follows from the small-country assumption and from the fixed exchange rate policy that was followed until then. This idea was a little more questionable in the 1980s, when Korea was trying to keep a purchasing power parity (PPP) rule in relation to a currency basket, with due consideration to current account developments. It might have been expected that this monetary policy would affect domestic inflation through its effect on the exchange rate, and ultimately on import prices. It was assumed that the unemployment rate was exogenous to any of the prices included in the model. It was much more questionable to assume that the excess demand variable was not related to the price variables in the model. This variable was never significant, however, and played a minor role in the model. The exogeneity of the four-quarter moving average of labor productivity in manufacturing ($\hat{q}_M$) and the lagged CPI ($\hat{P}_C$) does not need discussion.

An alternative model for studying the dynamic of inflation is the one initially formulated by Harberger (1963), which ties inflation to distributed lags in money growth, as well as output growth and an inflation acceleration variable. When a model selection test was used to compute an equation of this kind with a reduced form of the model presented in the paper, the model used here emerged as more favorable. (The comparison of the quasi-reduced form of the model presented in this paper with the Harberger-style model is presented in the appendix to this chapter.)

The Results

The results of the estimation of the individual equations are given in table 5-3. The bottom of the table shows the normalized weights for the variables that entered in polynomial distributed lag form.[2] These weights were used later as extraneous information in estimating the full model.

The results of the estimations are as expected. In the manufacturing price equation (5-2), the unit labor cost ($\hat{W}_M - \hat{q}_M$) has a coefficient of 0.247, the weighted price of imported raw materials ($P\hat{M}R$) a coefficient of 0.613. The large coefficient for materials indicates the heavy dependence of the Korean manufacturing sector on these imports. In the same equation the coefficient for the excess demand variable (DM) has the right sign but is not significantly different from zero.[3] The autoregressive coefficient is equal to 0.419 and is statistically significant.

In the wage equation (5-3) the reciprocals of both the contemporaneous and the lagged unemployment rates are statistically significant. In the same equation the coefficient of lagged inflation is equal to 0.651 and is highly significant. Surprisingly, the dummy variable for the wage persuasion variable, although it is not statistically significant, has a positive coefficient.[4] Thus, there is no direct evidence of a downward effect on wage growth from the "wage persuasion" dummy. The seasonal dummy, included to account for the fourth-quarter bonus, is highly significant and implies, other things being equal, a nearly 9 percentage point fall in the rate of change in manufacturing wages in the first quarter of every year, starting in 1978. The autoregressive coefficient is not significantly different from zero at the 10 percent level.

In the CPI equation (5-4) agricultural commodities have a coefficient of 0.254, manufacturing excluding energy products has a coefficient of 0.418, and the lagged CPI has a coefficient of 0.195. All these coefficients are highly significant. In contrast, the autoregressive coefficient is not significant.

The estimation of the full model appears in table 5-4. In comparison with the results of the single equation estimates for the unconstrained case given

Table 5-3. Quarterly Inflation Model, Least-Square Estimates

Manufacturing prices[a]		Manufacturing wages		Consumer prices		Energy prices[b]	
b_1	−0.003	c_1	−0.110	d_1	0.003	e_1	0.005
	(−0.140)		(−4.447)		(1.230)		(0.699)
b_2	0.247	c_2	0.378	d_2	0.254	e_2	0.660
	(1.944)		(5.096)		(4.901)		(11.490)
b_3	0.613	c_3	0.210	d_3	0.418	ρ_e	−0.074
	(8.24)		(2.962)		(6.734)		(−0.513)
b_4	0.0003	c_4	0.651	d_4	0.195		
	(0.013)		(4.629)		(2.404)		
ρ_b	0.419	c_5	0.009	ρ_d	−0.094		
	(2.760)		(1.149)		(−0.546)		
		c_6	−0.088				
			(−6.689)				
		ρ_c	−0.203				
			(−1.363)				
R^2	0.765		0.792		0.812		0.716
DW	1.79		2.06		1.99		1.85

Note: See the text for a definition of the coefficients.

a. In this equation, both the rate of change in the unit labor cost and the rate of change in the price of imported materials are restricted to a second-degree polynomial with three and two lags, respectively. In both cases, a far restriction is imposed. The normalized weights of the polynomial on the unit labor cost and their respective estimated t-coefficients are

$$0.122, \quad 0.300, \quad 0.339, \quad \text{and} \quad 0.239$$
$$(0.981) \quad (6.166) \quad (6.472) \quad \quad (6.335),$$

and the weights for the polynomial on the price of imported materials with their estimated t-coefficients are

$$0.549, \quad 0.317, \quad \text{and} \quad 0.134.$$
$$(6.931) \quad (6.637) \quad \quad (2.367)$$

b. In this equation, the coefficients of the price of imported petroleum products are restricted to a second-degree polynomial with far restrictions and two lags. The weights of the polynomial with their estimated t-coefficients in parentheses are

$$0.591, \quad 0.303, \quad \text{and} \quad 0.106.$$
$$(8.249) \quad (7.234) \quad \quad (2.132)$$

Source: Authors' estimates.

in table 5-3, four major changes can be noted. First, the coefficient of unit labor costs ($\hat{W}_M - \hat{q}_M$) becomes larger but less significant. Second, the coefficient of the previous quarter's CPI inflation becomes larger in the wage equation. Third, the coefficient of agricultural goods in the consumer price equation becomes smaller. Fourth, in the same equation the coefficient of lagged CPI becomes larger. There are no major changes with the single equation results for the other coefficients.

Before proceeding to the counterfactual simulations, a test for homogeneity of degree one in equations (5-2) and (5-4) was undertaken. The results are presented in the last two columns of table 5-4 (constrained cases). The homogeneity restriction cannot be rejected for equation (5-2); the computed χ^2 statistic for the null hypothesis is 1.18. For equation (5-4) the homogeneity restriction is rejected, and the computed χ^2 statistic is 4.37. Thus only the former restriction was imposed in the system. The

Table 5-4. *Quarterly Inflation Model, Simultaneous Estimation*

Coefficient	Unconstrained case	Constrained case $(d_2+d_3+d_4 = 1.0)$	Constrained case $(b_2+b_3 = 1.0)$
b_1	-0.002	-0.001	-0.007
	(-0.079)	(-0.035)	(-0.262)
b_2	0.280	0.269	0.386
	(1.695)	(1.554)	(6.173)
b_3	0.589	0.601	n.a.
	(9.703)	(9.499)	n.a.
b_4	-0.001	-0.002	-0.001
	(-0.026)	(-0.071)	(-0.025)
ρ_b	0.372	0.377	0.377
	(1.984)	(1.982)	(2.031)
c_1	-0.097	-0.097	-0.097
	(-3.247)	(-3.378)	(-3.414)
c_2	0.352	0.348	0.361
	(4.111)	(4.066)	(4.158)
c_3	0.193	0.193	0.187
	(2.511)	(2.628)	(2.828)
c_4	0.689	0.721	0.679
	(3.118)	(3.242)	(3.076)
c_6	-0.088	-0.089	-0.089
	(-3.612)	(-3.881)	(-3.653)
ρ_c	-0.166	-0.165	-0.171
	(-1.237)	(-1.274)	(-1.304)
d_1	0.004	0.0002	0.004
	(1.253)	(0.148)	(1.249)
d_2	0.118	0.118	0.120
	(2.303)	(2.272)	(2.337)
d_3	0.439	0.490	0.443
	(7.748)	(8.228)	(8.051)
d_4	0.318	n.a.	-0.317
	(3.269)	n.a.	(-3.350)
ρ_d	-0.408	-0.395	-0.414
	(-1.551)	(-2.006)	(-1.586)
LLF	433.731	431.546	433.142

n.a. Not applicable.
Note: The values of the estimated and asymptotic *t*-coefficients are in parentheses. *LLF* is the log of the likelihood function.
Source: Authors' estimates.

estimated coefficients under this restriction appear in the second-to-last column of table 5-4.

A set of counterfactual simulations was estimated to determine the factors that contributed to inflation. To this end, the model was completed with the estimation of equation (5-6) and the inclusion of identities (5-1) and (5-7), plus four more identities that provide the weights for equation (5-1):

$$(5\text{-}8) \qquad P_{A,t} \equiv P_{A,t-1} \left(1 + \hat{P}_{A,t}\right)$$

Figure 5-1. *Tracking Inflation, CPI: 1972-84*

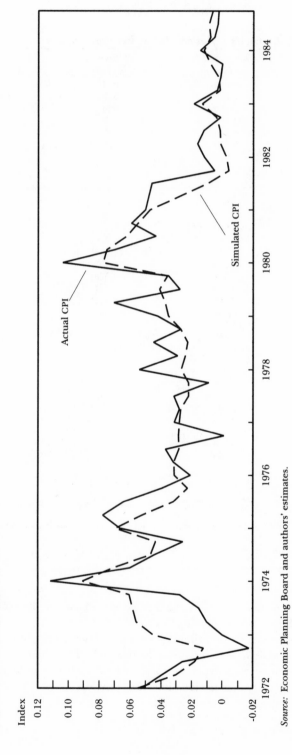

Index

Source: Economic Planning Board and authors' estimates.

(5-9) $$P_{M,t} \equiv P_{M,t-1}\,(1 + \hat{P}_{M,t})$$

(5-10) $$P_{E,t} \equiv P_{E,t-1}\,(1 + \hat{P}_{E,t})$$

(5-11) $$P_{W,t} \equiv P_{W,t-1}\,(1 + \hat{P}_{W,t}).$$

The results from the estimation of equation (5-6) appear in the last column of table 5-3. The coefficient of *PDL* ($P\hat{M}R1_t$) is equal to 0.66 and is highly significant.

Model Tracking How the model tracks changes in the CPI ($C\hat{P}I$) and WPI ($W\hat{P}I$) appears in figures 5-1 and 5-2, respectively. It can be seen that the tracking in the sample is quite good. In particular, the estimated model picks up most of the turning points in both series. The root-mean squared errors are 0.019 and 0.08, respectively. Furthermore, if Theil's decomposition of the root-mean squared errors is used, 0.958 of it is attributable to a different covariation of the series for both the $C\hat{P}I$ and $W\hat{P}I$ series.

Counterfactual Simulations The first simulation (which assumed no shock and no devaluation) studied the effect of the second oil shock and the post-1979 devaluation on inflation. It was followed by a second simulation (no post-1979 devaluation) of the effect of the second oil shock only. The third simulation (no second oil shock) assumed only the post-1979 devaluation. The fourth simulation (no slowdown in the rising price of imported raw materials after 1981) studied the effect of the moderation in the rate of change in the prices of imported raw materials ($P\hat{M}R$) in the post-1981 period. The fifth simulation (no slowdown in the real price of agricultural products after 1981) looked at the effect of the slowdown in the increase of the real price of agricultural products ($R\hat{P}_A$) in terms of the CPI after 1981. The final simulation addressed the joint effect of the slowdown in changes in the price of imported materials ($P\hat{M}R$) and in changes in the price of agricultural products ($R\hat{P}_A$) (no slowdown in either after 1981). The results of these counterfactual simulations are presented in table 5-5. The second-to-last column shows the effect on WPI inflation and the last column the effect on CPI inflation.

The first three simulations, as expected, show, in general, a deflationary effect, whereas the last three show an inflationary effect. In the first counterfactual simulation—no second oil shock and no post-1979 devaluation—the inflationary effect was -17.7 (-9.0) percentage points on the WPI (CPI) in 1980 and -4.1 (-3.9) percentage points in 1981. In the second simulation—no devaluation but a second oil shock—the inflationary effect was -9.0 (-4.5) percentage points on the WPI (CPI) in 1980 and -3.2 (-2.5) in 1981. For the third simulation—no second oil shock but a devaluation

Figure 5-2. *Tracking Inflation: WPI, 1972-84*

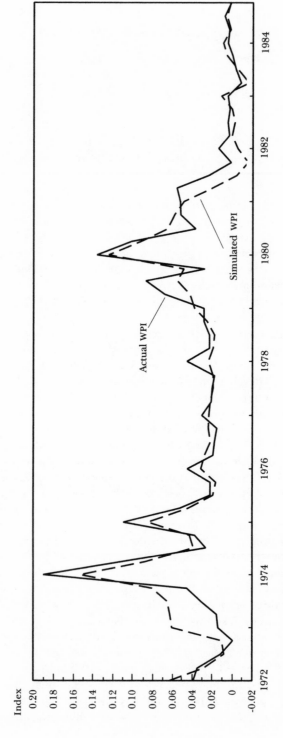

Index

Actual WPI

Simulated WPI

Source: Bank of Korea and authors' estimates.

Table 5-5. *Inflation Effects—Counterfactual Simulations*
(percentage points)

Simulation	Quarter	Change in WPI	Change in CPI
1. No second oil shock and no devaluation after 1979 (*PMR1* increases at 1.3 percent a quarter in 1980 and 1981)[a]	1980:1	−4.5	−1.6
	:2	−4.3	−2.2
	:3	−3.1	−2.0
	:4	−2.7	−1.8
	Annual[b]	−17.7	−9.0
	1981:1	−2.5	−1.7
	:2	−1.4	−1.2
	:3	−0.1	−0.6
	:4	−0.1	−0.2
	Annual	−4.1	−3.9
2. No devaluation after 1979 (*PMR1* increases at the rate of increase in the dollar price of imported petroleum and related products in 1980 and 1981)	1980:1	−2.5	−0.9
	:2	−1.9	−1.0
	:3	−1.4	−0.9
	:4	−1.5	−0.9
	Annual	−9.0	−4.5
	1981:1	−1.2	−0.8
	:2	−0.9	−0.7
	:3	−0.5	−0.5
	:4	−0.5	−0.4
	Annual	−3.2	−2.5
3. No second oil shock but devaluation after 1979 (*PMR1* increases at the rate of devaluation plus 1.3 percent a quarter in 1980 and 1981)	1980:1	−2.0	−0.7
	:2	−2.5	−1.2
	:3	−1.7	−1.1
	:4	−1.3	−0.9
	Annual	−9.4	−4.7
	1981:1	−1.3	−0.9
	:2	−0.5	−0.6
	:3	0.4	−0.1
	:4	0.4	0.1
	Annual	−1.0	−1.4
4. No slowdown in the price of imported raw materials after 1981 (*PMR1* increases at 12.64 percent a quarter in 1982, 1983, and 1984; *PMR2* increases at 5.3 percent a quarter in 1982, 1983, and 1984)[c]	1982:1	2.4	1.1
	:2	3.8	2.1
	:3	5.2	3.2
	:4	5.8	3.9
	Annual[d]	18.3	10.6
	1983:1	5.9	4.2
	:2	7.5	4.7
	:3	6.0	4.2
	:4	5.5	3.9
	Annual	27.3	18.5
	1984:1	5.7	4.0
	:2	5.7	4.0
	:3	5.8	4.2
	:4	6.2	4.5
	Annual	25.9	18.2

(*Table continues on the following page.*)

Table 5-5   *Continued*

Simulation	Quarter	Change in WPI	Change in CPI
5. No slowdown in the real price of agricultural	1982:1	0.9	0.6
products after 1981 (RP_A increases at 1.1	:2	0.3	0.4
percent a quarter in 1982, 1983, and 1984)[e]	:3	0.2	0.2
	:4	0.2	0.2
	Annual	1.6	1.5
	1983:1	−0.2	−0.1
	:2	0.6	0.4
	:3	0.9	0.7
	:4	0.8	0.8
	Annual	2.1	1.9
	1984:1	0.5	0.6
	:2	0.5	0.5
	:3	−0.4	−0.2
	:4	0.2	−0.01
	Annual	0.8	0.9
6. No slowdown in the price of imported	1982:1	3.3	1.8
materials or the real price of agricultural	:2	4.0	2.5
products after 1981 (combination of	:3	5.3	3.4
simulations 4 and 5)	:4	6.0	4.1
	Annual	20.0	12.3
	1983:1	5.7	4.0
	:2	8.1	5.1
	:3	6.8	5.0
	:4	6.2	4.7
	Annual	29.4	20.6
	1984:1	6.1	4.6
	:2	6.1	4.5
	:3	5.4	4.0
	:4	6.3	4.5
	Annual	26.4	19.2

a. Annual effect is fourth-quarter to fourth-quarter rate of change.

b. This is the quarterly average compounded growth rate of *PMR*1 between 1975:1 and 1978:4, a period in which the exchange rate was fixed.

c. These are the quarterly average compounded growth rates of *PMR*1 and *PMR*2 for the 1979:1 to 1981:4 period.

d. Annual effect is four-quarter compounded value.

e. This is the quarterly average growth rate of RP_A for the 1980:1 to 1981:4 period.

Source: Authors' calculations.

after 1979—the inflationary effect was −9.4 (−4.7) on the WPI (CPI) in 1980 and −1.0 (−1.4) in 1981.

Based on this set of simulations, the conclusion is that, given the structure of the transmission of inflation in the Korean economy, the acceleration of inflation in 1980 was attributable almost equally to the devaluation and the second oil shock. In 1981, however, the devaluation was much more important than the oil shock.

For the fourth simulation—no slowdown in the price of imported materials in the post-1981 period—the inflationary effect was 18.3 (10.6) percentage points on the WPI (CPI) in 1982, 27.3 (18.5) percentage points in 1983, and 25.9 (18.2) percentage points in 1984. Thus, for this period the moderation in the won price of imported materials was a major contributor to the slowdown in inflation. It is important to emphasize that this experiment includes the effects of the moderation in the international price of raw materials as well as the slowdown in the rate of devaluation of the won, the latter reflecting the moderate monetary and fiscal policies of the period.[5]

Based on the fifth simulation—no slowdown in the real price of agricultural products ($\hat{RP}_A$) after 1981—the slackening that occurred contributed to a slowdown in WPI (CPI) inflation of 1.6 (1.5) percentage points in 1982, 2.1 (1.9) percentage points in 1983, and 0.8 (0.9) percentage points in 1984. From the result of this simulation it can be concluded that the slowdown in $\hat{RP}_A$ contributed only marginally to the lessening of inflation.

Finally, the sixth simulation—no slowdown in the price of imported raw materials or in the real price of agricultural products after 1981—suggests that the combined effect of the actual moderation in the rate of change in the won price of imported materials and in the real price of agricultural products contributed to a lessening of WPI (CPI) inflation of 20.0 (12.3) percentage points in 1982, 29.4 (20.6) percentage points in 1983, and 26.4 (19.2) percentage points in 1984. Thus, the results of the best two simulations reveal that the slowdown in the rate of change in the won price of imported raw materials was a major factor in the successful stabilization of the Korean economy. Of course, the slowdown in the rate of change in the prices of imported materials was the result of restrictive monetary and fiscal policies that led to a much smaller need for an inflation tax and of the gains in the terms of trade attributable to the drop in the dollar prices of imported materials.

Conclusions

Two main conclusions emerge from this study. First, the devaluation initiated in 1980 and the second oil shock accounted for the acceleration in the rate of inflation in 1980. The contribution of each factor was similar. The devaluation was needed because the real appreciation that had developed in the late 1970s had become unsustainable. That is, observed inflation in the late 1970s had been repressed through an unsustainable appreciation, the same situation found in the Southern Cone countries of Latin America in the late 1970s and early 1980s (Corbo and de Melo 1987). Second, the slowdown in the rate of inflation during 1982–84 was primarily the result of the lessening in the rate of increase in the won price of imported raw materials. This moderation was the result of the collapse of the international price of primary commodities and the more stable nominal effective exchange rate that followed the moderate fiscal and monetary expansion that reduced the need for an inflation tax. A third, but less powerful factor was the slowdown in the rate of change in real agricultural prices brought about by the supply-side adjustment policies introduced in the agricultural sector and the return of more favorable weather conditions. The disinflation in wage growth was not found to be a significant factor in the quarterly model, but the moderation in wage growth helped to translate the sharp drop in the won price of raw materials into lower inflation.

Two important lessons emerge from the Korean experience that could be useful for other countries. First, to achieve a real devaluation when needed, it is necessary that it be accompanied by fiscal and monetary policies that avoid a permanent increase in the rate of inflation. Second, the use of the exchange rate to stabilize the economy without parallel contractionary fiscal and monetary policies is bound to result in an unsustainable real appreciation that will need to be corrected with a sharp nominal devaluation.

Appendix

The model used in the preceding sections to study the dynamics of inflation is that of a semiopen economy. An alternative specification is a model in which price inflation is determined mostly in the money market. In this kind of model—used by Harberger (1963), Vogel (1974), and Nam (1984)—the rate of inflation is a function of distributed lags of money growth, income growth, and the acceleration of inflation. This appendix looks at which of the two models provides a better explanation of inflation. The choice is treated as a nontested model selection procedure.

The two models will be called semiopen economy and monetarist. To obtain the semiopen economy model, equation (5-4) was replaced with equations (5-2) and (5-5) to generate the following equation:

$$(5\text{-}12) \qquad \hat{P}_{C,t} = g_1 + g_2 \, \hat{RP}_{A,t} + g_3 \, PDL(\hat{W}_{M,t} - \hat{q}_{M,t})$$
$$+ g_4 \, PDL(\hat{PMR}_t) + g_5 \hat{P}_{C,t-1} + g_6 DM_t.$$

The monetarist model is given by

$$(5\text{-}13) \qquad \hat{P}_{C,t} = h_1 + h_2 \, (PDL(M2_t) + h_3 \, PDL(Q\hat{S}A_t)$$
$$+ h_4 \, (\hat{P}_{C,t-1} - \hat{P}_{C,t-2}).$$

where

$M2$ = M1 plus time deposits
QSA = seasonally adjusted GNP.

The model selection procedure is the one developed by Davidson and McKinnon (1981). When equation (5-12) is the maintained hypothesis, the following artificial regression model is formed:

(5-14)
$$\hat{P}_{C,t} = (1 - \theta)(g_1 + g_2\hat{RP}_{A,t} + g_3PDL[\hat{W}_{M,t} - \hat{q}_{M,t}]$$
$$+ g_4PDL[\hat{PMR}_t] + g_5\hat{P}_{C,t-1} + g_6DM_t)$$
$$+ \theta(\tilde{h}_1 + \tilde{h}_2PDL[\hat{M2}_t]$$
$$+ \tilde{h}_3PDL[\hat{QSA}_t] + \tilde{h}_4[\hat{P}_{C,t-1} - \hat{P}_{C,t-2}])$$

where a tilde ($\tilde{}$) indicates the estimated value of the respective parameter obtained from the direct estimation of equation (5-13).

The model selection procedure consisted of estimating the artificial regression model given by equation (5-14) and testing the hypothesis $\theta = 0$. If the null hypothesis cannot be rejected, the conclusion is that equation (5-12) is correct. To complete the testing procedure, the models were reversed and the procedure repeated.[6]

When the artificial model of equation (5-14) was estimated, the result was $\tilde{\theta} = 0.37$, with an estimated error of 0.21. That is, it was not possible to reject the null hypothesis $\theta = 0$ at the 5 percent level, although it is rejected at the 10 percent level. When the models were changed and equation (5-13) was used as the maintained hypothesis, the results were $\tilde{\theta} = 0.86$ and an estimated error of 0.15. That is, the null hypothesis $\theta = 0$ is strongly rejected in this case. Therefore, the evidence for equation (5-12) is more favorable.

Notes

The authors are grateful to Jim Hanson and Sweder van Wijnbergen for their comments and to Inbom Choi for his assistance with the research.

1. For a review of Korea's macropolicies during this period, see Aghevli and Marquez-Ruarte (1985) and chapter 3 of this volume. For an analysis of the evolution of Korea's external balance, see chapter 4. Chapter 2 also provides a historical overview.

2. Because the joint estimation of a model with a polynomial distributed lag involves a difficult computational problem, equation (5-2) was first estimated in isolation using a polynomial distributed lag procedure. The estimated weights from the polynomial were then normalized to add up to one and were used as extraneous information in estimating the system of equations.

3. The curb market real interest rate was also included in the estimation of this equation (as in van Wijnbergen 1981), but it was not significant.

4. This result was robust for many alternative specifications of the wage equation.

5. The slowdown in the rate of nominal devaluation without significant real appreciation was the result of low inertia in wages and the supporting moderate fiscal and monetary policies.

6. In carrying out these tests, the coefficients for the *PDL*s in equation (5-12) were taken from the note to table 5-3. For equation (5-13), second-degree polynomials with three lags and no restrictions were used.

References

Aghevli, B. B., and Jorge Marquez-Ruarte. 1985. *A Case of Successful Adjustment: Korea's Experience during 1980–84.* IMF Occasional Paper no. 39. Washington, D.C.: International Monetary Fund.

Aukrust, Odd. 1977. "Inflation in the Open Economy: A Norwegian Model." In Lawrence Krause and Walter S. Salant, eds., *Worldwide Inflation—Theory and Recent Experience.* Washington, D.C.: Brookings Institution.

Beckerman, Wilfred, and Tim Jenkinson. 1986. "What Stopped the Inflation? Unemployment or Commodity Prices?" *Economic Journal* 96 (March):39–54.

Bruno, Michael. 1979. "Price and Output Adjustment: Microfoundations and Aggregation." *Journal of Monetary Economics* 5 (April):187–211.

———. 1980. "Imported Prices and Stagflation in the Industrialized Countries: A Cross-Section Analysis." *Economic Journal* 90 (September):479–92.

Calmfors, Lars. 1977. "Inflation in Sweden." In Lawrence Krause and Walter S. Salant, eds., *Worldwide Inflation—Theory and Recent Experience.* Washington, D.C.: Brookings Institution.

Corbo, Vittorio. 1974. *Inflation in Developing Countries.* Amsterdam: North-Holland.

———. 1985. "International Price, Wages and Inflation in an Open Economy: A Chilean Model." *Review of Economics and Statistics* 67 (November):564–73.

Corbo, Vittorio, and Jaime de Melo. 1987. "Lessons from the Southern Cone Policy Reforms." *World Bank Research Observer* 2 (July):111–42.

Davidson, Russell, and James G. McKinnon. 1981. "Several Tests for Model Specification in the Presence of Alternative Hypotheses." *Econometrica* 49:781–94.

Gordon, Robert. 1975. "Alternative Responses of Policy to External Supply Shocks." *Brookings Papers on Economic Activity* (1):184–204.

Harberger, A. C. 1963. "The Dynamics of Inflation in Chile." In C. Christ, ed., *Measurement of Economics.* Palo Alto, Calif.: Stanford University Press.

IMF (International Monetary Fund). 1982. *International Financial Statistics, 1982 Supplement.* Washington, D.C.

Lindbeck, Assar. 1979. "Imported and Structural Inflation and Aggregate Demand: The Scandinavian Model Reconstructed." In Assar Lindbeck, ed., *Inflation and Employment in Open Economies.* Amsterdam: North-Holland.

Nam, Sang-Woo. 1984. "Korea's Stabilization Efforts since the Late 1970s." Working Paper 8405. Seoul: Korea Development Institute.

Taiwan, China, Directorate General of Budget, Accounting, and Statistics (DGBAS). Various issues. *Monthly Bulletin of Statistics.*

van Wijnbergen, Sweder. 1981. *Short-Run Macroeconomic Adjustment Policies in Korea.* World Bank Staff Working Paper 510. Washington, D.C.

Vogel, Robert. 1974. "The Dynamics of Inflation in Latin America." *American Economic Review* 64 (March):102–14.

6 The Role of the Financial Sector in Korea's Structural Adjustment

YOON-JE CHO, World Bank
DAVID C. COLE, Harvard University

DID THE KOREAN FINANCIAL SYSTEM play a significant role in the distortion and restructuring processes in the late 1970s and the first half of the 1980s, or was it relatively passive and accommodating? Or, in the extreme, has the financial system been inconsequential and largely unaffected by the basic structural changes in the real economy? There is evidence that the financial system has played an important role in both the distortion and restructuring processes and has, in so doing, been changed substantially in structure.

The story, in brief, is as follows. In the second half of the 1970s the government used the banking system both to finance directly and to guarantee foreign financing of investments in the heavy and chemical industries. By the end of 1970s, interest rate subsidies, together with favored access to credit, led to excessive investment in these industries. With huge idle capacities, the enterprises had difficulty servicing their debts, and the banks accumulated nonperforming loans.

In the first half of the 1980s the government constrained the growth of bank credit to help control inflation. It also eliminated most low interest rate loan incentives, relaxed some of its allocative control over bank credit, and transferred five large commercial banks from government to private ownership. It continued the general controls over bank interest rates and the ceilings on the expansion of bank credit, however, and the burden of nonperforming loans carried over from the 1970s slowed growth and diminished the role of the banking system. [1]

Concurrently, a series of crises in the unregulated informal financial markets in 1982 led to a loss of confidence in, and a consequent withdrawal of funds from, those institutions. In addition, Korea's growing foreign debt and reduced supplies of loans from foreign banks limited foreign lending as an important source of corporate financing.

Despite the constraints on some financial sources, Korea's overall financial system grew dramatically in the first half of the 1980s, mainly because of the explosive expansion of nonbank financial institutions, such as investment and insurance companies, and of direct credit markets for corporate bonds and commercial bills. These institutions—which had few restraints on their size or the allocation of funds to particular industries and were either free from, or more able than banks to circumvent, the interest rate ceilings on both sources and uses of funds—attracted large amounts of financial savings and provided much of the new financing to support the growth of the Korean economy.

The shift in financing channels from the highly controlled banks to the less regulated nonbank financial institutions seems to have contributed more to the liberalization of the financial system and the integration of financial markets than did the government's limited efforts at deregulation and the transfer of ownership of the commercial banks.

Korea has been very cautious in opening the capital account. It has made substantial progress, however, in liberalizing its domestic financial markets. The opening of the capital account should be one of the last stages of liberalization.

This chapter presents the conceptual framework for analysis, followed by brief descriptions of the changing size, structure, and main operating characteristics of the Korean financial system, along with the major forces that have driven those changes. The broad trends in government policy affecting the financial system are then discussed, followed by a presentation of evidence of the effects of the changes in the financial system on the cost and availability of financing by industrial sector and size of firm, and the implications for the allocative efficiency of credit. The chapter concludes with a discussion of the lessons that can be derived from the Korean experience and some concerns for the future.

Conceptual Framework

The literature on financial development includes several themes of special relevance to the recent Korean experience. One stresses the broadening and deepening of financial markets to serve a wider range of customers more efficiently (Gurley and Shaw 1960). A related theme is the integration of previously segmented financial markets (Shaw 1973). Segmentation connotes the existence of several distinct financial markets that have significantly different prices for similar kinds of credit, varying accessibility for different categories of borrowers, and barriers to the movement of funds between markets or to the adjustment of prices that would normally tend to equalize the prices of claims bearing similar risks in an integrated market. Segmentation results in distorted prices and inappropriate market signals.

A third theme is that of financial repression resulting from excessive governmental controls, especially on interest rates, a situation that can be compounded by increased inflation (Shaw 1973; McKinnon 1973). The opposite of repression is liberalization, which implies reduced price controls and inflation, or at least the movement of controlled interest rates to a level above the rate of inflation. Repression tends to cause market segmentation and prevents or distorts the broadening of financial markets. Liberalization is expected to have the opposite effects.

A fourth theme, which emerged recently, suggests that financial liberalization, or "deregulation," is neither easy nor always successful (Taylor 1983; Edwards 1984; Diaz-Alejandro 1985; Corbo 1985; Park 1985). Complementary policy actions may be required in other parts of the economic system, either concurrently or sequentially, to support the financial changes. In addition, there is likely to be strong resistance from powerful groups to the loss of benefits derived from regulation, and these groups may include regulators as well as those regulated. Such resistance may frustrate or distort the liberalization process.

Finally, some degree of regulation is essential to the efficient functioning of the financial system and the maintenance of public confidence (Wallich 1986). The critical problem is to find the optimal mix of regulatory measures consistent with the economic and political structure and the developmental objectives of a particular country.

The concepts of repression and liberalization are frequently applied to the financial system as a whole. The conclusion here, however, is that they often bear more heavily on some financial sectors than others and that the responses of the more and less affected sectors are likely to be offsetting to a greater or lesser degree, although with some loss of efficiency. Substitution and fungibility are pervasive financial phenomena. Thus, for analytical purposes, it is useful to divide the Korean financial system into a number of subsystems according to the degree of governmental regulation and guidance. At one extreme are the banking institutions, which have traditionally been subject to the most extreme controls and guidance. At the other extreme are the informal, unlicensed financial institutions, which are largely unregulated but are occasionally subjected to strong governmental suppression. In between are various nonbank financial institutions (NBFIS), which have received varying amounts of governmental support or restriction over time.[2] This differential pattern of regulation across institutions and over time has led to erratic growth of the different subsectors and substantial shifts in the attempts of the government to use financial institutions to achieve development or political objectives.

For example, from 1965 to 1972, as part of the export-led, high-growth strategy, the Korean government tried to implement a controlled liberalization of the banking system by raising some deposit and loan rates above the rate of inflation. Bank time deposits, which had high real interest rates, expanded rapidly, as did bank loans with low or negative real rates for industrial exporters. Exports and bank assets both grew at high rates. Nevertheless, financial segmentation persisted, and the unregulated financial institutions continued to perform a substantial but unquantifiable portion of financial intermediation.

In 1972, when many large businesses were squeezed by the declining growth of exports, rising foreign debt service costs caused by devaluation, and constraints on domestic bank credit because of the credit ceilings imposed by the IMF standby arrangements, they turned to the unregulated markets for temporary relief. The government ultimately provided longer-term relief through a kind of financial shock treatment—sharply reduced bank loan and deposit rates, forced registration, rescheduled and reduced interest rates on all unregulated financial market credits, and authorization of new kinds of regulated nonbank financial institutions that were intended to replace the unregulated markets. This reversion to extreme repression of the banking sector and attempted repression of the nonregulated markets was compounded by the inflationary oil price shock of 1973. The result was a three-way segmentation of the financial markets throughout the remainder of the 1970s.

- Commercial and special purpose banks, which were highly regulated and directed and, with rising inflation and controlled low nominal interest rates, increasingly operated at negative real interest rates and therefore did not grow in relation to GNP.
- The new NBFIS—financial institutions such as investment and finance companies, mutual savings finance companies, and life insurance companies—which were allowed to pay and earn somewhat higher nominal interest rates, but nevertheless had difficulty keeping up with the high rates of inflation and grew slowly in relation to GNP.
- The unregulated financial markets, which responded to the inflation rates by maintaining high positive real interest rates, and thus recaptured an important but unknown share of the market.

This basic pattern of segmentation prevailed until 1981–82, when a number of policy and exogenous changes occurred. First, a sharp drop in the rate of inflation (the result of many factors, as discussed in chapter 5 of this volume) pushed the controlled interest rates of the banks and NBFIS from negative to significantly positive levels in real terms, despite a downward adjustment in nominal rates. Moreover, a scandal and financial manipulation in the unregulated financial markets raised the level of perceived risk for depositors. Further, the monetary authorities exercised greater restraint over the growth of bank credit, a step that limited the growth of the banking system. At the same time, the interest rates on commercial paper and corporate bonds, a substantial number of which were intermediated through the NBFIS, were further deregulated, and restrictions on entry into NBFIS were eased.

As a consequence of these changes, the NBFIS, which had no ceilings on either the mobilization of funds or on lending, were able to expand rapidly and fill the intermediate ground between the banks and the unregulated financial institutions. The result has been a substantial liberalization and integration of Korea's financial markets—less, however, as a consequence of conscious government efforts to reduce regulation than of the accelerated growth of the less regulated institutions in a favorable environment of reduced inflation.

Changing Size and Structure of the Korean Financial System

The growth of recorded, regulated finance in Korea between the mid-1970s and mid-1980s has been very rapid—roughly twice the rate of growth of GNP. This expansion occurred predominantly among the NBFIS, a pattern that has caused a sharp decline in the relative importance of banks, as their holdings dropped from roughly four-fifths of the regulated financial assets and liabilities to one-half. In recent years the unregulated financial institutions also seem to have declined in relative importance, although this trend cannot be quantified with any precision.

The growth and changing structure of the regulated financial sector are depicted in table 6-1. Total credit of these financial institutions (banks and NBFIS) was equal to 50 percent of GNP in 1974–75 and rose to 94 percent by 1984. The share of bank credit in total financial credit was just under 80 percent in 1974–75 but dropped to just over 55 percent by 1984, despite a 12 percentage point increase in the ratio of bank credit to GNP. The ratio of NBFI credit to GNP rose from 10 percent to about 42 percent between 1975 and 1985, a remarkable record.

On the liability side of the balance sheet of regulated financial institutions, there was a modest decline in M1 in relation to GNP; a moderate increase in M2 compared with GNP; and a near doubling of the M3-to-GNP ratio. M3 includes a small amount of the certificates of deposits and debentures of banks, as well as the deposits of all NBFIS, so the difference between M2 and M3 is not a precise measure of nonbank liabilities. Nevertheless, it roughly approximates the size of NBFI deposits, which accounted for much of the growth in the M3-to-GNP ratio, a finding that again confirms the important role of the NBFIS in the growth of the regulated financial system. Similarly, the share of bank deposits in total deposits declined from 86 percent in 1974 to 58 percent in 1984 (see table 6-2).

Among the NBFIS the investment and finance companies have been the most important, followed by the life insurance and investment trust companies. The investment and finance companies have been dealing in short-term commercial paper, whereas the insurance and investment trust companies have been attracting longer-term funds that they invest in corporate bonds or direct loans to businesses (see table 6-2 for the deposits of NBFIS).

The markets for corporate bonds and commercial paper have also grown rapidly in the 1980s, and their expansion has been facilitated by several factors. First, the corporate bond and commercial paper markets have not been subject to government price regulation. Interest rates have been determined relatively freely, depending on the market situation, and have been higher than the deposit rates at the banks. Second, the tight control

Table 6-1. *Financial Sector Development, 1974–84*

(percent)

Item	1974	1975	1976	1977	1978	1979	1980	1981	1982	1983	1984
M1/GNP	13	12	11	12	11	11	10	9	11	12	10
M2/GNP	33	31	30	32	33	32	34	34	38	39	38
M3/GNP[a]	40	36	38	42	42	43	48	51	60	65	69
Bond/GNP[b]	—	—	—	—	2	—	4	5	6	8	10
Bank credit/GNP	40	39	35	30	34	37	43	44	49	51	52
NBFI credit/GNP	11	10	10	16	17	19	25	28	33	37	42
Credit share											
Banks	78.4	79.6	77.8	65.2	66.7	66.1	63.2	61.1	59.8	58.0	55.3
NBFIs	21.6	20.4	22.2	34.8	33.3	33.9	36.8	38.9	40.2	42.0	44.7
National saving[c]	17.9	19.1	23.7	27.5	28.5	28.1	21.9	21.7	22.4	24.8	27.4

— Not available.

a. M3 is defined as M2, plus deposits at NBFIs, and commercial bills sold and certificates of deposits and debentures issued by deposit money banks.

b. Value of listed corporate bonds.

c. As a percentage of GNP.

Source: Various issues of Bank of Korea, *Economic Statistics Yearbook.*

Table 6-2. *Deposit Share of Banks and NBFIs, 1974–85*
(100 million won, unless otherwise noted)

Institution	1974	1975	1976	1977	1978	1979	1980	1981	1982	1983	1984	1985 February	1985 June
Bank[a]	21,933	27,922	37,824	51,732	68,831	87,659	115,375	149,162	188,474	220,956	248,188	211,620	275,127
Percentage share	85.7	84.1	82.1	81.1	79.3	76.1	73.3	68.9	64.6	60.9	57.6	57.0	58.6
Nonbank	3,666	5,276	8,131	12,066	18,014	27,458	42,085	67,280	103,305	144,745	182,679	189,943	194,714
Percentage share	14.3	15.9	17.9	18.9	20.7	23.9	26.7	31.1	35.4	39.1	42.4	43.0	41.4
Investment and finance companies	1,622	2,542	4,381	6,587	9,407	13,378	20,984	32,153	42,273	54,971	70,118	70,761	64,990
Investment and trust companies	53	148	425	1,244	2,413	3,615	6,351	13,542	27,683	36,536	43,129	45,051	49,027
Mutual savings finance companies	507	500	682	1,073	1,607	2,682	4,000	6,123	9,566	14,743	19,917	21,817	23,878
Life insurance companies	978	1,282	1,688	2,332	3,514	6,582	9,427	13,905	22,087	33,634	47,383	49,900	54,368
Other	506	804	955	830	1,073	1,201	1,323	1,557	1,696	1,861	2,286	2,414	2,451
Total	25,599	33,198	45,415	63,798	86,845	115,115	157,460	216,442	291,779	362,701	430,487	441,563	469,841

a. Includes money in trust, commercial bills, and demand certificates of deposit.
Source: Various issues of Korea, Ministry of Finance, *Fiscal and Financial Statistics.*

over domestic credit in the banking sector forced firms to turn either to the direct credit market or to NBFIS. Third, the guarantees of corporate bonds by the banks reduced the risk and helped the growth of these assets. The institutionalization of bond transactions on repurchase agreements in 1980 also encouraged the rapid growth of a secondary market. Compared with bond issues, new stock issues have been sluggish since 1980, despite government efforts to boost the market.

Government Financial Policies

The Korean government has used the banking system as one of its principal instruments of development policy, setting low interest rates on loans to certain categories of borrowers and directing loans to selected enterprises.[3] The apparent premise of the government has been that both the cost and availability of credit are important inducements to investment and production and that, without these direct interventions, either the level or pattern of investment and production would be suboptimal for the government's objectives. The form and relative intensity of application of these two mechanisms have varied over time, but they have been present constantly in some way since the 1950s.

In the latter half of the 1970s the government used bank credit instruments with greater than usual intensity to induce investment in selected heavy industries that probably would not have got started or grown so rapidly without that support. The consequence was a substantial increase in the share of total investment accounted for by heavy industries and an apparent misallocation of capital.

Partly in reaction to these trends, the Korean government changed direction in the 1980s and reoriented its financial policies. The intent of the financial policy shifts was to liberalize—to give financial institutions greater freedom to set their own prices and to attract and allocate funds. Accomplishing this shift turned out to be more difficult and gradual than anticipated, especially in the banking sector, which had been the most pervasively controlled part of the financial system and had carried the major burden of financing the heavy industry investment.

A central feature of the liberalization policy was the sale of the government's shares in the large commercial banks, which occurred between 1981 and 1983.[4] Continued government control of interest rates at all banks, however, along with the high proportion of nonperforming bank loans and heavy dependence on the Bank of Korea for low-cost funds to support their outstanding loans, has left the privately owned commercial banks very vulnerable. A substantial part of their outstanding loans is still policy-related. Highly indebted firms; declining industries such as shipping, ship-building, and construction; and industrial restructuring have continued to be seen by the government as justifying intervention in credit allocation, despite its intention to deregulate.[5] The banks cannot afford to ignore the government's suggestions, despite their shift to private ownership.

The NBFIS, in contrast, have always been privately owned and have been both less controlled and less protected by the government. They have had to mobilize their own funds in competitive markets and to earn enough on their loans and investments to cover the cost of their funds. There has been limited supervision of their operations, and the government has not been committed to assisting them, even when they have become insolvent. Thus, the NBFIS have had to live more by their own wits than banks, and they have been very effective in mobilizing funds and financing businesses. A combination of lax government supervision, unreliable accounting statements, and high growth has avoided or perhaps postponed serious problems. This is especially true for the insurance companies because their ultimate obligations and the value of their existing assets are difficult to estimate accurately.

Interest Rates

The rates of interest on most assets and liabilities of the organized financial institutions have been subject to direct governmental control or strong guidance. Only the unregulated financial institutions have been clearly outside government control, although some direct securities that are traded in the secondary markets have been relatively free of government intervention.

In recent years the most significant force affecting real interest rates has been changes in the rate of inflation. The government-controlled bank interest rates have been slow to respond to the changing rates of inflation, and even the semiregulated or "guided" rates on outstanding corporate securities and the liabilities of NBFIS have shown a lag. The maximum rates on these instruments have been subject to guidance from the Ministry of Finance. As a consequence, real interest rates have been low to negative when inflation has increased sharply, as in 1974–75 and 1978–80, but became very positive as inflation declined dramatically in 1982–84.

The real interest rate on curb market loans moved up from an average of about 16 percent from 1976 to 1981 to an average of 21 percent in 1982–84. (Real interest rates can be obtained from table 6-3 by the formula $[i - \pi] \div [1 + \pi]$ where i is the interest rate and π is the rate of inflation.) This rise coincided with an apparent decline in the relative size of the curb market and a shift from that market to the NBFIS for intermediation for less risky borrowers. Thus, the higher real interest rate in the curb market could reflect a higher risk premium on both loans and deposits. The higher rate would also have given an incentive to borrowers to rely more on NBFIS.

The real interest rates on corporate bonds, which were low to negative in the 1970s, have averaged 9 percent since 1981. Although this level is high by historical standards, it is still less than half the curb rate and probably represented an attractive source of financing for corporations large enough to use it.

Bank loan deposit rates were consistently negative in real terms throughout the 1974–80 period, but turned increasingly positive after 1981 as inflation declined. It is noteworthy that the big increase in M1, M2, and M3 occurred in 1982 (as shown in table 6-1), a year in which nominal bank interest rates on both deposits and loans were reduced sharply and real interest rates showed modest gains. Perhaps the most important change was a drop in the rate of inflation below 10 percent for the first time in many years. This decline, along with the collapse of some unregulated money lenders, seems to have led to a substantial increase in both bank and NBFI deposits. In 1983–84 the M2 ratio did not rise much further, despite a substantial increase in the real bank deposit rate. This pattern suggests that bank deposits, which were very sensitive to changes in real interest rates in the 1965–70 period (Cole and Park 1983), had become less responsive, partly because of the increased availability of other financial assets at even higher real interest rates and partly because of monetary policy restraints on the growth of bank deposits.[6]

An important policy change, introduced in June 1982, was to eliminate the preferential low bank loan rates for priority activities such as exporting. This change was accomplished primarily by reducing the general loan interest rate to the prevailing levels of preferential loans. This process was made easier by the decline in the rate of inflation (see table 6-3). Borrowers engaged in priority activities continued to have preferential access to bank

Table 6-3. *Interest Rates on Various Loans, 1974–85*
(percent)

Year	Curb market[a]	Corporate bonds	Bank loans General	Bank loans Export	Bank loans NIF[b]	Inflation (GNP deflator)
1974	40.6	—	15.5	9.0	12.0	29.5
1975	41.3	20.1	15.5	9.0	12.0	25.7
1976	40.5	20.4	18.0	8.0	14.0	20.7
1977	38.1	20.1	16.0	8.0	14.0	15.7
1978	41.2	21.1	19.0	9.0	16.0	21.4
1979	42.4	26.7	19.0	9.0	16.0	21.2
1980	44.9	30.1	20.0	15.0	19.5	25.6
1981	35.3	24.4	17.0	15.0	16.5	15.9
1982	30.6	17.3	10.0	10.0	10.0	7.1
1983	25.8	14.2	10.0	10.0	10.0	3.0
1984	24.8	14.1	10.0–11.5	10.0	10.0–11.5	3.9
1985	24.0	14.2	10.0–11.5	10.0	10.0–11.5	3.5

—Not available.
a. Bank of Korea figures.
b. National Investment Fund.
Source: Various issues of Bank of Korea, *Economic Statistics Yearbook.*

loans, but from 1982 to 1984 they did not benefit from special interest rates.

It is difficult to find unambiguous measures of the nominal interest rates on NBFI liabilities or assets. The Bank of Korea publishes tables showing the officially prescribed levels and ranges of rates, but there is no direct evidence of the interest rates actually paid. Nevertheless, there is some indirect evidence that such rates have exceeded the prescribed limits. One example is found in the insurance industry. Although the Bank of Korea says the range of prescribed rates in 1984 on insurance company loans was 12.0–12.5 percent, statistical reports of interest income in 1984 on loans made by insurance companies show an average rate of 13.4 percent, with one of the six main companies reporting an average of 14.4 percent (Life Insurance Association of Korea 1985, p. 15). Substantially higher rates must have been charged on some loans to result in these averages. All the rates are well above the prescribed ranges reported by the Bank of Korea, which suggests the prescribed rates are not indicative of reality.

Effects of Financial Changes on Corporate Financial Structure and Performance

Paralleling the changes in the relative importance of different kinds of financial institutions have been changes in the sources of business financing. This trend is shown in the composition of external funds raised by the corporate business sector (table 6-4). The distinctive feature of these changes is that the share of bank credit and foreign loans has decreased significantly, while that of NBFIs and direct financing has increased dramatically in the 1980s. This shift implies that the share of external funds (bank credit and foreign loans) of the corporate business sector with allocation that was *controlled or could have been controlled* by the government shrank to 29.3 percent in 1980–84 from 56.3 percent in 1975–79 and 63.7 percent in 1970–74,[7] while the share of external funds (NBFI credit and direct financing) with allocation that was not *controlled* by the government expanded to 67.4 percent in 1980–84 from 43.6 percent in 1975–79 and 35.8 percent in 1970–74.[8] In addition, even the controlled part of credit (bank loans and foreign loans) is subject to less intervention and has caused less distortion because its interest costs moved closer to the market equilibrium level following the elimination of most of the preferential lending rates. Therefore, the differential access to loans, although it still exists, does not cause as much distortion in the cost of capital as it did in the 1970s. The cost of foreign loans has also risen because of the high foreign interest rates and flexible exchange rates of the 1980s. The effective real interest rate on foreign loans has been close to the corporate bond rate in the 1980s, whereas it was the cheapest form of borrowing in the 1970s, equal to or

Table 6-4. *External Funds of the Corporate Business Sector, 1965–84*
(millions of won)

Source	1965–69	1970–74	1975–79	1980–84
Indirect financing	87.8	391.2	1,885.7	5,284.4
	47.4	*55.9*	*56.5*	*53.0*
Borrowing from financial institutions	87.8	387.9	1,883.7	5,001.8
	47.4	*55.4*	*56.5*	*50.2*
Banks	69.5	282.8	1,197.9	2,372.9
	37.5	*40.4*	*35.9*	*23.8*
Nonbanks	18.3	105.1	685.8	2,628.9
	9.9	*15.0*	*20.6*	*26.4*
Government loans	—	3.3	2.0	282.6
	—	*0.5*	*0.1*	*2.8*
Direct financing	27.1	145.3	767.9	4,083.7
	14.6	*20.8*	*23.0*	*41.0*
Stocks	26.4	124.6	458.0	2,059.3
	14.3	*17.8*	*13.7*	*20.7*
Bonds	0.7	12.0	216.5	1,441.9
	0.4	*1.7*	*6.5*	*14.5*
Commercial paper	—	8.7	93.4	582.5
	—	*1.2*	*2.8*	*5.8*
Foreign debts	70.2	163.3	681.1	601.6
	37.9	*23.3*	*20.4*	*6.0*
Total	185.2	699.8	3,334.7	9,969.7
	100.0	*100.0*	*100.0*	*100.0*

—Not available

Note: Data are annual averages. Numbers in italics represent percentages of the total. Noncorporate enterprises and government enterprises are included in the flow of funds accounts since 1980.

Source: Bank of Korea (1985).

even cheaper than policy-related loans such as export credit (Cho 1986). Consequently, the cost differentials of the different sources of borrowing have been greatly reduced.

In the 1970s the firms or industries that were favored by the government had greater access to subsidized credit—bank loans and foreign loans— which was tightly rationed. As a result, the cost of their capital was much lower than that of other firms or industries, which had to depend on different sources of borrowing with much higher costs. There were thus significant variations in the cost of capital across different firms and sectors of the economy that led to substantially different marginal rates of return on capital among the different sectors, and hence to a distorted allocation of capital. The financial policies of the 1980s reduced the gaps significantly, and capital allocation became less distorted.

Equalizing Access to Borrowing

The strategic sectors of the Korean economy in the 1970s were the export and heavy and chemical industries, which got high priority in the allocation of bank credit. In pushing its industrialization plan the government also favored large firms in the allocation of bank credit.[9] This pattern is clearly reflected in table 6-5, which shows the ratio of total bank and foreign borrowing to total assets calculated from the *Financial Statement Analysis* of the Bank of Korea.[10] Large firms had much greater access to subsidized credit than did small ones in the 1970s, as did export industries and the heavy and chemical industries compared with other domestic and light industries (table 6-5).[11] The gap, however, has been significantly reduced in the 1980s except for export versus domestic industries, a reflection of the government's efforts to reduce intervention in support of heavy industries and to correct past favoritism toward large firms.[12] Since 1982 small and medium-size firms have enjoyed slightly better access than large firms, while the gap has become almost negligible between the heavy and chemical and light industries.

Equalized Cost of Borrowing

As the financial market becomes more integrated and competitive, the cost of borrowing should be similar for different borrowers, except for the risk premium and transaction costs. Nevertheless, in an economy in which some financial markets are repressed and access is segmented because of government intervention, the cost of borrowing can diverge across sectors, depending on borrowers' access to the sources of borrowing.

In the 1970s the gap in the average cost of borrowing diverged substantially for different kinds of borrowers. This gap, however, has been greatly reduced in the 1980s (see table 6-6). The following factors, among others, have contributed to this development. First, the share of credit from the NBFIs and direct credit instruments, without discrimination against sectors in cost and allocation except with regard to risk, has expanded rapidly. In the past, government allocation of relatively low-cost bank and foreign loans gave rise to a substantial difference in the average cost of credit for favored and unfavored sectors. As the share of these sources of borrowing has diminished, the effect of the differential access of firms on the average cost of credit has also been reduced. Second, access to these sources of borrowing (bank and foreign loans) by different sectors has become far more equal in the 1980s. Third, the gap between bank or foreign loan rates and lending rates in the other credit markets has also been reduced. As a result, differential access to the various sources of borrowing, although it may still exist, does not have as much influence on the average cost of borrowing by different sectors as it did in the 1970s. Fourth, because of the abolition of the preferential lending rates for various types of band credit, which were available only to specific sectors, the range of bank loan rates was narrowed. In the 1970s the differential access to selected concessionary loans among bank loans made the average cost of borrowing of the various sectors quite different. Since 1982 all bank loans have carried roughly the

Table 6-5. *Access to Borrowing by Sector, 1972–84*
(percent)

Sector	1972	1973	1974	1975	1976	1977	1978	1979	1980	1981	1982	1983	1984
Total manufacturing	45.41	43.21	45.22	40.27	40.97	41.32	39.29	36.94	38.55	38.05	32.53	30.81	28.17
Large firms (A)	45.72	43.55	45.65	40.93	41.36	41.38	39.69	37.32	39.25	38.81	32.26	30.76	27.84
Small firms (B)	27.27	26.54	24.44	27.38	34.98	40.79	37.02	34.60	33.79	34.31	33.87	31.19	30.40
(B) − (A)	−18.45	−17.00	−21.20	−13.56	−6.38	−0.59	−2.67	−2.72	−5.46	−4.50	1.61	0.43	2.56
Export sector (C)	47.13	45.95	49.78	45.07	43.11	44.06	42.85	41.10	48.57	45.63	38.07	35.53	32.28
Domestic sector (D)	44.63	41.75	42.93	36.63	39.91	39.83	37.54	35.24	31.66	32.84	29.00	28.08	25.98
(D) − (C)	−2.50	−4.20	−6.85	−8.45	−3.20	−4.23	−5.31	−5.86	−16.90	−12.79	−9.07	−7.44	−6.29
Heavy industry (E)	49.20	43.43	41.25	38.52	41.59	42.53	41.60	37.07	39.67	40.86	32.81	31.08	27.72
Light industry (F)	42.30	43.02	49.05	41.96	40.32	40.04	35.94	36.79	37.11	33.89	32.13	30.41	28.96
(F) − (E)	−6.91	−0.42	7.79	3.44	−1.27	−2.48	−5.66	−0.28	−2.56	−6.96	−0.68	−0.67	1.25

Note: Data are the ratios of total bank loans and foreign loans to the total assets of each sector.

Source: Various issues of Bank of Korea, *Financial Statement Analysis.*

Table 6-6. *Average Cost of Borrowing by Sector, 1972–84*
(percent)

Sector	1972	1973	1974	1975	1976	1977	1978	1979	1980	1981	1982	1983	1984
Total manufacturing	12.00	8.60	10.50	11.30	11.90	13.10	12.40	14.40	18.70	18.37	15.97	13.63	14.42
Large firms (A)	11.98	8.48	10.49	11.19	11.80	11.91	11.91	14.42	18.42	18.30	16.08	13.71	14.45
Small firms (B)	14.16	11.59	11.41	13.92	14.39	13.80	15.55	14.16	20.74	18.77	15.38	12.95	14.13
(B) − (A)	2.18	3.11	0.92	2.73	2.59	1.89	3.64	−0.26	2.32	0.47	−0.70	−0.76	−0.32
Export sector (C)	11.06	9.78	9.82	9.82	11.34	12.87	12.68	15.70	16.01	15.81	13.55	12.39	12.91
Domestic sector (D)	12.46	9.84	10.88	12.60	12.25	13.24	12.25	13.80	21.03	20.36	17.59	14.37	15.20
(D) − (C)	1.40	0.06	1.06	2.78	0.91	0.37	−0.43	−1.90	5.02	4.55	4.04	1.98	2.29
Heavy industry (E)	10.53	8.65	10.38	10.24	10.14	11.50	10.09	12.51	17.58	17.49	15.29	12.93	14.3
Light industry (F)	13.31	10.90	10.59	12.16	13.70	14.29	15.85	16.62	20.05	19.64	16.93	14.63	14.46
(F) − (E)	2.78	2.25	0.21	1.92	3.56	2.79	5.76	4.11	2.47	2.15	1.64	1.70	0.07

Note: The average cost of borrowing is defined as the interest paid plus the discount, divided by total borrowing, which includes all sources: bank, NBFI, bond, foreign, and so forth.

Source: Various issues of Bank of Korea, *Financial Statement Analysis.*

Table 6-7. *Costs of Borrowing for Sixty-eight Manufacturing Industries, 1970–84*

(percent)

Year	Average	Variance
1970	17.92	83.18
1971	18.40	55.73
1972	15.05	43.14
1973	11.49	14.38
1974	12.47	17.56
1975	13.59	15.60
1976	14.58	16.13
1977	15.16	18.96
1978	15.52	14.50
1979	17.17	21.44
1980	20.47	20.99
1981	19.50	13.20
1982	16.89	8.33
1983	14.33	8.05
1984	14.46	5.91

Note: This table is based on the four-digit code classification of the Korea Standard Industry Classification.

Source: Various issues of Bank of Korea, *Financial Statement Analysis.*

same nominal interest rate, irrespective of the kind of lending. As a result, as of 1984 the average costs of borrowing were almost equalized across sectors, although the export sector has continued to enjoy lower costs because of its privileged access to bank loans.[13]

This narrowing of the gap is also observable in the trend of borrowing cost differentials among the industries in the manufacturing sector. A test of variance of the average costs of borrowing of sixty-eight manufacturing industries shows that it has been significantly reduced in the 1980s as compared with the 1970s (see table 6-7).

Improved Allocative Efficiency of Credit

The reduced disparity in the cost of credit appears to have contributed to a reduction in the variance of the rates of return across sectors. As shown in table 6-8, the rate of return on capital across sectors has become more equal in the 1980s (especially since 1982) compared with the 1970s.[14] In 1984 there was not much difference in the rate of return among the sectors. A test of the variance in the rate of return in the manufacturing industries also shows that the variance has fallen significantly since 1982 (see table 6-9).

Admittedly, it is the equalization of the marginal rates of return on capital that is the correct test of allocative efficiency, but such data are not available. Widely divergent average rates of return may well be consistent with allocative efficiency, at least in the short run, until new investment can bring about greater equality across sectors. Unless better data or more

Table 6-8. Rates of Return of Investment by Sector, 1972–84
(percent)

Sector	1972	1973	1974	1975	1976	1977	1978	1979	1980	1981	1982	1983	1984
Total manufacturing	10.55	12.77	10.91	9.50	10.42	10.27	11.03	10.74	9.14	9.98	8.80	9.59	9.67
Large firms (A)	10.55	12.75	10.86	9.43	10.37	10.06	10.82	10.57	8.84	9.70	8.82	9.50	9.59
Small firms (B)	10.42	13.61	12.81	10.87	11.22	12.25	12.23	11.10	11.10	11.44	8.68	10.30	10.21
(B) − (A)	−0.13	0.86	1.95	1.44	0.85	2.19	1.41	1.24	2.26	1.74	−0.14	0.80	0.62
Export sector (C)	10.44	15.14	8.21	7.75	9.10	8.75	8.53	8.55	9.22	10.65	7.94	8.91	9.82
Domestic sector (D)	9.23	11.62	12.25	10.82	11.08	11.12	12.33	11.68	9.08	9.54	9.33	9.98	9.58
(D) − (C)	−1.21	−3.52	4.04	3.07	1.98	2.37	3.80	3.13	−0.14	−1.11	1.39	1.07	−0.24
Heavy chemical industries (E)	7.92	10.06	12.45	9.34	9.41	8.96	9.69	9.32	7.36	9.11	8.56	9.20	9.75
Light industries (F)	11.00	15.30	9.45	9.65	11.50	11.57	13.80	12.50	11.40	11.28	9.13	10.15	9.52
(F) − (E)	3.08	5.24	−3.00	0.31	2.09	2.61	4.11	3.18	4.04	2.17	0.57	0.95	−0.23

Note: Data are the ratio of normal profits plus financial expenses to total assets. Inappropriate accounting of the effects of inflation, capital gains, and the like may have underestimated the real average return on investment. The purpose of this table is to compare the relative returns across sectors.

Source: Various issues of Bank of Korea, *Financial Statement Analysis.*

Table 6-9. *Rate of Return of Manufacturing Industries, 1974–84*
(percent)

Year	Mean	Variance
1974	12.63	39.76
1975	11.85	24.92
1976	12.12	14.34
1977	13.90	47.38
1978	13.75	19.73
1979	12.32	15.15
1980	10.74	24.15
1981	10.85	9.97
1982	9.24	8.43
1983	9.75	6.89
1984	10.44	7.34

Note: This table includes twenty-six manufacturing industries and is based on the three-digit code classification of the Korea Standard Industry Classification.
Source: Various issues of Bank of Korea, *Financial Statement Analysis.*

analysis can be obtained, perhaps the most that can be said is that, prior to 1982, government-directed loans went disproportionately to the industrial sectors that had the lowest rates of return. Since 1982 that disparity has been neutralized or reversed. Thus, there is negative evidence that the misallocation of credit to less efficient investments has diminished. The corollary is that more efficient allocation has increased.

Reduced Debt Ratio

The cheap cost of credit in the 1970s made debt financing very attractive to borrowers. The real cost of bank credit, which was a major source of corporate debt, was negative throughout most of the period. In addition, the government's risk partnership with the corporate sector through its control over bank credit decisions also made the cost of debt financing very cheap with regard to the risk of bankruptcy. Usually the advantage of debt in terms of tax deduction and interest costs is balanced by the high risk of bankruptcy incurred when a firm is highly leveraged. In that case there is a strong incentive for firms to keep the debt ratio below a certain level to reduce the risk of bankruptcy, particularly in a world of uncertainty where investment outcomes and interest costs are fluctuating. In Korea, however, strict low interest rate ceilings and an implicit government commitment to be a risk partner in the case of poor outcomes in favored sectors caused debt financing to be perceived as less risky.[15] As a result, the corporate sector's debt ratio became very high in the 1970s (table 6-10), and equity markets were slow to develop, despite government promotion.[16]

The high debt ratio made the corporate sector as a whole very vulnerable to external shocks and economic fluctuations that called for more and more government involvement in banks' credit allocation to bail out troubled firms and industries. Among other things, the rising real cost of debt,

Table 6-10. *Debt Ratio of the Manufacturing Sector, 1974–84*
(percent)

Year	Korea	United States	Japan	Taiwan	Federal Republic of Germany
1974	76.0	47.8	82.1	65.9	66.2
1975	77.2	49.7	83.0	61.6	67.8
1976	78.5	49.9	83.0	61.4	68.0
1977	78.6	49.3	82.6	63.2	68.3
1978	78.6	48.1	81.7	61.6	67.6
1979	79.0	46.0	80.7	61.6	67.9
1980	83.0	45.2	79.4	63.9	68.1
1981	81.9	44.0	79.1	63.8	68.9
1982	79.4	43.9	77.4	62.5	68.4
1983	78.3	45.9	76.4	61.3	68.5
1984	77.3	—	—	—	—

—Not available.

Note: Data are debt as a percentage of total assets.

Source: Bank of Korea, *Financial Statement Analysis* (1985).

together with reduced government commitment to being a risk partner in the case of bad performance, has caused firms to reduce their dependence on debt since 1980. In addition the government has attempted to reduce debt ratios by imposing constraints on the availability of bank loans to highly leveraged firms. As a result the debt ratio has diminished significantly since 1980, although it is still very high (see table 6-10).

Conclusions

There was both high growth and integration in Korea's financial markets in the first half of the 1980s, in contrast to the slow growth and continued segmentation in the latter half of the 1970s. Better integration of the domestic financial markets and the corresponding reduction in the divergence of interest rates appear to have contributed to a more efficient allocation of capital across sectors.

The reduced disparity in interest rates in the different financial markets was caused by two forces: the decline in nominal interest rates because of reduced inflation and the government's abandonment of the very low preferential interest rates (often negative in real terms) for priority sectors. Further, the government has encouraged greater competition among financial institutions by relaxing the entry barriers, allowed more diversified asset dealings, and limited deregulation of banks. The most important source of integration, however, has been the much more rapid expansion of the less regulated parts of the financial system, the NBFIS, and the corporate bond and commercial paper markets.

The low level of inflation and high real rate of return on financial assets since 1982 have increased the demand for all kinds of financial assets in relation to the demand for real goods. This trend has probably contributed further to the reduction of inflation with given increases in the money supply.

In 1973 McKinnon characterized the Korean experience from 1964 to 1970 as "financial reform without tears," because the rise in the nominal and real interest rates of banks brought not only rapid growth of the banking system but also apparently contributed to the fast growth of the overall economy. In the 1980s Korea has experienced financial liberalization and integration without much real liberalizing of the banks. Rather, as was indicated, the changes have been the result of the rapid growth in the more liberalized nonbank financial sector. This route may be easier than trying to free up the whole system in one stroke, as some countries have attempted to do.

A major obstacle to massive and sudden deregulation of all financial institutions is that some may have a significant amount of poor or nonperforming assets that will drag them under in a competitive environment. In addition, governments may feel a need for at least some institutions that can provide financing for low return or long-term payoff projects. In that case, they need to find some other way either to finance such projects or to retain institutions that are specifically charged with funding them. The biggest mistake in Korea was to hold the whole financial system, or the whole banking system, in a repressed state to finance a limited number of projects that could not be competitive.

Even now, the loosening of interest controls for Korean banks is being resisted because of the burden of nonperforming loans. Until some way is found to relieve that burden, the banks will continue to depend on the Bank of Korea and the government for special financing and will resist moving to market-determined interest rates.

Another area of concern is whether the NBFIS and financial markets will have the capacity and flexibility to meet the longer-term financing needs of investors. The banks have done this in the past on a risk-sharing partnership basis, backed by government and with central bank support. If this kind of support is reduced in the future, will the longer-term securities markets and life insurance companies be able to fill the gap, or will new financing instruments and institutions need to emerge? Certainly the less restricted and regulated the financial system is, the more likely it will be that new institutions will appear in response to changing needs.

A final concern is that the rapid growth of the NBFIS may lead to a deterioration in the quality of their assets and an increased risk of insolvency. It will be important for the financial authorities to have adequate capacity to monitor performance and regulate effectively, although not excessively.

This chapter has implicitly endorsed the view that integration into the world capital markets should be one of the last steps in liberalization of the economy and should not be taken until after the liberalization of the domestic financial markets and full consolidation of the stabilization effort.

Notes

The authors wish to express their appreciation to Vittorio Corbo, Shujiro Urata, Yung-Chul Park, Sang-Woo Nam, Sang-Mok Suh, Millard Long, and Edgardo Barandiaran for their helpful discussion; to officials from the Ministry of Finance and the Statistics Department of the Bank of Korea for data; and to Shirin Fozouni for assistance with the research.

1. The government took no immediate action on the nonperforming assets of banks. Consequently, those assets accumulated rapidly in the early 1980s. The accumulation of nonperforming loans also accelerated as a result of a decline in some industries, such as overseas construction and shipping, to which the government had also directed bank loans in the latter half of the 1970s. Eventually the government could no longer support the ailing firms through continuous rescheduling of bank loans, and it had to act to reduce the nonperforming loans by restructuring industrial firms. In the process, in 1985 the nation's seventh largest conglomerate went bankrupt, and during 1985–87, seventy-eight insolvent firms were dissolved or taken over. Their combined debts exceeded assets by $5.9 billion.

2. For a detailed description and history of the Korean financial system, see Cole and Park (1983) and Bank of Korea (1985).

3. At times the government has withdrawn or threatened to withdraw loans as a penalty for the failure of the borrowing enterprise to meet targets or other standards set by the government.

4. Although an effort was made to limit the concentration of ownership by the private purchasers of these shares, it is widely believed that the large conglomerate groups (*jaebul*) succeeded in gaining control of individual banks. (They also have controlling interests in some NBFIS, such as insurance companies and investment and finance companies.)

5. The percentage share of preferential credit to total credit of banks has been as follows: 1974, 44.5; 1975, 40.9; 1976, 41.4; 1977, 45.1; 1978, 51.0; 1979, 49.8; 1980, 49.1; 1981, 45.7; 1982, 40.3; 1983, 41.2; 1984, 40.7; and 1985, 39.1 (Korea, Economic Planning Board 1986).

6. See chapter 3 of this volume for an analysis of the excess demand for M1 and M2 since 1981.

7. The Korean government has made extensive and forceful use of a wide range of incentives to ensure private industry's compliance with its plans. Probably the most widely used incentive has been differential access to credit from the banks under government control. Foreign loans, which were also an attractive source of borrowing, required government authorization, and the government largely controlled the allocation of these funds.

8. Development institutions such as the Korea Development Bank, EXIM Bank, and Korea Long-Term Credit Banks are included in the nonbank flow of fund accounts. Since most of the expansion of nonbanks is attributable to the expansion of private NBFIS, however, the trend in changes in the share of the

controlled versus uncontrolled part of corporate finance is not much affected by the inclusion of these institutions.

9. Banks were often directed to give their loans to a specific large firm. In addition, the strict loan rate ceiling set by government-led banks favored large firms that had secured collateral, and their transaction costs were less. In the 1980s, however, the government has pushed commercial banks to allocate more loans to small and medium-size firms to reduce the concentration of bank loans to large firms.

10. The reason total bank and foreign borrowing has been divided here by total assets instead of total liabilities is that the different debt ratios across sectors can underestimate the real difference in access. For example, small firms, which have poor access to bank and foreign loans, usually have low debt ratios, and if total bank and foreign borrowing is divided by total debt, the result can overestimate their access to these sources of borrowings.

11. The *Financial Statement Analysis* by the Bank of Korea covers, in 1984 for example, 45 percent of the Korean corporate sector with regard to the number of firms and 92 percent with regard to the amount of total sales of the corporate sector. According to this source, large firms are those with more than 300 employees in the case of manufacturing firms and more than 200 in the case of the service industry. The heavy and chemical firms include: industrial chemicals, petroleum refineries, other nonmetallic mineral products, basic metals, fabricated metal products, machinery, electrical machinery, electronic machinery and appliances, transportation equipment, and precision equipment. A firm is classified as an export industry if exports constitute 50 percent or more of its total sales. Otherwise, it is classified as a domestic industry. Therefore, the distinction between domestic versus export industry is not as clear as are other classifications.

12. The Korean government still provides preferential access to bank credit to exporting firms by allowing automatic approval of export loans. In an economy in which domestic credit is tightly controlled, this privilege gives a great advantage to the export sector.

13. The gap between the export industry's and the domestic industry's costs of borrowing has been significantly reduced since 1983 because the export loan rate was equalized with the general loan rate in June 1982.

14. The ratio of normal profit plus financial expenses to total capital stock in each sector or industry is used as an approximate average rate of return for that sector or industry.

15. In the past, to reduce the disruptive effects on employment and financial transactions in the short run, the Korean government tried to prevent bankruptcies by industrial firms, especially big ones, by providing relief loans or rescheduling debt.

16. Although large and well-established firms could obtain financing through equity markets and could count on public demands for their stock, they did not have much incentive to do so because most were favored borrowers of cheap bank credit. In addition, the government-set prices on new stock issues (often based on the book value of net assets rather than on potential earnings) generated relatively little new capital at very high costs. In most cases new stock issues appreciated quickly on the secondary market, an indication that they were substantially under-priced at the time of issuance. This underpricing of new issues was part of a

government strategy to attract investors to the stock market. It appears to have been successful in the longer run, but in the short run the Ministry of Finance had to force companies to sell new equity in the market.

References

Bank of Korea. Various issues. *Economic Statistics Yearbook*. In Korean. Seoul.

———. Various issues. *Financial Statement Analysis*. Seoul.

———. 1985. *Financial System in Korea*. Seoul.

Cho, Yoon-Je. 1986. "The Effects of Financial Liberalization on the Development of the Financial Market and the Allocation of Credit to Corporate Sectors: The Korean Case." DRD Discussion Paper no. 166. Development Research Department, World Bank, Washington, D.C.

Cole, David C., and Yung Chul Park. 1983. *Financial Development in Korea, 1945–1978*. Cambridge, Mass.: Harvard University Press.

Corbo, Vittorio. 1985. "Reforms and Macroeconomic Adjustments in Chile during 1974–84." *World Development* 13 (August):893–916.

Diaz-Alejandro, Carlos. 1985. "Good-bye Financial Repression, Hello Financial Crash." *Journal of Development Economics* 19:(1–2):1–24.

Edwards, Sebastian. 1984. *The Order of Liberalization of the External Sector in Developing Countries*. Essays in International Finance, no. 156. Princeton, N.J.: Princeton University.

Gurley, John G., and Edward Shaw. 1960. *Money in a Theory of Finance*. Washington, D.C.: Brookings Institution.

Korea, Economic Planning Board, 1986. *Economic Statistics Yearbook*. Seoul.

Korea, Ministry of Finance. Various issues. *Fiscal and Financial Statistics*. Seoul.

Life Insurance Association of Korea. 1985. *Life Insurance Statistics Yearbook*. Seoul.

McKinnon, Ronald I. 1973. *Money and Capital in Economic Development*. Washington, D.C.: Brookings Institution.

Park, Y. C. 1985. "Economic Stabilization and Liberalization in Korea, 1980–84." In Bank of Korea, *Monetary Policy in a Changing Financial Environment*. Seoul.

Shaw, Edward. 1973. *Financial Deepening in Economic Development*. New York: Oxford University Press.

Taylor, Lance. 1983. *Structuralist Macroeconomics: Applicable Models for the Third World*. New York: Basic Books.

Wallich, Henry. 1986. "A Broad View of Deregulation." In Hang-Sheng Cheng, ed., *Financial Policy and Reform in Pacific Basin Countries*. Lexington, Mass.: Lexington Books.

7 Agricultural Policies and Structural Adjustment

DAE-HEE SONG, Korea Development Institute
BYUNG-SEO RYU, Sung Kyun Kwan University

A CONSTANT THEME in Korea's history between World War II and 1986 was government intervention in agriculture. Recently the goals of that intervention were adequate production of basic food grains, particularly rice, to achieve self-sufficiency; cheap and stable food prices for urban consumers; and parity between urban and rural incomes. Initially the key policies involved price supports for food grain producers and for fertilizers, subsidies for food grains for consumers, and protection of agriculture from imports. Later the government also emphasized rural industrialization and other rural development programs to provide off-farm income opportunities and to raise the rural standard of living.

Although agriculture expanded fairly rapidly until 1986, its rate of growth was below that of industry, the main source of economic development in Korea since the 1960s, and it was spurred mainly by demand from the rapidly developing urban sector. Within agriculture, food grains, despite being the priority, experienced a much slower rate of growth than did the sector as a whole. Between 1950 and 1981 the proportion of cereals in the total value of agricultural production fell from 67 percent to 43 percent, while horticultural and livestock production rose from 15 percent to 44 percent. The potential for raising the output of rice and barley, the main cereal crops, was limited compared with products such as fruit, vegetables, meat, milk, and eggs, which required less land, were more labor-intensive, and were subject to rapidly growing consumer demand. Farmers near big cities who shifted to these products reaped rapid increases in income, and increasing numbers followed suit. Although some initial success was made in achieving parity between rural and urban incomes, a gap in favor of urban areas reemerged in the 1980s.

By 1986 the future of agriculture in Korea raised a number of difficult issues. Despite government policy and incentives for cereals, production was lagging and self-sufficiency had been lost. At that stage in its economic development, Korea faced a growing comparative disadvantage in agriculture, given the scarcity of cultivable land and the shortage of labor, yet the sector continued to be favored by extensive protection that caused distortions in the allocation of resources and led to significantly higher food prices for urban consumers. There appeared to be a clear tradeoff between income maintenance for farm households and the welfare of the consumer. By the early 1980s the nominal rate of agricultural protection had reached about 100 percent (Anderson and Warr 1987), and the resulting misallocation of resources was probably very large. Although the price supports for producers of rice and barley and other rural programs had shored up rural incomes, they had not succeeded in maintaining parity with urban incomes, and there was evidence of an even larger gap between rural and urban standards of living. The funds used to operate the price support systems were running large deficits and were an important source of the macroeconomic imbalances of the early 1980s. Externally, Korea faced increasing pressure from trading partners such as the United States to open its markets to food imports.

The need for a change in agricultural policy, and concomitant policies for rural development, was clear. Many of the alternatives were politically explosive, however, and would require tradeoffs among the government's various goals and among different sectors of society. Although the focus here is on redressing the huge deficits in the agricultural price support system, which had severe macroeconomic consequences, other policies are reviewed as well, because it is impossible to separate that issue from others relating to rural development and social welfare.

Features of the Agriculture Sector

Korean agriculture has undergone profound changes since the 1950s, although an initial, major policy decision was made in 1948. At that time, the new government established three hectares as the maximum farm size. This led to the characteristic small size of Korean farms, which average only slightly over one hectare. Traditionally, the main crops were rice and barley, with rice accounting for about half of all farm income and of the calorie intake of farm households. Other important food crops were soybeans, pulses, potatoes, and miscellaneous cereals, which all together accounted for 25.4 percent of the cropped area and 7.4 percent of the total value of output. With the increase in income, higher-value-added farm products—such as fruits, vegetables, milk, eggs, and livestock—became increasingly popular with both producers and consumers, and more and more land was transferred to their production. These products were also highly protected through tariff barriers. The share of fruits, vegetables, and livestock in acreage and output value was increasing, and these products were responsible for a growing share of farm income, while the share of cereal crops was decreasing. Nevertheless, in 1984 rice was still the major crop, accounting for 35.8 percent of the total value of agricultural production and 45.5 percent of the total acreage planted. In 1981 rice accounted for 52 percent of agricultural receipts and 8 percent of GNP. Rice also accounted for 12 percent of the total expenditures of urban households.

Only one-third of farm income came from nonfarm sources, despite ongoing efforts of the government (see below) to change that ratio.

The cultivated land area for a farm household increased slowly. The use of machinery and fertilizer rose very rapidly, however, and farming became more capital-intensive and productive. Rice productivity continued to increase as a result of the expansion of irrigation, use of fertilizers and chemicals, planting of high-yielding varieties (HYVs), and better cultivation practices, rather than as a result of increases in land planted. Poor irrigation and drainage hindered increases in yields and the expansion of double-cropping. Greater reliance was placed on purchased inputs than on labor and land, largely in response to the rapid rise in wages and land values, scarce rural labor, and government policies.

Many of these shifts might have been even more extreme had it not been for the price supports initiated in the 1960s. At the same time, according to some, developments in agriculture in the mid-1980s may have been more the result of the protection of agriculture than of other factors.

Policy in the 1960s and 1970s

Until the latter part of the 1960s, economic policy in Korea had a distinct bias toward urban areas and industrialization. The government kept food prices low for urban consumers to restrain wage demands, and expenditures for rural programs were minimal. Export-oriented manufacturing was encouraged by aggressive government support. This urban bias and the unfavorable environment for agriculture encouraged migration from rural to urban areas, and the expanding urban labor supply also helped hold down wage demands. Industrialization did not spread to rural areas, in large part because of poor infrastructure. According to Moore (1984–85) the percentage of farm income derived from nonagriculture was only about 20 percent in the 1960s and early 1970s. One result of these conditions was a growing gap between urban and rural incomes—between 1965 and 1973 the income of farm households was only 60–90 percent that of nonfarm (urban) households.

In the late 1960s the government became increasingly concerned that the rapidly expanding gap between urban and rural incomes was a growing political liability. In addition, substantial food shortages required heavy imports, particularly of barley, wheat, corn, and raw cotton (table 7-1). Although in the 1950s and 1960s Korea could depend on the U.S. PL480 program to make up for shortfalls in the domestic production of food grains (table 7-2), it was anticipated that the program would soon be eliminated and that continuing growth in urban demand would force Korea to use scarce foreign exchange to pay for ever-increasing quantities of agricultural imports. These imports were also exacerbating the decline in rural income by contributing to the deterioration in the terms of trade for domestic

Table 7-1. *Deficits by Crop and Year, 1970–81*

(billions of won)

Period	Rice	Barley	Miscellaneous grains	Wheat flour price subsidy	Total
1970–76	37.5	108.4	5.5	128.0	279.4
1977	21.9	43.3	−2.1	0.0	63.1
1978	154.0	14.5	−9.4	0.0	159.1
1979	185.1	28.5	−4.9	0.0	208.7
1980	140.0	106.8	−5.1	0.0	241.7
1981	21.8	126.8	−4.5	0.0	144.1
Total	560.3	428.3	−20.5	128.0	1,096.1

Source: Ministry of Agriculture, Forestry, and Fisheries.

agricultural products. Korea came to see self-sufficiency in cereals as a high priority, a goal that was reinforced by the huge jump in international rice prices in the early 1970s. The country was also beginning a major drive toward heavy and chemical industrialization that was threatening to widen the gap between rural and urban incomes, while industry and urbanization in general were pulling more and more land out of cultivation.

In response to the problems of the low-income farm households, the growing imbalance between urban and rural areas, and the food deficits, from 1968 through the 1970s government policy emphasized agriculture and rural development. The basic objectives, which still held in 1986, were self-sufficiency in the production of basic foodstuffs, particularly rice; parity between rural and urban incomes; low urban food prices to restrain wage demands by urban workers (but not so low as to discourage agricultural production); and stabilization of agricultural prices within and across years.

Table 7-2. *Imports of Foreign Agricultural Products, Selected Years, 1975–85*

(millions of dollars)

Product	1975	1980	1982	1983	1984	1985
Agriculture and fisheries	1,030	2,270	1,976	2,190	2,163	1,893
Grains	689	1,073	887	1,013	1,044	912
Meat	12	23	159	155	72	21
Oilseeds	17	208	190	213	265	249
Animal and vegetable oils, fat	53	125	142	146	179	153
Vegetables	12	6	23	67	42	36
Live animals	1	10	37	30	40	9
Tea, coffee	8	37	37	30	42	60
Raw sugar	207	534	251	224	217	161
Tobacco	9	78	8	17	13	10
Oil cake and other vegetable residuals	2	3	31	74	47	20
Fisheries	9	34	55	49	60	79
Other	12	139	147	176	182	183

Source: Ministry of Agriculture, Forestry, and Fisheries.

**Table 7-3. *Public Investment and Loans to the Agricultural Sector,*
*1970–80***
(millions of won)

Year	Investment and loans		Marketing fund for price stability		Total	
	Amount	Index	Amount	Index	Amount	Index
1970	86,597	100.0	116,074	100.0	202,671	100.0
1971	113,799	131.4	130,930	112.8	244,729	120.8
1972	120,941	139.7	178,701	153.9	299,642	147.8
1973	129,827	149.9	230,242	198.4	360,089	177.7
1974	170,846	197.3	295,784	254.8	466,630	230.2
1975	269,176	310.8	468,488	419.1	755,644	372.8
1976	350,112	404.4	806,100	694.5	1,156,212	570.5
1977	420,970	486.1	922,521	794.8	1,343,491	662.9
1978	584,966	675.5	1,361,892	1,173.3	1,946,858	960.6
1979	818,441	945.1	1,484,031	1,278.5	2,303,472	1,136.0
1980	1,380,187	1,593.6	1,680,397	1,447.7	3,060,184	1,509.9

Source: Korea, Ministry of Agriculture, Forestry, and Fisheries (1986a).

In keeping with these goals, the government implemented four primary
programs during this period: price supports for producers of food grains;
intensive cultivation of HYVs of rice; increased expenditures for rural roads
and agricultural activities, such as irrigation, projects to boost the productivity of rice cultivation, and subsidies for fertilizers and pesticides and for
farm machinery and other labor-saving technologies required because of
the growing shortage of rural labor and the accompanying increase in real
rural wages; and support for local self-help programs such as the Saemaul
Undong. Major efforts were also made to improve the rural credit system.
In short, the government began to allocate a large portion of public funds
and loans to address the problems of the rural sector (table 7-3).

Price Support System

In 1968 the government adopted a policy of high prices for rice and barley,
intended to boost production and farm income.[1] That year the purchase
price of rice was increased by 17 percent over the 1967 level. The increases
in the years 1969 to 1974 were 23 percent, 36 percent, 25 percent, 13
percent, 15 percent, and 39 percent, respectively. Until 1975 the upward
trend in prices exceeded the index of prices paid by farmers (Myoung and
Lee 1988). Price supports were also provided for items such as red pepper,
garlic, apples, and sesame seeds, which were also imported in substantial
quantities.

The high grain prices put upward pressure on the general price level, a
trend that hurt urban consumers. In response, the government instituted a
two-tier pricing system for rice and barley in 1969. It continued the high
purchase price supports for producers and also provided subsidized prices

for consumers. This step marked the beginning of what would become an increasing burden on the government's budget as the gap between the producer and consumer prices widened steadily and the handling and storage costs for government inventories mounted.

In 1970 the government established a Grain Management Fund (GMF) to operate the price support system. The GMF purchased rice and barley and covered the handling and storage costs (called off-management costs). It then sold the rice, barley, and their byproducts to consumers, maintaining any surplus in storage. Any shortfall in operating costs was covered by loans from the Bank of Korea and, later, short-term grain bonds with a one-year maturity. In 1970 the government purchased about 8.9 percent of total rice production, a share that grew steadily.

As early as 1976 the government became concerned about the cost of this program, particularly in light of the need for investment funds for the heavy and chemical industrialization program and expanding social overhead. It tried to reduce the deficit by letting producer price increases fall behind the rate of inflation. Nevertheless, the deficit continued to grow every year, in large part because of the rising interest payments on the loans and bonds, as well as mounting grain purchases.

Another problem with the price support system was that Korean rice (and other agricultural products) was far more costly than imported rice—in 1970 the producer price of rice was about 65 percent higher than the world price, the urban price about 50 percent higher. In the case of barley, the producer price was two-and-a-half times the world price and the urban price was 30 percent above the world price. Although beneficial to rural producers, the subsidized prices amounted to a tax on urban consumers.

Because it is a major input, fertilizer was a central focus of agriculture policy, particularly after the introduction of HYVs, which were very responsive to fertilizer. Beginning in the early 1960s the government had encouraged the use of fertilizer through subsidies and purchase credits and had supported the construction of several fertilizer plants to end the country's dependence on imports. From 1965 to 1985 the rate of application of fertilizer doubled, with an average annual rate of growth of 5 percent. Moreover, by 1968 Korean plants began turning out domestic fertilizer, and by the mid-1970s the country achieved self-sufficiency and even began exporting, although at subsidized prices. As a result of protection of the local market, the factory-gate price was well above world levels—70 percent above in 1979. Contributing to the price was the use of naphtha as a base rather than natural gas and the unfavorable terms of the joint venture agreements.

The government operated another two-tier price system for fertilizer. To ensure an adequate domestic supply, the government guaranteed producers a reasonable profit, and they were required to sell all their fertilizer to the government through the National Agricultural Cooperative Federation

(NACF). In turn, the NACF sold and distributed the fertilizer to farmers at a price well below its purchase price plus handling costs. As noted, the government subsidized exports to ensure sales. The resultant deficit was again financed with loans from the central bank. In effect, the fertilizer price supports amounted to a general transfer to the fertilizer industry.

Cultivation of HYVs

Spurred by a strong desire to become self-sufficient in rice, in 1971 the government introduced HYVs and encouraged their cultivation. The price supports for rice and for fertilizers were limited almost exclusively to the production of HYVs. Access to credit was similarly contingent on planting HYVs. Emphasis in extension services was almost entirely on HYV production. Although consumers preferred traditional rice strains, which were also less costly to grow because they required fewer inputs, the government provided price subsidies only for HYVs. Under the onslaught of these incentives, producers gradually shifted to HYVs in the early 1970s, and by 1978, the peak year, some 76 percent of the cultivated rice area was under HYVs. Between 1971 and 1977, total rice production rose by 50 percent, or 7 percent a year on average. One problem, however, was that by the mid-1970s the difference between the market prices for HYVs and traditional strains began to narrow, which caused ill will, because farmers gained more profit from the traditional varieties.

Investment in Rural Development and Agriculture

Significant investment was plowed into rural infrastructure and improved extension services, consolidation and reclamation of land to increase the cultivable area, research to improve seeds, and promotion of agricultural mechanization through subsidized prices for farm machinery. Also introduced were programs to increase the availability of farm supplies, subsidies for fertilizers, and special projects to raise farm and fishery household income. To encourage farm mechanization, the government extended loans at favorable interest rates for 70 to 80 percent of the purchase price of power equipment. This measure was successful, although not sufficiently so to offset the scarcity of labor. Moreover, the small size and fragmented nature of farms constrained the spread of mechanization.

The major initiative here was the Saemaul Undong, the self-help movement. According to Moore (1984–85), it began as a purely rural program in the winter of 1970–71. Initially it involved the distribution of cement to villages for projects the villagers wanted. An important element in the early Saemaul ideology and practice was populism—properly motivated, the people would eliminate underdevelopment through "collective striving." Saemaul Undong was designed to motivate people by playing on their strong sense of a common national interest, the accepted leadership of the central government, the strong sense of solidarity within the individual village, and the egalitarian nature of farm ownership (in 1971, 67 percent of family farms were between one-half hectare and two hectares, 80 percent of farm households derived more than half their income from agriculture, and 78 percent of farm labor came from family members) (Moore 1984–85).

The program met with early success, and by 1972 the government had expanded it. The movement soon came to encompass a disparate range of activities, including political indoctrination, promotion of improved living environments, construction of collective facilities, conventional agricultural production programs, and a reforestation and beautification element. A Saemaul Factory Program, intended to promote the relocation of industries from the Seoul and Pusan metropolitan regions to rural areas, was begun in 1973. To bring industries to rural areas, the government pursued many policy measures, including financial and tax incentives for firms locating or expanding in rural communities with populations below 20,000. In addition, Saemaul factories received many benefits, such as priority in the installation of electricity and telephones, as well as managerial and technical advice from the Small and Medium Industry Promotion Corporation. In 1973 the government also initiated the New Community Movement, which, in its initial stage, aimed to improve the physical living environment of villages through self-help programs. Villagers built rural infrastructure such as community centers, public laundry places and baths, and farm roads.

In its later stages the Saemaul Undong focused on programs related to direct income generation, such as side business projects. In addition, the program moved to political and administrative levels above those of individual villages. According to Moore, the program appeared to become a national mobilization campaign, part of a broader drive to establish a kind of mass political party supporting the Park administration. Evidence of the program's growth was that the proportion of government expenditures for Saemaul Undong projects grew from 4 percent of the budget in 1972 to 38 percent in 1978.

Strengthening the Rural Credit System

The government had done much in the latter half of the 1950s and the early 1960s to consolidate the institutional framework for agricultural credit and to increase its supply. Despite these measures, problems remained. Throughout the 1970s the government pursued further measures to strengthen the rural credit system: rapid expansion of mutual financing through the basic agricultural cooperatives, strengthening of the lending role of the cooperatives and enhancement of their ability to raise funds on their own, and increased provision of medium- and long-term development loans. At the same time, the government took steps to improve the institutional framework, by establishing a creditworthiness guarantee system for poor farmers by providing collateral for their loans.

The Impact of the Policy Initiatives

How well did these measures do in restoring the balance between urban and rural incomes and in promoting the agricultural sector? Initially, it appeared they were working very well. In 1974 average farm household income exceeded average nonfarm household income, and in general rural incomes exceeded urban incomes in the mid-1970s, although the disparity was extremely small (table 7-4 and figure 7-1). Further, the agricultural sector showed strength. As a result of the food grains policy and favorable weather, agriculture experienced notable growth in value added overall until 1978 (table 7-5). In 1976 the rate of growth of agriculture was 9.4 percent; in 1977, thanks to a bumper crop, the value added of the sector reached its highest level of the decade—7,077 billion won (at constant market prices), compared with 6,900 billion in 1976. The value added in

Table 7-4. *Income of Farm and Nonfarm Households, 1970–85*

	Farm household income		Nonfarm household income		Farm household income as a percentage of nonfarm household income
Year	Won[a]	Growth rate (percent)	Won[a]	Growth rate (percent)	
1970	1,152,270	1.0	1,717,297	−1.7	67.1
1971	1,414,214	22.7	1,793,333	4.4	78.9
1972	1,528,093	8.0	1,841,281	2.7	83.0
1973	1,657,624	8.5	1,897,241	3.0	87.4
1974	1,868,285	12.7	1,785,374	−5.9	104.6
1975	1,931,268	3.4	1,901,150	6.5	101.6
1976	2,219,298	14.9	2,210,672	16.3	100.4
1977	2,496,183	12.5	2,447,875	10.7	102.0
1978	2,867,875	14.9	2,916,712	19.2	98.3
1979	2,866,773	−0.1	3,384,293	16.0	84.7
1980	2,693,110	−6.1	3,205,152	−5.3	84.0
1981	3,040,277	12.9	3,146,928	−1.8	96.6
1982	3,432,110	12.9	3,325,817	5.7	103.2
1983	3,812,821	11.1	3,710,462	11.6	102.8
1984	4,032,799	5.8	4,036,805	8.8	99.9
1985	4,068,260	0.8	4,288,247	6.2	94.9

a. Data are based on real 1980 consumer prices.

Note: It is difficult to estimate and compare precisely the level of income of rural and urban areas because of limitations of the official statistics published by the Ministry of Agriculture, Forestry, and Fisheries and the Economic Planning Board. Despite those limitations, these data do show the statistically approximate income trend in rural and urban areas in Korea.

Source: Ministry of Agriculture, Forestry, and Fisheries and Economic Planning Board.

Figure 7-1. *Household Income Trends, 1970-80*

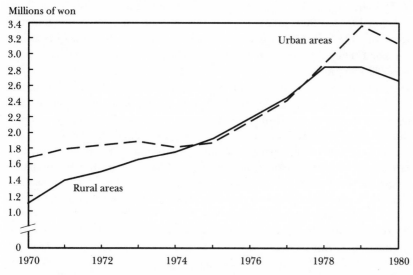

Millions of won

Source: Table 7-4.

agricultural products was 5,764 billion won, accounting for 81.4 percent of the total for the agriculture sector (the residual of 28.6 percent was divided between livestock and other products).

The farm credit reforms had enabled the agricultural cooperatives to increase their capacity to raise funds on their own, and they were able to make considerably more medium- and long-term loans. The cooperatives were able to rely more on their own resources for capital investment. Another important point was that the loans went to the growth sectors of agriculture. There is little question that the improvements in the farm

Table 7-5. *Value Added of the Agricultural Sector, Selected Years, 1970–80*

(billions of won)

Year	Amount	Growth rate (percent)	Index based on 1977 level
1970	4,066	−1.4	57.5
1975	6,308	4.9	89.1
1976	6,900	9.4	97.5
1977	7,077	2.6	100.0
1978	6,429	−9.2	90.8
1979	6,802	6.2	96.1
1980	5,372	−21.5	75.9

Note: Data are based on 1980 prices.
Source: Bank of Korea.

credit system contributed a great deal to the improvement of farm income and agricultural development.

The fertilizer subsidy policy had led to significant increases in fertilizer use. During the 1960s total fertilizer consumption was only 279,000 metric tons. In 1984 the figure was 762,000 metric tons. On the basis of fertilizer use per hectare, the yield in 1960 was only 130 kilograms; the 1984 level was 282 kilograms.

In spite of the favorable development reflected in the physical indicators, the different forms of intervention in favor of agriculture were increasingly costly in the economic distortions they caused. Inevitably, the good news did not last, and fundamental difficulties and changes in the agriculture sector emerged. In 1978 urban income again outpaced rural income: while farm income rose at an annual rate of 11.4 percent from 1975 to 1977, urban income rose at 13.2 percent. The gap continued to widen thereafter. Production of HYV rice was hit particularly hard by its susceptibility to pests and the early onset of cold weather that year. Then, in 1980, Korea experienced its worst drought of several decades, which badly damaged rice production. Crop production as a whole dropped 27.0 percent from the 1979 level, while the value added of agriculture was only 90 percent of the 1977 level.

Agriculture's value added was showing a similar trend. Up to 1978, as the economy developed and the industrial structure deepened, agriculture's share in value added was increasing in absolute amounts but decreasing in relative terms. In 1978 it decreased even in absolute terms, despite growth of 4.9 percent in forestry and 10.3 percent in fisheries.

Although the main reason for the decline was bad weather, there were other problems. Throughout the 1970s the amount of arable land was contracting as a result of the rapid urbanization and industrialization (table 7-6), despite the government's considerable efforts to increase the amount of farmland through the reclamation of slope and tidal zones. The new land, however, never exceeded that being pulled out of cultivation.

At the macroeconomic level, the deficits of the GMF and of the Fertilizer Fund had become unmanageable, despite the government's attempts to

Table 7-6. *Farmland Area, 1981–85*

(hectares, unless otherwise noted)

Item	1981	1982	1983	1984	1985
Total farmland area[a]					
(thousands of hectares)	2,188	2,180	2,167	2,152	2,144
Area transferred to nonfarm use	9,508	13,180	16,019	18,547	13,604
Newly developed area	1,952	4,927	2,568	4,099	5,662
Net effect	−7,556	−8,253	−13,451	−14,448	−7,942

a. At the end of the year.

Source: Ministry of Agriculture, Forestry, and Fisheries.

reduce them. Whereas the operating outlay of the GMF in 1975 was 495.5 billion won, in 1979 it was up more than threefold, having reached 1,493 billion won. The accumulated total deficit of the GMF by the end of fiscal 1980 was 971.9 billion won, the result of outlays for the dual price system and the growing off-management costs (table 7-7). Of the overall deficit, 53.7 percent, or 521.6 billion won, was attributable to the dual price system for rice and barley, and 46.3 percent, or 450.3 billion won, to the off-management costs. Of the 450.3 billion won, the interest payments on long-term loans from the Bank of Korea amounted to 95.8 billion won, and repayment and interest on the grain bonds totaled 246.9 billion won. Because the government financed the interest payments by printing money, a measure that increased the money supply, the deficits of the government funds were contributing to the growing problem of inflation. Thus, although the dual price system did increase farm income and alleviate the upward pressure on consumer prices, it did so at significant cost to the budget and to economic stability. The hopes embodied in the dual price system were not being met.

The problem of food imports—and the related effect on farm income—did not lessen. Despite serious efforts to expand agricultural production to achieve self-sufficiency, imports of foreign agricultural products still rose: in 1975 they amounted to about $1,030 million and in 1980 to $2,270 million.

Despite this concern with imports and even though grains accounted for about half the value of imported foods, by the end of the 1970s the government was no longer emphasizing HYVS. A major reason was that HYVS were very susceptible to pests and cold weather, as demonstrated in 1978.

Policy Responses and Issues in the 1980s

To address the problems caused by the external and domestic shocks to the Korean economy, including the agriculture sector, as well as the ongoing problems in the rural sector, the government implemented the Comprehensive Measures for Economic Stabilization (CMES) program. Although the economy experienced significant recovery in the early 1980s, the agriculture sector did not share in the recovery to the desired degree.

Concerned about the low level of rural income and the slow growth in agricultural value added, once again the government emphasized measures to promote agriculture. It had to do so within the context of constrained public resources, however, because of the unfavorable international economic climate and the impact of the second oil shock on the domestic economy. Initially the government pursued three primary policy measures to increase farm income: continuation of the high price supports for major agricultural products; intensive application of agricultural inputs, techno-

Table 7-7. GMF Deficit by Major Components, 1970–85
(billions of won)

Item	1970-75	1976	1977	1978	1979	1980	1981	1982	1983	1984	1985
Total deficit	249.0	50.3	63.1	159.1	208.7	241.7	144.1	1,305	3,370	4,059	3,450
Deficit from grain operation	85.2	20.8	37.9	113.3	142.5	121.9	12.4	−62	1,413	2,702	920
Sale of grains	50.2	9.3	23.4	94.3	113.6	89.7	−28.3	469	1,016	1,679	599
Handling costs	19.9	6.9	6.5	11.9	20.5	22.6	28.7	273	263	267	196
Management costs	15.1	4.6	8.0	7.2	8.4	9.6	12.0	134	133	126	125
Off-management costs	168.1	31.5	28.6	48.1	72.5	121.9	138.5	1,696[a]	2,057[a]	2,151[a]	2,896[a]
Interest	19.2	21.1	27.9	45.1	56.9	76.7	98.0	—	—	—	—
Price subsidy	128.0	0.0	0.0	0.0	0.0	0.0	0.0	0.0	—	—	—
Other	22.4	8.9	0.7	3.0	15.6	45.2	40.5	210	591	537	1,268
Off-management revenue	−4.3	−2.0	3.4	−2.3	−6.3	−2.1	−6.8	−329	−100	−164	−366

— Not available.
a. The decomposition of the off-management costs was not available after 1982.
Source: Ministry of Agriculture, Forestry, and Fisheries.

Table 7-8. *Government Purchase Price for Rice and Barley, 1971–85*

	Rice		Barley		
Year	Price (won per 80 kilogram)	Rate of increase (percent)	Price (won per 76.5 kilogram)	Rate of increase	Wholesale price increase (percent)
1971–75	10,555	25.5	6,272	22.4	17.9
1976–80	27,060	18.4	16,020	19.3	15.0
1981	45,750	25.0	26,400	20.0	44.2
1982	52,160	14.0	29,700	12.5	11.8
1983	55,970	7.3	33,780	13.7	0.2
1984	55,970	0.0	33,780	0.0	0.7
1985	57,650	3.0	39,181	16.0	0.9

Source: Ministry of Agriculture, Forestry, and Fisheries.

logical innovation, and diversification of farm activities to improve agricultural productivity; and promotion of rural off-farm income through rural industrialization.

Price Support Policy

From 1979 until 1982 the government increased its purchase price for rice an average of 19.1 percent a year. In a radical but necessary departure from past policy, from 1983 to 1985 it permitted an increase of only 3.3 percent a year (table 7-8). This measure was seen as one way to achieve structural adjustment, reduce the distortions in agriculture, and contribute to the overall stabilization program by lowering the deficit of the GMF. In real terms, the purchase price decreased 0.03 percent a year on average during 1983–85, while wholesale prices rose at an annual average rate of 0.6 percent. During the same period the overall wholesale price index grew at an average annual rate of 0.06 percent a year and the consumer price index increased at an annual average rate of 2.7 percent a year.

Measures to Increase Agricultural Productivity

In part because of the need to compensate for the change in the price support policy and its detrimental effect on farm household income, the government acted to boost agricultural productivity. Among the measures adopted were intensification of agricultural practices through greater use of inputs, technological innovation, new seeds, and intensive extension services and the diversification of farm activities.

The intensification of agricultural practices, or improvement in the ratio of farmland utilization, became increasingly important. Technological improvements in the 1980s have continued to emphasize rice production, as they did in the 1970s, but they also focused on vegetables, fruits, special crops, and livestock, all higher-value-added products. The government

Table 7-9. *Improvement of Farmland, Selected Years, 1970–85*
(thousands of hectares)

	1970	1975	1980	1982	1983	1984	1985
Total paddy area	1,195	1,277	1,307	1,311	1,316	1,320	1,325
Irrigated paddy	745	790	893	917	929	935	949
Ratio of irrigated paddy to total (percent)	62	62	68	70	71	71	72
Consolidated paddy	144	277	369	400	415	431	447
Consolidated paddy ratio (percent)[a]	20	39	52	57	59	61	63
Improved drained area	22	8	20	27	30	31	33
Ratio of improved drained area (percent)[b]	1.5	6	16	21	23	24	26

a. Consolidated paddy ratio is consolidated paddy divided by total possible consolidated area. Total possible consolidated area is 706,000 hectares.

b. Ratio of improved drained area is improved drained area divided by total possible area for improving drainage. Total possible area for improving drainage is 127,000 hectares.

also increased the paddy under irrigation and consolidated the land. In 1985 the ratio of irrigated paddy to total paddy was 72 percent, but the ratio for upland paddy was very low. In that same year the ratio of consolidated to unconsolidated land was 63 percent, the ratio of drained to undrained paddy 26 percent (table 7-9). Although some of these efforts may bear fruit, since the 1970s the ratio of land utilizatio: has decreased: in 1970 it was 142 percent and in 1984 only 125 percent The reason for the decline was decreased production of barley and soybeans.

Agricultural extension services—such as the introduction of new HYVS and higher-value-added products, development of new storage technologies, development of high-yield breeds of livestock, and development of Korean agricultural machines at competitive prices—have played an important role in enhancing the productivity of Korean agriculture during the past two decades, as shown in table 7-10.

Systematizing the provision of agricultural materials and chemicals was another method used to promote agricultural productivity. The major agricultural materials were farm machinery and vinyl film for greenhouse cultivation. In 1980 the total number of farm machines held by farm households was 1,069,200; in 1984, the figure was 1,650,000, or 54.4 percent greater. Important aspects of the mechanization program were that the farm machinery industry was developing equipment suitable for Korean agriculture and that the system of distribution and repair was well organized. On the down side, while mechanization helped raise agricultural production by compensating for the decline in farm labor, it also increased farm debt. One reason was that, in the early 1980s, as part of the structural adjustment program, the government discontinued the preferential low rate of interest for agricultural credit. The mechanization program was slowed by other factors as well, such as low capital efficiency, the high

Table 7-10. *Indexes of Terms of Trade for Agricultural Products, Land Productivity and On-Farm Income, 1964–85*

(percent)

Year	Terms of trade		A/B × 100 (percent)	Land productivity[a]	On-farm income
	Price farmers received (A)	Price farmers paid (B)			
1964	6.8	6.7	101.5	113.5	50.6
1965	7.3	9.3	78.4	97.9	39.6
1966	7.9	9.9	79.8	111.8	41.4
1967	8.9	10.7	83.2	96.5	43.2
1968	10.3	12.0	85.8	97.2	45.9
1969	11.6	13.7	84.6	117.3	55.7
1970	14.7	15.6	94.2	114.2	49.8
1971	17.8	17.8	100.0	116.6	66.0
1972	21.7	20.4	106.4	115.6	71.6
1973	24.1	22.3	108.1	123.8	76.6
1974	31.6	30.0	105.3	128.4	85.5
1975	39.2	37.1	105.7	133.6	90.1
1976	48.7	46.3	105.2	149.8	100.7
1977	56.8	54.2	104.8	170.9	102.7
1978	74.0	70.5	105.0	164.0	117.8
1979	82.0	80.2	102.4	156.7	112.3
1980	100.0	100.0	100.0	100.0	100.0
1981	128.2	128.5	99.8	143.9	116.3
1982	137.1	144.3	95.0	151.6	132.8
1983	140.3	156.2	89.8	152.9	141.1
1984	139.1	150.1	92.7	160.2	153.2
1985	138.2	146.4	94.4	157.8	149.5

a. Yield of rice for 0.1 hectare is used as the proxy variable for land productivity.

Source: National Agricultural Cooperative Federation and Ministry of Agriculture, Forestry, and Fisheries.

level of uncertainty about the expected return on capital, and the low level of assets of individual farmers.

The government responded to these problems, after 1983, by pursuing a policy of farm management diversification to boost agricultural productivity (table 7-11). In that year 225 areas were selected for intensive diversification farming based on the principle of suitable-crop-to-suitable-area, and 900 demonstration villages were chosen to receive intensive government support. In 1984 the number of diversification farming areas was increased to 300 and the number of demonstration villages to 1,200. In keeping with the emphasis on the development of livestock under the farm diversification project, the government imported many calves and distributed them to the general farms.

The diversification program did not prove very successful. For example, as the number of beef cattle increased rapidly, their price fell dramatically from 1 million won for baby beef cattle in 1983 to 355,000 won in 1985, so that the effect of the program was the opposite of that intended. Anderson

Table 7-11. Status of Farm Diversification Project, 1983–86

Designation	Unit	1983	1984	1985	1986
Farming	Each	225	300	401	540
Villages	Each	900	1,200	1,586	2,054
Households	Each	16,276	20,500	−7,870	33,698
Specified areas for cash crops	Hectare	7,118	15,956	28,507	42,69
Livestock	Each	25,000	47,786	44,876	—
Financial support	Millions of won	26,367	53,258	58,741	54,049
Production	Millions of won	21,867	44,258	57,431	52,049
Marketing	Millions of won	4,500	9,000	1,310	2,000

—Not available.
Source: Ministry of Agriculture, Forestry, and Fisheries.

(1986) noted that the protection of livestock had been initiated to provide rice farmers with a supplementary source of income. In the 1980s, however, livestock were increasingly raised on specialized farms, further evidence that this program did not work as intended. Other problems with the diversification program were seasonal labor shortages and the low level of farm mechanization.

Measures to Raise Off-Farm Income

Farm household income is usually divided between on-farm and off-farm (table 7-12). On-farm income is defined as net earnings from crops and livestock production on a family's own farm. In general, gross farm earnings are estimated by multiplying crop quantities by their unit prices and subtracting input costs. At a more detailed level, on-farm income depends on the terms of trade for farm products and on land productivity. Land productivity, in turn, is influenced by investments in the agricultural sector. Given a certain level of production costs and land productivity, unit prices must increase to raise on-farm income. Alternatively, given a certain level of prices and production costs, land productivity must be expanded. If the level of production and prices remains constant, then production costs have to decrease to improve the level of farm income.

The relationship among farm income, terms of trade, and farm productivity was estimated using regression analysis, with sample data from 1962 to 1984. Given an elasticity for farm income with respect to land productivity of about 0.4967, as estimated by regression analysis, the implication is that a 10 percent increase in the growth of agricultural land productivity would boost on-farm income by 4.967 percent. Given an estimated elasticity for on-farm income with respect to the terms of trade for farm products of 0.9323, a 10 percent increase in the relative price would increase on-farm income by 9.3 percent. Thus, between farm productivity and terms of trade, on-farm income has a higher degree of response to improvements in the terms of trade than to an increase in productivity.

Table 7-12. *Farm Household Income by Source, 1970–85*
(thousands of won)

Year	On-farm income	Off-farm income	Total	Off-farm income as a percentage of total
1970	874	279	1,153	24.2
1971	1,159	254	1,413	18.1
1972	1,256	270	1,526	17.7
1973	1,345	314	1,659	18.8
1974	1,501	366	1,867	19.6
1975	1,582	350	1,932	18.1
1976	1,768	453	2,221	20.3
1977	1,805	692	2,497	27.7
1978	2,064	805	2,869	28.0
1979	1,970	896	2,866	31.2
1980	1,755	938	2,693	34.2
1981	2,041	998	3,039	32.8
1982	2,330	1,102	3,342	32.1
1983	2,477	1,336	3,813	35.0
1984	2,688	1,344	4,032	33.0
1985	2,623	1,445	4,068	35.5

Note: Data are based on 1980 consumer prices.
Source: Ministry of Agriculture, Forestry, and Fisheries.

A third factor in on-farm income is land. In Korea, as in most developing countries, the amount of cultivated land was probably the single most important determinant of farm household income. Surveys of farm households showed that on-farm income increases with farm size: the on-farm income of farm households with 2.0 hectares or more of cultivated land in 1985 was 5.5 times that of farm households with less than 0.5 hectare of cultivated land. As noted earlier, the average farm size was just over 1 hectare.

Unfortunately, the potential for using the three factors cited to boost on-farm income in Korea was very low. There was a limit to the capacity of the agricultural sector in Korea to absorb the supply of rural labor and sustain the ratio of farm to nonfarm income through increased farm size and agricultural productivity, and there was little remaining new cultivable land. Although the enhancement of agricultural productivity through technological innovation was promising, it was not sufficient.

Given that reality, the government looked to rural nonfarm activities as an alternative, or supplementary, source of income. Moreover, because off-farm income varied inversely with farm size, it had a tendency to equalize average farm household income across farm size groups, an important characteristic. When off-farm income was added to on-farm income, the average income of farm households with 2.0 hectares or more of cultivated land in 1985 was 2.1 times greater than that of those with less than 0.5 hectare (table 7-13). Similarly, because off-farm income raised total farm income and tended to equalize average total farm household income across farm size groups, it was commonly believed to improve income distribu-

Table 7-13. *Farm Household Income by Size of Farm, 1985*
(won)

Hectares	Total income	On-farm income	Off-farm income
Less than 0.5	4,078,409	1,322,203	2,756,206
0.5–1.0	4,901,787	2,571,052	2,330,735
1.0–1.5	5,779,791	3,975,003	1,804,788
1.5–2.0	6,982,476	5,431,621	1,550,855
More than 2.0	8,621,890	7,207,347	1,414,543
Average	5,736,246	3,698,936	2,037,310

Source: Korea, Ministry of Agriculture, Forestry, and Fisheries (1986b).

tion, both within the rural sector and between the rural and urban sectors. Opportunities for nonfarm employment permitted households with small farms to raise their income by using part of their labor off the farm to compensate for the lack of land.

Rural off-farm income included side business income, wages and salaries, and income from wealth and donations. Income from wealth and donations consisted of rent for land and other property, interest payments, donations by family members, allowances, subsidies, and domestic receipts. Among these, the proportion donated by family members was the largest. During the latter half of the 1970s, the proportion of side business revenues in farm income was about 20.3 percent, that of wages and salaries 9 to 14 percent, and that of income from wealth and donations 6 to 15 percent. In recent years the proportion of wages and salaries has increased rapidly.

Off-farm income can be specified as a function of the expansion of the nonagricultural sector. Given an elasticity of off-farm income with respect to the growth rate of nonagricultural sector GNP of about 0.521, as estimated by regression analysis, a 10 percent increase in the growth of nonagricultural sector GNP would raise off-farm income by 5.21 percent.

There was ample potential in Korea for raising off-farm income: in contrast to the 63.4 percent share of off-farm income in farm household income in Japan in 1970 and the 59.5 percent share in Taiwan in 1977, farm household surveys in Korea indicated a level of only 35.5 percent in 1985 (table 7-12; the per capita income level of Korea in 1985 was similar to that of Japan in 1970 and Taiwan in 1977).

The principal policy measure the Korean government pursued from 1980 through 1986 for increasing off-farm income was rural industrialization. In 1984, 71.3 percent of all industrial firms were situated in urban areas, only 28.7 percent in rural areas. Moreover, employment in manufacturing was more concentrated in urban than in rural areas: 79.2 percent of total manufacturing employment in 1984 was in urban areas.

To reduce this imbalance and provide opportunities for off-farm employment, in the 1970s the government initiated rural industrialization efforts such as the Saemaul Factory Program described earlier in this chapter, the Farm Household Side Business Program, and the Folkcraft Development Program. Although they were still active in the 1980s, they did not prove successful because of unfavorable conditions such as inadequate rural infrastructure, limited availability of skilled labor, inefficient utilization of market and technological information, and inadequate access to capital. Moreover, because most rural areas were unsuitable for sustained industrial activity, the Saemaul factories still in operation in 1984 were heavily concentrated in the rural areas contiguous to large metropolitan zones. By 1984 the Saemaul movement was essentially moribund. Protectionist policies, by increasing the reservation wage for rural labor, also limited the potential for labor-intensive rural industrialization. Side businesses also proved unable to increase productivity and improve product quality on a sustained basis because of unskilled labor and low-performance equipment.

In promoting the folkcraft industry, the government designated ninety-five firms with good business prospects as strategic producers and provided them with special assistance. Compared with other small industries, however, the folkcraft industry had limited potential for absorbing the rural labor force and raising rural off-farm income because of its small market size. The 907 manufacturers of folkcrafts active at the end of 1984 accounted for only 2.9 percent of Korea's small and medium-size industries. Altogether the companies employed 23,000 people, but 61.4 percent had 10 or fewer employees. Most were cottage industries, 79.4 percent of them based in private homes.

Given the problems and slow progress under the initial rural industrialization programs, the government decided that rural industrialization needed to be a long-term policy goal within an integrated urban-rural development plan. Against this background, it introduced a new concept for rural industrialization: the small and medium-size rural industrial park, to be located at the center of a rural employment zone. The underlying premise was that rural industrialization required at least a spatial clustering of plants at a site where locational requirements would be met. In addition, the local rural industrial park, with its employment opportunities in manufacturing and services, had to be linked to a rural employment zone or to farm villages within commuting distance. The roads that connected the villages with the local rural industrial parks would be improved so that villagers could commute easily and cheaply to places of employment. The size of the rural employment zone would depend on both the distance between the areas and the efficiency of the transportation network.

Factories built in these parks would be entitled to preferential financial and tax treatment over a certain period, as well as technological and managerial advice. Selection of the optimum industrial sites would be the most important factor in the success of rural industrialization. In the past the choice had often been based on political compromise among localities eager to attract manufacturing plants. Instead, selection should have been based on the presence of the basic requirements of an industrial location.

Historically, many of the industries looking for a new site in rural areas tended to be polluters. Thus the movement from metropolitan to rural areas raised the possibility that environmental pollution might become dispersed. To deal with this threat, the law required that all factories cited in rural industrial parks install pollution control facilities.

As of the end of 1985, seven rural industrial parks had been designated and were under construction. This program is likely to improve rural income, although its potential impact on rural industrialization may be only marginal.

The Impact of Policy in the 1980s

As noted, the government used its agricultural and rural development policies in pursuit of several goals: parity of rural and urban income; low prices for basic foodstuffs; stability of agricultural prices; and self-sufficiency in basic foodstuffs, particularly rice. What emerges from various analyses of the effect of government policies, some of which are described briefly below, is that none of these goals was met. Instead, the policies brought significant known and hidden costs, such as higher food prices and hence lower income for some groups, unsustainable burdens on the budget and scarce government resources, and distortions in the allocation of the factors of production.

Despite the price supports, the level of farm household income has been lower than that of nonfarm households in every year since 1978 except 1982 and 1983 (table 7-4). Thus, the price support policy did not succeed in maintaining urban and rural parity.[2] Schrader (1986) believes that the rural standard of living was even lower than is indicated because the income figures were misleading. There is also some question whether the price system could ever result in income parity, particularly in the face of the policy then of holding producer prices down. Although the price supports did contribute to stabilizing the general level of consumer prices, which rose only 2.7 percent annually from 1983 to 1985, the cost to farmers was considerable because the low rate of increase in the government purchase price for rice and barley hurt the terms of trade for farm products (table 7-8). For major grain products, however, domestic producer prices were still substantially above international CIF prices, indicative of significant protection of agriculture and a potential for resource misallocation (table 7-14).

Another negative result is that the price supports and other production incentives did not bring about self-sufficiency. On the contrary, as national income rose and urbanization expanded, demand for foodstuffs continuously exceeded supplies, and the government had to permit imports. By

Table 7-14. *Comparison of Domestic and International Prices for Major Grains, 1980–85*

(dollars per metric ton)

Grain and year	Domestic price[a] (1)	International price[b] (2)	Ratio (1 ÷ 2)
Rice			
1980	926.1	439.9	2.1
1981	991.5	487.3	2.0
1982	959.2	314.3	3.1
1983	924.4	349.9	2.6
1984	911.6	325.3	2.8
1985	929.6	316.7	2.9
Barley			
1980	481.5	182.3	2.6
1981	525.9	187.8	2.8
1982	557.8	144.3	3.9
1983	540.8	146.4	3.7
1984	536.1	150.1	3.6
1985	528.5	126.7	4.2
Soybean			
1980	800.4	313.8	2.6
1981	1,094.5	304.8	3.6
1982	971.1	256.1	3.8
1983	1,014.0	293.3	3.5
1984	964.3	297.5	3.2
1985	869.6	239.1	3.6
Corn			
1980	295.3	167.7	1.8
1981	305.6	166.5	1.8
1982	280.7	134.7	2.1
1983	293.8	161.0	1.8
1984	333.5	164.3	2.0
1985	316.0	136.5	2.3

a. Producers' price.
b. CIF price.
Source: Korea, Ministry of Agriculture (1987).

1984 $2,163 million worth of farm products entered the country, compared with $1,030 million in 1975, or an increase of 110 percent (table 7-2).[3]

Trade liberalization began in 1978 and has since been expanded. The Korea Development Institute estimated that the nominal rate of protection for agricultural and fishery products in 1978 was 43.4 percent (the effective rate of protection was 57.0 percent). By 1985, 455 of a total of 715 items were imported subject to a tariff only. As the international prices of rice and barley were decreasing in the 1980s (table 7-14), the big winners from the liberalization of agriculture—the lifting of nontariff barriers—were consumers, who benefited from lower prices and lower inflation. Other authors found still higher levels of nominal protection. Anderson and Warr (1987), for example, calculated nominal protection of agriculture in the early 1980s at around 100 percent. Anderson (1986) cited estimates that the economic rate of return for rice rose from 15 percent to 300 percent and for barley from 7 percent to 450 percent between 1967–69 and 1977–79. Anderson concluded that the rate of agricultural protection at that time was similar to that in the most protectionist industrial countries.

Anderson and Ahn (1984) calculated the foreign exchange costs of the protection for rice using the domestic resource cost (DRC) methodology. A DRC greater than 1 indicated that it would be socially desirable to shift some resources out of rice production. Although the DRC for rice was 1 in 1968, it rose to 2 in 1977 and 3 in 1980. That is, for every unit of foreign exchange saved by growing rice domestically, two units could have been earned by using the resources in an activity with a stronger international comparative advantage. Moreover, the authors noted that the DRC was more unfavorable for small farmers than for large farmers. This was an indication of the cost to the Korean economy of the policy of keeping the price of rice at a level close to three times the international price. This distortion was true not only for rice: as a result of the price support system and protection for agriculture, according to Anderson and Ahn (1984), in the early 1980s the prices of both grain and livestock were over two times the international level. As shown in table 7-14, in the case of the major grains, domestic producers were isolated from the drop in international prices, and the gap between domestic producer prices and CIF prices increased. Fruits and vegetables were also costly, and the nominal rates of protection for red pepper and garlic, two main nongrain crops, were 275 percent and 580 percent, respectively, in 1980–82 (Anderson and Ahn 1984). In contrast, the prices of manufactured products were close to the border prices. According to another source (*Business Korea* 1986), the prices of local beef, milk, rice, barley, red beans, and soybeans were two to three times higher than international prices, peanuts four times higher, and red peppers and garlic six times higher. *Business Korea* commented that "the desirable effect of strict import quotas and outright bans is an income transfer from urban consumers to farmers but on the other side of the coin consumers face high food prices."

Using a general equilibrium model and assuming that labor was mobile across sectors, as seemed to be the case, Anderson and Warr (1987) concluded that agricultural protection favored unskilled labor and landowners at the expense of skilled labor. It also encouraged a sector—agriculture—in which Korea did not have a comparative advantage, discouraged manufacturing, and encouraged more skill-intensive activities in both sectors compared with what would have occurred under free trade because of the decrease in the wage differential between skilled and unskilled work. The authors surmised that protection may have been one reason for the rapid expansion of skill-intensive manufacturing. Although protection may have promoted greater income equality in urban areas, in rural areas the impact may have been the opposite because it benefited large landowners more.

Finally they suggested that by decreasing the gap between skilled and unskilled labor, not only did protection lower national income in a comparative static sense, it also weakened the incentives for workers to invest in human capital, which may have led to a lower overall rate of economic growth.

Schrader (1986) noted that as national income grew, the demand for rice and barley fell with increased demand for other products, such as vegetables, meat, and milk. As a result the government had to acquire larger stockpiles of rice and barley—in 1985, 1.44 million tons of surplus rice were in inventory at a cost of about 167,000 won a ton. The estimated deficit of the GMF was 1.53 trillion won, the largest single deficit in the budget. Schrader further pointed out that had Korea suddenly developed rice surpluses, the operational and inventory costs of the GMF would have escalated even more dramatically. Anderson (1986) claimed that from 1974 to 1980 the consumer prices for rice and barley averaged 20 percent and 40 percent below what the government paid. The result was that the deficit of the GMF (including the interest on accumulated debt) was 4 to 5 percent of the government's expenditures.

Myoung and Lee (1988) carried out an analysis that estimated the costs of the grain policy, as well as what would have happened in its absence. Using a standard partial equilibrium framework, they looked specifically at the tradeoff in welfare between consumers and producers, the effect on government revenues and expenditures, the net losses in social efficiency, and the foreign exchange balance. They, too, found that the government had incurred a substantial loss from the price support system, equivalent to 20 to 25 percent of the total costs for rice acquisition, or about 15 percent of the annual government budget. They give the cumulative total in 1985 as 14.6 trillion won. When the cost of handling was included, the deficit for each 80-kilogram bag of rice was 33 percent of the purchase price in 1984. Although keeping the prices low reduced the taxation to consumers arising from the price support system, this policy conflicted directly with the government's goal of monetary and financial stability because the government was repaying the loans to the GMF and the Fertilizer Fund from the central bank by printing money, a practice that boosted the money supply and inflation.

Myoung and Lee also noted that the domestic consumer and producer prices of rice were generally above the border prices except in 1970–71 and 1973–75, with the highest level of distortion in 1985. They estimated that in 1985 the producer welfare gains were $3,807.6 million, while consumers lost $3,445.2 million. Therefore, there was a net social welfare loss of $418.4 million. Over the period 1970–85, they estimated the aggregate total producer gain at $19.5 billion. This was offset, however, by a total consumer welfare loss of $19.6 billion. In the same period the accumulated total government earnings were $7.2 billion and the possible foreign exchange savings $1.3 billion. The net total efficiency losses were $2.54 billion (Myoung and Lee 1988, p.72).

The authors then calculated what would have happened in 1970–85 had the government not intervened. Rice production would have slightly exceeded recorded levels up to 1977, except in 1973, but would have fallen below them in 1978–85. The self-sufficiency ratio would have fallen below 50 percent in the 1980s, and the additional imports would have cost $2.54 billion. Total agricultural production would have exceeded actual levels by 0.4 percent in 1970 and 3.4 percent in 1975. Thereafter, free rice production would have boosted nonrice production, although not commensurately in value. Total agricultural value added would have fallen 24.2 percent in 1983 and 28.2 percent in 1984. Some 500,000 jobs would have been lost by the end of the 1970s, and 1 million farm workers would have left the farm sector by the 1980s to maintain their income. An open rice market might have resulted in a 5 to 6 percent drop in wages in the nonfarm sector. As 250,000 to 350,000 jobs were created in the nonfarm sector, rural unemployment would have increased, with some 661,300 people displaced by 1985. It is unlikely that the economy could have grown sufficiently to provide new jobs for these people and have financed the $2.6 billion in grain imports. The authors concluded that Korea would have faced serious foreign exchange and unemployment problems without the price intervention. The authors, however, did not consider crops that could have been substituted for rice and could have absorbed part of the labor displaced from agriculture.

Another disappointment in the 1980s was the record of the Fertilizer Fund. It continued to produce huge deficits that reached 711.7 billion won in 1984. That deficit was met by borrowing from the Bank of Korea and NACF funds. Government efforts to eliminate the deficit did not solve the problem.[4]

A final point by Anderson (1986) is worth mentioning. He noted that it is important to recognize that factors other than protection also played a role in the rise in farm income and food self-sufficiency in the 1970s. One was that farmers responded rapidly to the increase in manufacturing wages, with many turning to nonfarm jobs on a part- and full-time basis. Another was on-farm adjustments, with a significant substitution of capital for labor. Third was the adoption by many farmers of new agricultural technologies. In sum, farmers were willing and able to adjust quickly to new conditions.

A New Policy Initiative: 1986

In 1986, with farmers earning only 88 percent as much as urban dwellers, the government proposed a new plan to make the rural economy an equal partner in industry. The plan called for expenditures of 1.56 trillion won for infrastructure, education, medical care, and other projects. The government planned to move from direct assistance through subsidies to indirect capital assistance. The aim was to increase nonfarm income with support for rural industrialization, a strategy that was expected to bring the price support deficits down and keep food prices low. This program, according to Schrader (1986), suggested that the government saw a need to separate income policy from commodity pricing policy. Under the new policy it would be more difficult for urban industries to expand in urban areas, and the government would offer tax breaks, soft loans, and easier land use requirements for locating in rural areas. There were 100 new industrial estates under development. The program faced the major obstacles of inadequate schools and medical facilities and a limited pool of skilled labor. It was also proving difficult to attract people back to rural areas. The plan encouraged farmers to shift from rice to higher-value-added commodities and made it easier for them to do so.

As other sources of nonfarm income developed, the final objective was to lower agriculture protection to improve resource allocation and reduce the Fund deficits.

Alternatives in Agricultural Policy

It was clear that policy changes were needed. It was equally clear, however, that the needed reforms were politically explosive. Rice production still accounted for 43 percent of farm household income, and a "commitment to rural-urban income parity [was] now firmly entrenched in social policy with the grain price support system as its cornerstone" (Schrader 1986, p.22). Complete liberalization would be politically unfeasible because it would increase Korea's dependence on food imports and cause the value of farm capital assets to fall (Anderson 1986). This section reviews some of the analyses of the impact and issues involved in reform of current agricultural and rural policy.

Braverman, Ahn, and Hammer (1983) carried out a comprehensive analysis of five alternative agricultural pricing policies that considered six effects.[5] They found that there was no way the government could satisfy all its objectives simply by changing the prices of products supported by the GMF and the Fertilizer Fund. The incomes of larger farmers, of the entire rural sector perhaps, and the goal of self-sufficiency were best served by maintaining current rural grain prices and raising urban consumer prices. Reducing the Fund deficits, moderating the cost of living in urban areas, raising national income, and improving the standard of living of the very poor would be furthered by reducing the support prices for farmers. Thus, if the only policy instrument was pricing, the government would have to choose between the rural and urban sectors.

Braverman, Ahn, and Hammer (1983) concluded that "priority should be given to expanding the number of policy instruments available in order to allow the government to satisfy more of its objectives simultaneously"

(p. 79). For example, if the aim was to use the GMF to reduce migration to urban areas, the government could opt instead for off-farm employment, decentralized industry, urban amenities and planning in rural areas, and social services and agricultural extension. Whatever options were chosen, the government would need to specify in its policy options not just that the distribution of income was important, but also how important it was compared with other objectives.

The authors noted that most of the policy alternatives produced a proportionately far greater effect on the Fund deficits than on private sector production and income. Lowering rural prices in particular had a strong impact on the deficits compared with comparable increases in urban prices. The substitution possibilities in both supply and demand moderated the impact of the policy alternatives on consumers and producers but exacerbated the effect on government expenditures. The greater the substitution possibilities on the supply side, the greater would be the mediating effect on incomes.

The most crucial decision that Braverman, Ahn, and Hammer saw as potentially confronting the government was whether to forgo self-sufficiency as a goal. The deficits in the grain and rice markets could have been eliminated by closing the price gap between the rural and urban sectors. If that measure had been taken in a closed economy, however, the government would have lost both potential revenues from import tariffs and the possibility of a substantial drop in food grain prices. "To a large extent, the basic tradeoff between the rural sector on the one hand and the government budget and urban sector on the other hand, involves the decision of how much agricultural imports to allow" (p. 32).

Anderson and Ahn (1984) pointed out that cognizance had to be taken of other factors as important as, if not more important than, the price support system in raising farm income and food self-sufficiency in the 1970s. Farmers responded rapidly to the increase in real wages in the manufacturing sector, seeking part-time and full-time work in industrial jobs. The authors estimated that the percentage of the labor force leaving agriculture rose from less than 3 percent a year in the late 1960s to about 5 percent in the mid-1970s and more than 7 percent in the late 1970s. Producers also adjusted to the changing conditions on their farms. As wages rose, many turned to mechanization, a process that contributed to a 9 percent rise in productivity in the 1970s compared with the 5.6 percent gain of the late 1960s. They also took advantage of new farm technologies and higher-value-added products.

Anderson and Ahn (1984) concluded that to stem just the current decline in farm income and self-sufficiency would require ever greater protection. That policy was costly, however, and they suggested that it might be worth supporting the natural process of adjustment instead. In light of the proven ability of Korean farmers to adjust to new agricultural conditions, the government might have emphasized assistance for adjustment rather than continuing the losing battle of protection and price supports. The authors recognized, however, that powerful political and economic forces would continue to exert strong pressure for protection, because any significant change would have important outcomes in the distribution of income and the economy in general.

Clifford (1988) commented that Korea needed to consolidate the small farm plots in order to raise productivity, but he recognized that doing so was politically dangerous, particularly given the strength of rural farmers, especially through the NACF. Moreover, the farmers were supported by the urban sector, which seemed to value self-sufficiency over lower food prices. Clifford also argued for liberalization of agricultural imports. Although this policy would hurt farmers, it would also channel labor to industries with a long-term comparative advantage, and the new supply of labor would keep wages low.

Van Wijnbergen (1984) stated that because changes in food grain prices affected so many aspects of the economy, from the distribution of income to the external balance, it was important to coordinate macroeconomic policy to minimize the problems of agricultural reform. He saw reforms leading to the use of world prices causing a substantial drop in urban food costs and both macroeconomic benefits and gains in efficiency. The transitional costs, however, would necessitate compensatory measures on the part of the government.

Van Wijnbergen also estimated the impact of increases or decreases in real food prices. Further increases would lead to upward pressures on wages and a consequent loss in competitiveness unless accompanied by gains in productivity. Because such gains are a direct result of investment, a 10 percent rise in prices would necessitate a matching increase of 75 percent of one year's investment. Decreasing consumer and producer prices gradually (over one year) to world levels would cause inflation to fall and the real money stock to rise, with a positive impact on investment. Private savings, however, would fall and the current account would deteriorate. With investment and consumer expenditures both rising and stimulating aggregate demand, however, real growth would rise. The lower food prices would mean lower wage claims, but there would be a two-quarter lag between wages and export prices. Thus, the effect on competitiveness in the short term and on the real growth in exports would not be significant. The results of a simulation of a decline in food prices to world levels over two years showed a strong positive effect on competitiveness and export growth.

Anderson (1986) discussed four alternative agricultural policies: lowering the cost of producing food, especially through advances in technology; pursuing other ways to achieve food security, particularly through greater dependence on imports, with mechanisms to offset some of the resulting

Table 7-15. *Rice Purchase and Selling Prices, Selected Years,*
1970–85

(won per 80 kilograms)

Year	Purchase price	Handling costs	Total (A)	Selling price (B)	Deficit (B - A)
1970	5,150	578	5,728	5,400	−328
1975	15,760	1,488	17,248	13,000	−4,248
1980	36,600	7,126	43,960	32,000	−11,960
1981	45,750	9,750	55,500	44,000	−11,500
1982	52,160	10,184	62,344	53,280	−9,064
1983	55,970	9,358	65,328	52,280	−13,048
1984	55,970	14,782	68,592	52,280	−16,312
1985	57,650	16,262	73,912	54,260	−19,652

Source: Ministry of Agriculture, Forestry, and Fisheries.

insecurity; facilitating the mobility of labor, with an emphasis on parity between rural and urban incomes, particularly through rural industrialization; and more efficient policy instruments that could yield welfare gains without reducing the support for producer prices.

The authors of this chapter see several alternatives with respect to the GMF deficit. One is to eliminate it by narrowing the differential between the purchase and selling prices by raising the selling price to the level of the purchase price, with a margin sufficient to cover actual handling costs. In contrast, up to 1986 the government had increased the selling price at a slower rate than the purchase price in order to support general price stabilization (tables 7-15 and 7-16). The second way is to increase the government selling price so that it reflects seasonal variations, a step that would raise the selling price during periods of shortage and lower it during periods of harvest, but with an overall increase in the average price. Although this policy would reduce the deficit of the GMF, it would increase the losses for consumers and could put pressure on wages and inflation. A third alternative is to allow the government purchase and sales prices to move according

Table 7-16. *Barley Purchase and Selling Prices, Selected Years,*
1970–85

(won per 76.5 kilograms)

Year	Purchase price	Handling costs	Total (A)	Selling price (B)	Deficit (B - A)
1970	3,348	439	3,787	2,750	−1,037
1975	9,901	1,412	10,503	6,900	−3,603
1980	22,000	9,618	31,618	10,120	−21,498
1981	26,400	12,546	38,946	18,475	−20,471
1982	29,700	13,691	43,391	19,355	−24,036
1983	33,780	9,473	43,253	28,000	−15,253
1984	33,780	10,009	43,789	30,800	−12,989
1985	39,181	10,490	49,671	31,420	−18,251

Source: Ministry of Agriculture, Forestry, and Fisheries.

to current market prices. The government would buy grains at market prices during harvesttime, when the market price is low, and release them at market prices during the off-season, when the market price is high. Supply and demand would be adjusted through the government's food grain market operations, and the price could be stabilized. Accordingly, the seasonal price fluctuation would be minimized and the losses reduced. A fourth alternative is to decrease the amount of grain acquired.

Summary and Conclusions

In the early 1960s, government policy for agriculture and rural development focused on the expansion of agricultural production through greater land productivity and the expansion of farmland and self-sufficiency in staple food grains. In the second half of the 1960s the priority was to narrow the rural-urban income gap, to stabilize food grain prices, and to promote rural development, along with the previous goals. As a result, government policy on rural development shifted toward the enhancement of farm household income through the maintenance of high farm prices and fertilizer price subsidy programs.

The pricing policy for agricultural products proved ineffective, despite significant transfers of public funds from the nonfarm sector to the agricultural sector. Moreover, the farm price support policy created increasing deficits for the GMF and ultimately caused monetization and accelerating inflation. It did not eliminate the imbalance between rural and urban areas.

The core of farm income policy since the early 1980s has been to increase off-farm income in rural areas through rural industrialization. Through the mid-1980s this strategy did not meet with great success.

When looking at the future of agriculture and the implications for policy, several factors must be considered. Korea will need to reassess its policy of self-sufficiency in favor of greater efficiency in production and maintaining the access of its manufactured products to foreign markets. Improvements in the situation of rural households can be addressed through policies that encourage increases in efficiency and the diversification of production to activities in which Korea can compete with average protection similar to that provided to the manufacturing sector. Off-farm income should be encouraged through the development of physical and social infrastructure in rural areas. To improve efficiency it is likely that some form of consolidation of small farms will be necessary.

It is also important to be realistic about agriculture's position in the economy. In the mid-1980s real agricultural value added in domestic prices was rising at 5 percent a year. At the same time, however, agriculture's share in GNP fell from almost 50 percent in the late 1950s to only 16.5 percent in 1981 and 12.7 percent in 1986. Whereas two-thirds of the Korean labor force was employed on farms in the 1960s, the figure was less than one-third in 1986. Agriculture's share in Korea's all-important exports was negligible. Although production continued to rise, demand rose even faster, so that food imports remained high. Korea's self-sufficiency ratio fell and likely would have fallen even lower had it not been for the subsidies for domestic producers and consumers. As many economists have pointed out, Korea's comparative advantage in agriculture had fallen dramatically, despite the heavy protection, and was likely to continue to decline. This decrease in the share of agriculture in GDP is a normal characteristic of development, especially in a high-growth country like Korea.

Under these circumstances, even with heavy protection it is very difficult to keep agriculture profitable without undue resource misallocation and large financial costs. The alternative of moving consumer prices to the level of the protected producer prices would have caused large consumer losses and pressures on wages and inflation.

Many economists have pointed out that the government was trying to meet too many goals with a single policy measure—price supports—and needed to begin looking at a range of policies and measures. The comprehensive program enacted in 1986 to eliminate the shortcomings of previous government rural industrialization programs seemed to be an appropriate means of accelerating rural development and improving farm income. Nevertheless, some factors may limit the success of that new program. Industrialization in Korea was concentrated in the Seoul and Pusan areas (Seoul, Pusan, Gyeonggi, and Gyeong Nam). In rural areas, small commercial and service establishments, industrial workshops, and homecraft activities had not developed, migration to urban areas depleted the human capital, credit was difficult to obtain, and the rural infrastructure was underdeveloped. For these reasons it is questionable whether rural industrialization could be successful in increasing rural income.

The farm management diversification policy pursued since 1983 is another approach to eliminating the decrease in farm income experienced in 1980. Although the small-scale farming system made it possible for this policy to maintain farm household income, such diversification will not be desirable in the long run, when a specialized, commercial, large-scale farming system develops.

Government efforts to increase agricultural production after the poor harvests of 1979 and 1980 produced surpluses of rice, barley, vegetables, and fruits (but not of wheat, soybeans, and food grains). Once the current account of the balance of payments showed a steady surplus, however, the government should have accelerated structural transformation of the agricultural production sector by moving prices closer to the international level to achieve a more efficient allocation of production resources.

The government established and supported institutions to control the domestic demand for and supply of food grains and to stabilize grain prices to increase farm income and protect the welfare of urban consumers. Although the dual price policy, with its higher price for farmers and lower price for urban consumers, may have increased farm income and alleviated the upward pressure on consumer prices, it also increased government costs for the grain operation at an accelerating pace. In response, the government began in 1980 to adjust the dual price system to eliminate the GMF deficit. This policy, however, had a negative direct effect on rural families. If the objective of government policy was to improve the income participation of these families, the government should have implemented expenditure and transfer policies that benefited rural families. Among these policies are those that promote the development of rural infrastructure and social services for the rural population. The price system itself is more effective in achieving efficiency in resource allocation.

It seems evident that elimination of the deficits will require difficult choices among goals and income groups. These transition costs can, however, be alleviated by compensatory measures.

Notes

1. Intervention in the rice market actually goes back to at least 1948, when the new Korean government passed the Grain Purchase Law. It required that producers and landowners sell to the government all their output that they did not consume themselves. In 1950 the legal authority for the government's food grain policy was established with the Grain Management Law. The aim was to stabilize prices, keep prices low for urban consumers, and provide adequate incentives for producers. U.S. PL480 imports, especially of wheat and barley, were crucial to keeping prices low in the 1950s and 1960s, while at the same time generating funds for investment.

2. Anderson (1986) concluded that this objective had been met: since 1974, when farm income achieved parity with urban income, the two had remained within 4 percent of each other, except in 1979–80 when crop yields were low. He also noted that this success was achieved in part through progressive increases in domestic prices for food, which were made possible because of the rising protection against food imports. Farmers thus benefited at the expense of consumers. Anderson calculated the implicit tax on nonfarm households at $1,500, or one-sixth of total household income. This transfer itself was highly inefficient, because only half that amount actually reached the farmers, while the rest was a deadweight loss in economic welfare.

3. Anderson (1986) claimed that Korea achieved food security in rice and other foods except wheat and ruminant meat. In the case of rice and barley, however, it did so on the basis of imports of raw materials for chemical fertilizers, and in the case of livestock production, through an increasing reliance on feedstuffs, most of which were imported. He concluded that there was only a "veneer of food security" (p.49).

4. Anderson (1986) noted that the fertilizer policy would likely change in 1987 when the government's obligation to protect fertilizer producers was to end.

5. Their analysis took into account the various objectives underlying current policies (redistribution of income, public revenues and ease of collection, market failures, and production incentives) and major institutional characteristics (such as the dual rice markets—traditional strains and HYVs). Only the highlights of their studies are presented here to give an idea of the effects involved and the issues the alternatives raise.

References

Anderson, Kym. 1986. "Food Policy in Korea, 1955 to 1985." University of Adelaide, Department of Economics.

Anderson, Kym, and In-Chan Ahn. 1984. "Protection Policy and Changing Comparative Advantage in Korean Agriculture." *Food Research Institute Studies* 19 (2):139–51.

Anderson, Kym, and Peter G. Warr. 1987. "General Equilibrium Effects of Agricultural Price Distortions: A Simple Model for Korea." *Food Research Institute Studies* 20 (3):245–63.

Braverman, Avishay, Choong Young Ahn, and Jeffrey S. Hammer. 1983. *Alternative Agriculture Pricing Policies and the Republic of Korea: Their Implications for Government Deficits, Income Distribution, and Balance of Payments.* World Bank Staff Working Paper 621. Washington, D.C.

Business Korea. 1986. "Liberalization to Come Slowly." *Business Korea* 3(10) (April):26.

Clifford, Mark. 1988. "Poor Future on the Land: South Korea Faces Difficult Policy Decisions on Farming." *Far Eastern Economic Review* (Hong Kong) 141 (July):56–57.

Korea, Ministry of Agriculture. 1987. *Major Statistics of Agriculture and Fisheries.* Seoul.

Korea, Ministry of Agriculture, Forestry and Fisheries. 1986a. *Major Agricultural Policy Indicators.* Seoul.

———. 1986b. *Report on the Results of the Farm Household Economy Survey.* Seoul.

Moore, Mick. 1984–85. "Mobilization and Disillusion in Rural Korea: The Saemaul Movement in Retrospect." *Pacific Affairs* 57(4) (Winter):577–98.

Myoung, Kwang-Sik, and Jung-Hwan Lee. 1988. "Evaluation of the Korean Market Intervention System." In Asian Development Bank, *Evaluating Rice Market Intervention Policies: Some Asian Examples.* Manila.

Schrader, Erwin. 1986. "Growing Pains on the Farm." *Business Korea* 3(10) (April):21–25.

van Wijnbergen, Sweder. 1984. "Short-Run Macro-economic Effects of Agricultural Pricing Policies." Discussion Paper 43. Development Economics Research Centre, University of Warwick, Coventry, U.K.

8 Import Liberalization and Industrial Adjustment

SOO-GIL YOUNG, Korea Development Institute

DESPITE KOREA'S LONG RECORD of unprecedentedly rapid growth, by the end of the 1970s many Koreans believed that the government's pursuit of heavy industrialization had created an unsound structure for manufacturing and that there was an urgent need for structural adjustment.[1] One response of the government was to adopt a policy of import liberalization. This chapter examines the significant aspects of this policy and the ways in which industries and firms have adjusted to it.

Although import liberalization had long been official policy in Korea, it was not seriously implemented until 1978, when domestic aggregate demand became too high and the current account balance was improving. The effort was soon interrupted, however, by the economic difficulties that arose in 1979–80. When import liberalization was resumed in the early 1980s, it provoked acrimonious debate among various circles of society. Although proposed as a way to remedy the unhealthy structure of heavy industries, it provoked a fear of massive dislocation of domestic industries, among other effects.

Contrary to these fears, import liberalization has, at least on the surface and up to 1986, caused no serious economic difficulties. This observation raises the question, however, of whether any adjustment has taken place. Some foreign critics argue that the measures taken have been cosmetic and ineffectual and that no serious industrial adjustment has occurred. At the same time, many Korean intellectuals and business leaders believe that imports are being liberalized beyond the nation's capacity and that industrial adjustment has taken place at considerable cost to firms and workers.

These conflicting views suggest that basic questions about Korea's recent import liberalization program have yet to be answered satisfactorily. How substantive was it in scope and depth? Did it have material effects on Korean industries? On the whole, were the effects beneficial or destructive? How did firms respond to import liberalization? What remains to be done? This chapter addresses these questions.

Unfortunately, a well-designed survey of how firms have responded to import liberalization was not possible. Instead, this chapter draws upon a few anecdotes about industry, the responses of firms to the government's policy, and a recent survey of subjective firm opinions on the impact of import liberalization. An obvious and important shortcoming of this chapter is the absence of a clear framework for analysis. As a consequence of these limitations, the chapter merely establishes a broadly valid picture of the depth and effect of import liberalization in the context of Korea's recent industrial adjustment.

This chapter has five sections. The first reviews the historical background of import liberalization, presenting it essentially as part of the industrial adjustment issue stemming from the drive for heavy industrialization in the 1970s. The second section examines the specifics of the import liberalization policy in place since the late 1970s and evaluates its scope and substance. The third section analyzes the pattern of recent changes in the structure of manufacturing industries. The analysis develops a hypothesis about the role played by import liberalization in the context of these changes. The fourth section discusses evidence concerning the way firms have been adjusting to import liberalization. The chapter concludes with an overall evaluation of the policy.

Background on the Recent Import Liberalization

The Korean government declared import liberalization to be official policy in 1967, but did not make a serious attempt to implement it until ten years later, after Korea had successfully ridden out the difficulties caused by the first oil shock and the subsequent world recession.[2] The economy was booming, with strong export performance by the light manufacturing industries, a high level of investment in heavy industry, and successful penetration of the Middle East construction market. As a result the current account balance was improving rapidly. Nevertheless, the government was worried that pressure from domestic demand was building. Seeing import liberalization as one way to relieve this pressure, the government liberalized imports of a large number of commodities in several successive phases between 1978 and 1979.[3]

In 1979 a dramatic downturn in the economy forced the government to discontinue import liberalization. The severity of the recession in the next two years was largely the result of a triple assault: the second oil shock, the sociopolitical instability associated with the assassination of President Park Chung Hee and the establishment of a new government, and the unprecedented crop failure in the summer of 1980. These shocks had, however, been preceded by problems of declining export performance and decreasing capacity utilization in many manufacturing industries. Those trends began in late 1978 and aggravated the effects of the three shocks. Together these factors resulted in negative growth of the economy in 1980.

The problems that developed in Korea's manufacturing industries toward the end of the 1970s can be explained in the context of a general decline in international competitiveness. As the table shows, Korea suffered a sudden and large loss in its international market share in 1979–80.[4]

This downturn has been attributed largely to the government policy that preceded it: the promotion of heavy industries.[5]

				Korea's share in manufactured exports (percent)					
1963	1973	1977	1978	1979	1980	1981	1982	1983	1984
1.1	11.9	16.9	17.3	15.8	15.3	17.0	19.0	19.4	19.5

The dominant concern of the government authorities responsible for economic policy in the 1960s had been the promotion of exports. In the 1970s, and especially since 1973, however, they became preoccupied with the promotion of "nontraditional" industries, broadly defined as heavy industries. Exports were still important, but their promotion was seen as secondary to, and in fact contingent upon, the promotion of heavy industries.

This change in policy priorities was accompanied by a vigorous campaign to promote investment in manufacturing sectors identified as heavy and chemical, or strategic, industries. Essentially, they included all the nontraditional industries, ranging from chemical, nonferrous metal, and steel to machinery, electronics, automobiles, and shipbuilding. Various discriminatory incentives in the form of special tax treatment, preferential credit allocation, and state provision of industrial infrastructure were introduced to promote investment. These industries were also protected from foreign competition by high import barriers.

The policy was fully implemented as intended, but, at least at the time, its effect seemed very different from that intended. By the late 1970s the heavy and chemical industries were suffering from serious excess capacity and a worsening financial structure and were increasingly dependent on government assistance and the rescheduling of bank loans. The promotion of heavy industries also created a demand-pull inflation of wages that caused losses of international competitiveness for light manufacturers. This situation is apparent in table 8-1, which shows a decline in the unit-labor-cost–adjusted real exchange rate of 26 percent compared with the United States between 1975 and 1979.

In an environment of political and economic crisis, the new government initiated a series of economic reforms to promote industrial adjustment. As a short-term measure and in immediate response to what appeared to be urgent problems of industry, the government sought to reduce the excess capacity in major heavy industrial sectors—such as copper refineries, power generators and other heavy electrical machinery, automobiles, diesel engines, and electronic switchboards—by forcing a realignment of investment among firms and by liquidating some plants.

As a long-term measure, the government sought to reform the industrial incentive system. As a result, industry-specific incentives were largely eliminated, although the general incentives for small firms and the regula-

Table 8-1. Macroeconomic Indicators of the Korean Economy, Selected Years, 1975–85

Year	GNP growth[a] (percent)	Unemployment (percent)	Manufacturing wage increase (percent)	Nominal exchange rate index (won/dollar)	Real exchange rate index[b]	Imports/GDP	Trade deficit (percent of GNP)	Trade deficit (billions of dollars)
1975	6.8	4.1	27.0	79.7	115.9	36	8.0	1.7
1979	7.0	3.8	28.6	79.7	85.6	35	7.1	4.4
1980	−4.8	5.2	22.7	100.0	100.0	41	7.3	4.4
1981	6.6	4.5	20.1	112.1	116.8	42	5.5	3.6
1982	5.4	4.4	14.7	120.4	112.3	38	3.7	2.6
1983	11.9	4.1	12.2	127.7	121.4	38	2.3	1.8
1984	8.4	3.8	8.1	132.7	138.3	38	1.3	1.0
1985	5.4	4.0	9.5	143.2	146.4	36	0.0[c]	0.0

a. The calculation of GNP for the years beginning with 1980 is based on the new system of national accounts.
b. The deflator used is the ratio of Korea's manufacturing unit labor costs to those in the United States.
c. Preliminary estimate.
Source: Korea, Economic Planning Board (1986) and database of the Korea Development Institute.

tion of large firms were strengthened. In addition, efforts were made to privatize and deregulate commercial banking. All these measures, which constituted a new industrial policy, were thought to strengthen the market mechanism and discourage the misallocation of resources. At the same time, a multiyear program of import liberalization—a resumption of the earlier effort—was initiated, a step that proved particularly controversial.

Another important and successful policy development was the move by the government to adjust and stabilize the real exchange rate (see chapter 3 in this volume). The government also implemented a successful campaign to stabilize wages and prices through income policy and fiscal and monetary restraint. Table 8-1 shows that, as a result, the real exchange rate was maintained at a competitive level.

Given the generally held view that heavy industries have been oversubsidized and overprotected, the heated national debate provoked by the import liberalization proposal was unexpected.[6] The debate about import liberalization was very confused initially, but eventually it became clear that the key issue was the appropriate speed and manner of liberalization and that nothing would satisfy everyone.[7]

The debate revolved around three major concerns that the optimal import liberalization program should address. One was the potentially heavy costs of adjustment that would have to be borne by firms and workers. This concern was the basis for the massive dislocation argument against import liberalization. According to this argument, any significant import liberalization program at this stage of industrial development would result in a flood of more competitive foreign goods, would bankrupt domestic firms in the affected industries, and would create serious structural unemployment.

The second concern was the need to promote industrial sophistication. Opponents of import liberalization argued that free trade would retard technological development—and hence industrial sophistication in general—and the growth of infant industries.

The third widely held concern was the balance of payments impact of import liberalization. A popular argument was that with the dislocation of many import-competing industries, imports would surge while exports would not increase, a disparity that would cause serious current account difficulties. This argument had special appeal to the public, given the heightened alarm about Korea's large international debt. According to those holding this view, imports would surge without accompanying growth in exports because the upper-income class had both an "irrational" preference for goods imported from advanced countries and ample purchasing power. Import liberalization would unleash both at the expense of domestic savings.

Proponents of import liberalization shared these concerns but argued that a preannounced, medium-term, across-the-board program of import liberalization, with allowance for a limited number of exceptional commodities and a substantial level of residual transparent protection, could be implemented without undue shock to industry. A preannounced, medium-term program would not necessarily lead to a surge in imports, and firms would have sufficient time to prepare for adjustment. Furthermore, anticipation of the exposure to international competition would force firms to reduce X-inefficiency and become more innovative. As a result, their international competitiveness would be strengthened and technological development accelerated.

Proponents also argued that although Korea had overinvested in heavy industries and needed to carry out industrial adjustment, it was nonetheless also rapidly gaining international competitiveness in this sector. Accordingly, although a reallocation of resources was not only inevitable but also a major aim of import liberalization, the adjustment would be largely intra-industrial rather than interindustrial. Such adjustment need not be very painful, and, with the help of efforts by firms to become more competitive and to upgrade their technologies, the costs of adjustment could be largely eliminated.

A further argument of the supporters of liberalization was that, except perhaps in the very short term, the current account balance was a macro-economic problem that could be handled with an appropriate real exchange rate policy that maintained the international competitiveness of Korean goods in general. Overall, depending on how it was managed, import liberalization would be only moderately painful at worst and could induce necessary industrial adjustment.

Although the adjustment of industries and firms to import liberalization is discussed further in subsequent sections, it should be pointed out that Korea's recent balance of payments record supports the proponents' view of import liberalization. Stabilization of the real exchange rate at an internationally competitive level was a paramount concern of the government through the mid-1980s. For this reason it adjusted the nominal exchange rate rather flexibly, while successfully seeking to stabilize wages and prices through austerity measures. As a result, as shown in table 8-1, the trade account improved steadily even before the yen-dollar realignment and the decline in oil prices and international interest rates.

This experience does more than vindicate the view that import liberalization should not be held responsible for the balance of payments problems. It also—and more appropriately in the present context—demonstrates that Korea's exchange rate and domestic macroeconomic policies were favorable to import-competing and exporting firms in general and thereby minimized the problems of adjustment. In this regard, Korea's import liberalization program was well supported by macroeconomic policies.

Table 8-2. *Imports by Use, 1981 and 1985*

	1981		1985	
Item	*Value (billions of dollars)*	*Composition (percent)*	*Value (billions of dollars)*	*Composition (percent)*
Total	26.1	100.0	31.1	100.0
Imports for export use	6.2	23.9	13.2	42.5
Imports for domestic use	19.9	76.1	17.9	57.5
Raw materials	16.3	62.2	17.4	56.2
Crude oil	6.5	24.4	5.6	18.0
Capital goods	6.2	23.6	11.0	35.3
Ships for export	0.9	3.4	3.1	10.1
Others	5.3	20.3	7.9	25.3
Consumer goods	3.7	14.2	2.6	8.5
Grains	2.0	7.5	1.2	3.8

Source: Ministry of Trade and Industry.

Policy Approach to Import Liberalization

Korea's import regime had a dual structure in the sense that it purported to accord a relatively free import regime to exporters while being generally restrictive with imports for domestic use. Exporters operated under a tariff drawback system: upon completion of exports, they were, in principle, refunded any tariffs they had paid on imports. In addition, quantitative restrictions applied much less stringently to materials brought in for processing for exports.

Table 8-2 shows that imports for domestic use accounted for nearly 60 percent of Korea's total imports in 1985. Largely because of Korea's poor natural resource endowment, raw materials accounted for just over 56 percent of imports and consumer goods for around 9 percent, with those other than grains accounting for less than 5 percent. These figures suggest that the import restrictions were the most severe for consumer goods.

To discuss protection in Korea it is useful to classify it into two categories, structural and contingency. There were two ways in which structural protection was provided. First, it was implemented through legislated tariff rates, with a basic structure determined by the general tariff rates that applied to imports from all sources. Wherever relevant, the general tariff rates were superseded by concession rates at the General Agreement on Tariffs and Trade (GATT) negotiations. The GATT concessions covered only a small portion of traded commodities, and more often than not the general tariffs were below the concession rates.

Another way structural protection was provided was through two complementary discretionary import licensing systems: general and discriminatory. General import licensing was administered through a "trade notice." For each one-year period starting July 1, the Ministry of Trade and

Industry announced a revised list of the commodities for which import approval had to be requested. Approval was not given unless it could be shown that the commodity to be imported had no domestic substitute and was essential for the operation of export or other important industries. In this way the authorities administered quantitative restrictions on imports from general sources.[8]

The Ministry of Trade and Industry also maintained an "import source diversification notice," a list of commodities that required approval for import from Japan. The government justified discrimination against imports from Japan with the huge and chronic current account deficit that Korea had been running with Japan since the early years of industrialization.

Two instruments of contingency protection were also used. One was a flexible tariff adjustment system that allowed the government to vary the tariff rates under specified circumstances. The reasons for which tariff adjustment could be invoked to protect domestic industries included emergencies, dumping, subsidy countervailance, and adjustments. Emergency tariffs were the Korean version of safeguards. Adjustment tariffs allowed for a temporary increase in the rate for a product above the general rate when general discretionary import licensing had been liberalized during the preceding three years. Flexible tariff adjustments were allowed in retaliation for unfair discrimination abroad, most-favored-nation treatment of non-GATT signatory countries, and tariff adjustment to stabilize the domestic prices of specific commodities. The last of these provisions was ordinarily used to reduce tariffs below the general rates rather than to raise them.

As to the so-called import surveillance instrument of contingency protection, related products were announced periodically, with the government monitoring their import for possible quantitative restraint whenever they appeared to be having disruptive effects on the domestic market. Historically, Korea did not use contingency protection much; structural protection was the instrument used most often. In the Korean context, import liberalization always meant a reduction of structural protection, effected through the liberalization of basic tariffs and import licensing.

Until the mid-1960s the purpose of tariff policy was to maximize the protection of domestic industries. As a result, the level and structure of tariff rates grew increasingly complex.[9] In the late 1960s the policy was reversed, and the government tried to rationalize the structure of tariffs.[10]

Table 8-3 shows the changes in the tariff system. It was reformed three times in the 1970s: in 1972, 1976, and 1978. In 1972 and 1978, in particular, tariff reduction was one of the main objectives. In this connection, it may be added that while the average level of tariffs was lowered, those for selected products were often raised. In 1976, for example, and especially in 1978, the tariffs on heavy industry products were increased.

Table 8-3. *Structure of General Tariff Rates, Selected Years, 1952–84*

Year	Simple average (percent)	Coefficient of variation
1952	25.4	0.70
1957	30.3	0.70
1962	40.0	0.77
1968	39.1	0.71
1973	31.5	0.70
1977	29.7	0.61
1979	24.8	0.69
1984	21.9	0.61

Source: Kim (1991, table 3.4).

The tariff system was reformed once again in 1984 to pave the way for introduction of a five-year program of preannounced tariff cuts. As shown in table 8-4, the tariffs on industrial products were to be reduced by about 25 percent during the period and were to be somewhat uniform across different stages of processing. Agricultural products were exempted from the cuts in tariffs, and some agricultural tariffs were raised.

The liberalization of import licensing was accomplished through periodic revisions of the trade notice. There were two possible approaches to preparing the trade notice. One was to list products subject to automatic import approval, the other to list products subject to discretionary import approval. The government used the former, "positive list," system until 1967, when it adopted the latter, "negative list," approach. This change followed the declaration of import liberalization as formal policy. It was intended to signal the government's determination to liberalize imports and was accompanied by a significant liberalization of licensing. This import liberalization policy was in effect suspended almost immediately, however, and was even reversed as the balance of payments on the current account worsened.

In 1978–79 substantial liberalization of the general import licensing was implemented for the first time since the adoption of the new trade notice system. It was followed by another significant liberalization measure in 1981. Finally, a multiyear program of liberalization of general import licensing that covered the period up to 1988 was announced in 1983–84.

Table 8-4. *Structure of General Tariff Rates, 1983, 1984, and 1988*
(percent)

Category	1983	1984	1988
Nonagricultural products	22.6	20.6	16.9
Raw materials	11.9	10.6	9.5
Finished products	26.4	24.7	18.9
All products	23.7	21.9	21.3

Source: Korea, Ministry of Finance (1984).

Table 8-5. *Import Licensing Liberalization Ratio (ILLR), 1967–84*
(percent at year's end)

Year	ILLR
1967	58.8
1968	56.0
1969	53.6
1970	52.8
1971	53.5
1972	49.5
1973	50.7
1974	49.3
1975	47.8
1976	49.6
1977	49.9
1978	61.3
1979	69.1
1980	70.1
1981	75.5
1982	77.4
1983	81.2
1984	85.4

Note: The ILLR indicates the proportion of items subject to automatic import approval under the regular trade notice, based on the classification of goods into 1,097 items at the four-digit level of the Customs Cooperation Council Nomenclature (CCCN).
Source: Kim (1991, table 3.6).

Preannouncement of the plans for each commodity for licensing liberalization each year was an important feature of this program.

One way to quantify the extent of import liberalization is to calculate what may be called the import licensing liberalization ratio (ILLR), popularly termed the "import liberalization ratio" in Korea. This ratio is obtained by dividing the number of commodity classes subject to automatic import approval by the total number of commodity classes at a given level of commodity classification. Table 8-5 expresses the progress of the general liberalization of licensing through this ratio.

Table 8-6 shows the structure of the import licensing liberalization program. The ILLR was to be raised to 95 percent at the end of the program. Some 360 products out of a total of 7,915 were to remain under general discretionary licensing at the end of the period. They were to include about 270 items in the class of primary products and food and beverages; 65 items such as jewelry, ornaments, and collector goods; 23 raw silk and silk products; and a few others. These figures reflect the degree of exemption of agricultural products from the import licensing liberalization in progress.

Table 8-6 suggests that by 1988 most mainstream industrial products were to be free of quantitative restrictions. This interpretation is subject to a few qualifications, however. According to table 8-7, the import source diversification notice, which included mostly manufactures, covered 16 percent of the total commodity classes in 1985, a significant amount. The table also indicates, however, that the commodity coverage of the diver-

Table 8-6. Structure of the Import Licensing Liberalization Program, 1981–88

Commodity class	Number of items[a]	Percentage of items subject to automatic import approval under the regular trade notice							
		1981	1982	1983	1984	1985	1986	1987	1988
Primary products, food, and beverages	1,386	68.5	70.6	73.2	75.8	78.2	79.7	80.1	80.5
Chemical products, paper, and ceramics	2,182	93.4	94.0	94.4	95.0	95.6	97.7	99.1	99.6
Steel and metal products	802	88.9	89.7	90.9	92.8	95.6	99.4	100.0	100.0
General machinery	1,414	64.2	65.5	68.7	78.0	83.0	89.4	93.3	100.0
Electrical and electronic machinery	495	40.9	46.1	53.6	62.4	73.0	87.0	95.5	100.0
Textile products, including leather garments	1,089	65.4	68.4	80.4	90.3	93.1	95.1	96.0	97.8
Others	547	71.2	75.7	81.2	82.1	82.8	85.7	88.2	88.2
Total	7,915	74.7	76.6	80.4	84.8	87.7	91.6	93.6	95.4

Note: All figures are as of July 1 of each year. The program for 1986–88 is an announced plan.
a. At the eight-digit level under the CCCN as of 1984.
Source: Ministry of Trade and Industry.

Table 8-7. *Number of Commodity Classes on the Import Source Diversification Notice, 1980–85*

Year	Number[a]	Commodity coverage[b] (percent)
1980	195	19.3
1981	205	20.3
1982	209	20.7
1983	174	17.2
1984	168	16.6
1985	160	15.8

a. At the four-digit level of the CCCN.
b. Relative to the total of 1,010.
Source: Ministry of Trade and Industry.

sification notice declined gradually from 1983 to 1985. In terms of commodity coverage, import surveillance was not important. According to table 8-8, the proportion of commodity classes covered by import surveillance decreased in 1984 and 1985 and as of 1986 did not exceed 2 percent. Nevertheless, by targeting "sensitive" agricultural products and manufactured consumer goods that held potential for a surge in imports, this provision was instrumental in discouraging rapid increases in imports of specific commodities.

It is often suggested that the effects of import licensing liberalization were largely offset by the flexible tariff system. This does not seem to be true. For example, according to the Ministry of Finance, in the first half of 1986 only three items fell under emergency protection and two under adjustment tariff protection. There were no other cases of tariff increases.

The present examination indicates that the approach of Korea's current import liberalization program, which dates back to 1978, was very cautious, as demonstrated in several ways. It was a gradual program that spanned ten years; in addition, at least since 1983, it followed a preannounced commodity schedule of tariff reductions and licensing liberalization. Thus, import licensing liberalization affected a very small portion of

Table 8-8. *Commodity Coverage of Import Surveillance, 1981–85*

Year	Total commodity classes (number)	Commodity classes under surveillance	
		Number	Percentage of total
1981	7,465	193	2.6
1982	7,460	201	2.7
1983	7,460	161	2.1
1984	7,915	125	1.6
1985	7,915	118	1.5

Note: All figures are year-end data.
Source: Ministry of Trade and Industry.

Table 8-9. *Proportion of Imports of Newly Liberalized Items in Total Imports, 1978–84*

(percent)

Year liberalized	Initial year	Second year	Third year	Fourth year
1978	17.8	17.3	14.3	13.0
1979	3.5	3.1	2.7	2.6
1980	2.1	2.6	2.3	2.1
1981	1.8	1.5	2.4	2.2
1982	1.7	1.7	1.3	1.2
1983	3.9	4.6	3.8	—
1984	3.1	2.8	—	—

— Not available.

Note: Newly liberalized items are defined in terms of general import licensing liberalization based on the trade notice.

Source: Ministry of Trade and Industry.

imports each year, as table 8-9 demonstrates. Furthermore, this approach allowed producers ample time to adjust, a pattern that shows up in table 8-6. For example, among the areas in which the ILLR rose most slowly were primary products and food and beverages, as well as the two industrial product categories of general machinery and electrical and electronic machinery. The preannouncement also permitted revision of the plan in response to criticism.

The caution taken with the import liberalization program was also evident in the willingness to leave general tariff rates relatively high at the end of the period. In addition, the import licensing liberalization took place in the presence of not only the general tariffs, but also other devices that could have offset its impact. The import source diversification and import surveillance system, as well as the emergency and adjustment tariffs, served as precautions that could prevent disastrous changes.

These considerations suggest that minimization of the costs of adjustment was a paramount concern of Korea's import liberalization policy. As a result it may have been too cautious to have had a pervasive effect on the structure of industries—at least until 1986. The intention seems to have been to liberalize imports after adjustments were made.

The Pattern of Industrial Development and the Effect of Import Liberalization

For purposes of this review, the years since the beginning of the 1970s are divided into three periods. In the first period, 1970–75, the drive for heavy industrialization had not yet been launched and industrial development largely reflected the thrust of the generally across-the-board promotion of exports initiated in the 1960s. In the next period, the late 1970s (specifically 1976 to 1978–79), the promotion of heavy industry was in full progress. In

Table 8-10. *Growth of Manufacturing Output, Valued
at 1980 Prices, 1971–83*

(percent per year)

Category	1971–83	1971–75	1975–80	1980–83
Light industries	11.0	16.5	10.5	5.0
Food, beverages, and tobacco	9.6	10.6	12.0	6.8
Textiles	12.7	21.8	10.5	4.8
Apparel	13.2	25.8	8.0	6.4
Leather products	16.2	38.0	8.0	4.5
Footwear	14.9	33.5	10.6	0.4
Wood products	6.6	11.1	8.7	−2.3
Rubber products	18.8	20.7	26.6	4.6
Miscellaneous products of petroleum	6.9	7.4	8.0	4.4
Plastic products	10.4	13.2	24.9	2.4
Printing and publishing	9.1	11.2	10.9	3.7
Professional and scientific equipment	23.4	49.2	18.5	2.5
Miscellaneous products	10.1	16.8	8.8	3.7
Heavy industries	16.5	22.6	16.6	8.5
Paper products	12.4	16.2	13.1	6.4
Industrial chemicals	17.6	29.0	16.7	5.1
Other chemical products	15.0	22.4	13.8	7.7
Petroleum products	8.2	7.1	12.6	2.7
Nonmetallic mineral products	12.4	15.9	12.6	7.6
Iron and steel products	22.6	38.7	18.7	9.7
Nonferrous metal products	24.5	28.2	23.7	21.0
Fabricated metal products	19.5	26.2	21.9	7.3
General machinery	21.8	33.2	20.3	10.5
Electrical machinery	25.3	44.1	21.3	9.7
Transport equipment	20.4	28.4	22.4	7.5
Total manufacturing	13.8	19.3	13.7	7.0

Note: The data for each period are the averages of annual figures; the annual figures are the average of the year in question, the year before, and the year after.

Source: Bank of Korea.

the final period, from 1980 through 1986, that policy direction was reversed.

Table 8-10 shows the strong growth of manufacturing since the beginning of the 1970s, particularly in the nontraditional, skill-intensive sectors. The seven fastest-growing industries during 1971–83 were electrical machinery, nonferrous metal products, precision ("professional and scientific") equipment, iron and steel products, general machinery, transport equipment, and fabricated metal products. All but precision equipment were heavy industries. In contrast, the growth of such traditionally important sectors as textiles and apparel was much slower.

Table 8-10 distinguishes between light and heavy industries as defined by the government. It shows that heavy industries began to grow rapidly in the early 1970s, if not sooner. That is to say, the phenomenon of heavy industrialization was already well under way by the time the government's drive was launched, and it was continued after. As a result, through the mid-1980s all heavy industries except paper products, industrial chemicals,

Table 8-11. *Composition of Manufacturing Output, Selected Years, 1971–83*

(percent)

Item	1971	1975	1980	1983
In real terms[a]				
Light industries	56	51	44	42
Heavy industries	44	49	56	58
In nominal terms				
Light industries	62	52	45	43
Heavy industries	38	49	56	57

Note: The annual figures are the average of the year in question, the year before, and the year after. Numbers do not always sum to 100 because of rounding.

a. Output is valued at 1980 prices.

Source: Tables 8-13 and 8-14.

and petroleum products continued to have relatively high rates of growth in contrast to the rest of the manufacturing sector. Such light industries as footwear, wood products, plastic products, precision equipment, and miscellaneous products lagged well behind. At the same time, the growth of output in both the light and heavy industries slowed. Thus, heavy industrialization was associated with a continued slowdown in industrial growth.

The pattern of heavy industrialization in Korea's manufacturing is clearer in table 8-11: heavy industries increased their share of nominal manufacturing output by 20 percentage points between 1971 and 1983. Further details in table 8-12 show that iron and steel products, electrical machinery, transport equipment, and general machinery experienced large real increases in their share of output, while wood products and food, beverages, and tobacco recorded the opposite trend. According to table 8-13, in the course of the push for heavy industrialization, nearly all light industries suffered a decrease in their share of nominal output. In particular, food, beverages, and tobacco, textiles, and wood products experienced sharp declines in their shares. Meanwhile, iron and steel products, petroleum products, electrical machinery, industrial chemicals, transport equipment, and general machinery emerged as major industries. Despite their decline, the shares of such sectors as food, beverages, and tobacco, and textiles and apparel were still large.

These tables make clear that Korean manufacturing experienced both rapid but decelerating growth and heavy industrialization in the 1970s. Through the mid-1980s, however, according to tables 8-11, 8-12, and 8-13, the changes in output share were very small or reversed.

Table 8-14 indicates the role that exports played in the heavy industrialization process: they expanded faster than manufacturing as a whole. Closer examination shows, however, that the role of exports as an engine of growth was pronounced in both the light industries and heavy industries only in the early 1970s. In the late 1970s exports failed to generate dynamic

Table 8-12. *Composition of Manufacturing Output, Valued at 1980 Prices, Selected Years, 1971–83*

(percent)

Category	1971	1975	1980	1983
Light industries	56	51	44	42
Food, beverages, and tobacco	23	17	14	14
Textiles	13	14	13	12
Apparel	4	5	4	4
Leather products	1	1	1	1
Footwear	1	1	1	1
Wood products	4	3	2	2
Rubber products	1	1	2	2
Miscellaneous products of petroleum	4	2	2	2
Plastic products	2	2	2	2
Printing and publishing	2	1	1	1
Professional and scientific equipment	0	1	1	1
Miscellaneous products	2	2	1	1
Heavy industries	44	49	56	58
Paper products	2	2	2	2
Industrial chemicals	5	7	8	7
Other chemical products	3	3	3	3
Petroleum products	16	10	10	9
Nonmetallic mineral products	5	4	4	4
Iron and steel products	4	8	10	11
Nonferrous metal products	1	1	1	2
Fabricated metal products	1	2	2	2
General machinery	2	2	3	4
Electrical machinery	3	6	8	9
Transport equipment	3	4	6	6
Total manufacturing	100	100	100	100

Note: The annual figures are the average of the year in question, the year before, and the year after.

Source: Bank of Korea.

growth in either sector. In the 1980s an asymmetry developed, with significant export-led growth only in the heavy industries.

This asymmetry suggests that Korea had exhausted the room for further increases in the international competitiveness of light industries in the late 1970s. It also suggests that the growth of heavy industries was based on the domestic market in the late 1970s, presumably because of the import-substitution bias of new investments since the mid-1970s and the weakness of market conditions abroad.

Table 8-15 shows that, unlike the export-output ratio, the import penetration ratio, that is, the proportion of imports in apparent domestic consumption, was relatively stable. Nevertheless, a pattern of change can be observed. In the case of light industry, in the early 1970s the changes in the import penetration ratio varied among industries but were generally limited in magnitude. In the heavy industries, however, the import penetration ratio generally decreased, an indication of a definite tendency toward import substitution.

Table 8-13. *Composition of Manufacturing Output, Valued at Current Prices, Selected Years, 1971–83*
(percent)

Category	1971	1975	1980	1983
Light industries	62.3	51.5	44.5	42.7
Food, beverages, and tobacco	21.8	16.0	14.9	15.3
Textiles	18.2	15.5	12.5	11.4
Apparel	5.3	5.1	4.3	4.7
Leather products	0.5	1.0	1.1	1.0
Footwear	0.4	0.7	0.7	0.6
Wood products	4.9	3.1	2.2	1.6
Rubber products	1.3	1.7	2.0	1.9
Miscellaneous products of petroleum	3.0	1.8	1.8	2.0
Plastic products	2.3	1.9	1.6	1.4
Printing and publishing	1.8	1.4	1.2	1.1
Professional and scientific equipment	0.6	1.2	0.8	0.6
Miscellaneous products	2.3	2.1	1.4	1.2
Heavy industries	37.7	48.5	55.5	57.3
Paper products	3.1	2.9	2.1	2.0
Industrial chemicals	4.2	6.5	7.6	7.0
Other chemical products	4.6	4.2	2.8	2.7
Petroleum products	4.4	7.0	9.5	9.8
Nonmetallic mineral products	4.2	3.8	3.9	4.1
Iron and steel products	4.0	7.0	10.1	10.1
Nonferrous metal products	0.6	0.8	1.4	1.8
Fabricated metal products	2.1	1.7	2.3	2.5
General machinery	1.6	2.1	3.2	3.3
Electrical machinery	4.9	8.0	8.4	8.2
Transport equipment	4.0	4.5	4.3	5.8
Total manufacturing	100.0	100.0	100.0	100.0

Note: The annual figures are the average of the year in question, the year before, and the year after.
Source: Bank of Korea.

In the late 1970s import substitution in heavy industry continued. Through the mid-1980s, import penetration grew in nearly all areas, with the important exceptions of food, beverages, and tobacco; iron and steel products; and nonferrous metal products. This pattern indicates that effective import liberalization was under way.

According to table 8-16, heavy industrialization was more dramatic in the export sectors than in manufacturing as a whole. The share of manufactured exports of heavy industry rose from 22 percent to 56 percent over the 1971–82 period. This trend was, however, natural, given that heavy industrialization was led by exports.

According to table 8-17, at the beginning of the 1970s textiles dominated Korea's exports of manufactures. Textiles, apparel, and wood products accounted for half of total exports and two-thirds of exports of light manufactures. Light manufactures themselves accounted for nearly 80 percent of the exports of manufactures. Since then, however, the share of textiles has been halved, while exports of wood products nearly disappeared. As a

**Table 8-14. *Export-Output Ratio by Industry, Selected Years,
1971–83***

(percent)

Category	1971	1975	1980	1983
Light industries				
Food, beverages, and tobacco	2	7	8	6
Textiles	26	38	38	41
Apparel	46	70	74	67
Leather products	23	48	42	40
Footwear	51	30	63	100
Wood products	41	45	33	18
Rubber products	28	45	38	28
Miscellaneous products of petroleum	0	1	2	2
Plastic products	4	18	10	8
Printing and publishing	1	9	7	8
Professional and scientific equipment	11	35	62	68
Miscellaneous products	61	49	64	64
Heavy industries				
Paper products	1	4	6	4
Industrial chemicals	7	6	11	12
Other chemical products	1	2	2	3
Petroleum products	3	7	1	7
Nonmetallic mineral products	5	14	15	12
Iron and steel products	16	22	21	22
Nonferrous metal products	16	9	13	8
Fabricated metal products	10	39	45	53
General machinery	15	21	17	28
Electrical machinery	25	36	33	45
Transport equipment	4	22	46	90
Total manufacturing	15	24	24	28

Note: The export data in the Standard International Trade Classification (SITC) have been
reclassified by the Korean Standard International Trade Classification (KSIC) and converted at
the average exchange rate for each year. The annual figures are the average of the year in
question, the year before, and the year after.

Source: Author's calculations using Korea Development Institute trade tapes and Bank of
Korea.

result, the export share of light manufactures itself fell drastically. In the
meantime, transport equipment, electrical machinery, iron and steel products, and fabricated metal products emerged as the major export products
and sharply raised the overall share of heavy industry in exports.

Table 8-16 is somewhat surprising because it shows limited but clear
heavy industrialization in imports that parallels the heavy industrialization
of domestic production. According to table 8-18, at the beginning of the
1970s imports of manufactures came mainly from heavy industry. Since
then, despite the growth of heavy industry in Korea, the preponderance of
imports of those products continued to grow, with increases in the shares of
electrical machinery and transport equipment. This trend stopped during
the late 1970s but picked up again in the 1980s.

Table 8-15. *Import Penetration Ratio by Industry, Selected Years, 1971–83*

(percent)

Category	1971	1975	1980	1983
Light industries	13	14	14	13
Food, beverages, and tobacco	14	11	13	7
Textiles	20	21	17	19
Apparel	1	1	1	4
Leather products	25	56	49	58
Footwear	0	0	0	0
Wood products	2	2	4	8
Rubber products	3	3	4	6
Miscellaneous products of petroleum	1	1	3	3
Plastic products	3	3	2	4
Printing and publishing	4	3	4	4
Professional and scientific equipment	44	40	59	75
Miscellaneous products	15	13	22	27
Heavy industries	34	30	25	27
Paper products	18	19	21	19
Industrial chemicals	45	36	29	30
Other chemical products	10	10	13	14
Petroleum products	4	4	7	7
Nonmetallic mineral products	5	6	6	7
Iron and steel products	43	31	19	16
Nonferrous metal products	44	45	33	25
Fabricated metal products	33	27	27	27
General machinery	77	69	56	56
Electrical machinery	39	35	29	40
Transport equipment	38	42	45	81
Total manufacturing	23	24	21	22

Note: The import data in the SITC have been reclassified by the KSIC and converted at the average exchange rate for each year. The annual figures are the average of the year in question, the year before, and the year after.

Source: Author's calculations using Korea Development Institute trade tapes and Bank of Korea.

Table 8-16. *Composition of Trade in Manufactures, Selected Years, 1971–82*

(percent)

Category	1971	1975	1980	1982
Exports				
Light industries	78	65	56	44
Heavy industries	22	35	44	56
Imports				
Light industries	30	25	26	23
Heavy industries	70	75	74	77

Note: The annual figures are the average of the year in question, the year before, and the year after.

Source: Tables 8-12 and 8-13.

Table 8-17. *Composition of Manufactures Exports, Selected Years, 1971–83*

(percent)

Category	1971	1975	1980	1983
Light industries	78	65	56	44
Food, beverages, and tobacco	3	5	5	3
Textiles	31	25	20	17
Apparel	16	15	13	11
Leather products	1	2	2	2
Footwear	1	1	2	3
Wood products	13	6	3	1
Rubber products	3	3	3	2
Miscellaneous products of petroleum	0	0	0	0
Plastic products	1	1	1	0
Printing and publishing	0	1	0	0
Professional and scientific equipment	0	2	2	2
Miscellaneous products	9	4	4	3
Heavy industries	22	35	44	56
Paper products	0	0	1	0
Industrial chemicals	2	2	4	3
Other chemical products	0	0	0	0
Petroleum products	1	2	0	3
Nonmetallic mineral products	1	2	2	2
Iron and steel products	4	7	9	8
Nonferrous metal products	1	0	1	1
Fabricated metal products	1	3	4	5
General machinery	2	2	2	3
Electrical machinery	8	12	12	13
Transport equipment	1	4	8	18
Total manufacturing	100	100	100	100

Note: The annual figures are the average of the year in question, the year before, and the year after. Numbers do not always sum to 100 because of rounding.

Source: Korea Development Institute trade tapes.

Parallel increases in heavy industries' share in both exports and imports show that domestic heavy industries were not integrated vertically. There was a high degree of international vertical intraindustry specialization in heavy industry, with domestic productive activities devoted largely to the processing and assembly of imported materials and parts. The import composition shown in table 8-2 suggests this pattern as well. The implication is that, to an important degree, Korea's imports were complements to, rather than substitutes for, domestic production. Insofar as import liberalization in Korea covered heavy industries, one of its consequences was thus increased intraindustry specialization in these industries, leading to increases in both domestic production and imports of heavy industry goods.

Table 8-19 shows the incidence of import licensing liberalization by industry from 1977 through 1984. It reveals that the program deeply affected heavy industries as well as light industries, although protection may initially have been relatively less important in such sectors as textiles. Table

Table 8-18. *Composition of Manufactures Imports, Selected Years, 1971–83*

(percent)

Category	1971	1975	1980	1983
Light industries	30	25	26	23
Food, beverages, and tobacco	13	8	10	6
Textiles	13	11	8	8
Apparel	0	0	0	0
Leather products	1	3	3	4
Footwear	0	0	0	0
Wood products	0	0	0	1
Rubber products	0	0	0	0
Miscellaneous products of petroleum	0	0	0	0
Plastic products	0	0	0	0
Printing and publishing	2	2	3	3
Professional and scientific equipment	1	1	1	1
Miscellaneous products	1	1	1	1
Heavy industries	70	75	74	77
Paper products	3	3	3	2
Industrial chemicals	13	15	13	13
Other chemical products	2	2	2	2
Petroleum products	1	1	3	4
Nonmetallic mineral products	1	1	1	1
Iron and steel products	10	10	9	7
Nonferrous metal products	2	3	3	3
Fabricated metal products	4	2	2	2
General machinery	17	16	17	15
Electrical machinery	9	12	12	15
Transport equipment	9	11	9	13
Total manufacturing	100	100	100	100

Note: The annual figures are the average of the year in question, the year before, and the year after. Numbers do not always sum to 100 because of rounding.

Source: Korea Development Institute trade tapes.

8-20 shows the index of intraindustry trade for the years since 1976 using both the Grubel-Lloyd and the Michaely indexes. (The Grubel-Lloyd index increases, and the Michaely index decreases, with the intensity of intraindustry trade.) By either measure, intraindustry trade has increased significantly since 1976, and especially since 1978. Thus, substantial progress has been made in intraindustry specialization since the import liberalization was begun.

The relative export-import ratio shown in table 8-21 should reflect both Korea's comparative advantage and policy distortions, such as import restrictions. The table suggests that Korea had an undisputedly strong comparative advantage in such products as footwear, apparel, rubber products, miscellaneous products, and textiles in the early 1970s. Overall, light industries continued to enjoy a comparative advantage, but their strength declined steadily from the early 1970s through the early 1980s. In contrast, heavy industries in general lacked a comparative advantage, although spe-

Table 8-19. *Import Licensing Liberalization Ratio (ILLR)*
by Industry, Selected Years, 1977–84

Category	Total imported items, 1977	ILLR (percent)			
		1977	1980	1983	1984
Light industries					
Food, beverages, and tobacco	191	49	45	60	61
Textiles	227	40	70	81	90
Apparel	75	21	42	74	91
Leather products	32	66	87	91	100
Footwear	9	44	100	100	100
Wood products	50	72	82	90	100
Rubber products	26	39	92	91	92
Miscellaneous products of petroleum	12	92	100	100	100
Plastic products	14	0	93	100	100
Printing and publishing	17	82	88	94	94
Professional and scientific equipment	72	57	60	67	75
Miscellaneous products	62	34	54	64	70
Heavy industries					
Paper products	42	45	88	93	93
Industrial chemicals	305	48	77	83	84
Other chemical products	107	87	96	97	98
Petroleum products	17	94	100	100	100
Nonmetallic mineral products	99	58	86	91	91
Iron and steel products	92	57	76	80	84
Nonferrous metal products	76	82	90	89	89
Fabricated metal products	82	61	85	94	95
General machinery	278	49	54	65	70
Electrical machinery	137	20	29	48	56
Transport equipment	81	32	31	37	46
Total manufacturing	2,093	50	67	76	80

Note: The import licensing liberalization ratio is the number of items automatically approved for import relative to the total number of items imported. Commodities have been counted in accordance with Korea's tariff lines.
Source: Trade tapes of the Office of Customs Administration.

cific products such as iron and steel products, fabricated metal products, and transport equipment (ships at that time) rapidly improved their position during the period.

It is interesting to note that starting from very low bases, the relative export-import ratios for such sectors as paper products, industrial chemicals, nonferrous metal products, and electrical machinery increased for a while but then declined in the early 1980s. The recent import liberalization seems to have been a factor in this process.

The preceding analysis suggests that the pattern of Korea's trade and industry responded rather sensitively to the changes in industrial and im-

Table 8-20. *Index of Intraindustry Trade for all Industries, Selected Years, 1976–84*

(percent)

Year	Grubel-Lloyd index	Michaely index
1976	52.0	95.7
1978	52.3	95.8
1979	55.6	88.7
1980	58.0	82.2
1981	56.4	82.7
1982	55.5	84.7
1983	58.7	75.4
1984	62.7	66.5

Note: Grubel-Lloyd index $= 100 \cdot \dfrac{\sum ([X_i + M_i] - |X_i - M_i|)}{\sum (X_i + M_i)}$

Michaely index $= 100 \cdot \sum |\dfrac{X_i}{\sum X_i} - \dfrac{M_i}{\sum M_i}|$

where X and M denote exports and imports, respectively, and the subscript i signifies the ith industry.

Source: Korea Development Institute trade tapes.

port policies. Korea's heavy industrialization, which was well under way by the mid-1970s, was associated with a decreasing level of import penetration in heavy industry in general throughout the 1970s. During that period Korea's import policy remained essentially protectionist, and import liberalization was initiated only toward the end of the decade. From 1975 to 1980, in particular, the share of imports of heavy industry manufactures stopped rising. Meanwhile, the level of intraindustry trade remained stationary.

After the liberalization of imports began at the end of the 1970s, however, import penetration rose, particularly in heavy industries, and heavy industries' share of manufactured imports also grew. The index of intraindustry trade rose at the same time. It is not possible to pinpoint the role of import liberalization in these developments, but there is a strong presumption that it has played a substantial part in promoting Korea's industrial adjustment since the late 1970s, especially with respect to intraindustry specialization in heavy industries.

Pattern of Adjustment to Import Liberalization at the Firm Level

It is the individual firm that bears the brunt of import liberalization. Given an actual or anticipated flow of imports, import-substituting producers try to survive international competition at home by cutting production costs, improving product quality, developing new varieties of products, and developing new production and marketing technologies in support of these

Table 8-21. *Relative Export-Import Ratio by Industry, Selected Years, 1971–83*
(percent)

Category	1971	1975	1980	1983
Light industries	2.58	2.21	2.17	1.92
Food, beverages, and tobacco	0.21	0.64	0.51	0.57
Textiles	2.35	2.27	2.55	2.25
Apparel	262.33	178.57	225.54	36.54
Leather products	1.53	0.74	0.64	0.51
Footwear	829.03	455.98	1,376.62	811.49
Wood products	70.33	52.49	9.74	1.79
Rubber products	20.58	30.46	14.23	4.15
Miscellaneous products of petroleum	0.14	0.53	0.56	0.56
Plastic products	2.48	7.29	3.71	1.66
Printing and publishing	0.55	3.27	1.48	1.48
Professional and scientific equipment	0.26	0.80	0.66	0.50
Miscellaneous products	14.90	6.35	5.43	3.49
Heavy industries	0.31	0.46	0.60	0.73
Paper products	0.06	0.16	0.20	0.13
Industrial chemicals	0.15	0.11	0.27	0.23
Other chemical products	0.20	0.16	0.15	0.13
Petroleum products	1.38	1.97	0.12	0.70
Nonmetallic mineral products	1.65	2.79	2.18	1.26
Iron and steel products	0.43	0.63	0.99	1.07
Nonferrous metal products	0.41	0.21	0.26	0.19
Fabricated metal products	0.39	1.70	1.94	2.21
General machinery	0.09	0.11	0.14	0.23
Electrical machinery	0.88	1.04	1.03	0.90
Transport equipment	0.12	0.37	0.90	1.45
Total manufacturing	1.00	1.00	1.00	1.00
Export ÷ imports	0.58	1.01	1.16	1.37

Note: The ratio for all manufactures is defined as 1.00. The annual figures are the average of the year in question, the year before, and the year after.
Source: Korea Development Institute trade tapes.

efforts. Should these attempts fail, import-substituting firms will cut their production, sales, employment, and investment. Depending on the severity of their difficulties, they may even cease operation. Closure or contraction in operation releases resources for reallocation to other more competitive lines of production and thereby affects what may be called interfirm industrial adjustment.

Central to the policy debate on import liberalization was concern about the possible adverse effects on import-substituting firms and the scope of the consequent interfirm adjustments. Contrary to the fear expressed by critics, however, there is no evidence that much interfirm adjustment resulted from import liberalization. One study reports that Korea Optics, the only domestic producer of the 16-millimeter camera, went out of operation in 1982 because of competition from imports (Oh and Kim 1986). Import licensing of that product, however, was not liberalized until 1984. Clearly liberalization of import licensing was the result rather than the cause of the bankruptcy of Korea Optics. Government reports do not contain a single case of firm failure that is specifically attributable to import liberalization (Korea, Ministry of Finance 1984 and Korea, Ministry of Trade and Industry 1985).

In contrast, success stories abound. Washing machines, refrigerators, and tape recorders are examples of products where the effects of international competition were much feared. Table 8-22 provides examples of improvements in quality that enabled domestic producers to survive international competition. Liberalization of import licensing must have provided a strong incentive to improve product quality.

The lack of clear-cut cases of firms adversely affected by import liberalization may be explained by several factors other than sampling errors. First, the measures that were implemented added up to an import liberalization program that had limited success, as discussed earlier in this chapter. Second, in the case of many of the commodities covered by the program, Korea either was already internationally competitive, as in many light industry products, or had no domestic substitutes, as was the case with many heavy industry products, especially those of "upstream" industries. The Ministry of Trade and Industry regarded such items as targets of early import liberalization (Young 1984a; Kim 1991). Third, import liberalization measures were administered gradually and cautiously, as noted, to avoid any serious hardship for domestic firms. The effect of import liberalization was cushioned by the flexible adjustments of the exchange rate and the stabilization of wages and prices at the macroeconomic level, among other measures. It was also blunted by the government's increased support for small and medium-size firms. In addition, the government provided firm-specific support.

The government seems to have wanted any adjustment caused by import liberalization to be of the intrafirm variety and made efforts to ensure that

Table 8-22. *Product Improvement Following Import Licensing Liberalization*

Product	Year of liberalization	Changes, 1980–85
Washing machines	1983	Consumption of electricity dropped by 20 percent, that of water by 10 percent. Product made rust-proof.
Refrigerators	1983	Temperature control made flexible for both cooling and freezing. Energy saving of 38 percent. Noise level reduced by 40 percent.
Tape recorders	1984	Output level raised from 1 watt to 2.4 watts. Noise-removal function added. Knob-gilding made corrosion-free.

Source: Office of Industry Promotion, Ministry of Trade and Industry.

Table 8-23. *Adjustment Indicators for the Home Kitchen and Table Glassware (CCCN 7013) Industry, 1976–85*

Year	General tariffs (percent)	Number of firms	Tons of total production (A)	Tons of domestic shipments (B)	Tons of imports (C)	Korean domestic market share, B/(B + C)
1977	80 (60)[a]	45	24,901	23,818	165	99.3
1978	60	47	35,451	33,666	439	98.7
1979	60	43	34,208	31,567	2,265	93.3
1980	60	39	33,098	27,774	625	97.8
1981	50	40	15,851	8,195	579	93.4
1982	50 (85)[b]	39	17,918	10,422	1,272	89.1
1983	50 (60)[b]	46	15,761	8,793	1,513	85.3
1984	40	—	—	—	—	—
1985	40	—	—	—	—	—

— Not available.

Note: The general discretionary import licensing was liberalized in 1978; import surveillance was introduced in July 1979; import diversification notice in July 1984; import licensing was completely liberalized in July 1985.

a. Tentative contingency tariff.

b. Emergency contingency tariff.

Source: Korea Glassware Producers' Association.

existing firms survived import liberalization. The focus of these efforts was small and medium-size firms, which, as mentioned, received special support. In addition, the Office of Industry Promotion under the Ministry of Trade and Industry adopted a special program to assist efforts by these firms to improve products threatened by import liberalization. It has been reported that import liberalization of a product—or its mere announcement—invariably was accompanied by increased requests to the office for such assistance (Korea, Ministry of Trade and Industry 1985).

Furthermore, import liberalization itself was often delayed as long as firms were having difficulty adjusting. This approach may be illustrated by the experience of import liberalization in the area of home kitchen and table glassware (Customs Co-operation Council Nomenclature, or cccn, 7013). This category was taken off the trade notice in 1978. After a subsequent fivefold increase in imports, it was placed under import surveillance, and import growth was reversed. In 1981 its general tariff rate was reduced from 60 percent to 50 percent. Once again, imports rose, a trend that prompted the Ministry of Finance to raise the tariffs to 85 percent in 1983 under the emergency tariff provision. In the meantime, however, as table 8-23 shows, industrial adjustment was proceeding gradually. In 1984 the government lowered the general tariff to 40 percent and the emergency tariff to 60 percent; at the same time, it moved the products from the import surveillance notice to an import diversification notice. In 1985 their licensing was completely liberalized.

There are also many cases in which import liberalization was postponed indefinitely because of adjustment difficulties. The problems of the synthetic fiber, alloyed steel, automobile, heavy construction equipment, diesel engine, and heavy electrical machinery industries dated back to the heavy industrialization drive of the 1970s. None of these industries could have been taken off the trade notice, and only recently did the government announce three-to-four-year rationalization plans for them.

The foregoing discussion suggests that the Korean government took maximum precautions to prevent import liberalization from forcing negative adjustment on domestic firms. As a result, it appears that the import liberalization program itself was left rather ineffectual. At the same time, there is also some evidence that import liberalization affected many domestic firms and induced their intrafirm adjustment. The results cited earlier in this chapter are consistent with this hypothesis, and the episodes discussed at the beginning of the present section provide further evidence.

This conclusion is confirmed by a survey of Korean firms conducted by the Overseas Development Institute (odi) of Dongkuk University. The odi selected 311 products from among those with liberalized imports in 1983 and 1984. The items involved all had shown substantial import volume and rapid import growth.[11] The odi then chose 207 firms that produced one or more of these products and asked them to answer questions about their

Table 8-24. *Responses of Firms to the Survey on the Impact of Import Liberalization*

Item	Unaffected	Raised	Lowered
Total sales	52.6	21.3	26.0
Domestic sales/total sales	82.1	5.3	12.6
Domestic market share	77.4	2.9	19.7
Output prices	76.3	7.2	16.5
Production costs	88.8	6.9	4.3
Net profit/sales	82.8	2.3	14.9
Marketing expenses	57.8	39.8	2.4
Technology development	46.8	48.4	4.8
Technology level	50.7	45.5	3.8
Product quality	57.4	39.0	3.6
Competitiveness	48.4	26.3	33.5

Source: Overseas Development Institute (1985).

impressions of the import liberalization and the steps they had taken to adjust to it. A total of 987 responses was collected, a figure that may be interpreted as the number of respondent firms weighted by the number of products they produced.

Table 8-24 provides a brief summary of the survey results, which revealed that import liberalization affected total firm sales in about 47 percent of the cases, representing a large but not overwhelming number. It did not, however, affect the proportion of domestic sales in total sales or the domestic market share in more than three-quarters of the cases. Moreover, in the vast majority of cases, output prices, production costs, and the net profit-sales ratio remained unaffected. Import liberalization thus did not affect the market performance of a majority of the import-competing producers.

Nevertheless, it did influence the behavior of the firms. For instance, import liberalization affected marketing strategy in 77 percent of the cases surveyed, as evidenced in part by a rise in marketing expenses. In addition, in close to a majority of cases import liberalization stimulated technological and other development efforts. In a very large number of cases firms reported that they had upgraded both their technology and product quality.

In cases where import liberalization affected market performance, the result was more often negative than positive from the point of view of the firm. Total sales, domestic sales, domestic market share, output price, and net profit ratio all declined, while production costs increased.

The ODI survey produced other interesting results, as reported in summary form in table 8-25. Technology development was identified as a major response of firms to import liberalization, and in most cases quality improvement and new product development received the highest priority in these efforts. Development and substitution of new materials and productivity improvement were also important aims of the technological efforts.

In the ranking of factors that discouraged technological efforts, fear of an irrational consumer preference for foreign products was the most fre-

Table 8-25. *Distribution of Firm Responses to Survey on the Impact of Import Liberalization*

Response	Percent
Technological development stimulated	
by import liberalization	
Quality improvement	36.9
New product development	35.3
Substitution of materials	14.7
Productivity improvement	10.2
Other	2.9
Sources of new technology	
Own development	52.9
Foreign technology licensing	32.6
Joint development with domestic research institutes	6.1
Joint investment with foreigners	5.7
No response	2.7
Factors that discourage technological efforts	
Fear of irrational consumer preference	24.5
Fear of dumping by foreigners	12.2
Insufficient time	11.0
Reduced profitability	9.7
No response	42.6
Factors that prevent import liberalization from raising	
international competitiveness	
Technological incapability	21.0
Firm too small in size	17.8
Outdated equipment	13.0
Insufficient government incentives	8.3
Managerial incapability	6.8
No response	33.1

Source: Overseas Development Institute (1985, tables 14, 15, 16, and 10).

quently cited; foreign dumping was also identified as a real threat. Some firms thought that import liberalization came too early for them to be interested in technology and market developments.

Finally, the table lists the factors that prevented import liberalization from leading to strengthened international competitiveness, including lack of technological capability, inadequate firm size, outdated equipment, lack of government support, and lack of managerial capability.

The ODI survey had shortcomings. One was its exclusive reliance on the respondent firms' subjective opinions. Another was the multiple-choice format of the questionnaire. Nevertheless, it is quite useful because it confirmed that import liberalization has touched a large number of firms in each affected industry.

Conclusions

This chapter examined Korea's current import liberalization program, as well as some evidence about the related patterns of adjustment by industries and firms. The program was adopted and strengthened to promote industrial adjustment, especially in heavy industry, where government intervention and protection had nurtured inefficient and excessive import substitution.

This chapter has not shown a specific pattern of industrial adjustment to import liberalization, but it has established a strong presumption that the program contributed to an acceleration of heavy industrialization in recent years, in particular promoting intraindustry specialization.

A striking conclusion is that, at least as of 1986, Korea's import liberalization had not led to broad-based industrial dislocation or much interfirm adjustment. A major reason seems to have been that the program involved largely the liberalization of the general discretionary import licensing of manufactures and took place in the presence of relatively high tariffs and other safeguards. Its salient characteristic was gradual liberalization over a number of years according to a preannounced, phased timetable. Thus, the program, which was to be completed in 1988, left a level of protection that was still substantial, and it allowed postponement of real import liberalization where adjustment presented difficulties to firms. For all these reasons, the program should be regarded as rather modest in the effective import liberalization it was to achieve.

The discussion in this chapter has also shown that modest as the program may have been, it led to some real adjustment. It facilitated imports of commodities in which there were no import-competing firms. The production and trade statistics suggest that this trend occurred in such heavy industry sectors as electrical machinery and transport equipment. As a result there was an increase in intraindustry specialization and trade in heavy industry.

Where there were import-competing domestic firms, there seems to have been a substantial degree of interfirm adjustment. While the speed of adjustment was often moderated considerably by offsetting protection, some firms curtailed their operations, and a larger number seem to have tried to gain international competitiveness through technological advances and other measures.

These patterns of import liberalization and the consequent industrial adjustment show that the Korean government assigned an important role to import liberalization as an instrument of industry promotion. It tried to minimize interfirm adjustment while promoting intrafirm adjustment with assistance from supportive macroeconomic and industrial policies. Viewed in this way, Korea's approach to import liberalization since the late 1970s may be characterized as one that minimized the cost of adjustment but maximized the role of import liberalization as an instrument of infant-industry promotion. The assumption associated with the latter point is that domestic firms lacking international competitiveness were either X-inefficient, infant firms, or both. Under this assumption, gradual import liberalization under a preannounced program would promote the firms by pressuring for the removal of the X-inefficiencies and for learning by doing.

The evidence seems to indicate that this approach to import liberalization worked to a significant degree. This success does not mean that inter-firm adjustment to import liberalization can be avoided altogether. While the need for such adjustment can be reduced, it cannot be eliminated entirely. Some firms and industries will simply prove unviable and will have to go. Adjustment of this nature seems to have been postponed under the import liberalization program and will have to be addressed in the next phase.

Another phase of import liberalization is necessary to complete the initial industrial adjustment effort. Progress will have to be made along at least three lines in this phase. First, all the remaining manufactured products will need to be removed from the trade notice, including those with so-called rationalization problems. Second, the roles and administration of the import-source diversification and import surveillance systems will have to be critically reviewed and possibly reformed in the spirit of import liberalization.[12] Surveillance seems to be redundant in view of the availability of the contingency tariff protection. Third, the level of the general tariffs on manufactures will have to be lowered substantially to complement the liberalization of quantitative restrictions. In addition, rationalization of agricultural protection is a matter that has to be seriously addressed within a long-term perspective despite the immediate political and social constraints. Further, the system of contingency tariff protection may have to be reformed in order to minimize the potential for protectionist abuse.

Finally, it is acknowledged that this chapter does not offer a fully satisfactory study of the impact of import liberalization. Future exploration of the considerable amount of objective information on the responses to import liberalization of individual firms producing specific commodities would be helpful. The most useful information would include knowledge about nominal and effective protection and the way it has changed over time, as well as detailed disaggregated statistics on production, trade, and employment.

Notes

This paper was first drafted when the author was visiting the Trade Policy Research Center in London during 1985–86 as a Ford Foundation fellow. The author acknowledges his indebtedness to Seong-Yun Kang of the Korea Development Institute for his most able research assistance and also thanks Johannes F. Linn and Chong-Hyun Nam of the World Bank for their helpful comments on an earlier draft.

1. This assumption underlay the Fifth Five-Year Plan, 1982–86 (Korea, Economic Planning Board, 1981).

2. See K. S. Kim (1991) for a discussion of economic conditions in Korea during the 1970s and early 1980s.

3. See the next section for a further discussion of this period of liberalization.

4. Data are from various issues of Korea, Economic Planning Board, *Major Economic Statistics*; various issues of General Agreement on Tariffs and Trade, *International Trade*; and various issues of Organisation for Economic Co-operation and Development, *Foreign Trade by Commodities*.

5. There has been no vigorous analysis of the heavy industrialization policy of the 1970s. Young and others (1982) provide a critical perspective, while Kim (1984) also provides a historical perspective.

6. Young and others (1982) contains the proposal.

7. The debate is summarized in Young (1984a and 1984b).

8. Discretionary import licensing was based on the Trade Transactions Law. There were thirty-seven other laws of a regulatory nature—so-called special laws—that authorized the appropriate ministries to restrict trade in specific commodities for particular purposes (Pharmacist Law, Food Hygiene Law, Quarantine Law, Grain Management Law, Livestock Law, Law Regarding Imports and Circulation of Foreign Periodicals, Law for Safety of Electrical Appliances, Industrial Standards Law, and Law for Quality Management of Manufactured Products are examples). Protection of domestic industries was not by itself a formal objective of these laws, except in a few cases such as the Grain Management Law and Livestock Law. These examples, however, suggest that even when exceptions are put aside, whether intended or not, these laws afforded considerable room for protection of domestic industries.

9. See Kim and Westphal (1976) on Korea's early import policy.

10. The history of Korea's import policy since the early 1970s is discussed in detail in Young (1984a) and Kim (1991).

11. Imports in excess of $100,000 at the cccn eight-digit level.

12. The special laws mentioned in note 8 should also be reviewed critically from this perspective.

References

General Agreement on Tariffs and Trade. Various issues. *International Trade*. Geneva.

Kim, Kihwan. 1984. *The Korean Economy: Past Performance, Current Reforms and Future Prospects*. Seoul: Korea Development Institute.

Kim, Kwang Suk. 1991. "Korea." In Demetris Papageorgiou, Michael Michaely, and Armeane M. Choksi, eds., *Liberalizing Foreign Trade*. Vol. 2, *The Experience of Korea, the Philippines, and Singapore*. Cambridge, Mass.: Basil Blackwell.

Kim, Kwang Suk, and L. E. Westphal. 1976. *The Exchange and Trade Policies of Korea*. Seoul: Korea Development Institute.

Korea, Economic Planning Board. 1981. *The Fifth Five-Year Plan for Economic and Social Development, 1982–1986*. Seoul.

———. 1986. *Major Statistics of Foreign Economy*. Seoul.

———. Various issues. *Major Economic Indicators*. Seoul.

Korea, Ministry of Finance. 1984. *Efforts of Economic Liberalization*. Seoul. In Korean.

Korea, Ministry of Trade and Industry. 1983. *Guidelines for Preparation of the Trade Notice for 1983–1984*. Seoul. In Korean.

―――. 1985. *Import Liberalization and Appropriate Responses*. Seoul. In Korean.

Oh, Dong-hee, and Dae-sik Kim. 1986. *Effects of Import Liberalization*. Seoul: Korea Institute for Economics and Technology. In Korean.

Organisation for Economic Co-operation and Development. Various issues. *Foreign Trade by Commodities*. Geneva.

Overseas Development Institute. 1985. *An Analysis of the Impact of Import Liberalization*. Dongkuk University, Seoul. In Korean.

Young, Soo-Gil. 1984a. "Problems of Trade Liberalization in Korea." Paper presented at research meeting on Participation of the Developing Countries in the International Trading System, Trade Policy Research Centre, Wiston House, United Kingdom, October 1984. (Forthcoming as a Thames Essay, Trade Policy Research Centre.)

―――. 1984b. "Import Liberalization and the Management of Economy." *Korean Economic Journal* 23(4)(December). In Korean.

Young, Soo-Gil, Jung-ho Yoo, Seung-jin Kim, and Jae-won Kim. 1982. *The Basic Role and a New Direction of Industrial Policy*. Seoul: Korea Development Institute. In Korean.

9 Industrial Organization: Issues and Recent Developments

KYU-UCK LEE, Korea Development Institute
SHUJIRO URATA, Waseda University
INBOM CHOI, The World Bank

THE DEVELOPMENT POLICY pursued by the government of Korea in the 1960s and 1970s included major initiatives to achieve rapid economic growth in a short period. As part of this effort, the government set quantitative targets in every economic area. Reaching these targets became the highest priority, and the quantitative aspect of production was strongly emphasized. Little attention was given to the qualitative aspects of this quantitative growth. Government policy stressed industrial structure (the relationship among different sectors, such as machinery and textiles) rather than industrial organization (the relationship among firms within one sector or across sectors) throughout the period of rapid economic growth in the 1960s and 1970s.

In the early 1980s the Korean economy was beset by adverse changes in both the domestic and international economic environment. Global stagflation following the second oil shock and new protectionism aggravated the economic conditions facing the country. Within Korea, supply and demand imbalances, caused largely by aggressive policies to promote heavy and chemical industrialization, started to appear. In addition to these economic problems, Korea had to deal with abrupt political changes. In the midst of all these events, the most important task was to set the economy on a proper long-term track.

With the scale of the economy growing bigger and industrial relationships becoming more complicated and diversified, the market began to replace government planning as the mechanism for allocating resources. As this change took place the importance of industrial organization loomed large. The general consensus was that the economy had to be ruled by the free interplay of economic agents in the market to enhance efficiency. At the same time, more attention had to be paid to promoting equity among various sectors and groups.

The government set about addressing these issues in the 1980s. For example, it launched a liberalization policy in all areas of the economy, along with measures to support this initiative. During this period the government-led economy that had prevailed until then was rapidly transformed into what was supposed to be a market economy.

This chapter focuses on the background and substance of the liberalization policy within the framework of industrial organization and assesses the changes in the relationships between market structure and market performance before and after the change in policies. The analysis considers only static efficiency, although the effects of the changes in policies over time should also be measured. The chapter first describes and discusses the market structure by focusing on domestic factors in the 1970s and 1980s (see chapter 8 of this volume for an analysis of foreign trade). The second section summarizes the main characteristics of the industrial organization policies adopted during the period. Market performance is then analyzed in light of the changes in market structure and industrial organization policies. Both domestic and foreign factors influencing the market structure are examined. Concluding comments are presented in the final section.

Market Structure in the 1970s and 1980s

The 1970s were a period of dramatic and rapid economic growth for Korea. To pursue the basic economic strategy of expanding the scale of the economy as quickly as possible, manufacturing rather than agriculture, export industry rather than domestic industry, and large corporations rather than small ones received high priority. The government intervened deeply in the market mechanism, designating steel, machinery, chemicals, and shipbuilding as the strategic industries and assisting their growth through various measures, including financial, fiscal, and trade policies. The government could not, however, avoid side effects such as monopolistic or oligopolistic market structures, concentration of economic power, and disruption of market functions. These byproducts can be considered characteristic of industrial organization in Korea.

A useful starting point in analyzing this new policy is to look at the sequence of changes in the level of concentration, an important indicator of market structure, and then at the reasons for these changes. Table 9-1 shows that in the 1970s the market share of manufacturing of the top 100 firms (overall concentration ratio) increased steadily to as much as 46.8 percent in 1982 when measured by shipments. The magnitude of the concentration seems to have been even more prominent, considering that the number of firms rose substantially throughout the 1970s. A comparison of Korea with Japan and Taiwan in table 9-2 indicates that the level of concentration in Korea was significantly higher. The differences are mainly attributable to different government policies: unlike the policy in Japan or Taiwan, in Korea the government strongly encouraged the establishment of large firms during the 1970s to take advantage of scale economies in the heavy and chemical industries (Scitovsky 1985).

In Korea a monopolistic and oligopolistic structure was most evident in the commodity market. Defining as monopolistic or oligopolistic a market

Table 9-1. *Overall Concentration Ratio, 1970, 1977, and 1982*
(percent)

Item	1970	1977	1982
Market share of manufacturing by shipment			
Top 50 firms	33.8	35.0	37.5
Top 100 firms	44.6	44.9	46.8
Market share of manufacturing by employment			
Top 50 firms	15.4	16.9	16.0
Top 100 firms	28.7	23.9	31.9
Share of top 100 firms in total number of manufacturing firms[a]	0.41	0.38	0.28

Note: Data for 1970 are for plants; data for 1977 and 1982 are for corporations.
a. Share = (100/total number of firms) × 100.

in which the top three firms account for more than 60 percent of the total share, the ratios of the commodity markets in Korea so characterized in 1970, 1977, and 1982 were all around 85 percent in the number of products and 65 percent in the value of shipments (table 9-3).[1] It is noteworthy that the total number of commodities increased by about 720 items (about 49 percent) between 1970 and 1977, while the number of competitive commodities increased by only 67.

The share of commodities classified as monopoly increased between 1970 and 1977 and then declined between 1977 and 1982, while the share classified as oligopoly increased dramatically between 1977 and 1982 after a slight decline between 1970 and 1977. These developments can be explained by the behavior of business groups during the period. As will be reviewed in detail later, business groups intensified operations in their specialized fields from 1970 to 1977, which led to greater concentration at

Table 9-2. *Overall Concentration Ratio by Shipment in Korea, Japan, and Taiwan, Selected Years, 1970–82*
(percent)

	Korea		Japan	Taiwan	
Year	Top 50 firms	Top 100 firms	Top 100 firms	Top 50 firms	Top 100 firms
1970	33.8	44.6	—	—	—
1975	—	—	28.4	15.8	21.7
1977	35.0	44.9	—	15.2	22.4
1980	—	—	27.3	16.4	21.9
1982	37.5	46.8	—	—	—

— Not available.
Source: For Korea, K. U. Lee (1984); for Japan, Senoo (1983); and for Taiwan, Chou (1985).

Table 9-3. *Commodity Market Structure, 1970, 1977, and 1982*

Year	Item	Monopoly	Duopoly	Oligopoly	Competitive	Total
1970	Commodities					
	Number	442	279	495	276	1,492
	Percentage share	29.6	18.2	33.2	18.5	100
	Shipments					
	Billions of won	110	204	439	498	1,252
	Percentage share	8.7	16.3	35.1	35.9	100
1977	Commodities					
	Number	667	425	674	343	2,219
	Percentage share	31.6	20.1	32.0	16.3	100
	Shipments					
	Billions of won	2.2	1,536	4,716	5,404	13,920
	Percentage share	16.3	11.0	33.9	38.8	100
1982	Commodities					
	Number	533	251	1,071	405	2,260
	Percentage share	23.6	11.1	47.4	17.9	100
	Shipments					
	Billions of won	5,649	3,275	24,967	15,481	49,372
	Percentage share	11.4	6.6	50.6	31.4	100

Note: The following definitions are used for the market structure: monopoly if $CR1 > 80$ percent, $S1/S2 < 10$; duopoly if $CR2 > 80$ percent, $S1/S2 < 5.0$, $S3 < 5$ percent; oligopoly if $CR3 > 60$ percent (monopoly and duopoly are excluded from the market share); and competitive if $CR3 < 60$ percent, where CRi indicates i-firm concentration ratio and Si indicates market share of the largest ith firm.

Source: K. U. Lee (1984).

the sectoral level; from 1977 to 1982 they expanded into new sectors, a process that made the market structure oligopolistic.

In addition to the monopolistic market characteristic of individual organization in the 1970s and 1980s, there was also significant concentration of economic power in Korea: a group of companies with a large number of affiliates exercised control over a major part of the economic resources or activities of the overall economy. When such a business group is owned by a small number of families, the concentration is called a *jaebul*.

Table 9-4 shows the share of the top business groups in the manufacturing sector. The twenty leading groups continued to increase their share of shipments after 1974, with an especially sharp rise between the late 1970s and the early 1980s.[2] The share of employment in manufacturing was far lower than the share of shipments and did not show any significant change over the years. These two observations indicate, among other things, a capital deepening in production by business groups (see Lee, Lee, and Kim 1984 for details). The capital deepening seems to have been made possible by low-cost financial resources made available by government policy (see chapter 6 of this volume).

Many factors led to the concentration of market structure (see Leff 1979). By introducing mass production techniques from abroad into a small domestic market at an early stage of economic development, large

Table 9-4. The Concentration of Economic Power in the Manufacturing Sector, 1974, 1977, 1982

Business group	Percentage share of shipments			Percentage share of employment		
	1974	1977	1982	1974	1977	1982
Top 5	—	15.7	22.6	—	9.1	8.4
Top 10	—	21.2	30.2	—	12.5	12.2
Top 15	—	25.6	33.9	—	14.4	14.5
Top 20	24.6	29.3	36.6	13.5	17.4	16.0
Top 25	—	31.9	38.8	—	18.9	17.1
Top 30	—	34.1	40.7	—	20.5	18.6

— Not available.
Source: K. U. Lee (1985).

corporations gained a monopolistic or at least highly concentrated oligopolistic position in the market. They were also able to retain comparatively superior human and physical resources and were protected from domestic and international competition by institutional barriers erected to limit new entry into the market. These corporations formed many monopolistic enclaves in the economy. They easily entered the new market and diversified their operations, taking advantage of the excess capacity in human, natural, and financial resources that they had accumulated in the existing market. It might be expected that the more the business groups are diversified, the more severe the competition among them becomes. This pattern was demonstrated clearly in the late 1970s, when a large number of business groups rushed simultaneously into overseas construction, financing, and heavy and chemical industries.

The government's economic policy sometimes caused a further acceleration of economic concentration. It might have been possible to alleviate a monopoly or oligopoly by letting in new companies as the size of the market increased. But this possibility was practically eliminated by an institutional barrier that was introduced to prevent overlapping investment in the most important industrial branches. In a bid to promote rapid economic growth, the government designated certain industries as strategic. These industries happened to require large-scale technical, financial, manpower, and organizational capabilities that could be mustered more easily by a business group than by a single corporation. It is not an overstatement to say that the advantages of the protection and incentive policies—involving taxation, banking, and commercial policy measures—were enjoyed almost exclusively by the business groups. In short, government policies designed to facilitate rapid economic growth further promoted the expansion of the business groups that originally enjoyed competitive advantages and naturally embarked on diversification.

Business groups expanded not only through the growth of their existing affiliate firms but also by adding to the number of those affiliates. Table 9-5

Table 9-5. *Integration of the Thirty Largest Business Groups,*
1970–82

(number of firms)

Type of change	1970	1971–79	1980–82
Addition of subsidiaries			
New firms	n.a.	202	30
Acquisition	n.a.	135	25
Loss of subsidiaries			
Internal merger	n.a.	27	31
Sales	n.a.	7	51
Net increases	n.a.	303	−27
Number of affiliated firms	126	429	402

n.a. Not applicable.
Note: The thirty largest business groups were selected on the basis of total assets.
Source: K. U. Lee (1985).

shows the trend in the integration of the firms under thirty leading business groups, selected on the basis of their assets in 1982. The number of affiliated firms in each business group dramatically increased from 4.2 to 14.3 from 1970 to 1979, a period of rapid growth of the Korean economy. What was distinctive about the integration process during 1970–79 was that the number of newly established subsidiaries was overwhelmingly larger than the number of corporate takeovers or acquisitions, in contrast to 1979–82, when the number of subsidiaries decreased.

It was more advantageous, especially at an early stage of economic development, to set up a new firm than to acquire the outdated facilities of an existing one that had been shaken out of the market. At the same time, as the economy grew, new firms were pushed vigorously as a means of entry into the new markets that were emerging in great numbers.[3] Under a slowly growing economy, however, business groups realigned their overall organizations by selling and internally merging unprofitable firms.

The advantage of a business group is best demonstrated in the multimarket activities through integration: it creates a synergistic effect because the business group can reallocate scarce resources internally and thereby seize economic opportunities as they arise. This capacity to improve resource allocation internally could permit Korea to deal more easily with the structural adjustment problems it currently faces. If, however, the business groups cling to business lines that have lost comparative advantage, structural adjustment could be very difficult. To make structural adjustment less painful, policy should emphasize manpower retraining, debt-liquidating mechanisms, and other measures that lower the exit barriers.

At the same time, a business group has a negative side. Since it tends to have higher bargaining power and better market position than a single firm, it may eliminate individual firms, a trend that could lead to a loss of allocative efficiency in the overall economy. In addition, the general public views the concentration of ownership and the rapid expansion of business groups with disfavor.

The increasing magnitude of concentration did limit the level of competition. Competition in the 1970s was also constrained by the trade associations, both formal and informal, whose numbers increased from 95 in 1970, to 130 in 1978, and to 235 in 1982 (Lee and Lee 1982). Most trade associations, such as the cooperatives of small and medium-size firms and the exporters' associations, were decreed by special laws. In many cases they had big corporations as members—not the original intent. These associations acted as a channel between the government and individual firms in implementing the government's industrial policies. The government occasionally allowed them to behave like cartels, and some trade associations took concerted group actions of questionable economic justification, such as determining prices, adjusting production, and restricting the number of newcomers to the industry. Even the trade associations that were organized voluntarily did approximately the same thing under the guise of government administrative guidance or ad hoc industry protection laws. The 1979 study of group actions taken by a sample of seventy-four trade associations revealed five cases of restriction of the creation or expansion of new companies, eighty-nine cases of control of the procurement of raw materials, five cases of regulation of production activities, five cases of central coordination of the acquisition of funds, and eighty-eight cases of restriction of sales activities (Korea, Economic Planning Board 1984).

Industrial Organization Policies in the 1970s and 1980s

Problems related to industrial organization were not viewed as critical before 1973, because until then the economy was growing steadily. They came to the forefront in 1974, however, when the country was hit by the first oil crisis. The severely distorted market mechanism and a sharp increase in the price of imported raw materials caused inflation and demand-supply imbalances in a large number of markets. To tackle this problem, the government placed heavy emphasis on microeconomic policy in addition to traditional macroeconomic policy. The government attempted to monitor selected individual product markets and apply pertinent policy measures as the need arose. The Act Concerning Price Stabilization and Fair Trade[4] (hereafter called the Price Stabilization Act) was the legal foundation for this new economic policy.

The Price Stabilization Act had two objectives: price control and ensuring fair trade. Regarding price control, the following three actions were stipulated: the fixing of price ceilings for daily necessities, regulation of the prices of monopolistic or oligopolistic firms, and emergency measures such as rationing or stockpiling for demand-supply adjustment. To ensure fair trade, the government prohibited unfair practices and the restriction of competition.

Once the act was implemented, price control and the prohibition of a few categories of unfair trade practices were stressed. Extensive price regulation of about 150 products that enjoyed a monopolistic or oligopolistic market was carried out every year until 1979, when the Overall Economic Stabilization Program was implemented (Korea Development Institute 1981). In addition, a price ceiling system was put into place starting with anthracite briquettes; between 1977 and 1978 it was extended to more than twenty items of daily necessity. In 1979, however, coverage was reduced to briquettes only again (K. U. Lee 1979).

With respect to the restriction of unfair trade practices, 100 cases were investigated between 1976 and 1979. Almost all of the eighty-five cases that were actually prosecuted, however, involved hoarding and cornering at the time of the 1979 fluctuations in agricultural prices.[5] In contrast, not a single case of undue restriction of competition was tried. In fact, the stipulation against restricting competition came up in only one case; ironically, the case involved four attempts to legalize the cartel in the cement industry in the name of antirecession or industry rationalization measures.[6]

The Price Stabilization Act had unexpected side effects because it placed greater emphasis on the regulation of prices, an element of market performance, than on the structural aspects of the market. Because of the wide range of commodities covered, the scope of the direct price controls exceeded the government's administrative capacity and led to a series of problems. Long-lasting price controls severely disturbed the price mechanism and gave rise to such phenomena as dual pricing, deterioration in quality, and chronic excess demand. Producers lost interest in expanding production because their products were under price control. As a result, they did not emphasize capital investment, a stance that weakened their ability to weather business cycles. Because prices intermittently went up sharply in a stop-and-go pattern, consumers had neither reasonable expectations about prices nor the ability to plan their consumption rationally.

The second oil crisis in 1979 made the situation even worse, and the government was forced to come up with a functional system. The Overall Economic Stabilization Program, which took effect in April 1979, was intended to rectify the distortions created by the government's policy of rapid economic development and to establish a more flexible economic system with greater reliance on the market mechanism. The program called for such comprehensive measures as a realignment of monetary and fiscal policy, introduction of antimonopoly measures, stabilization of wages and real estate prices, and coordination of investment in the heavy and chemical industries. It can be considered as a preparatory policy package that laid the foundation for Korea's entrance into an era of liberalization in the 1980s.

At the same time, the government undertook piecemeal measures in 1979 and 1980 to mitigate the economic concentration that had become one of the major industrial organization issues of the 1970s. To ensure the soundness of the financial structure of firms affiliated with *jaebuls*, the government attempted to induce them to go public by introducing favorable bank loan and tax policies. The government also encouraged the firms to procure operating funds by selling parts of their companies and stockholdings. Control over new loans was tightened for companies that did not offer stocks to the public. The government also issued "Measures to Improve Corporate Financial Structure," which advocated reduction of real estate ownership by large corporations, streamlining firms affiliated with *jaebuls*, cutting relief financing by banks, and strengthening credit controls.

The aim of these measures was to improve the fragile financial situation of some large corporations, limit their expansion, and restrict their real estate ownership. Strictly speaking, they cannot be considered policies to prevent economic concentration, and the measures were temporary. In addition, the government institutions responsible for implementing them were not clearly defined, which made it impossible to carry them out continuously.

In the early 1980s, with the Comprehensive Measures for Economic Stabilization (CMES) program of 1979 as its symbolic starting point, the government moved the country into a new economic system that respected the workings of the free market and the freedom of people to make their own decisions. The government vigorously promoted its policy of economic liberalization on both the domestic and foreign fronts. Financial deregulation measures included putting the management of most city banks into private hands, providing more freedom to bank management, eliminating policy loans, and simplifying the term structure of interest rates. On the foreign front, the government made more vigorous attempts to attract foreign direct investment and to liberalize imports and the foreign exchange markets.

As part of the economic liberalization measures, the Fair Trade and Anti-Monopoly Act (hereafter referred to as the Monopoly Regulation Act) was enacted in April 1981 in the belief that a new economic order was necessary to adapt to the changing economic environment. The Monopoly Regulation Act does not employ direct price regulation as did the Price Stabilization Act, and it gives more weight to the regulation of market structure.

Two important issues arose when the Monopoly Regulation Act was being formulated. First, although it was desirable in principle to allow prices to be determined by the market mechanism, reliance on the market would have caused prices to rise unless the pricing policies of the firms in monopolistic and oligopolistic markets changed. For instance, there was always a strong possibility, at least in the short run, that an unfettered monopolist would raise its price by a wide margin. Because the majority of product markets were noncompetitive in structure and price stabilization was regarded as the primary economic goal, the Monopoly Regulation Act came to include a clause that dealt with undue pricing activities by market-dominating firms.

The second issue was whether or not to use the Monopoly Regulation Act as a legal tool to attack directly the problem of the concentration of economic power. When the draft of the law was discussed, most people believed that the *jaebul* issue should be addressed as well. This view was clear in the first article of the law, which identified preventing the concentration of economic power as one of its purposes. The act, however, did not include a clause restricting conglomerate integration—the most powerful means of expanding economic power. It did not do so for two reasons. First, there was concern that such policies would harm enterprises that had fallen on hard times following the recession that began in 1979. Second, the problem of the concentration of economic power was too complicated and difficult to solve with the Monopoly Regulation Act alone. [7]

The provisions of the Monopoly Regulation Act forbade abuse of a market-dominating position, restricted corporate integration, prohibited undue concerted activities, forbade unfair trade practices, and restricted the conclusion of improper international agreements. Forbidding abuse of a market-dominating position meant eliminating injuries that would arise from a monopolistic market structure. This prohibition applied to monopolistic or quasimonopolistic firms that unduly set, maintained, or changed prices, made unjustified sales adjustments, harmed the activities of other businesses, or installed new or additional capacities to preempt potential competition. Parallel price increases among oligopolists were also to be given close scrutiny. [8]

The restriction on corporate integration was intended to prevent markets from becoming monopolistic by regulating the roots of monopoly. In addition to the typical methods of corporate integration—such as stock acquisitions, interlocking directorates, mergers, or asset acquisition—the law uniquely and specifically designates the establishment of new enterprises. In Korea, where the market was (and still is) growing rapidly, the acquisition of existing enterprises was not as important a means of expansion as the establishment of new enterprises. Corporate integration was restricted where its effect might have led to a substantial injury to competition in any market or if the method of integration would have been unfair. There could be exceptions to this rule, however. Despite the accompanying restriction of competition, corporate integration was permitted for purposes of rationalizing industry and strengthening international competitiveness. This kind of exception shows that rather than being the result of unconditional respect for the ideal of competition, the Monopoly Regulation Act was introduced with the objective of developing the national economy. Both horizontal and vertical integrations were restricted by the act, but the act barely addressed conglomerate integration.

The concerted activities of firms in a marketplace were to be registered to prevent them from turning a competitive market into a monopolistic one through collusion. Although restrictions on competition were prohibited in any market, concerted activities were permitted when needed to overcome temporary recessions or to rationalize industry. The concerted activities prohibited by the law in principle were cartel activities such as the setting of prices, conditions of sale, quantities, distribution channels, plants and equipment, standards, and quality.

Unfair trade practices are not necessarily related to market power: they can be observed between producing firms and between producers and consumers. The Monopoly Regulation Act restricted the refusal to deal, price discrimination, boycotts, unduly high or low prices, coercion to deal, exclusive dealing or tie-in selling, and abuse of a market-dominating position, as well as false, misleading, and exaggerated advertising.

The Monopoly Regulation Act, to eliminate some of the side effects that would accompany the opening-up of the Korean market, prohibited the conclusion of international agreements that would have restricted competition or resulted in unfair trade practices. This clause attempted to maintain fair competition in the domestic market while strengthening the bargaining stance of domestic entrepreneurs in their dealings with foreigners.

From April 1981, when the Monopoly Regulation Act went into effect, to the end of 1985, numerous cases were handled by the Fair Trade Committee. Although the number of firms designated by the government as dominant in their respective markets increased greatly—from 105 in 1981 to 216 in 1985—no more than 10 were accused of abusing their market-dominating position and served with cease and desist orders. In the case of restrictions of corporate integration, all 1,172 applications were approved except for 2 involving horizontal integration.[9]

The act was applied to eighty cases of concerted activities. Of these, 10 cases were approved, the cement joint transportation cartel[10] and liquor spirits syndicate the most noteworthy among them. The remaining seventy cases were disapproved with cease and desist orders. In addition, administrative recommendations and orders were issued to forty-one trade associations that had clauses permitting undue concerted activities in their articles of incorporation.

In the 238 cases involving a violation of the provisions against unfair trade practices, 113, or 48 percent, concerned subcontracting practices. The importance of this problem was reflected in the passage of the Act Concerning Fair Subcontracting Transactions in 1985.

There were 2,640 applications for international agreements between 1981 and 1985, of which 931, or 35.3 percent, were judged to contain provisions restricting competition or calling for unfair trade practices and were revised accordingly. There were 1,850 applications for agreements on importing technology, the most common kind of agreement, and 811, or 43.8 percent, of these applicants were ordered to make revisions.

Table 9-6. *Import Liberalization Rate and Tariff Rate, 1983–85*
(percent)

Item	December 1983	July 1984	July 1985
Import liberalization rate			
All items	80.3	84.8	87.7
Market-dominating items	52.0	62.4	78.0
Customs rate			
All items	23.7	21.9	21.3
Market-dominating items	40.9	33.2	32.9

Source: Ministry of Finance.

Although several measures relating to industrial organization were implemented simultaneously with the enactment of the Monopoly Regulation Act, as discussed above, further action was also taken to increase the level of competition in monopolistic markets: competition from abroad was introduced into markets dominated by a few enterprises. Table 9-6 shows that although the average import liberalization rate of affected items was still lower than that of other commodity items, the pace of their liberalization was accelerated, and their tariff rates have been decreasing rapidly (see chapter 8 of this volume).

Small and medium-size firms have been a favorite target of government policy initiatives in the past few decades, in part because this stance has been politically attractive. Nevertheless, because the overall economic policy has been oriented toward big businesses and because of the very large number of small and medium-size firms, not enough resources or attention has been directed toward the latter.

Because international competitiveness requires that big firms produce items of superior quality at cheaper prices, the development of small and medium-size firms has become crucial to the survival of the large assembling firms and to self-sustained economic growth. In other words, small firms badly need to become the basis of industrial restructuring.

This process will be expedited as small and medium-size firms realize that their own efforts will determine whether they survive and as an increasing number of innovative entrepreneurs emerge with venture businesses. Big firms will also find it more economical to support and rely on small firms that produce parts than to manufacture the parts themselves or to import them. The competitive pressure on large firms, either from other firms or from foreign competitors, is encouraging them to mold a cooperative relationship with small and medium-size firms, which gives the smaller firms an impetus to improve. It is gradually being demonstrated that competition is better for all.

Industrial organization policy generally takes a long time before it has a visible impact on the market. Since only a few years have passed, it may be premature to evaluate the effects of the policy, especially in quantitative terms.

Although some temporary policy measures have been used intermittently to back the operations of big businesses, it is clear that the general policy line has shifted against concentration. Therefore, it is possible to argue that the degree of concentration has finally hit a ceiling. At the same time, vigorous promotion of fair trade and robust implementation of the relevant laws have also enhanced the degree of competition in the market. The competitive spirit can be felt among existing firms, as well as in potential competitors. Although this conclusion cannot be proved with concrete data, without a doubt it should manifest itself in more competitive conduct and eventually in a more competitive market structure. The next section presents the tentative results of an empirical study that demonstrates one aspect of this process.

Market Performance

In this section market performance in the 1970s and 1980s is analyzed by taking market structure into consideration. Market performance here refers only to static efficiency in resource allocation and is measured by profitability; resource allocation is considered statically optimum if there is zero excess profit.

It would be expected that competition leads to lower excess profitability. In the absence of a good measure of the level of competition, which is determined by firms' conduct, various characteristics associated with market structure can be used as a proxy.[11] The level of concentration can be used to represent the level of competition among domestic producers, while the magnitude of import share and level of import protection can be used to capture the extent of competition from abroad. To analyze the market structure and performance relationship statistically, a data base was built for three years (1973, 1978, and 1983) for sixty-five Korean manufacturing sectors selected from the Korean Standard Industrial Classification (KSIC) four-digit level industries. The years 1973, 1978, and 1983 were chosen for two reasons. First, these three years encompass two important developments in recent Korean economic history: a period of substantial government intervention (1973–79) and a period of liberalization (1980–86). Second, the choices were constrained by the availability of data.[12]

The first step is to compare profitability, domestic concentration, and foreign competition across the census years. As table 9-7 shows, between 1973 and 1978 there was a statistically significant decrease in the weighted averages of price-cost margins,[13] accompanied by a slight decline in the level of concentration, as measured by either the three-firm concentration ratio ($CR3$) or the Herfindahl index. Both export and import shares declined during this period,[14] while the intraindustry trade index showed a drop in intraindustry specialization in international trade. A comparison of the same variables between 1978 and 1983 reveals a near reversal in the

Table 9-7. *Profitability, Concentration, and Exposure to Trade for Sixty-five Korean Manufacturing Sectors*

Variable	Year	Mean[a]	Standard deviation	Difference in mean 1978-73	Difference in mean 1983-78
Price-cost margin (*PCM*)	1973	0.328	0.121		
	1978	0.292	0.111		
	1983	0.260	0.107	−0.036[c]	−0.32[b]
Three-firm concentration ratio (*CR3*)	1973	0.547	0.209		
	1978	0.541	0.215		
	1983	0.626	0.200	−0.006	0.085[c]
Herfindahl index (*H*)	1973	0.179	0.124		
	1978	0.119	0.119		
	1983	0.241	0.170	−0.008	0.070[b]
Export share (*XPS*)	1973	0.268	0.242		
	1978	0.209	0.205		
	1983	0.205	0.201	−0.059	−0.004
Import share (*MPS*)	1973	0.210	0.216		
	1978	0.159	0.170		
	1983	0.155	0.146	−0.051	−0.004
Actual tariff rate (*ATR*)	1973	0.115	0.206		
	1978	0.200	0.355		
	1983	0.134	0.097	0.085[b]*	−0.066*
Intraindustry trade (*IIT*)	1973	0.463	0.331		
	1978	0.389	0.260		
	1983	0.515	0.302	−0.074	0.126[d]

Note: The variables are defined as follows:

PCM = (sales − input costs − wages)/sales; XPS = exports/sales; MPS = imports/(sales − exports + imports); IIT = 1.0 − (exports − imports)/(exports + imports); ATR = actual tariff duty collected/imports. For the entries followed by an asterisk (*), the equality of variance is rejected at the 1 percent level. Satterthwaite's (1946) approximation to degrees of freedom is used to construct the *t*-statistic when the equality of variances is rejected.

a. Weighted averages using the value of shipments as weights.

b. Significant at the 10 percent level.

c. Significant at the 5 percent level.

d. Significant at the 1 percent level.

Source: Authors' calculations.

direction of the changes except for profitability. There was little change in export and import shares, but there were increases in concentration and intraindustry specialization.[15] Although unexpected, between 1978 and 1983 a decline in profitability was accompanied by an increase in concentration and a decrease in the import share. One possible explanation is the overall macroeconomic effect, which cannot be captured by the variables in this analysis. Another possibility is that trade liberalization in the form of a reduction in nominal tariff rates as well as in nontariff barriers increased the level of potential competition from abroad, which restrained firms from exercising market power.

Table 9-8 shows the mean price-cost margins for different kinds of market structures. As expected, industries faced with greater competition gen-

Table 9-8. *Performance of Different Market Structures, 1973, 1978, and 1983*

Market structure	Year	Number of sectors	Price-cost margin Mean	Price-cost margin Standard deviation	Value
Monopoly/	1973	30	0.328	0.099	
oligopoly	1978	28	0.320	0.160	
	1983	34	0.262	0.134	
Competitive	1973	35	0.327	0.134	
	1978	37	0.276	0.068	
	1983	31	0.259	0.065	
Difference in mean	1973				0.001
between market structures	1978				0.044*
	1983				0.003*
High import	1973	25	0.313	0.046	
competition	1978	28	0.260	0.048	
	1983	25	0.249	0.042	
Low import	1973	40	0.336	0.148	
competition	1978	37	0.310	0.132	
	1983	40	0.267	0.132	
Difference in mean	1973				−0.023*
between market structures	1978				−0.050[a]
	1983				−0.018*
Highly protected	1973	25	0.431	0.185	
	1978	22	0.385	0.156	
	1983	34	0.302	0.139	
Less protected	1973	40	0.290	0.047	
	1978	43	0.257	0.059	
	1983	31	0.231	0.063	
Difference in mean	1973				0.141[b]*
between market structures	1978				0.128[b]*
	1983				0.071[b]*
High export	1973	23	0.273	0.049	
share	1978	20	0.246	0.037	
	1983	24	0.251	0.036	
Low export	1973	42	0.370	0.142	
share	1978	45	0.314	0.128	
	1983	41	0.266	0.133	
Difference in mean	1973				−0.097[b]*
between market structures	1978				−0.068[b]*
	1983				−0.015*

Note: The following definitions are used for the market structure: monopoly/oligopoly if $CR3 > 0.6$; competitive if $CR3 < 0.6$; high import competition if $MPS > 0.210, 0.159, 0.155$ (weighted means of the years 1973, 1978, and 1983, respectively), low import competition otherwise; highly protected if $ATR > 0.113, 0.196, 0.133$ (weighted means of each year, respectively), less protected otherwise; high export share if $XPS > 0.268, 0.209, 0.205$ (weighted means of each year, respectively), low import share otherwise. For the entries followed by an asterisk (*), the equality of variance is rejected at the 1 percent level. Satterthwaite's (1946) approximation to degrees of freedom is used to construct the t-statistic when the equality of variance is rejected.

a. Significant at the 5 percent level.
b. Significant at the 1 percent level.

Source: Authors' calculations.

erally show lower profitability than those faced with less competition.[16] For example, sectors that are identified as competitive among domestic producers (sectors with $CR3 < 0.6$) showed lower price-cost margins than sectors in the category of monopoly/oligopoly ($CR3 > 0.6$). Especially in 1978, the difference in the mean was statistically significant. With regard to competition from abroad, industries were separated into high import competition compared with low import competition sectors and highly protected sectors in contrast to less protected ones by using each year's weighted averages of import shares and actual tariff rates, respectively, as the cutoff point.[17] As indicated by the statistically significant differences in the mean, the high import competition sectors showed lower price-cost margins than the low import competition sectors, while industries with higher tariff protection displayed higher profitability than the less protected industries. According to these observations, both domestic and foreign competition were negatively associated with profitability. This finding tends to support the import discipline hypothesis, which is described below.

To go beyond an analysis of descriptive statistics, a cross-sectoral regression analysis is proposed. Because the main interest here lies with the effect of market structure on market performance, the focus is on the profitability equation. The profitability equation is described below with the expected signs:

(9-1) $$PCM = f(H, RDR, XPS, MPS, GR, KSR)$$
$$+ \quad + \quad ? \quad - \quad + \quad ?$$

where

PCM	=	price-cost margin [(value added − wages)/sales]
H	=	Herfindahl index of concentration in sales
RDR	=	research and development (R&D) ratio (R&D expenditure/sales)
XPS	=	export share (export/sales)
MPS	=	import share [import/(sales − exports + imports)]
GR	=	growth rate of sales (simple average growth rate of preceding four years, except for 1973 data, for which the average growth rate of 1972 and 1973 is used)
KSR	=	capital/sales ratio (total fixed assets/sales).

In the profitability equation the Herfindahl index is included as a measure of concentration. The index is expected to have a positive effect on the price-cost margin because an industry with a high concentration offers an easy environment for collusion, which can yield a higher price-cost margin. This positive relationship between the price-cost margin and the Herfindahl index has been suggested theoretically, and a number of empirical studies have supported it (for the theoretical treatment, see Cowling and Waterson 1976 and Clarke and Davies 1982).

The export and import shares are included in the profitability equation as measures of foreign influence. It is generally expected that the price-cost margin is negatively related to the import share because greater competition from abroad should depress the market power of domestic firms. This effect is often referred to as the import discipline hypothesis. There is, however, a possibility of a positive relationship between the price-cost margin and the import share when the conduct of firms (conjectural variations) is incorporated explicitly (see Geroski and Jacquemin 1981; Urata 1984; de Melo and Urata 1986; Choi 1986). Nevertheless, most empirical studies have reported a negative relationship between the price-cost margin and the import share.

The effect of the export share on profitability is also ambiguous. A negative relationship can be expected between the price-cost margin and the export share if domestic oligopolists cannot segregate the foreign market from the domestic market because the oligopolists are likely to face a more elastic world demand curve. This relationship could be positive if the exporting domestic oligopolists were able to discriminate between the domestic and foreign markets and thereby profit from price discrimination. Accordingly, empirical studies have shown diverse results.

The capital-output ratio is included as a measure of capital intensity to take into account the components of the opportunity cost of capital (for example, the normal rate of return) that are included in the measure of price-cost margin used here. A positive relationship between the capital-output ratio and price-cost margin could be expected, but Caves, Porter, and Spence (1980) point out that a negative relationship is possible because the capital-intensive sector's marginal cost is more likely to fall below the average cost than is the case with a less capital-intensive sector.

A measure of the growth rate of sales is included as a determinant of profitability because actual growth is positively correlated with the difference between realized and expected growth, and thus is positively correlated with windfall profits or losses (Caves, Porter, and Spence 1980; Pugel 1978).

R&D-sales ratios are included as a possible source of an entry barrier, although this variable is not likely to show significance in Korean manufacturing industries, because their R&D expenditures were generally very low.

In the estimation, three variables—*H, RDR,* and *MPS*—are treated as endogenous, as suggested by earlier theoretical as well as empirical studies (for example, Caves, Porter, and Spence 1980; Pugel 1978). The results of the *OLS* and *2SLS* regressions are reported in table 9-9.[18] In general the results are in accordance with many other cross-section estimates calculated in market structure and performance studies, although the predictive power of the profitability equation for 1973 is weak.

Two major findings are noteworthy. First, for the 1983 estimation, there is a statistically significant positive effect of concentration on profitability,[19] the result under many other empirical studies.[20] There have been two

Table 9-9. *Regression Estimates of the Profitability Equation*

Explanatory variable	OLS estimate			2SLS estimate		
	1973	*1978*	*1983*	*1973*	*1978*	*1983*
Constant	0.410[a]	0.309[a]	0.264[a]	0.503[a]	0.320[a]	0.206[a]
	(8.79)	(6.07)	(5.98)	(6.57)	(4.99)	(3.04)
H	−0.097	0.031	0.201[a]	−0.251	−0.015	0.403[a]
	(−1.01)	(0.27)	(2.86)	(−1.32)	(−0.08)	(2.88)
RDR	−0.862	2.823	4.801	−10.431	−13.577	38.852[b]
	(−0.25)	(0.31)	(0.82)	(−1.04)	(−0.46)	(2.51)
XPS	−0.172[b]	−0.224[a]	−0.013	−0.143	−0.255[a]	0.037
	(−2.27)	(−3.56)	(−0.23)	(−1.44)	(−3.33)	(0.44)
MPS	−0.026	−0.206[a]	−0.116[c]	−0.090	−0.344[b]	−0.360[b]
	(−0.38)	(−2.90)	(−1.71)	(−0.44)	(−2.29)	(−2.00)
GR	−0.013	0.127[c]	−0.087	0.003	0.216[b]	−0.037
	(−0.43)	(1.82)	(−0.98)	(0.07)	(1.72)	(−0.29)
KSR	−0.006	0.031	−0.013	−0.018	0.068	−0.126
	(−0.14)	(0.34)	(−0.18)	(−0.39)	(0.61)	(−1.20)
R^2	0.150	0.278	0.206	n.a.	n.a.	n.a.
F	1.64	3.59[a]	2.42[b]	1.86	2.68[b]	2.43[b]

n.a. Not applicable.

Note: The *t*-values are in parentheses. The variables are defined as follows: H = Herfindahl index of concentration of sales; RDR = R&D expenditures/sales; XPS = exports/sales; MPS = imports/(sales − exports + imports); GR = growth rate of sales; KSR = capital/sales ratio.

a. Significant at the 1 percent level.
b. Significant at the 5 percent level.
c. Significant at the 10 percent level.

Source: Authors' calculations.

radically different interpretations of the positive correlation between concentration and profitability in the recent literature on industrial organization (see Donsimoni, Geroski, and Jacquemin 1984 for details). The structuralist view asserts that the positive correlation is evidence of rent-seeking behavior by firms in oligopolistic industries. It also maintains that larger firms do not have a substantial efficiency advantage over their smaller rivals. In contrast, the efficiency-based view argues that the positive relationship reflects the superior performance of large firms (see, for example, Clarke, Davies, and Waterson 1984). The empirical evidence supports the structuralist view for manufacturing industry, because it has been shown that the efficiency of small and medium-size firms caught up with that of large firms by the end of the 1970s (Kim 1985).

The second major finding is the negative effect of import competition on profitability in all three years, with statistically significant estimates for 1978 and 1983.[21] This result confirms that the import discipline hypothesis is applicable to Korean manufacturing industry.[22]

These findings (the positive effect of concentration and the negative effect of import competition on profitability) have significant implications for industrial organization policymaking: liberalization policies to increase both domestic (for example, through the encouragement of small and me-

Table 9-10. *Structural Change Test*

	OLS		2SLS	
Variable	*1973–78*	*1978–83*	*1973–78*	*1978–83*
D. constant	−0.101	−0.045	−0.183[c]	−0.114
D.H	0.128	0.170	0.236	0.418[c]
D.RDR	3.685	1.978	−3.126	52.409
D.XPS	−0.052	0.211[b]	−0.112	0.292[c]
D.MPS	−0.180[c]	0.090	−0.254	−0.017
D.GR	0.141	−0.214[c]	0.213	−0.253
D.KSR	0.036	−0.044	0.087	−0.195
R^2	0.207	0.272	n.a.	n.a.
F	2.246[b]	3.217[a]	2.543[a]	4.161[a]

n.a. Not applicable.

Note: Only the differences in the values of the coefficients are reported here. The test on R^2 is on the whole equation. D = dummy variable (1973 = 0 and 1978 = 1 for 1973–78 test, and 1978 = 0 and 1983 = 1 for 1978–83 test); *D*. constant = $D \times$ constant; $D.H = D \times H$; $D.RDR = D \times RDR$; $D.XPS = D \times XPS$; $D.MPS = D \times MPS$; $D.GR = D \times GR$; $D.KSR = D \times KSR$. The variables are defined as follows: H = Herfindahl index of concentration of sales; RDR = R&D expenditures/sales; XPS = exports/sales; MPS = imports/(sales − exports + imports); GR = growth rate of sales; KSR = capital/sales ratio.

a. Significant at the 1 percent level.

b. Significant at the 5 percent level.

c. Significant at the 10 percent level.

Source: Authors' calculations.

dium-size firms) and foreign competition improve the allocative efficiency of the economy.

Table 9-10 gives the results of the tests for a structural shift in the coefficients in the profitability equation across the years. The null hypothesis of no structural change across the years is strongly rejected.[23] This result suggests that the pattern of profitability across sectors changed significantly during the 1973–78 and 1978–83 periods. In particular, significant increases in the coefficients of concentration, R&D, and export share are noticeable between 1978 and 1983.

The significant positive correlation between the price-cost margin and concentration in 1983 compared with earlier years seems to reflect the declining importance of direct government intervention in pricing behavior. At the same time, this finding argues in favor of tightening the provisions of the Monopoly Regulation Act. The increased influence of R&D expenditures on profitability in 1983 indicates that Korean manufacturing was shifting from production that makes intensive use of low-skilled labor to production that makes intensive use of skilled labor and R&D.

Finally, the significant increase in the magnitude of the coefficient on the export share reflects an increasing share of differentiated products in Korean exports, as was indicated by the increase in the intraindustry trade index in table 9-7.

Conclusions

The Korean government shifted its development policies from highly interventionist to more liberal in the early 1980s. There was a shift in industrial policies from the quantitatively oriented to the qualitatively oriented.

This chapter has examined industrial organizational issues, past and present, and presented some implications for the future. The results of the quantitative analysis of the factors influencing market performance, which used sectoral data, show that the new liberal policies should improve the efficiency of resource allocation by increasing competition.

There are, however, two important issues facing policymakers as well as economists that are not fully analyzed here: the effect of business groups on the economy and the issue of R&D in the industrial organization. Careful and rigorous analyses of these issues should help policymakers in formulating industrial policies.

The impact of business groups on the economy was examined in terms of their size, as measured by such indicators as sales or employment, but not in terms of their influence on market performance. Several factors make the latter analysis difficult. First, it is hard to obtain reliable data on business groups because of the extensive intragroup transactions in financial resources as well as inputs and outputs. Second, there have been no testable models that explain business group behavior.

R&D investment is one of the most important issues in Korea. It plays a very important role in the development and application of the new technology that enables producers to improve their competitiveness. Because Korea's comparative advantage is shifting from unskilled-labor-intensive goods to skilled-labor-intensive goods, it is not an overstatement to say that Korea's future economic development depends on technological progress.

An issue here is whether competition increases R&D investment. Two somewhat opposing views have been presented on this point. It has been argued that competition results in higher R&D expenditures because producers under competitive pressure seek to establish a technological advantage that enables them to reap profits. This conclusion suggests that antimonopoly measures should be adopted to induce R&D investment. Some experts argue against such measures—they claim that firm size may be important to R&D investment because of its indivisibility. The R&D issue gets more complicated with regard to formulating government policies, because the government as well as private firms expends a large amount on R&D investment.

Finally, it should be noted that the issues of business groups and R&D investment are closely related. Firms belonging to business groups are moving rapidly into R&D-intensive sectors.

Notes

The authors are grateful to Vittorio Corbo, Danny M. Leipziger, and Peter Petri for their helpful comments and suggestions.

1. As with the overall concentration ratio, the sectoral concentration ratio in Korea may be higher than that in Japan or Taiwan. The weighted averages of the 3-firm concentration ratio are as follows: Korea (1981), 62.0 percent; Japan (1980), 49.3 percent; and Taiwan (1981), 49.2 percent. (See table 9-2 for the sources.)

2. The size of Korean business groups is very large compared with firms in other developing countries. Ten Korean business groups are among twenty-seven private firms in developing countries on the *Fortune* 500 list of the largest non-U.S. industrial companies (see Y. K. Lee 1985).

3. Such a phenomenon is nothing more than the progression of diversification. Comparing 1974 with 1982, the number of commodities shipped by subsidiaries per business group for the sixteen largest business groups increased from 22.2 to 52.4.

4. Even before this law was enacted, a limited number of items such as textbooks, alcohol, naphtha fraction, foodstuffs, and the like were regulated by special laws.

5. Of the eighty-five cases, five involved charges of false and exaggerated advertising; three, refusal to deal; seventy-three, hoarding and cornering; and four, other matters.

6. Cement manufacturers were authorized to engage in concerted activities in transportation, sales, and pricing, as well as in creating production quotas, for the following reasons: geographic concentration of producers, high transport costs, seasonal fluctuations in demand, and the difficulty associated with adjusting the production schedule.

7. In 1986 this act was amended to regulate intercompany shareholding and to prohibit holding companies.

8. This clause was removed in the 1986 amendment of the Monopoly Regulation Act.

9. The two cases of integration were disapproved in January and February 1982. The first involved duopolists in the hydrogen peroxide industry; the second involved the two largest firms in the polyvinyl chloride stabilizer industry. In both cases the Fair Trade Committee concurred that the long-term injury to competition outweighed any possible antirecession effect expected from these integrations.

10. See note 6 for details.

11. Several studies estimated conjectural variations that are considered to represent firms' conduct. That approach is beyond the scope of this chapter. See, for example, Iwata (1977) and Gollop and Roberts (1979).

12. The years for which industrial census and input-output tables are available are 1973, 1978, and 1983.

13. Although there are alternative measures of profitability, the price-cost margin is customarily used as a measure of profitability in the field of industrial organization.

14. The reason is not the observations omitted (for various reasons) from the analysis. Based on all the manufacturing sectors in the tables, export and import shares also declined from 15.5 percent and 16.9 percent in 1973 to 14.3 percent and

15.4 percent in 1978. One possible explanation is that 1973 was an exceptionally strong boom year throughout the world, which might have contributed to high export and import ratios. In addition, by the mid-1970s Korea was losing its international comparative advantage. See chapters 2 and 3 in this volume.

15. The direction of the changes in concentration between the years found here is consistent with the findings in table 9-3. Some explanations for these changes were given earlier.

16. Although they are not shown in table 9-8, the research and development sales ratios were, in general, higher in industries with higher degrees of competition (both domestic and foreign); advertising intensity tended to be higher for industries with low foreign competition; and the production of consumer goods yielded higher price-cost margins than did the production of producer goods.

17. See the notes in table 9-8 for the actual cutoff points used in differentiating among the categories of market structure.

18. The instruments used for 2SLS are *XPS, GR, KSR, MKSR (KSR* interacted with minimum efficient scale), *ATR* (actual tariff rate), *EMP* (employment), *MESI* (minimum efficient scale index), *ADCG* (advertising intensity interacted with consumer good index), *VA* (value added), *KLWR* (capital-labor ratio), *SLL* (skill level index of labor), and *CGI* (consumer good index). For a discussion of the estimation procedure applied here, see Pugel (1978).

19. The negative and insignificant estimate of the Herfindahl index in the 2SLS estimation for 1978 can be attributed to the fact that the prices of a large number of commodities were controlled in 1978 because the producers were monopolistic firms.

20. Several cross-sectional studies of market structure and performance in Korean manufacturing industry have found a significant positive relation between concentration and profitability. See K. U. Lee (1977), Choi (1986), and S. S. Lee (1985).

21. An interaction term, $MPH (= MPS \times H)$, was also tried in lieu of *MPS,* with similar results. But when both *MPH* and *MPS* were entered together in the profitability equation, the overall regression results were worse.

22. Several studies yielded results that support the import discipline hypothesis. See, for example, de Melo and Urata (1986) on the effect of Chilean liberalization on market structure and performance.

23. The Chow test of structural change is applied. The null hypotheses are

$$H_o: A_i^{t_1} = A_i^{t_2}$$

where A_i refers to the coefficients in the profitability equation, and t_1 and t_2 to the years being tested. This test is an F_n-test:

$$\frac{(RRSS - URSS)/K + 1}{URSS/(n_1 + n_2 - 2K - 2)} \sim F_{n_1+n_2-2K-2}^{K+1}$$

where *RRSS* and *URSS* refer to the residual sum of the squares of the restricted and unrestricted models, respectively, $K + 1$ is the number of restricted coefficients, and n_1 and n_2 are the number of observations for each year. The F-statistics are 8.98 for 1973 versus 1978 and 7.02 for 1978 versus 1983, while the critical F-value at the 1 percent significance level is 2.811.

References

Caves, R. E., M. Porter, and M. Spence. 1980. *Competition in the Open Economy: A Model Applied to Canada.* Cambridge, Mass.: Harvard University Press.

Choi, Inbom. 1986. "Effects of Foreign Trade on Domestic Market Structure and Performance." Ph.D. dissertation. Georgetown University, Washington, D.C.

Chou, T. C. 1985. "Industrial Organization in the Process of Economic Development, The Case of Taiwan, 1950–80." Department of Economic Science, Catholic University of Louvain, Belgium.

Clarke, R., and S. W. Davies. 1982. "Market Structure and Price-Cost Margins." *Economica* 49:277–87.

Clarke, R., S. W. Davies, and M. Waterson. 1984. "The Profitability-Concentration Relation: Market Power or Efficiency?" *Journal of Industrial Economics* 32(June):435–50.

Cowling, K., and M. Waterson. 1976. "Price-Cost Margins and Market Structure." *Economica* 43:267–74.

de Melo, Jaime, and S. Urata. 1986. "The Influence of Increased Foreign Competition on Industrial Concentration and Profitability." *International Journal of Industrial Organization* 4:287–304.

Donsimoni, M. P., P. Geroski, and A. Jacquemin. 1984. "Concentration Indices and Market Power: Two Views." *Journal of Industrial Economics* 32 (June):419–34.

Geroski, P., and A. Jacquemin. 1981. "Imports as Competitive Discipline." In P. Geroski and A. Jacquemin, eds., *Recherches Economiques de Louvain* 47:197–208.

Gollop, F. M., and J. Roberts. 1979. "Firm Interdependence in Oligopolistic Markets." *Journal of Econometrics* 10:313–31.

Iwata, G. 1977. "Measurement of Conjectural Variations in Oligopoly." *Econometrica* 42:947–66.

Kim, J. W. 1985. "The Rate of TFP Changes in Small and Medium Industries and Economic Development: The Case of Korea's Manufacturing." Korea Development Institute Working Paper 8501. Seoul.

Korea, Economic Planning Board. 1984. *White Paper on Fair Trade Policies.* Seoul. In Korean.

Korea Development Institute. 1981. *Collection of Documents and Study Reports in Relation to Economic Stabilization Policies.* Seoul. In Korean.

Lee, K. U. 1977. *Market Structure and Monopoly Regulation.* Seoul: Korea Development Institute. In Korean.

———. 1979. "Market Structure and Regulating for Monopoly and Oligopoly." Korea Development Institute, Research Series, no. 18. Seoul. In Korean.

———. 1984. "Market Segmentation and Market Structure." Seoul: Korea Development Institute. In Korean.

———. 1985. "Business Integration and Concentration of Economic Power." Seoul: Korea Development Institute. In Korean.

Lee, S. S. 1985. "International Trade and Domestic Market Structure in Korea." Seoul: Korea Development Institute. In Korean.

Lee, Y. K. 1985. "Conglomeration and Business Concentration: The Korean Case." A paper presented at the 1985 Joint Conference on Industrial Policy of the Republic of China and the Republic of Korea, Seoul, Korea, November 21–22.

Lee, K. U., and Jae-Hyung Lee. 1982. "Roles of Trade Association and Its Regulation." *Korea Development Review* 4 (December). In Korean.

Lee, K. U., J. H. Lee, and Joo-Hoon Kim. 1984. "Market Structure of the Manufacturing Sector in Korea." *Korea Development Review* 6 (April). In Korean.

Leff, N. H. 1979. "Monopoly Capitalism and Public Policy in Developing Countries." *Kyklos* 32:718–38.

Pugel, T. A. 1978. *International Market Linkages and U.S. Manufacturing: Prices, Profits and Patterns*. Cambridge, Mass.: Ballinger Press.

Satterthwaite, F. W. 1946. "An Approximate Distribution of Estimates of Variance Components." *Biometric Bulletin* 2:110–14.

Scitovsky, Tibor. 1985. "Economic Development in Taiwan and South Korea: 1965–81." *Food Research Institute Studies* 19(3):215–64.

Senoo, Akira. 1983. *Industrial Concentration in Contemporary Japan: 1971–1980*. Tokyo: Nippon Keizai Shimbunsha. In Japanese.

Urata, Shujiro. 1984. "Price-Cost Margins and Imports in an Oligopolistic Market." *Economics Letters* 15:139–44.

10 Structural Adjustment and the Role of the Labor Market

TARSICIO CASTANEDA, World Bank
FUNKOO PARK, Korea Development Institute

To CLARIFY THE ROLE of the labor market in the recent structural adjustment of Korea, this chapter will address two sets of issues. The first is how the Korean labor market fared in the years of adjustment, a process that has often been accompanied by a massive increase in unemployment, a reduction in the real wages of workers, and disruptive shifts in labor-management relations. In the case of Korea, the structural adjustment took place without large increases in unemployment or a deterioration in real wages. The focus here is on the adjustments the labor market did undergo in employment, redeployment of labor, structure of the labor supply, and wage flexibility.

Second, this chapter investigates the ways the labor market contributed to the successful management of Korea's structural adjustment. The two questions posed are: how did the labor market contribute to the price stabilization efforts and to what extent did labor productivity improve and contribute to the gain in Korea's international competitiveness and overall economic growth? To answer these questions, the labor market policies pursued affecting wages, education and training, and redeployment are reviewed.

Overview of Adjustment

Table 10-1 reviews the changes in the key labor market variables in Korea over the period 1975–1985. After 1979, employment started to grow at a much slower rate in comparison with that observed earlier in the 1970s. Although total employment increased at an average annual rate of 3.8 percent for the period 1970 to 1979, the pace fell to an average of 1.7 percent during 1980 to 1985. In 1984 there was even a drop from the level of the previous year, although a marginal one.

Employment in manufacturing, which had more than doubled in the 1970s, dropped from its 1979 level for two consecutive years and did not regain that level until 1983. In the 1980s the expansion of employment occurred mostly in the service sector, for which the annual rate of growth from 1979 to 1985 was almost identical to that for the period between 1970 and 1979.

Employment in agriculture showed the largest drop in the 1980s, through 1985, a trend that may explain the slower growth in total employment in this decade. Agricultural employment, which increased continuously until 1976, began to decrease thereafter, with only a temporary reversal in the trend around the 1980–81 recession years. After 1982 it dropped steadily at the rate of 6.2 percent a year until 1985.

Against this series of changes in total and sectoral employment, the rate of increase in the labor supply in the 1980s was far slower than in the 1970s. Although labor supply, measured by the number of economically active people, grew at around 3 percent a year during the 1970s, the rate of increase during the period from 1980 through 1985 was only 1.5 percent a year.

Reflecting these changes in employment and labor supply, the rate of unemployment in Korea remained reasonably low during and after the 1980 recession. At the peak of the expansion in 1978 the rate of unemployment was 3.2 percent; the rate of unemployment at the trough of the 1980 recession was 5.2 percent. Although the growth of total employment following the 1980 recession was negligible, the rate of unemployment remained around 4 percent.

The wage trends observed in the 1980s also differed sharply from the pattern in the 1970s. In the latter part of the 1970s, nominal wages increased over 30 percent a year. Thereafter, the annual rate of wage increase decreased gradually, maintaining a level of around 8 to 9 percent after 1984. During the course of adjustment, the level of real wages dropped in 1980 and 1981 because of severe inflation, then returned to a substantial rate of increase as a result of sustained price stability.

From the observations about the labor market, it can be concluded that Korea adjusted fairly well to the external shocks and structural adjustment around the turn of the 1980s. Although the speed of employment generation in the overall economy slowed, the rate of unemployment was maintained at a reasonable level; real wages dropped in the period 1980–81, but they established a course of steady growth of 6 to 7 percent afterward.

Labor Supply and Employment Generation

This section reviews in detail the pattern of changes in the Korean labor market through an examination of labor supply and employment expansion during the period from 1975 through 1985. As noted in the previous section, unemployment was maintained at a reasonable level, even during the recessionary period. The primary focus of the following discussion is identification of the trends in labor supply and employment, the factors behind them, and the kinds of labor market adjustments pursued.

Table 10-1. Labor Market Trends, 1970–85
(thousands)

Year	Economically active population		Employment increase								Unemployment rate		Wage increase rate	
			Total		Agriculture		Mining and manufacturing		Services		Total	Nonfarm	Nominal	Real
1970	10.199	*3.1*	9.745	*3.5*	4.916	*1.9*	1.395	*3.6*	3.434	*5.9*	4.5	8.9	n.a.	n.a.
1975	12.340	*2.2*	11.830	*2.1*	5.425	*-2.8*	2.265	*9.8*	4.140	*5.1*	4.1	6.6	29.5	3.4
1976	13.061	*5.8*	12.556	*6.1*	5.601	*3.2*	2.743	*21.1*	4.212	*1.7*	3.9	6.3	35.5	17.6
1977	13.440	*2.9*	12.929	*3.0*	5.405	*-3.5*	2.901	*5.8*	4.623	*9.8*	3.8	5.8	32.1	19.9
1978	13.932	*3.7*	13.490	*4.3*	5.181	*-4.1*	3.123	*7.7*	5.186	*12.2*	3.2	4.7	35.0	18.0
1979	14.206	*2.0*	13.664	*1.3*	4.887	*-5.7*	3.237	*3.7*	5.540	*6.8*	3.8	5.6	28.3	8.5
1980	14.431	*1.7*	13.706	*0.3*	4.654	*-4.8*	3.079	*-4.9*	5.951	*7.4*	5.2	7.5	23.4	-4.1
1981	14.683	*1.7*	14.048	*2.5*	4.801	*3.2*	2.983	*-3.1*	6.239	*4.8*	4.5	6.5	20.7	-0.5
1982	15.032	*2.4*	14.424	*2.7*	4.612	*-3.9*	3.143	*5.4*	6.624	*6.2*	4.4	6.0	15.8	7.9
1983	15.118	*0.6*	14.515	*0.6*	4.315	*-6.4*	3.375	*7.4*	6.816	*2.9*	4.1	5.4	11.0	7.4
1984	14.997	*-0.8*	14.417	*-0.8*	3.914	*-9.3*	3.491	*3.4*	7.024	*3.1*	3.8	4.9	8.7	6.3
1985	15.592	*4.0*	14.935	*3.6*	3.733	*-4.6*	3.659	*4.8*	7.578	*7.9*	4.0	4.9	9.2	6.6

n.a. Not applicable.

Note: The figures in italics are percentage rates of increase.

Source: Korea, Economic Planning Board, *Annual Report on the Economically Active Population Survey* (1985) and Korea, Ministry of Labor, *Yearbook of Labor Statistics* (1985).

Labor Supply

One of the most noticeable structural changes in the Korean labor market was the slowdown in the growth of the supply of labor. This trend was largely responsible for the low unemployment rates observed in the 1980s. The slowdown in the labor supply in 1980–85 was the combined result of a slowdown in population growth, especially the size of the population fourteen years of age or older, and a reduction in the labor force participation rate.

The population fourteen years of age or older grew at a substantially lower annual rate between 1980 and 1985 than between 1970 and 1980. Whereas between 1980 and 1985 this growth was 2.4 percent a year, between 1970 and 1980 it was 3.0 percent (table 10-2). The rapid population growth of the 1970s was the result of the post–Korean War "baby boomers" entering the labor force, and the recent slowdown was attributable to the lower fertility rates that Korea began to experience after the mid-1960s.

As seen in table 10-2, the labor force participation rate in the 1980s dropped by 3 to 4 percentage points from the peak of 1978. The rapid decline between 1979 and 1984 was mainly responsible for the relatively low unemployment rates recorded in those years. For instance, had the participation rate of 1979 remained the same between 1980 and 1985, the rates of unemployment would have been substantially higher than those recorded: 6.1 percent in 1980 and 1981 instead of the actual 5.2 percent and 4.5 percent; 5.6 percent in 1982 instead of 4.4 percent; 7.1 percent in 1983 instead of 4.1 percent; and close to 10 percent in 1984 and 1985 instead of 3.8 percent and 4.0 percent. According to these figures, the adjustment of these years appears to have been more painful than is usually shown, with 1984 the worst in terms of unemployment.

A number of factors explain the drop in the labor force participation rate. First, the participation rate for the younger age group, especially those between the ages of fourteen and nineteen, both male and female, as well as males between twenty and twenty-four, dropped significantly between 1975 and 1984 (table 10-3). Because this younger age bracket constituted a large share of the total population, its decline had a strong effect on overall trends in the participation rate. The decline of the labor force participation rate of the younger age group was a reflection of the rapid increase in school enrollment, which continued through 1985.[1] Enrollment in secondary education increased gradually as the general income level of the nation rose, and tuition support for poor families was expanded. College enrollment increased rapidly after 1980, when the college quota was extended to meet the ever-increasing demand for higher education.[2] The size of enrollment in colleges, including two-year junior colleges, increased from 560,000 in 1980 to around 1.2 million in 1985.

Table 10-2. *Labor Force, Employment, and Annual Rates of Growth, 1970–85*

Year	Population age fourteen and over (thousands)	Economically active population (thousands)	Participation rate (percent)					Unemployment rate (percent)	
			Average	Male	Female	Farm	Nonfarm	Total	Nonfarm
1970	18,253	10,199	55.9	75.1	38.5	60.9	51.5	4.5	8.9
1975	21,833	12,340	56.5	74.6	39.6	62.7	52.2	4.1	6.6
1976	22,549	13,061	57.9	74.6	42.3	64.8	53.3	3.9	6.3
1977	23,336	13,440	57.6	75.9	40.7	63.3	54.0	3.8	5.8
1978	24,024	13,932	58.0	75.0	42.2	63.9	54.6	3.2	4.7
1979	24,678	14,206	57.6	74.1	42.2	63.6	54.4	3.8	5.6
1980	24,463	14,431	57.1	73.6	41.6	62.5	54.4	5.2	7.5
1981	25,100	14,683	56.6	73.2	41.1	62.6	53.8	4.5	6.5
1982	25,638	15,032	56.8	72.5	42.2	61.9	54.7	4.4	6.0
1983	26,212	15,118	55.8	70.9	41.6	59.8	54.2	4.1	5.4
1984	26,861	14,997	53.9	69.4	39.5	59.3	52.2	3.8	4.9
1985	27,553	15,592	54.6	69.6	40.6	59.7	53.1	4.0	4.9
Annual growth rates (percent)									
1970–75	3.65	3.88							
1975–80	2.30	3.18							
1980–85	2.41	1.56							

Source: Korea, Economic Planning Board, *Annual Report on the Economically Active Population Survey* (1985) and Korea, Ministry of Labor, *Yearbook of Labor Statistics* (1985).

Table 10-3. *Male and Female Labor Force Participation Rates by Age Group, Selected Years, 1970–84*
(percent)

Age group	1970	1975	1980	1983	1984
Male					
14–19	41.2	33.7	22.9	15.0	12.6
20–24	77.3	78.5	76.4	68.2	64.7
25–29	92.2	95.1	95.1	92.2	90.9
30–34	95.6	97.3	97.6	96.9	96.4
35–39	95.9	96.7	97.2	96.6	96.2
40–44	95.3	95.6	96.1	95.1	95.1
45–49	93.1	92.9	94.3	93.7	93.2
50–54	87.8	90.5	90.5	89.8	87.9
55–59	77.1	83.4	80.1	78.4	77.3
60–64	58.8	63.4	63.7	—	—
Total	75.1	74.6	73.6	70.9	69.4
Female					
14–19	38.7	36.4	29.0	21.5	18.2
20–24	47.3	47.3	53.5	54.1	52.5
25–29	34.7	29.5	32.0	32.5	33.3
30–34	38.4	37.0	40.8	44.5	42.2
35–39	42.7	48.0	53.0	52.8	51.3
40–44	46.9	51.6	56.7	60.8	56.4
45–49	46.6	50.9	57.3	60.4	57.1
50–54	41.1	50.8	54.0	55.5	51.8
55–59	37.1	44.8	46.2	48.0	45.3
60–64	22.8	28.1	32.2	—	—
Total	38.5	39.6	41.6	41.6	39.5

—Not available.

Source: Various issues of Korea, Economic Planning Board, *Annual Report on the Economically Active Population Survey.*

The effect of the increased enrollment on the labor supply can be seen in the ratio between the additional high school and college enrollment and the additional population over fourteen years of age—about 22 percent each year from 1976 to 1979, it rose to more than 40 percent from 1980 to 1982 (table 10-4). Had the ratio observed during the 1976–79 remained the same during 1980–82, the rate of recorded unemployment would have been 5.7 percent in 1980, 5.6 percent in 1981, and 5.2 percent in 1982. The implication is that the increase in enrollment contributed to the lower recorded unemployment by as much as 0.5 percentage point in 1980, by 1.1 percentage points in 1981, and by 0.8 percentage point in 1982. Because the rate of increase in enrollment started to slow in 1983, it ceased to be a significant factor in reducing the labor supply and in the recorded unemployment rate.

Another factor that affected the overall decline in the labor force participation rate was the acceleration in rural-urban migration in the 1980s. As a result of the migration, the size of the population fourteen years or older in the farm sector dropped to about 6.4 million in 1985 from a peak of around 9.1 million in 1976. Because the average rate of participation in the farm

Table 10-4. *Annual Changes in Enrollment
and in Population Age Fourteen and Over*
(thousands)

Year	Change in population age fourteen and over (1)	Change in enrollment[a] (2)	(2)/(1) (percent)
1970	614[b]	78[b]	12.7
1976	716[c]	160[c]	22.3
1977	787	137	17.3
1978	688	157	22.8
1979	654	138	21.1
1980	215	290	42.9
1981	637	318	49.9
1982	538	248	46.1
1983	574	226	39.4
1984	649	184	28.4
1985	692	143	20.7

a. Includes high school (general and vocational), junior college, junior teachers' college, and college, university, and graduate school.

b. Change from 1969.

c. Change from 1975.

Source: For population: various issues of Korea, Economic Planning Board, *Annual Report on the Economically Active Population Survey;* for enrollment: Korea, Economic Planning Board (1985), which cites the Ministry of Education as a primary source of data.

sector stayed about 8 to 10 percentage points higher than that in the nonfarm sector, this change in the composition of the total population had a negative effect on the overall reduction in the participation rate.

Although there are no concrete data on the size of migration and the characteristics of migrants, table 10-5 indicates the nature of rural-urban migration in the period from 1975 to 1985. Most noticeable is that the size of the economically active population in the age group fourteen to twenty-four in the farm sector declined by one-third. This trend did not necessarily

Table 10-5. *Economically Active Population by Age Group
in the Farm Sector*

Year	Total	Age group 14–24	Age group 25–54	Age group 55+
Number (thousands)				
1975	5,673	1,391	3,400	882
1980	5,169	895	3,288	986
1985	3,836	421	2,493	922
Ratio				
1980/1975	0.91	0.64	0.97	1.12
1985/1975	0.68	0.30	0.73	1.05
1985/1980	0.74	0.47	0.76	0.94

Source: Korea, Economic Planning Board, *Annual Report on the Economically Active Population Survey* (1985).

imply, however, that the reduction was solely the result of out-migration, because secondary education in the rural sector also expanded. Another point to be noted from table 10-5 is that the labor force in the farm sector aged very fast: the share of the labor force fifty-five years or older went from 15.5 percent to 24.0 percent over the period from 1975 to 1985.

Employment

Total employment in Korea grew more slowly after 1979 in contrast to the period between 1970 and 1979 (table 10-6). This slower growth can be attributed not only to an acceleration in the decline of employment in agriculture but also to the slower growth in manufacturing and services. Employment in manufacturing even declined in 1980 and 1981.

Agriculture Agricultural employment started to decline in relative terms beginning in the mid-1960s but did not decrease in absolute numbers until the mid-1970s. The reversal of the trend in agricultural employment that appeared in 1981 probably was a response to the decline in employment in manufacturing. After 1982 employment in agriculture continued to decline at an even faster pace than in the past. As a result it was only 25 percent of total employment in 1985, half the level of 1970.

Because unemployment rates in agriculture were low, the decline in employment was associated with rural-urban migration. As seen in table 10-7, migration boosted the urban labor force by about 350,000 each year between 1977 and 1980 and by around 600,000 annually between 1982 and 1984.[3]

The rural-urban migration that took place from the late 1960s up to 1980 can be explained by economic factors. In the late 1960s the rate was high because the terms of trade in agriculture deteriorated, while the employment prospects in manufacturing improved (table 10-8). From 1972 to 1976 migration slowed primarily because the agricultural terms of trade improved and urban unemployment increased. From 1977 to 1980 migration rose again, mainly because of the decline in urban unemployment as manufacturing and services expanded.

The rural-urban migration of the 1980s can also be explained by economic factors. During 1981 migration stopped in response to the decline in manufacturing employment in the two previous years. Then, from 1982 to 1984, it increased tremendously, probably because of the rapidly declining terms of trade in agriculture and the recovery of employment growth in manufacturing and services.[4]

Although the slower growth in employment in the mid-1980s may be explained by the reduced GNP growth rate, changes in the structure of the economy may also have affected its capacity to absorb labor. These changes included the capital deepening observed in manufacturing and the acceler-

Table 10-6. *Sectoral Employment Trends, 1970–85*
(thousands, unless otherwise noted)

Year	Total employment	Percentage change over previous year	Agriculture[a]	Percentage change over previous year	Mining and manufacturing	Percentage change over previous year	Services[b]	Percentage change over previous year
1970	9,745	n.a.	4,916	n.a.	1,395	n.a.	3,434	n.a.
1975	11,830	3.9[c]	5,425	2.0[c]	2,265	9.7[c]	4,140	3.7[c]
1976	12,556	6.1	5,601	3.2	2,743	21.1	4,212	1.7
1977	12,929	3.0	5,405	-3.5	2,901	5.8	4,623	9.8
1978	13,490	4.3	5,181	-4.1	3,123	7.6	5,186	12.2
1979	13,664	1.3	4,887	-5.7	3,237	3.6	5,540	6.8
1980	13,683	0.1	4,654	-4.8	3,079	-4.9	5,951	7.4
1981	14,023	2.5	4,801	3.2	2,983	-3.1	6,239	4.8
1982	14,379	2.5	4,612	-3.9	3,143	5.4	6,624	6.2
1983	14,505	0.9	4,315	-6.4	3,375	7.4	6,816	2.9
1984	14,429	-0.5	3,914	-9.3	3,491	3.4	7,024	3.1
1985	14,970	3.7	3,733	-4.6	3,659	4.8	7,578	7.9

n.a. Not applicable.
a. Includes agriculture, forestry, and fisheries.
b. Includes construction, public utilities, commerce, finance, and community and personal services.
c. Average rate between 1970 and 1975.
Source: Korea, Economic Planning Board, *Annual Report on the Economically Active Population Survey* (1985).

ation in the decline of agricultural employment. (The recent trends in employment in agriculture, manufacturing, and services are reviewed below.)

The decline in the terms of trade was the result of (a) changes in agricultural policies to reduce the price supports for rice and other crops and

Table 10-7. *Rural-Urban Migration, 1965, 1970, and 1975–85*
(thousands, unless otherwise noted)

Year	Recorded farm populaton[a]	Population growth rate (percent)	Predicted farm population[b]	Estimated net off-farm migration[c]
1965	8,985	2.55	9,118	133
1970	8,540	2.13	8,795	255
1975	9,054	1.67	9,138	84
1976	9,128	1.61	9,205	67
1977	9,023	1.57	9,275	252
1978	8,734	1.53	9,165	431
1979	8,492	1.53	8,868	376
1980	8,269	1.56	8,622	353
1981	8,313	1.57	8,398	85
1982	7,848	1.57	8,443	595
1983	7,571	1.58	7,971	400
1984	6,749	1.57	7,691	943
1985	6,428	1.55	6,855	427

a. Age fourteen and over.

b. Calculated as the recorded farm population (age fourteen and over) of the previous year multiplied by the population growth rate.

c. The difference between the predicted and recorded farm population.

Source: For recorded farm population: various issues of Korea, Economic Planning Board, *Annual Report on the Economically Active Population Survey;* for growth rate of the population: Korea, Economic Planning Board (1985).

Table 10-8. *Ratios of Prices Received and Paid by Farmers, 1966, 1970, and 1975–84*

Year	Prices received/ prices paid by farmers[a]	Prices received/prices paid for farm supplies	Prices received/ paid wages
1966	90.0	78.6	202.5
1970	94.2	82.1	168.9
1975	105.7	99.2	168.2
1976	105.2	91.0	165.1
1977	104.8	88.7	155.2
1978	105.0	80.8	142.8
1979	102.4	93.6	105.1
1980	100.0	100.0	100.0
1981	99.8	86.0	103.6
1982	95.0	83.1	106.4
1983	89.8	74.7	102.8
1984	92.7	84.5	97.9

a. Prices received for sales of grains (including potatoes), fruits and vegetables, livestock, and poultry products. Prices paid for purchases of farm supplies, household goods, and farm labor.

Source: Korea, Economic Planning Board (1985).

the subsidies for inputs in 1980 and (b) the sharp increase in farm wages. This decline most probably affected the less productive farmers who, although not employing much hired labor, were probably unable to compete with farmers who had increased their productivity by introducing machinery and high-yield varieties into farming in the late 1970s.[5]

Manufacturing The manufacturing sector became a major source of employment growth when industrialization began in the 1960s, a trend that continued up to the mid-1970s. The average annual rate of manufacturing employment expansion during 1971–76 was 12.2 percent. The rate slowed considerably, however, in the late 1970s: the average annual rate of growth of employment in manufacturing during 1977–85 was only 3.3 percent, and in 1980 and 1981, it fell by 3.4 percent each year. Even when growth as a whole resumed, manufacturing employment showed no significant gains.

The slowdown in manufacturing employment growth in the late 1970s was partly a response to the slower expansion in manufacturing output. Manufacturing GNP increased at around 15 to 20 percent a year until 1978 and at only 6.8 percent between 1979 and 1985. There is also a strong indication that structural changes were responsible for this trend. Table 10-9 shows the trends in employment elasticity—the ratio of growth rates between employment and GNP—for the period 1972–85. It is not easy to identify any distinctive trends in manufacturing after 1980 because the fluctuations were great. It can be observed, however, that employment elasticity in the first part of the 1970s was significantly higher than in the latter part.

Table 10-9. *Employment Elasticity, 1972–85*

Year	All industries	Mining and manufacturing	Services
1972	0.86	0.39	−0.29
1973	0.39	0.75	0.07
1974	0.52	0.90	1.00
1975	0.30	0.80	0.91
1976	0.43	0.96	0.13
1977	0.23	0.37	0.62
1978	0.44	0.38	1.01
1979	0.20	0.40	1.36
1980	−0.06	2.93	−4.13
1981	0.38	−0.40	8.27
1982	0.50	1.35	0.90
1983	0.05	0.61	0.27
1984	−0.08	0.16	0.38
1985	0.71	1.26	1.32

Note: Elasticity = percentage change in employment/percentage change in GNP.
Source: Authors' calculations.

The pattern of change can be more clearly observed when the changes in GNP and employment are compared for a longer time period. Although the employment output elasticity in manufacturing during the period from 1970 to 1976 was 0.583, it dropped to 0.254 during 1979–85.[6]

Several factors led to the slower employment absorption of manufacturing. Most important was the shift in the composition of manufacturing output toward more capital-intensive products. The share of heavy manufacturing output increased from 30 percent in 1970 to 55.7 percent in 1983. The shift in the composition of manufacturing output toward heavy manufacturing was primarily the result of the government policy to promote the heavy and chemical industries. Also important in explaining the trend of capital deepening in Korean manufacturing was the continued growth in the level of real wages, which caused a steady decline in the relative price of capital compared with labor.[7]

Also noteworthy in explaining the trend of declining employment absorption in Korean manufacturing are changes in management attitudes. To survive the 1980 recession, Korean firms had to emphasize managerial efficiency with respect to manpower, which had been controlled somewhat loosely in the rapidly expanding period of the 1970s. This change in managerial attitude persisted even after the economy resumed a normal growth path after 1983. Changes in the perspective of management toward labor-management relations were also an issue: the number of labor disputes increased and became more difficult to handle in the late 1970s.[8] Although it is difficult to measure their impact on management practices, labor disputes encouraged management to replace employees with machines at a faster pace.

Employment in manufacturing at a more disaggregated level is shown in table 10-10.[9] As of 1983, textiles and wearing apparel and fabricated metal products, machinery, and equipment were the two largest manufacturing subsectors, accounting for more than 50 percent of total manufacturing employment. Although textiles and wearing apparel was, as of 1983, the subsector with the highest level of employment, the number of workers did not increase much after 1975. In the fabricated metal products, machinery, and equipment subsector, however, employment grew rapidly. Further, inasmuch as this subsector will be the leader within manufacturing, it will soon be the largest manufacturing subsector.

Table 10-10 presents the employment figures by manufacturing subsector obtained from the establishment surveys. An interesting point is that the share of manufacturing employment within firms with more than five workers increased over the period between 1975 and 1983. This phenomenon, which can be described as a diminution of the nonformal sector, may be one of the structural changes within manufacturing that was responsible for the decreasing employment absorption.[10] At a disaggregated level, the

Table 10-10. *Employment Composition in Manufacturing, 1975–83*
(thousands, unless otherwise noted)

Item	Population census[a]			Annual rate of increase (percent)		Establishment survey[b]					
	1975 (1)	1980 (2)	1983 (3)	1975–80 (4)	1980–83 (5)	1975 (6)		1980 (7)		1983 (8)	
Total	2,211	2,797	2,893	4.8	1.1	1,420	64.2	1,998	71.4	2,134	73.8
Food and beverages	222	248	311	2.2	7.8	150	67.6	136	54.8	150	48.2
Textiles, wearing apparel	827	950	834	2.8	-4.3	504	60.9	651	68.5	684	82.0
Wood	126	148	173	3.3	5.3	52	41.3	63	42.6	58	33.5
Paper and printing	101	158	172	9.4	2.9	69	68.3	95	60.1	96	55.8
Chemicals	213	263	321	4.3	6.9	182	85.4	234	88.9	265	82.6
Minerals, nonmetallic	90	120	132	5.9	3.2	60	66.7	89	74.2	93	70.5
Basic metals	59	108	90	12.9	-5.9	47	79.7	72	66.7	51	56.7
Equipment and machinery	451	681	742	8.6	2.9	295	65.4	577	84.7	652	87.9
Miscellaneous	119	119	119	0.0	0.0	57	47.8	71	59.7	82	68.9

Note: The figures in italics are percentages (survey figure divided by census figure for the year in question).

a. Census employment figures are the basis for the employment reported for 1975 and 1980; the 1983 figure comes from the 1983 Special Employment Census.

b. Employment data come from the Ministry of Labor's Establishment Surveys, which covered firms with more than five workers, except for 1975, for which the Economic Planning Board's Mining and Manufacturing Survey results were used (the Mining and Manufacturing Survey covers firms with more than five workers as well).

diminution of the nonformal sector is not observed in all subsectors. The trend is visible, however, in the two largest, textiles and fabricated metal products.

Social Overhead Capital and Services Although the share of employment in social overhead capital (SOC) and services[11] remained constant at around 35 percent during the first half of the 1970s, it rose steadily thereafter, reaching 50 percent by 1985. After the mid-1970s, SOC and services was the fastest growing sector in employment: the average rate during 1971–76 was 3.5 percent, compared with 6.8 percent for the period from 1977 to 1985.

For the period 1970–76, employment and output in this sector grew by 22.7 percent and 61.4 percent, respectively, only to jump to 63.5 percent and 52 percent, in 1977–85. The employment output elasticities for the two periods were 0.36 and 1.22, respectively, evidence that employment absorption in the tertiary sector increased greatly.

Table 10-11 shows the composition of employment in SOC and services.[12] A majority of employment in this sector was found in commerce, which comprises the retail and wholesale trades and restaurants and hotels (42 percent), and in community, social, and personal services (25 percent). In the commerce and service industry subsector, the small traditional operation was typical, and employment of nonpaid family workers was prevalent.

The number of workers in firms employing more than five persons is available from the Establishment Surveys. When these figures are compared with total employment for 1983, it is seen that 11.3 percent of the total employment in commerce and 18.1 percent in services was in firms with more than five workers. Compared with these figures, the transportation and banking sectors showed a much higher portion of workers employed in the large modern sector.[13]

As noted above, tertiary sector employment increased steadily after the mid-1970s, a trend that continued even during the serious business downswings of the 1980–81 period. In 1980 employment in the tertiary sector increased by 7.4 percent although sector GNP fell by 1.8 percent. That trend probably was a result of the urban informal service sector's absorbing the workers displaced from other sectors as a form of underemployment.

A more important question, it seems, is what forms the increase in tertiary sector employment took. Detailed data indicating its trends are lacking. The census report shows that during 1975–83 employment in the public utility, construction, and financial subsectors, which tended to employ highly paid, highly skilled workers, grew much faster than did the tertiary sector on average, an indication that over the period the service sector was gradually institutionalized into the formal sector. It cannot be

Table 10-11. Composition of Tertiary Sector Employment, 1975–83
(thousands)

Item	Population census					Establishment survey					
	1975	1980	1983	1975–80	1980–83	1975		1980		1983	
Total	4,169	4,999	6,171	3.7	7.3	422	*10.1*	1,133	*22.7*	1,410	*22.8*
Electricity, gas, water	35	36	67	0.6	23.0	10	*28.6*	23	*63.9*	24	*35.8*
Construction	484	664	860	6.5	9.0	89	*18.4*	236	*35.5*	198	*23.0*
Sales, restaurants, hotels	1,694	2,059	2,608	4.0	8.2	37	*2.2*	231	*11.2*	295	*11.3*
Transportation, storage, communications	432	551	657	5.0	6.0	161	*37.3*	268	*48.6*	343	*52.2*
Finance, insurance, real estate	151	286	409	13.6	12.7	66	*43.7*	168	*58.7*	265	*64.8*
Community, social, personal services	1,373	1,403	1,571	0.4	3.8	59	*4.3*	207	*14.8*	285	*18.1*

Note: The figures in italics are percentages (survey figures divided by census figure for the year in question).
Source: Economic Planning Board, *Population and Housing Census Report*; and Ministry of Labor, *Report on Labor Conditions of Establishments*.

ignored, however, that 45 percent of a net increase in tertiary employment of about 2 million from 1975 to 1983 came from commerce.

Employment Adjustment

It was noted that labor market adjustment was quite successful in avoiding massive unemployment and that the adjustment came mainly through changes in supply-side conditions. It should also be noted that during 1980 and 1981 real wages dropped, a downturn that brought with it demand-side adjustment. The magnitude of the adjustment should depend on the size of the demand elasticity for labor, but it is apparent that wage flexibility contributed to relieving the pressure on employers to reduce employment substantially. [14]

Another point to be noted regarding labor market adjustment is the structure of the labor market nexus among permanent and temporary workers and the informal sector. [15] The pattern of manpower redeployment in developing countries is that temporary workers are laid off during contractions and are absorbed into the large informal sector. In the process, massive unemployment can be avoided at the aggregate level.

There is no clear-cut answer to the validity of this argument in the Korean case. As was seen, absorption of laid-off workers by the informal sector was a critical element in labor market adjustment to maintain the aggregate level of employment. Nevertheless, the notion that workers in the formal sector were divided into temporary and permanent status according to job security arrangements and that temporary workers were laid off as a means of employment adjustment does not seem to describe the Korean labor market. With respect to job security arrangements, there is no clear-cut distinction between temporary and permanent workers. [16]

Adjustment of the size of employment in Korea was often accomplished by simply not filling vacancies. Turnover among production workers was high (4 to 5 percent a month) even during the recessionary period, and a 20 to 30 percent employment reduction is thus possible within a short time without deliberate layoffs.

Another form of employment adjustment involved the use of subcontractors. In such labor-intensive industries as wearing apparel, shoes, and the like, a portion of output was produced through subcontractors. When demand declined, the subcontract was terminated. Thus, employment security could be maintained in the ordering firms, although jobs in the subcontractors' firms fluctuated severely.

Wages and Productivity

This section reviews the pattern of wage changes and productivity trends observed in the course of adjustment in the Korean labor market in the period 1975 through 1985. The major issues are the ways in which wage policy was employed to curb wage trends, changes in wage structures, and productivity trends and their effect on the competitiveness of Korean exports.

Wages Over the course of the period from 1975 through 1985, the level of wages in nominal as well as real terms shows a positive trend, with a drop from the trend in 1980 and 1981 (table 10-12). Particular patterns are worth noting. First, the increase in nominal wages, which was around 30 percent a year in the latter half of the 1970s, fell to less than 10 percent after 1984. Second, the level of real wages dropped in both 1980 and 1981 but increased steadily thereafter, despite reduced nominal wage growth. The rapid wage increases in the latter half of the 1970s were a reflection of changes in labor market conditions. The expansion of employment in all sectors of the economy created upward pressure on the labor market, and labor shortages were acute among college graduates, highly skilled occupations in various manufacturing industries, and construction jobs. In construction, for instance, nominal wages jumped by more than 80 percent in 1976.[17]

The trade union movement, which expanded considerably in the 1970s with the increase in employment in the modern sector, played only a limited role in the rapid wage increases.[18] In industries such as textiles and transportation, the role of the trade union in collective bargaining was more pronounced than in others. Nevertheless, because of a relatively short history, inadequate social acceptance and support for the role of the trade union, a low level of awareness, and a lack of participation on the part of the workers, the effectiveness of trade union activities in Korea was reduced.

Table 10-12. *Wage Trends, 1975–85*
(percent)

	All industries		Manufacturing	
Year	Nominal	Real	Nominal	Real
1975	29.5	3.3	27.0	1.4
1976	35.5	17.5	34.7	16.8
1977	32.1	19.9	33.8	21.5
1978	35.0	18.0	34.3	17.4
1979	28.3	8.4	28.6	8.7
1980	23.4	−4.1	22.7	−4.7
1981	20.7	−0.5	20.1	−1.0
1982	15.8	7.9	14.7	6.9
1983	11.0	7.4	12.2	8.6
1984	8.7	6.3	8.1	5.7
1985	9.2	6.6	9.9	7.3

Note: Data show percentage changes from the previous year.
Source: Various issues of Korea, Ministry of Labor, *Yearbook of Labor Statistics.*

Table 10-13. *Annual Increases in Nominal Wages in Manufacturing and Government, 1971–85*

(percent)

Year	Manufacturing		Government	
	Total[a]	Negotiated over basic wage	Total[a]	Negotiated over basic wage
1971	16.2	—	14.0	—
1972	13.9	—	19.0	—
1973	18.0	—	24.0	—
1974	35.3	—	48.0	—
1975	27.0	—	28.0	—
1976	34.7	—	55.0	—
1977	33.8	36.0	25.0	32.0
1978	34.3	29.7	26.0	20.0
1979	28.6	26.8	23.0	15.0
1980	22.7	21.5	22.0	10.0
1981	20.1	16.1	17.0	10.0
1982	14.7	9.5	9.9	9.0
1983	12.2	6.9	8.5	6.0
1984	8.1	—	—	0.0
1985	9.9	—	—	3.0

— Not available

a. Includes bonus payments and fringe benefits.

Source: Data for manufacturing are from the Ministry of Labor's Monthly Wage Survey. The government totals are from the Economic Planning Board, and the "negotiated over basic wage" data are from Nam (1984).

Nominal wage increases in the 1980s, up to 1986, were much slower than in the 1970s; the slowdown was particularly pronounced after 1983. One reason was the price stability apparent after 1982. Because of the much lower rate of inflation, real wages rose at a substantial rate, even with the much slower growth in nominal wages.

In pursuing its wage policy, the government emphasized that the burden of curtailing inflation should be borne by all people. Wage increases in the public sector were minimal, and their rate was suggested as a guideline for the private sector. The government raised the purchase price for grain as little as possible, and it urged firms to keep their dividend payments to a minimum. Government wage-setting behavior, however, does not appear to have been responsible for the behavior of aggregate wages between 1971 and 1985 (see table 10-13). From 1971 to 1980 the changes in public sector wages were quite different from those in manufacturing. The implication is that the public sector did not provide leadership in setting wages for the rest of the economy (Lindauer 1984). From 1981 to 1985, when public sector wage increases were recommended to the private sector for the first time, the increases in total wages in the private sector were also quite different from those in the public sector.

As to trends in the wage structure, there was a drastic change between 1975 and 1985, as outlined in table 10-14. The relative wages of high-

Table 10-14. *Relative Monthly Earnings by Occupation, 1971 and 1975–84*

(production workers = 100)

Year	Professionals, technicians	Managers	Clerical	Sales	Service	Production workers
1971	280	428	243	140	107	100
1975	266	458	215	123	104	100
1976	291	474	222	112	103	100
1980	243	395	162	89	100	100
1981	230	367	163	96	100	100
1982	241	345	158	134	102	100
1983	241	343	155	129	101	100
1984	235	336	153	128	101	100

Note: Data include regular pay, overtime, and special earnings (bonus payments).
Source: Ministry of Labor, Occupational Wage Survey, 1972–85.

paying jobs—such as those of professionals and technicians and managers —increased faster than those of production workers during 1975–76, but declined strongly during 1980–81 and maintained a comparable level thereafter. In 1980, for instance, while the real wages of professionals and technicians declined by 12.5 percent, and managers by 17.2 percent, those of production workers fell by 8.8 percent. The same pattern can be observed in table 10-15, where it can be seen that the relative wage level of college and university graduates increased over that of primary and middle school graduates during 1975–76 and then declined significantly in 1980 and 1981. In 1980 the real wages of college graduates declined by 12.5 percent, those of high school graduates by 10.3 percent, and those of middle and primary school graduates by 8.7 percent.

As seen in tables 10-16 and 10-17, there are strong indications that market forces have been the main factors behind the changes in the struc-

Table 10-15. *Relative Male Monthly Earnings by Education, Selected Years, 1975–84*

(primary school = 100)

Year	College, university	Junior college	High school	Middle school	Primary school
1975	306	200	154	109	100
1977	305	206	148	106	100
1979	280	187	135	104	100
1980	256	170	127	—ᵃ	—ᵃ
1981	256	168	127	—ᵃ	—ᵃ
1982	252	161	126	—ᵃ	—ᵃ
1983	245	156	124	—ᵃ	—ᵃ
1984	240	145	121	—ᵃ	—ᵃ

Note: Data include regular pay, overtime, and special earnings (bonuses).

a. Primary school = 100, except in the case of 1980–84, for which middle school and below = 100.

Source: Ministry of Labor, Occupational Wage Survey, 1976–85.

Table 10-16. *Labor Force by Education, 1980–84*

(thousands)

Year	Total	Primary school		Middle school		High school		College or higher	
1980	14,454	7,250	*50.2*	2,944	*20.4*	3,287	*22.7*	973	*6.7*
1981	14,710	7,166	*48.7*	3,025	*20.6*	3,498	*23.8*	1,021	*6.9*
1982	15,080	6,708	*44.5*	3,279	*21.7*	3,910	*25.9*	1,183	*7.8*
1983	15,128	6,395	*42.3*	3,292	*21.8*	4,180	*27.6*	1,261	*8.3*
1984	14,984	5,811	*38.8*	3,212	*21.4*	4,526	*30.2*	1,435	*9.6*

Note: Figures in italics are percentages.

Source: Various issues of Korea, Economic Planning Board, *Annual Report on the Economically Active Population Survey.*

ture of wages. The supply of skilled labor increased rapidly in the late 1970s and at the beginning of the 1980s, whereas demand, after increasing rapidly at the end of the 1970s, showed slower growth in the 1980s. The labor supply increased as a result of the large expansion of general high school and vocational education. In 1980, for instance, 43 percent of the work force had a secondary education (middle and high school), a large increase from the 27 percent of 1970. By 1984 that proportion reached 52 percent of the total work force. Although the proportion of those with college educations did not rise appreciably between 1970 and 1980, it started to rise rapidly after 1982.

The demand for skilled labor rose more slowly in the 1980s compared with the 1970s. The number of technicians and managers, for instance, which had grown at 6.4 percent a year between 1975 and 1980, grew at 5.1 percent from 1980 to 1983. Similarly, the number of clerical workers, after increasing by 7.1 percent a year between 1975 and 1980, increased by 4.1 percent between 1980 and 1983.

The increase in the demand for skilled workers in the mid-1970s can, as noted, be attributed to the expansion of heavy industries and the larger firms in manufacturing and construction and to the expansion of services

Table 10-17. *Employment by Occupation, 1970–83*

Year	Technicians	Managers	Clerical	Sales	Service	Production workers
Number (thousands)						
1970	322.8	95.8	593.5	1,028.1	678.6	2,197.8
1975	417.4	102.3	844.2	1,317.1	815.8	2,890.7
1980	580.9	133.6	1,203.2	1,531.1	894.6	3,569.7
1983	715.0	119.0	1,362.0	2,022.0	1,149.0	3,824.0
Annual rates of growth (percent)						
1970–1975	5.1	1.3	7.0	5.0	3.7	5.5
1975–1980	6.6	5.3	7.1	3.0	1.8	4.2
1980–1983	6.9	−3.8	4.1	9.3	8.3	2.3

Source: 1970, 1975, and 1980 Population Census and Korea, Economic Planning Board (1984).

Table 10-18. *Wage Payment System, Selected Years, 1971–84*
(percent)

Year	Basic wage	Overtime pay	Bonus
1971	78.4	16.6	5.0
1975	74.6	17.3	8.1
1980	70.9	17.0	12.1
1984	71.3	16.1	12.6

Source: Ministry of Labor, Occupational Wage Survey.

such as insurance, finance, and community and social services. The slower increase in the 1980s can be attributed to less expansion of the larger manufacturing and construction firms and to the slower growth of services (including public administration), especially after 1982.

⌈To gain more insight into the wage issue in Korea, it is helpful to look at the structure of compensation. As table 10-18 shows, in addition to basic wages, workers receive overtime pay, annual or seasonal bonuses, and other allowances. A notable feature of Korea's compensation system is the magnitude of the allowances and bonuses. According to the Occupational Wage Survey by the Ministry of Labor, an average worker received 71 percent of his cash payment in basic wages in 1984. The remainder was roughly divided between overtime and bonus payments.⌋

There was nothing unusual about Korean overtime payments compared with those of other countries. Over the years, however, the annual bonus payment came to represent a larger share of the total payment and was provided almost uniformly by all but very small firms. The size of the bonus, often paid as some percentage of the basic wage, varied across establishments and depended on business conditions. In the case of civil servants, a minimum 400 percent of the basic wage was paid as an annual bonus and was a fixed portion of their total wage bill.

There are a number of reasons that Korean firms used the annual bonus as an important element in the structure of compensation. First, given the relative infrequency of the bonus payment, firms could control their wage funds longer and thereby enhance their cash flow. Second, in Korea a variety of compensation benefits were tied to the basic wage instead of total pay. A firm could minimize total labor costs by granting large bonuses and minimizing basic wages. Third, and perhaps most important, the bonus system enabled firms to adjust their labor costs with changing business climates. The bonus system may have worked as a profit-sharing program in good years and a cost-reduction one in bad years.

Productivity and Unit Labor Costs

The trend in productivity as measured by the output for each worker in manufacturing during 1975–85 is shown in table 10-19.[19] The average rate

Table 10-19. *Productivity and Unit Labor Cost in Manufacturing,*
1975–85

(1980 = 100)

Year	Nominal wage	Output per worker	Unit labor cost (won)	Wage		Unit labor cost (dollars)
				Dollars	Index	
1975	26.2	58.6	44.7	79.3	35.7	60.9
1976	35.2	62.8	56.1	106.8	48.0	76.4
1977	47.2	69.6	67.8	142.9	64.3	92.4
1978	63.3	78.0	81.2	191.9	86.3	110.6
1979	81.5	90.3	90.3	246.9	111.1	123.0
1980	100.0	100.0	100.0	222.3	100.0	100.0
1981	120.1	118.1	101.7	251.5	113.1	95.8
1982	137.8	127.3	108.2	269.9	121.4	95.3
1983	154.6	144.6	106.9	285.1	128.3	88.7
1984	167.2	159.8	104.6	296.4	133.3	83.4
1985	183.8	171.1	107.4	302.9	136.3	79.7

Note: Unit labor cost = index of nominal wages/index of output per worker.
Source: Various issues of Korea, Ministry of Labor, *Yearbook of Labor Statistics.*

of productivity increase was around 11 percent a year, and there was no
distinctive difference in the productivity trends between the latter part of
the 1970s and the first half of the 1980s. It should be noted that even during
the years of recession in 1980–81, output per worker increased at a substantial rate, mainly because the reduction in employment was faster than the
reduction in output.

There were many reasons manufacturing in Korea was able to maintain
such a high level of productivity increase in this period. The most important factors were the trend of gradual capital deepening in all sectors of
manufacturing and the shift in the composition of manufacturing production toward products with greater value added. Both trends increased labor
productivity.

In explaining the large increase in labor productivity, it should also be
noted that the Korean labor market maintained a high degree of flexibility
and that there was continuous investment in human capital in both the
public and private sectors. Labor market flexibility—firms' ability to adjust their labor pool and wage bill in keeping with changes in economic
conditions—derived from the weakness of the Korean trade unions compared with those in Western countries and the fact that social policies and
regulations concerning labor matters were less rigid in Korea.

Korea's consistent comparative advantage in both quality and quantity
of resources has also been noted frequently. Mass education at the primary
level was achieved in the 1950s, and secondary education, even at the
upper level, expanded rapidly as well. There was also a significant increase
in technical education at the secondary level, and the public vocational
training system was expanded in the 1970s to meet the ever-increasing

demand for skilled workers in manufacturing and construction.[20] Although government-sponsored technical education and vocational training programs have been criticized for not reflecting market needs adequately, there would have been serious bottlenecks in the supply of skilled workers in the newly emerging industries of the 1970s without those programs.

Private efforts in manpower development at the firm level were also enhanced in the 1970s by a special government act promoting vocational training, which made in-plant vocational training programs in selected industries compulsory.[21] In conjunction with the in-plant training program, a training levy system was introduced for firms that opted not to have their own training programs. The funds made available from the levy system were utilized to develop training materials, research vocational training, and subsidize public training programs. No data exist that permit an assessment of the balance of training within and outside the firms.

A point of interest in the trends in wages and productivity is the effect of wage increases on international competitiveness. Table 10-19 shows the trends in unit labor costs for the manufacturing sector in won and U.S. dollars.[22] Unit labor costs by either measure more than doubled between 1975 and 1979. Even with the steady increase in worker output, the wage increases in those years were high, creating pressure in the domestic market and seriously dampening the competitiveness of Korean products in the international market.

The slower wage increases in the 1980s led to a much slower rise in unit labor costs: in won, they rose by only about 10 percent over the period from 1980 to 1985. In addition, because of the continued devaluation of the Korean won in the 1980s, unit labor costs in U.S. dollars declined by about 20 percent. Based on this observation it can be said that wage increases had little impact on the competitiveness of Korean export products through 1986. The steady increase in labor productivity, lower nominal wage increases, and the won-dollar exchange rate were all favorable to Korean exports.

Lessons and Emerging Issues

This chapter reviewed how the labor market fared in the years of structural adjustment and the extent to which it contributed to the achievement of successful macroeconomic adjustment. It was argued that the labor market adjusted to the difficult years without any serious prolonged setback in unemployment and wages. Unemployment was contained at a reasonably low level, even during the recessionary period, and resumed a normal 4 percent level of growth thereafter. Containment of unemployment during the recessionary period meant a reduction in employment in manufacturing in the formal sector and an increase in underemployment in the service sector instead of a drastic increase in open employment. Also important is the lucky coincidence that although employment growth in the 1980s was slower than in the previous period, growth of the labor supply also slowed considerably as a result of a reduction in population growth, expansion of educational enrollment, and continuous rural-urban migration.

The real wages of Korean workers suffered for only a short period, a decline that contributed to the slow growth of unemployment, and then resumed a steady increase after 1982. Wage adjustment during the recessionary period was particularly difficult because the recession entailed severe inflation following the second oil shock.

It is not easy to quantify the contribution of the labor market to Korea's successful macroeconomic adjustment, which comprised price stabilization, improvement of the external balance, and resumption of steady economic growth. It is possible, however, to identify a number of contributions. First, the containment of wage increases in the early 1980s as a result of long-term labor market forces, labor market flexibility, and flexible bonus system payments played an important role in achieving price stability.

Second, labor productivity in Korea was maintained at a significant rate during the period concerned. This factor, together with the much slower increase in wages, contained the rise in unit labor costs and reduced the cost-push pressure. Moreover, given the favorable exchange rate policy pursued in the 1980s, unit labor costs in dollars helped maintain and upgrade Korea's competitiveness in the international market.

A third point is that the rise in labor productivity was possible not only because of the hard work of Korean workers, but also because of the extensive investment in human capital in general and technical education and training, which became widespread and was continuously upgraded in the 1970s.

Against this background, it is worth looking at the labor market issues that will emerge as critical in the coming years. The first point is the imbalance between the labor supply and the expansion of employment. As discussed earlier, employment absorption in the Korean economy through the mid-1980s was much slower than in the 1970s. This trend will continue into the foreseeable future as the capital intensity of manufacturing continues to grow and the service sector becomes increasingly organized. At the same time, the supply pressure in the labor market will continue. Female labor, especially employment of married women, will continue to rise, and a sizable number of workers can still be released from the agricultural sector as farm mechanization continues.

Supply and demand imbalances will emerge as critical at the disaggregated level as well. The rapid expansion of higher education brought about a severe surplus of college graduates, a trend that will persist for some time. Also important is that structural unemployment will become more serious as the structural adjustment of the economy proceeds at a faster rate. Microeconomic labor policy measures such as employment service functions, vocational training, and retraining will emerge as more important issues.

The second point of concern is how well Korea can maintain its comparative advantage in human capital in a manner compatible with its long-term development strategy. It is well known that Korea's relative advantage in human capital has been the main source of its economic success and that this was made possible by the expansion of general and higher education. As the economy faces growing skill intensity in manufacturing as well as services, the traditional strategy for manpower development may no longer be sufficient. The quality of higher education, which did not improve with the massive expansion in size in recent years, will need to be upgraded, especially in the fields of science and engineering. Technical training and education, with content developed to suit the manpower requirements of the 1970s, need to be widely revised and upgraded to reflect the changing skill intensity and diversity of the economy. Investment in manpower development by individual firms should be further expanded not only for production workers but also for engineers and other R&D personnel.

Low wages and long work hours are the third issue. Average work weeks were around 54 hours and rising. The wage differential among Korean workers decreased, but the number of poorly paid workers was still considerable. To address the low wages, the government was preparing to introduce a minimum wage system beginning in 1988. The system will need to be approached cautiously if it is not to cause a major disruption in the labor market. The low-wage issue can also be addressed through the structural adjustment of industries and the subcontracting system. Government regulation of labor standards and work hours might well be reviewed and employers encouraged to use labor more efficiently. Lessons can be drawn from the experience of Japan in the 1960s, where the issues of low wages and long working hours were resolved gradually without burdening the overall economy.

Finally, there is the matter of labor-management relations and the need to devise a proper mechanism for the peaceful resolution of labor disputes. In the process of rapid industrialization, a wide variety of labor-management issues emerged. Their resolution often involved excessive government intervention and illegal wildcat strikes. Industrial conflicts will become more visible and significant as Korea's industrialization continues, and the lack of a self-regulating mechanism for settling labor problems will become more and more costly to Korea's economic performance.

Notes

1. For the population twenty to twenty-four years of age, enrollment in colleges and universities between 1978 and 1984 went from 18.4 percent to 40.5 percent for males and 4.2 percent to 11.6 percent for females. A related trend is that the proportion of high school students who continued on to higher education increased from 27.2 percent to 37.8 percent between 1980 and 1984.

2. One reason given for the increase in the quota was that the education authorities were concerned about the large and increasing wage differences between college and high school graduates. These large wage differences are well documented in Lindauer (1984) and in the several studies on the rates of return on education in Korea (F. Park 1976; S. Park 1982; Park and Park 1984). These studies show that the rate of return on a college education is much higher than that on lower levels of education, in contrast to the findings in other countries (Psacharopoulos 1985).

3. The figures in table 10-7 should not be interpreted as the size of migration, because only farm population fourteen years and over is reported. Given the importance of the subject, work has to be done to (a) document the actual magnitude of migration by making the 1985 census figures compatible with those of the Economically Active Population Survey (EAPS) and the First Employment Structure Survey (FESS) of 1983, (b) document the characteristics of migrants, and (c) establish why they migrated.

4. The terms of trade referred to in the text correspond to the ratio of prices received to prices paid by farmers. The prices received are for sales of grains (including potatoes), fruits and vegetables, livestock, and poultry products. Prices paid are for purchases of farm supplies, household goods, and farm labor. The trend in the terms of trade so defined is different from that shown by the ratio of farm to nonfarm income, which suggests an improvement in the terms of trade. The latter figures may, however, suffer from several problems: reliable data on farm income are difficult to obtain, because more than 85 percent of the workers are self-employed or family workers; and the figures obtained probably overrepresent paid workers, whose salaries increased rapidly in agriculture. For these reasons the price figures may be more reliable. In addition, for the "marginal farmer," prices may be the relevant variable when he or she has to decide whether to work as a salaried employee, to continue on the farm, or to go to the city.

5. The use of machinery in farming increased rapidly between 1975 and 1980: the number of tractors rose fourfold and the number of power tillers and other machines owned by farmers increased threefold (the figures are from Korea, Economic Planning Board 1985, p. 78).

6. In mining and manufacturing, employment and GNP increased by 96.6 percent and 165.8 percent during 1970–76. For the period 1977–85, however, employment and GNP increased by 26.0 percent and 102.4 percent.

7. That the cost of borrowing was heavily subsidized between 1975 and 1980 is shown in chapter 6 by Cho and Cole. The unit cost of labor, in turn, increased in dollars by 78 percent between 1976 and 1979, the largest increase of the Asian newly industrialized economies—Taiwan, Singapore, and Hong Kong (Nam 1984).

8. The number of labor disputes, mostly wildcat strikes, was around 100 a year during the latter part of the 1970s, but increased, numbering 407 in 1980 alone. The incidence in 1980 was strongly related to the political and social circumstances that prevailed in the period between the death of the late President Park Chung Hee and the establishment of the new government. Labor disputes fell in number and scale in the early 1980s, but they became more frequent again in 1985.

9. The size of employment by industry subsector within manufacturing is not available on an annual basis. The data quoted were obtained from the Census and Special Employment Survey of 1983. It should also be noted that the size of

manufacturing employment obtained from the annual Household Survey (Economically Active Population Survey) differs somewhat from the employment figure found in the census report: manufacturing employment in the former in 1980 was 2,972,000, while in the latter it was 2,797,000.

10. In the sense that the labor-output ratio in small nonformal establishments is generally much larger than in large formal ones.

11. This classification covers employment in public utilities; construction; sales, restaurants, and hotels; transportation, storage, and communications; financing, insurance, and real estate; and community, social, and personal services.

12. The same kind of statistical problem arises here: the census employment figures for SOC and services are quite different from those reported in the annual household survey. In 1980 the difference was around 1 million workers.

13. Note that the employment figure from the Establishment Survey for 1975 covers only firms employing more than ten workers. In the 1980 and 1983 surveys the coverage was expanded to firms with more than five workers.

14. This point was made by Professor Ruth Klinov of the Hebrew University of Israel in comments on the preliminary draft of this chapter. A study by Mohabbat and Dalal (1983) gives a demand elasticity within a range of -0.27 and -0.34. A recent estimate by Kim (1986) shows that, for manufacturing, demand elasticity with respect to real wages was -0.24.

15. This point was also raised by Klinov.

16. The general employment practice was to hire workers on a provisional basis for a short period (three to six months) and to give them regular status afterward. In the Household Employment Survey (Economically Active Population Survey of the Economic Planning Board), employment is classified into regular and temporary workers, with a temporary worker defined as one whose employment contract is shorter than one year. In the actual survey, however, those who have worked in the current job for less than one year are classified as temporary workers. In the context of this practice, temporary workers will increase as the economy expands and new hires are increased. Also to be noted is that there is no differentiation of workers by employment status within the legal provision of the labor standards law. The labor standards law provides that notice should be given one month before a worker is laid off.

17. This jump reflected the rapid rise in the demand for construction workers as a result of the expansion of overseas construction in the Middle East, as well as the domestic construction boom.

18. The size of union membership doubled in the 1970s, reaching around 1.1 million in 1979. The effect the union had on wage determination is discussed in S. Park (1983).

19. The productivity index quoted here is based on data generated by the Korea Productivity Center. One major drawback of this index is that the size of the labor input is measured in man-days instead of man-hours. Consequently, fluctuations in working hours, especially overtime, are not captured in the measurement of input. Considering that the average working hours in manufacturing increased gradually over the years, the productivity index series can be judged to be somewhat overestimated. For further discussion of the productivity data, see Lindauer (1984).

20. In 1985, 70,000 people graduated from the technical high schools and 10,000 workers were trained in the public training centers.

21. Compulsory in-plant training was to be provided at firms in the mining, manufacturing, construction, public utilities, transportation and communication, and service industries. Firms employing more than 300 workers were under this program, with some exceptions.

22. Unit labor cost is the ratio of the index of nominal wages to the index of output per worker.

References

Kim, Choong-Soo. 1986. "Quarterly Econometric Model for Korean Labor Market." Korea Development Institute Working Paper 8612. Seoul.

Korea, Economic Planning Board. 1973, 1975b, and 1980. *Population and Housing Census Report,* vol. II: *Economic Activity.* In Korean. Seoul.

———. 1984. *Report on the First Employment Structure Survey.* Seoul.

———. 1985. *Major Statistics of Korean Economy.* In Korean. Seoul.

———. Various issues. *Annual Report on the Economically Active Population Survey.* In Korean. Seoul.

———. Various issues. *Korea Statistical Yearbook.* Seoul.

Korea, Ministry of Labor. Various issues. *Report on Labor Conditions of Establishments.* Seoul.

———. Various issues. *Yearbook of Labor Statistics.* Seoul.

Lindauer, David L. 1984. *Labor Market Behavior in the Republic of Korea.* World Bank Staff Working Paper 641. Washington, D.C.

Mohabbat, K. A., and A. J. Dalal. 1983. "Factor Substitution and Import Demand for South Korea: A Translog Analysis." *Weltwirtschaftliches Archiv* 119(4):709–23.

Nam, Sang-Woo. 1984. "Korea's Stabilization Efforts since the Late 1970s." Working Paper 8405. Seoul. Korea Development Institute.

Park, Fun-Koo. 1976. "Returns to Education in Korea." *Journal of Economic Development* 6(1).

Park, Fun-Koo, and Seil Park. 1984. *Wage Structure in Korea.* Seoul: Korea Development Institute. In Korean.

Park, Seil. 1982. "Social and Private Rates of Return to Education in Korea." *Korea Development Review* 4(3). In Korean.

———. 1983. "The Effects of Labor Unions on Relative Wage and Productivity in Korea." *Korea Development Review* 5(2). In Korean.

Psacharopoulos, George. 1985. "Returns to Education: A Further International Update and Implications." *Journal of Human Resources* 20(4):583–604.

11 Energy Policy and Adjustment

JULIO J. ROTEMBERG, Massachusetts Institute of Technology
SEOK-HYUN HONG, Korea Development Institute

[KOREA IMPORTS most of its energy. Its only important domestic energy source is anthracite coal, which is used mainly for household heating and contributes only marginally to industrial development.] Given that imported energy plays such a central role in Korea's economy, the country's principal energy policy has involved domestic pricing. This chapter describes and evaluates the policy through the mid-1980s. In particular, it looks at the extent to which government pricing helped or hindered the adjustment of the Korean economy to the two large increases in the price of oil in the 1970s.

This analysis is of general interest because the approach to pricing of energy in most oil-importing countries, including Korea, has been somewhat unusual, at least in relation to standard neoclassical theory. These countries have made use of the substantial tax (or subsidy) component of energy prices to cushion their domestic energy prices against fluctuations in world prices. The World Bank's *World Development Report 1981* states that, for oil importers generally, the ratio of domestic petroleum product prices to international prices fell from 2.7 in 1972 to 1.8 in 1978 and 1.4 in 1980. Comparable numbers for Korea are 2.7, 1.9, and 1.8, respectively.[1] Thus, in comparison with other oil importers, Korea "passed through" a slightly larger fraction of the increase in oil prices in 1974 (its internal price tripled, while the foreign price quadrupled) and a substantially larger fraction in 1979 (both the internal price and the international price essentially doubled). This study assesses the social costs and benefits of this pass-through.

The benefit of having the same effective exchange rate for all imports, including oil—that is, from completely passing through the change in the relative price of oil—is that it promotes the conservation of energy. If the demand is completely inelastic, there is essentially no social cost to having the wrong price for oil. The amounts used and imported do not change; except for the distributional effects, the economy is in principle capable of achieving the same allocation. If the distributional effects were offset with lump-sum transfers, in principle it would be possible to reestablish the same equilibrium as with a complete pass-through. If the demand for oil is price-elastic, however, a policy curtailing domestic price increases leads to too much energy consumption. The private benefits from this extra energy consumption are lower than the social cost of obtaining the energy from abroad.

A first step in measuring the social costs of an incomplete pass-through is to measure how much more energy is used because of this policy. To make this determination and to maintain the focus on imported energy, a relatively simple function that gives the aggregate demand for imported petroleum products was estimated. One important consideration in this function was the speed at which energy demand adjusted to changes in price. With slow adjustment, the economy first responds to a one-time increase in energy prices as if demand were relatively inelastic at first. This does not mean that maintaining low domestic energy prices forever is costless, because the long-term response to higher prices can be substantial.

Advocates of an incomplete pass-through argue that it is a temporary policy to ease the adjustment. This assertion leads to a consideration of policies that result in a gradual increase in domestic energy prices. How should private agents respond to such policies? In both households and industries, energy is needed to operate capital goods (in the case of households, these goods include cars and refrigerators). Moreover, a large fraction of the adjustment of energy demand is accomplished by changing the mix of these capital goods. Therefore, the issue for firms and households investing in new equipment is whether to purchase energy-thirsty equipment appropriate for current low prices or energy-conserving items with an eye to tomorrow's higher prices.

Paradoxically, the higher the cost of changing the energy intensity of existing capital, the more investors should be concerned about future energy prices. If any decision on energy intensity has a long-run effect, energy intensity should be responsive to the future conditions in which the capital will be operated. If people expect gradual increases in domestic petroleum prices, they should respond more to the current increase in international energy prices than if energy prices were expected to stay low forever. Therefore, if adjustment costs are high, postponing energy price increases has only relatively mild effects on energy consumption.

These costs of adjustment are considered explicitly in the analysis of the extra imports of energy generated by a policy of postponing necessary price increases. The conclusion is that a policy of simply postponing the entire increase in domestic energy prices for one year has, with forward-looking firms and households, very small effects on the path of current accounts.

The next point to be considered is the benefits of postponing energy price increases. They are of essentially two kinds. First, there are the potential distributional effects, which are large when a significant subset of the population is engaged in the production of energy. In the United States, for example, the residents of Texas and Oklahoma benefit substantially from higher energy prices. In Korea, however, energy production (anthracite mining) is a small industry subject to extensive regulation, so that any effects on its income can easily be offset by other policies.

Thus, the only distributional effects that could be of concern are those across different categories of consumers. It would be cause for concern if some important groups consumed energy disproportionately to their total consumption. The work of Stoker (1986) suggests that, at least in the United States, these "consumption" distribution effects are not very large. In particular, it does not appear that poor families suffer disproportionately more from energy price increases. Whether this conclusion would also be true for countries like Korea is an open question. The difficulty of quantifying these distributional effects for Korea precludes their complete analysis here.

The second benefit from postponing energy price increases is that they are associated with significant macroeconomic dislocations. "Supply shocks" such as energy price increases tend to produce simultaneous increases in inflation and slowdowns in economic activity. These effects are probably the result of the rigidity of prices and wages, which postpones the needed fall in real wages and in the relative prices of nonenergy goods. Thus, an economy without rigidities would experience falls in nominal nonenergy prices and wages in response to increases in the price of a single good such as energy. These reductions would prevent real money balances from declining and prevent a contraction in aggregate demand. In contrast, an economy with important nominal rigidities would feature drops in real money balances as nonenergy prices and wages fail to decline and even increase.

Although we discuss the theoretical reasons for the macroeconomic consequences of energy price increases, the focus here is empirical: to measure whether energy price increases in Korea have been associated with economic slowdowns as they have been in the United States (see Hamilton 1983). The finding is that this association is statistically significant in Korea as well. The resulting estimates are then used to gauge the costs of alternative paths of domestic energy prices. The estimates suggest that postponing energy price increases does indeed delay economic declines, a pattern that can be counted as a social benefit. But this benefit is somewhat dampened because the recessionary effects of energy price increases appear to be less than proportional to the price increase itself. An extremely large increase in the domestic price of energy tends to generate a proportionately milder recession than does a small increase. That is, the cumulative decline in output is smaller when the entire increase in energy price is passed through at once than when the pass-through is gradual. Thus, although policies to postpone the entire energy price increase are attractive, policies to effect a gradual increase in domestic energy prices are not.

The Korean Energy Sector

The phenomenal growth of the Korean economy since the mid-1960s has increased Korea's consumption of energy dramatically. Korea has very few resources of its own: as mentioned, its only major domestic source of energy is anthracite. By some criteria, anthracite could be said to provide a substantial fraction of Korea's energy needs. For example, when measured in oil equivalent units, anthracite provided 21 percent of Korea's primary energy consumption in 1984.[2] Nevertheless, anthracite is used almost exclusively for residential and commercial heating and cooking, particularly in the traditional sector of the economy. Of the 24 million metric tons consumed in 1984, more than 21 million were used for these purposes. The other sources of domestic energy are hydroelectricity, which accounted for 1 percent of 1984 energy consumption measured in oil equivalent units, and firewood, which accounted for 4 percent.

It may therefore be concluded that the bulk of energy is imported. Another important point is that marginal energy needs are overwhelmingly being met by imported energy, as is reflected in the fact that the relative importance of anthracite has declined steadily as Korea has grown (anthracite provided 43 percent of Korea's energy needs in 1965).

Of the imported sources of energy, the most important by far has been oil, which in 1984 accounted for 52 percent of Korea's primary energy consumption. Recently, however, oil has been losing its preeminence. One of Korea's responses to the oil price increases of the 1970s has been to diversify the portfolio of energy imports. Nuclear energy was introduced in 1977 and by 1984 accounted for 5 percent of energy consumption; imported bituminous coal, which accounted for only about 22 percent of energy consumption in the mid-1970s, represented 16 percent in 1984.

Not surprisingly, a large fraction (42 percent in 1984) of Korea's energy is consumed by industry. It is noteworthy that this fraction is substantially larger (55 percent) when anthracite is omitted. This again reflects the use of anthracite primarily for residential and commercial purposes.

Korea's first energy policy response to the energy price shocks of the 1970s was to encourage alternative energy sources, such as nuclear energy and bituminous coal. The second was the promotion of energy conservation along two tracks. First, firms that invest in energy conservation equipment have been given access to subsidized credit. Second, the government has financed educational campaigns and energy audits to disseminate information about conservation.

The last prong of Korea's energy policy has been domestic pricing of imported energy, shown in table 11-1. The first column gives the international price of oil in won, calculated as the product of the dollar price of a light-24 barrel of Saudi Arabian oil and the won-dollar exchange rate. The second column gives the deflator for petroleum products, which can be viewed as a measure of the domestic price of imported energy. The third column gives the ratio of these two price indexes. Finally, the last column gives the average revenue per kilowatt hour from electricity sold in Korea.

The first point to note in the table is that although Korea passed through a substantial part of the price increases resulting from both energy shocks,

Table 11-1. *Domestic and International Prices, 1970–84*

Year	International price per barrel (won)	Petroleum deflator	Ratio of deflator to international price (percent)	Electricity price (won per kilowatt hour)
1970	545	4.7	0.86	6.3
1971	780	5.8	0.74	6.4
1972	949	7.4	0.78	7.4
1973	1,173	8.5	0.72	7.3
1974	4,743	24.1	0.51	10.6
1975	5,460	31.2	0.57	17.1
1976	5,774	33.4	0.58	19.4
1977	6,263	33.9	0.54	21.8
1978	6,321	35.2	0.56	22.4
1979	8,693	48.7	0.56	32.2
1980	20,404	100.0	0.49	50.9
1981	24,924	134.9	0.54	64.3
1982	25,504	145.4	0.57	69.9
1983	23,785	138.0	0.58	67.7
1984	24,060	135.4	0.56	67.4

Source: Various issues of Korean Institute of Energy and Resources, *Yearbook of Energy Statistics.*

prices did not rise by the full amount of the international increase. When the international price quadrupled in 1974, the national price tripled and then rose more gradually up to 1979. Similarly, the price of electricity rose substantially in 1974 and 1975 and then continued rising more gradually to catch up to the international price.

The analysis here focuses almost exclusively on pricing policy, with energy prices a central variable. An effort is also made to account for the effects of conservation policies. Because of the difficulty of quantifying the energy substitution policies, however, this effort is not very successful. As a result, the effects of the prices estimated here may be somewhat biased because they may include the simultaneous effects of the subsidization of alternative energy sources.

Energy Demand

This section reviews both a traditional and a more modern method for estimating the demand for imported oil and the application of these methods to annual Korean data. It closes with an analysis of the implications of the estimates for alternative pricing policies. Since the focus is mainly on energy imports, the emphasis is on petroleum products because they constitute the bulk of such imports.

The traditional approach to estimating the demand for a set of commodities such as petroleum products is to run a regression that explains the level of petroleum consumed by a variety of variables, such as the relative price of these products and the level of aggregate activity. This regression is generally derived by starting from a plausible model of the amount that would be demanded in the long run if conditions stayed forever as they are at time t. This long-run, or static, demand can be specified in log linear form as:

$$(11\text{-}1) \qquad e_t^* = a + by_t + cp_t + fz_t + u_t$$

where

e_t^* = the logarithm of "long-run" energy imported at t
p_t = the logarithm of its relative price
y_t = the logarithm of GNP
z_t = a vector of other variables affecting energy imports
u_t = an error term.

The constants a, b, c, and f are parameters to be estimated. The parameters b and c can, in principle, be interpreted as demand elasticities.

The price and output variables included in equation (11-1) deserve comment. If energy is viewed exclusively as an input to production, these variables could be the driving forces behind cost minimization efforts. These efforts take the following form. First, firms solve their profit maximization problems and derive an optimizing path for all their inputs and outputs. The aggregate of their outputs corresponds closely to y. A necessary condition for this path of output to be profit-maximizing is that the path of inputs the firm chooses minimize its costs, subject to the need to produce that path of output. For econometricians, it is often much easier to deal with this second problem directly because the profit maximization problem involves a variety of market imperfections, such as the lack of perfect competition and costs of changing prices, that are difficult to deal with when estimating the demand for energy. Because the cost minimization problem is dealt with here, energy demand has to be conditioned on the level of output. But it also means that the relevant prices are those of energy compared with the prices of other outputs, such as wages, rental rates of capital, and the like. In contrast, the direct demand for energy by households presumably depends on total household expenditures (which are only a subset of the expenditures reported in GNP) and on the price of energy compared with other consumable goods.

In either case, there are sound theoretical reasons to expect that an equation such as (11-1) will not be a good description of energy use if "long-run" imports e_t^* are replaced with actual imports e_t. When such a replacement is carried out and an attempt is made to estimate equation (11-1) by, for instance, ordinary least squares, the signs of misspecification abound. In particular, the degree of serial correlation is too large to be attributed simply to the existence of unobservable shocks to the demand for energy. The theoretical reason for such a serial correlation is that energy demand cannot be expected to adjust immediately to changes in economic conditions. The main reason is that energy tends to be used together with other, longer-lived inputs, such as capital or consumer durables. At a fixed level and composition of these long-lived goods, the demand for energy is not very sensitive to either y or p.

Changes in y and p, however, have strong effects on the level and composition of these goods, which does translate into substantial changes in energy use. Another way of phrasing this situation is that an equation such as (11-1) also requires variables on the right-hand side that describe the range of capital goods available at a given time in order to describe the short-run determination of e_t. The quantities of these goods also evolve as a function of p and y. To obtain a complete model of e, the choice of energy-using durable goods must be modeled together with the energy intensity with which these goods are used. The microeconomic study of Hausman (1979) and the macroeconomic model of Pindyck and Rotemberg (1983) take this approach.

Although eminently desirable, this approach is taxing in its data requirements. There are, however, at least two possible shortcuts that avoid these data difficulties. The first is to postulate, as Pindyck (1979) has, that e_t gradually adjusts toward e_t^*. Pindyck uses adjustment equation of the form:

$$(11\text{-}2) \qquad e_t - e_{t-1} = (1 - g)(e_t^* - e_{t-1})$$

where g is between 0 and 1.

The coefficient $1 - g$ gives the "speed of adjustment," or the fraction of the difference between e^* and the previous e that is adjusted in any given period. The idea of equation (11-2) is that changes in p and y are not immediately reflected by changes in e because durable goods using energy must first be replaced.

Although the approach embodied in equation (11-2) has the advantage of extreme simplicity, it has two disadvantages. First, if e^* grows deterministically over time, equation (11-2) embodies the implication that e never catches up with e^*, even though the movements in e^* are entirely predictable. The second is that an equation such as (11-2) does not allow agents to respond to future changes in the price of energy. This drawback is serious if households and firms are rationally anticipating these changes when they make irreversible decisions concerning durable goods.

An alternative approach is to postulate explicitly the costs associated both with having an energy consumption different from e^* and with changing individual energy consumption drastically (this approach is discussed more fully in the appendix). This approach leads to an estimating equation of the form:

$$(11\text{-}3) \qquad e_t = e_t^* - d[(e_t - e_{t-1}) - \delta E_t(e_{t+1} - e_t)]$$

where

E_t = expectations conditional on information available at t
δ = a discount factor
d = a parameter to be estimated.

The parameter d gives the relative importance of adjusting energy consumption and being away from e^*. If d is zero, e always equals e^*, so that the costs of adjustment are nonexistent.

Equation (11-3) implies that at optimum, firms will be indifferent to the choice between adjusting their energy input slightly more today and waiting until tomorrow. Such a postponement leads to costs, given by the left side of equation (11-3): energy input is further from e^*, and some adjustment costs must be paid tomorrow. In contrast, the right side gives the costs of the alternative approach of adjusting energy input immediately.

With respect to the data used in this study, the variable e is given by the logarithm of the sum of the crude oil and petroleum products exported, with magnitudes measured in thousands of barrels. Although the aggregation of different petroleum products with crude oil is problematic in principle, in practice the difference between the noncrude petroleum products imported and those exported is negligible compared with the imports of crude.[3] Thus, the measure of e is essentially equal to the logarithm of crude oil imports. The variable y is the logarithm of real GNP in 1980 won, and the variable p is defined as the difference between the logarithm of the wholesale price index for petroleum and related products and the logarithm of the GNP deflator. These data are annual and cover the period from 1963 to 1984.

One issue that must be confronted before the estimation can begin is the extend to which p and y are correlated with disturbances in the demand for oil. For y, it is easy to believe that random disturbances in the demand for oil have relatively little effect on GNP itself, particularly because energy production is such a small component of the Korean economy. The variable p, the relative price of oil products, is affected by three forces. The first is the international price of oil, which can be viewed as exogenous. The second is the array of domestic tariffs and other taxes levied by the government. The third is the exchange rate. These factors permit an incomplete pass-through of the changes in the international price. Unfortunately it is probably incorrect to view changes in government policy as exogenous. For instance, if there is a demand shock that raises the demand for energy, such as a very cold winter, the government may well decide to lower the domestic price of petroleum products. To accommodate these factors an eclectic approach is adopted, in which estimation procedures such as ordinary least squares that assume that u is uncorrelated with the included variables, as well as instrumental variable procedures, are used.

The first step is to estimate an equation based on the partial adjustment equation (11-2), which leads to:

$$(11\text{-}4) \qquad e_t = (1 - g)a + (1 - g)by_t + (1 - g)cp_t + (1 - g)fz_t$$
$$+ ge_{t-1} + u_t.$$

Estimation of equation (11-4) by ordinary least squares still leads to an unacceptably high serial correlation in the residuals, so this equation is quasidifferenced, with the result:

$$(11\text{-}5) \quad e_t = 1.13 + 0.34y_t - 0.04p_t + 0.61e_{t-1}$$
$$\phantom{(11\text{-}5) \quad e_t =} (1.05) \quad (0.18) \quad (0.06) \quad (0.08)$$

$$\rho = 0.66\,(0.05);\ \text{observations: 1964 to 1984}$$

where the standard errors are in parentheses.

This equation has a long-run elasticity of energy demanded by income level of 0.87 and a long-run elasticity with respect to relative price of 0.10. In addition, petroleum demand adjusts rather slowly—after a change in y or p in a given year, only half the adjustment toward the long run has taken place by the following year. The elasticities as well as the speed of adjustment used here are similar to the results of Ahn and Lee (1980) for total energy demand in Korea.

Alternative variables (z_t) have been considered. The first is a crude measure of the conservation efforts of the Korean government after 1980. There were two kinds of conservation efforts. First, the government gave subsidized loans and tax credits to enterprises that invested in equipment capable of conserving energy. Second, the Energy Management Corporation was commissioned to conduct programs in support of energy conservation, including energy audits and educational efforts. The budgetary outlays of the Energy Management Corporation for these purposes are added to the costs of the loan subsidies and tax credits to obtain a measure of expenditures for what is termed here "energy conservation capital." This capital is measured in millions of 1980 won using the GNP deflator. It is assumed that this capital depreciates at a rate of 20 percent a year, so that the current level of this capital i_t is current expenditures plus 80 percent of the previous capital. When the estimate of this capital is included in equation (11-5):

$$(11\text{-}6) \quad e_t = 0.26 + 0.45y_t - 0.02p_t - 1.1E - 4i_t + 0.59e_{t-1}$$
$$\phantom{(11\text{-}6) \quad e_t =} (1.2) \quad (0.21) \quad (0.06) \quad (9.3E - 5) \quad (0.09)$$

$$\rho = 0.64\,(0.06)$$

The inclusion of i_t raises the response of e to y and reduces that to p. The direct effect of i_t however, is not only statistically insignificant but also economically negligible. For example, it takes 4,500 million 1980 won to reduce oil imports by 1 percent.

An alternative variable for inclusion in equation (11-4) is the price of petroleum products relative to the price of anthracite briquettes. This relative price would be important if there were substantial substitution between these products. This relative price o_t is computed as the difference between the logarithm of the deflator for petroleum products and the logarithm of the housegate price of anthracite briquettes. The results are:

$$(11\text{-}7) \quad e_t = \begin{array}{ccccc} -1.2 & + 0.34y_t & - & 0.006p_t & - & 0.04o_t & + & 0.6e_{t-1} \\ (1.1) & (0.19) & & (0.19) & & (0.22) & & (0.09) \end{array}$$

$$\rho = 0.68 \, (0.06)$$

The point estimates seem to indicate that the substitution with briquettes is bigger than the substitution with the products contained in the GNP deflator. Yet the overall elasticity of the demand for imported oil with respect to its own price, with all other prices kept constant, changes little when o_t is included. For this reason, and because the coefficients are somewhat more precisely estimated when o_t is excluded, more weight is given to the specification of equation (11-5).

In the estimation of equation (11-3), by using (11-1) and rearranging, (11-3) becomes:

$$(11\text{-}8) \qquad e_t = a + by_t + cp_t + fz_t - d[(e_t - e_{t-1}) \\ - \delta(e_{t+1} - e_t)] + u_t + v_t$$

In equation (11-8) the actual value of e_{t+1} is used instead of the expected value as in equation (11-3), so that a forecast error must be added. Equation (11-8) cannot then be estimated by ordinary least squares because the forecast error is obviously correlated with e_{t+1}. Therefore, two-stage least squares are used. In principle, any variable known at t is a valid instrument for this procedure because it cannot be correlated with the (rational) forecast error v_t. In practice, only instrumental variables dated $t - 1$ or earlier were used. One reason for doing so is that this may reduce the bias from the misalignment of the observations with the decision period of firms and households.

All the parameters of equation (11-8) are estimated by instrumental variables except the discount factor δ, whose value is constrained during estimation. The omission of δ from the list of free parameters has two advantages. First, it makes equation (11-8) linear in the parameters, which considerably simplifies the estimation. Second, estimation of society's discount rate from an equation such as (11-8) tends to lead to implausible results because (11-8) is not ideally suited for the estimation of this important parameter. As shown below, however, the precise value of δ has little effect on the other estimated parameters.

Table 11-2. *Estimates of Petroleum Demand Based on Equation (11-8)*

Coefficient	δ			
	0.99	*0.95*	*0.90*	*0.85*
a	−20.5	−19.8	−18.9	−18.2
	(7.7)	(6.6)	(5.5)	(4.6)
b	3.07	3.00	2.93	2.86
	(0.72)	(0.62)	(0.52)	(0.44)
c	−1.57	−1.52	−1.50	−1.41
	(0.84)	(0.76)	(0.67)	(0.60)
d	3.06	2.85	2.61	2.39
	(3.99)	(3.63)	(3.23)	(2.89)
DW	1.95	1.92	1.87	1.83
R^2	0.853	0.864	0.876	0.886
α	0.57	0.57	0.56	0.56

Note: Figures in parentheses are *t*-statistics.
Source: Authors' calculations.

The results of estimating equation (11-8) are presented in table 11-2. The instruments include e_{t-1}, y_{t-1}, p_{t-1}, and a constant. The results are quite stable across the discount rates. As can be seen from table 11-2, the long-run elasticities with respect to y and p are substantially larger than when the approach of equation (11-4) is used. The elasticities with respect to y hover around 3, while those with respect to p are near 1.5.

The estimates of d have the right sign but are statistically insignificant. Its magnitude suggests that the cost of having to adjust energy use by 1 percent is between one-and-a-half and three times as large as the cost of being away by 1 percent from the long-run optimal level of energy use. Such apparently large costs of adjusting energy use should not be regarded as implausible—as long as input factors are reasonably interchangeable in production, the cost of having only an approximately optimal factor mix should be small. Although d is statistically insignificant, constraining d to equal zero considerably worsens the serial correlation of the residuals. Constraining d to zero is equivalent to estimating equation (11-1) with the actual level of energy use e_t on the left side. This equation exhibits extreme serial correlation, so that the inclusion of a nonzero d makes it possible to deal very parsimoniously with the dynamics of adjustment.

The last row of table 11-2 gives the smallest root of the characteristic equation associated with equation (11-8). As discussed in the appendix to this chapter, 1 minus the smallest root interprets the speed of adjustment to permanent changes in y or p. The speed of adjustment of about 0.43 is similar to that estimated with the standard partial adjustment model of equation (11-4).

Once again, an experiment involving the inclusion of some alternative variables in z_t was run. The first of these variables is the measure of energy conservation capital. The results using this measure are shown in table

Table 11-3. *Estimates of Petroleum Demand with Conservation Capital Added*

Coefficient	δ			
	0.99	0.95	0.90	0.85
a	-20.3	-19.7	-19.0	-18.3
	(7.7)	(6.8)	(5.8)	(5.0)
b	3.05	2.99	2.92	2.86
	(0.72)	(0.63)	(0.54)	(0.46)
c	-1.69	-1.65	-1.59	-1.54
	(0.98)	(0.90)	(0.81)	(0.73)
d	-2.90	-2.75	-2.57	-2.39
	(3.95)	(3.67)	(3.35)	(3.05)
f	$4E-4$	$3E-4$	$3E-4$	$3E-4$
	$(6E-4)$	$(6E-4)$	$(6E-4)$	$(5E-4)$
DW	1.95	1.93	1.89	1.86
R^2	0.847	0.856	0.867	0.877

Note: Figures in parentheses are *t*-statistics. $E - i = 10^{-i}$.
Source: Authors' calculations.

11-3. As can be seen, the coefficient of i_t, f, is of the wrong sign (more capital is associated with more energy consumption) and statistically insignificant.

Table 11-4 reports the estimates in which the price of petroleum products relative to anthracite briquettes is included instead of energy conservation capital. This inclusion does not materially affect any of the estimates reported in table 11-2. The coefficient of o_t, f, is now both less important economically and statistically than the coefficient on p_t, c. As such, the specification without z_t is retained as the preferred specification.

Table 11-4. *Estimates of Petroleum Demand with the Price of Anthracite Added*

Coefficient	δ			
	0.99	0.95	0.90	0.85
a	-22.1	-21.1	-19.9	-18.8
	(12.8)	(10.9)	(8.9)	(7.2)
b	3.22	3.13	3.02	2.92
	(1.2)	(1.0)	(0.84)	(0.68)
c	-1.53	-1.48	-1.42	-1.38
	(0.97)	(0.88)	(0.79)	(0.71)
d	-3.75	-3.45	-3.08	-2.74
	(6.11)	(5.49)	(4.78)	(4.17)
f	-0.22	-0.20	-0.16	-0.12
	(1.29)	(1.21)	(1.11)	(1.02)
DW	2.04	2.00	1.95	1.89
R^2	0.823	0.840	0.859	0.875

Note: Figures in parentheses are *t*-statistics.
Source: Authors' calculations.

Macroeconomic Consequences of Pricing Policies: Theory

The oil price shocks of the 1970s preceded the worst recessions in the industrial countries since World War II. Some theoretical explanations for this phenomenon are explored here.

The first potential explanation is that even with completely flexible prices, the increase in the price of an input is the kind of "productivity shock" that drives classical (or "real") models of the business cycle (see, for instance, Long and Plosser 1983). This explanation is appealing because it does not require any rigidities, and it allows a certain smug attitude about the recessions: they do not mean the economy is operating at anything other than a Pareto optimum.

This explanation is difficult to reconcile with the empirical magnitudes of the ensuing recessions. The main problem is that if energy is an input with no substitute, GNP should not change at all in response to oil price increases, except insofar as they lead the owners of the factors of production, such as labor and capital, to supply less of those factors. The reason is that GNP measures the flow of goods produced with domestic factors of production such as capital and labor. With a given supply of these factors, GNP does not change as long as the factors are not used to take the place of imported energy. Thus, the only macroeconomic effect is a loss in real income, which equals $S/(1 - S)$ times the percentage increase in energy prices, where S is the share of energy in real GNP (around 0.08 for the United States and 0.09 for Korea). This loss in real income represents the payment of a larger fraction of the goods and services produced for the oil imported. With energy perfectly substitutable for labor and capital there is no loss in real income, but GNP falls by this magnitude when the price of imported energy goes up.

This extreme case is unrealistic. For a price elasticity of the demand for energy of 1.5 (as computed in the previous section), it can be expected that a 1 percent increase in the real price of energy leads to a 1.5 percent reduction in imported energy and a less than 0.10 percent reduction in GNP. The fall in real income is much more substantial.

This analysis assumes that the supply of capital and labor is fixed. This assumption is not completely reasonable. As energy becomes more expensive, the real payments for workers and the owners of capital fall. Thus, they might decide to supply fewer of these factors. The existing estimates, however, point to relatively modest responses of labor supply to long-term changes in real wages (Ashenfelter 1984) and to modest responses of savings to relative prices.

Although long-run responses have been addressed, the short-run responses to oil shocks are substantially larger. The question is whether a classical explanation can be found for this. In some sense, the prospects for this explanation do not appear promising. In the short run, energy is even less interchangeable with other inputs. This means, as already discussed, that the decline in GNP for given levels of other inputs is smaller.

Precisely because energy is not rapidly substituted for these inputs in the short run, the demand for the inputs that represent alternatives to energy rises only gradually. For example, if firms use more labor as a substitute for energy, the demand for labor will gradually shift outward, and workers can expect higher wages when the adjustment is complete. This pattern, in turn, might encourage them to take leisure now and postpone working.

Although such an explanation has some theoretical plausibility, it is unlikely to be important empirically. First, there are some costs to changing employment that make firms unwilling to have workers leave, only to return shortly thereafter. Second, the empirical evidence of Pindyck and Rotemberg (1983, 1984) shows that, at least in the United States, the demand for workers shifts outward immediately after an increase in the price of energy and thereafter changes only negligibly.

Thus, there must be an alternative explanation for the apparently vast macroeconomic consequences of the increases in energy prices. One logical question is whether the sort of Keynesian wage and price rigidities that can explain the deleterious effects of a fall in aggregate demand can also explain those attributable to energy price increases. This explanation of recessions caused by "supply shock" is explored critically in Rotemberg (1983), Fischer (1985), and Pindyck and Rotemberg (1984). A natural consequence of Keynesian rigidities in prices and wages is that increases in some prices resulting from exogenous forces necessarily lead, at least in the short run, to increases in the level of prices. This is as likely to occur after the increase in the price of a commodity as after an increase in indirect taxes.

The reason for this is easiest to understand in the context of the problem studied in Poterba, Rotemberg, and Summers (1986), which looked at the effect of an increase in indirect taxes matched by an equal decline in revenues from direct taxes. In principle such a shift in the source of taxation should not affect anything, including the price level. It is just as if the government ceased collecting a sales tax on a producer and started levying it on the consumer at the time of purchase. A shift from direct to indirect taxes, however, requires that producers lower the prices they charge so that prices after taxes remain constant. With any kind of nominal rigidity, either some prices or some wages will not fall, and there will be an increase in the price level.

Similarly, suppose that an increase in the price of oil has no long-run consequences on aggregate activity or the price level. The increase in the price of oil will then have to be matched by a decline in other prices. Insofar as these prices are rigid and do not fall, the price level rises. The resulting increase in the price level has the usual contractionary effect: it lowers real money balances, thus requiring an increase in interest rates to make people satisfied with the lower money balances. The rise in interest rates causes a drop in investment and output. This scenario is theoretically attractive because it accounts very simply not only for the recessions induced by the oil price increases, but also for the inflation that accompanied them. It also fits in well with the evidence of Poterba, Rotemberg, and Summers (1986) that neutral shifts from direct to indirect taxes raise the price level.

There are two difficulties with this simple explanation, however—one theoretical, the other empirical. The theoretical difficulty is that there are good reasons to expect the price level to increase in the wake of an increase in oil prices even if all prices and wages are flexible. These stem from the declines in real income and GNP that must materialize in the long run. Insofar as the demand for real money balances depends on real income (because households want to keep a fraction of their income in assets that enable them to make purchases easily) or on domestic absorption, the fall in real income leads to a fall in the amount of real money balances demanded. With an unchanged money supply, this decline in money demand requires an increase in the overall index of prices.[4] Insofar as the demand for money depends on the level of output, a similar fall in money demand will be observed, although to a lesser extent.

Thus, in this case the increase in the price index does not prove that nominal rigidities are causing a recession. Moreover, in the presence of nominal rigidities, it might be true that the overall index of prices fails to rise enough in response to an increase in oil prices. In that case, nominal rigidities would imply that the short-run response of GNP to the oil price increases is dampened instead of accentuated. For example, suppose that the price level needs to rise by 1 percent in response to an increase in oil prices of 1 percent. Suppose further that the direct effect of this increase in oil prices on the price level is β percent, where this direct effect is what keeps all other prices constant. Then the crucial issue is whether α is bigger or smaller than β. Suppose that both the fall in real income and the elasticity of the demand for money with response to real income are big enough so that β is smaller than α. If domestic prices and wages are rigid in the short run, they will fail to rise enough. Compared with the long-run results, real money balances and thus aggregate demand will be larger, implying a higher GNP than would be realized in the long run.

The question is whether the case in which α exceeds β is a theoretical curiosity or is consistent with other macroeconomic evidence. The latter case is argued here. Assume that energy imports do not respond to the increase in the price of energy and that the price of energy rises 1 percent. As discussed, real income falls by $S/(1 - S)$ percent. With a unitary elasticity of money demand with respect to real income, the price level must rise by $S/(1 - S)$ percent. It is not implausible, however, to imagine that the price level would rise by only S percent if all nonenergy prices stayed constant, as they would in a world of completely rigid prices and wages.[5] Because S is smaller than $1 - S$, α exceeds β (this example is only illustrative). If energy were substitutable for other inputs, real income would fall by less. Moreover, the elasticity of money demand with respect to real income would probably be less than 1. There is, however, no reason to be sure that α is bigger or smaller than β.

There is a crude method for ascertaining whether α is bigger or smaller than β. It is known that in models in which wages alone are rigid (Fischer 1977) and are set by rational agents, they move gradually to their long-run values. If prices alone are rigid (Rotemberg 1983) and are set to maximize the present discounted value of profits, they move gradually to their long-run values. Direct observations of the changes in prices and wages after energy price shocks might thus convey information about whether, in the short run, nonenergy prices and wages are too low or too high. It seems that both price and wage inflation accelerate after oil price increases. For instance, average gross hourly earnings in the nonagricultural sector in the United States rose 6 percent from 1972 to 1973 and then 8 percent and 7 percent the following two years, while the consumer price index (CPI) rose 11 percent from 1973 to 1974 and another 9 percent the following year. It might be deduced that, if anything, prices and wages did not increase enough in the immediate aftermath of the oil shocks.

This conclusion poses an empirical difficulty for the simple Keynesian model of recession induced by supply shock outlined above. Although the model can explain why output falls more in the short run than in the long run, it requires simultaneously that, all else being equal, prices rise by more in the short run than in the long run. This latter phenomenon is clearly counterfactual.

Nor is it easy to pin the blame for the increased inflation on expansionary macroeconomic policies. First, in the United States, the government pursued contractionary policies after both oil shocks. For instance, M1 rose by only 4 percent from 1973 to 1974 and 5 percent the following year. Second, if these government policies were viewed as expansionary, the size of the recessions would be difficult to explain.

These theoretical and empirical difficulties suggest a third explanation for the mixture of inflation and recession that seems to have followed the oil price increases. This explanation relies on somewhat less rational pricing than that assumed in the rigid price and wage models alluded to above. It assumes that in the aftermath of increases in input prices, at least some firms raise their nonenergy prices (they "pass through" the price increase of inputs) and at least some workers see a deterioration in their real wages and insist on wage increases. Firms respond in this way perhaps because they cannot disentangle the increase in energy prices, whose macroeconomic effects require price drops, from other increases in input prices that have no such macroeconomic consequences. For these other increases, passing the price increase through is appropriate. Workers respond as above because they do not expect real wages to drop as a result of all the increases in input prices. Thus, wages and prices rise in response to the increase in oil prices until the impending recession slows and reverses the price increases.

The appropriateness of various macroeconomic and energy price policies depends on which of these three theoretical explanations is right. Suppose that the recession is attributable simply to the change in the Pareto optimal competitive equilibrium brought about by the increase in oil prices. Then the appropriate policy is one of noninterference. Slowing the rate of domestic increases in energy prices has no advantageous macroeconomic consequence.

Suppose, instead, that the simple Keynesian story outlined after discussing the classical model is valid. Temporarily slowing the rate of growth of domestic energy prices has the advantage of dampening the increase in the price level. This result both slows inflation and expands output. The policy has even more striking benefits if the agents are forward-looking in their pricing policies (so that they set today's prices in part as a function of the environment they expect for tomorrow) and anticipate that the government will eventually allow domestic energy prices to be in line with world energy prices. They will start to reduce nonenergy prices when the energy price is still low because they anticipate its eventual increase. This policy might not only postpone the needed recession, but also make it less severe when it takes place.

The advantage of postponing energy price increases at home are less apparent if the third (and preferred) explanation is valid. In that case it seems likely that the agents would increase their prices whenever the domestic energy price was allowed to rise. Thus, postponing domestic energy price increases simply postpones the recessionary effect of these increases. The delay might be attractive if the future is discounted. Because the advantages are smaller, however, the disadvantages, outlined in the previous section, loom larger by comparison.

Moreover, there is a potential disadvantage in postponing the energy price increases: these one-time increases cause recessions only because they are confused with the ordinary rises in input prices that have negligible effects on the macroeconomy. Thus, the government would like to increase the agents' awareness of these macroeconomic consequences. It is at least possible that this awareness can be achieved more effectively with one big energy price increase than with a succession of little ones. The next section turns to this empirical question.

The Macroeconomic Consequences of Pricing

This section gauges empirically the macroeconomic effects of domestic energy price increases. The approach is simple. Regressions are given that explain changes in GNP and the GNP deflator by, among other things, increases in the domestic price of petroleum products. The approach closely parallels that of Hamilton (1983), whose work shows that increases in the price of oil in the United States have tended to precede recessions.

In Korea, just as in the United States, increases in the deflator for petroleum products are correlated with subsequent declines in GNP and with increases in the GNP deflator. These statistical associations are taken here as causal—they are interpreted as the effect on output and the price level of the combination of changes in the international prices of energy and of the pass-through policy dictated by the government. This interpretation is of course open to dispute. For instance, the analysis here cannot disprove that the energy price increases and poor macroeconomic performances are not the joint response to some third (or fourth) excluded variable. This problem is more acute with Korean data than with U.S. data. Because Korean data are more limited, there is less room to consider alternative variables that might cause the movements in both GNP and petroleum prices. Nonetheless, a sufficient number of experiments can be carried out to ascertain that the relations found here are fairly robust.

These experiments are shown in table 11-5. The first column reports the regression of the logarithm of GNP on its own lagged value; a quadratic

Table 11-5. *Reduced Forms for the Logarithm of GNP*

Variable	(1)	(2)	(3)	(4)	(5)	(6)
Constant	2.4	4.5	3.1	2.6	2.5	2.7
	(1.2)	(1.5)	(1.4)	(1.0)	(1.3)	(2.5)
$y(-1)$	0.71	0.48	0.63	0.68	0.70	0.69
	(0.15)	(0.18)	(0.17)	(0.12)	(0.16)	(0.14)
t	0.06	0.07	0.07	0.06	0.06	0.06
	(0.02)	(0.02)	(0.02)	(0.02)	(0.02)	(0.04)
t^2	−0.001	−0.001	−0.001	−0.001	−0.001	−0.001
	(0.0003)	(0.0003)	(0.0003)	(0.0003)	(0.0003)	(0.0003)
dp	−0.18	n.a.	−0.15	−0.10	−0.16	−0.16
	(0.05)		(0.06)	(0.05)	(0.06)	(0.05)
dp^2	0.08	n.a.	0.06	0.04	0.07	0.08
	(0.03)		(0.03)	(0.03)	(0.03)	(0.02)
$dp(-1)$	n.a.	−0.1	−0.04	n.a.	n.a.	n.a.
		(0.06)	(0.05)			
$dp^2(-1)$	n.a.	0.04	0.01	n.a.	n.a.	n.a.
		(0.03)	(0.03)			
de_t	n.a.	n.a.	n.a.	−0.23	n.a.	n.a.
				(0.08)		
de_{t-1}	n.a.	n.a.	n.a.	0.01	n.a.	n.a.
				(0.03)		
dm_t	n.a.	n.a.	n.a.	n.a.	−0.0003	n.a.
					(0.0006)	
dm_{t-1}	n.a.	n.a.	n.a.	n.a.	0.0005	n.a.
					(0.0006)	
li_t	n.a.	n.a.	n.a.	n.a.	n.a.	0.79
						(0.42)
li_{t-1}	n.a.	n.a.	n.a.	n.a.	n.a.	−0.81
						(0.61)

n.a. Not applicable.

Note: Figures in parentheses are *t*-statistics.

Source: Authors' calculations.

trend; the current value of the change in the logarithm of the petroleum products price index (dp); and the square of dp (dp^2). Further lags of GNP proved insignificant in all the specifications tried. Increases in the petroleum price index reduced GNP, but the reduction was less than proportionate. For example, a 1 percent increase in this price lowered GNP by 0.18 percent. A 100 percent increase in p, however, lowered GNP by only 10 percent (instead of by 18 percent, as it would have if the coefficient of dp^2 had been zero). This finding is consistent with the view that large increases in energy prices alert households and firms to possible macroeconomic consequences and make them more cautious in their pricing decisions.

The second column repeats the regression of the first column but uses lagged changes in the petroleum price index. The results are considerably weaker, although the two coefficients have the same sign as before and are still jointly significant at the 5 percent level.

The third column shows the results using both current and lagged values of dp. The approach of taking current values for dp is more open to criticism than is the case when dp is endogenous. Changes in the current values of dp, however, to the degree that they depend on governmental decisions about energy policy that are somewhat divorced from macroeconomic considerations, are exogenous at least to some extent. Insofar as they are exogenous, it is more plausible that dp would have effects within one year of the changes in dp. Further indication that this conclusion is correct is obtained when current and lagged dp's are included; the lagged ones do not matter significantly. This result suggests that the dynamic repercussions of the energy price increases are similar to those of any other shock that affects GNP.

To analyze the contribution of the endogeneity of dp to the significant coefficients in the first column, some further variables are added. The first addition is the current and lagged rates of growth of the exchange rate, de (see column 4). The fifth column considers the effects of including the current and lagged rates of growth of M1 (dm) and the last column includes the current and lagged values of GNP in the industrial countries. The inclusion of these variables does not affect the significance of dp. It might also be said that the effect of dp is a proxy for the effect of the overall increases in domestic prices. Yet, as the literature of the Phillips curve makes clear, increases in the overall index of prices tend to be associated with high, not low, GNP. Indeed, when the current and lagged rates of growth of the GNP deflator are added to the regression, their coefficients are positive, and their presence does not weaken the results of the effects of energy price increases.

The effects of changes in energy prices on the general index of prices are econometrically much more difficult to measure because many variables that, when they change, require the general index of prices to rise also tend to raise the index of domestic petroleum prices. As will be seen, this simultaneous determination is not too important when analyzing the costs of various paths of energy prices as long as the increase in the overall index of prices is not taken as a cost.

Regressions of the rate of change of the GNP deflator dd on lags of that rate of change and on changes in petroleum prices tend to have a coefficient on the current rate of change of petroleum prices of about 0.08. A typical example is the following:

$$(11\text{-}9) \qquad dd_t = 0.88 + 0.29dd_{t-1} + 0.08dp_t + 0.01dp_{t-1}$$
$$\phantom{(11\text{-}9) \qquad dd_t =} (0.03) \quad (0.21) \qquad (0.02) \qquad (0.03)$$

$$DW = 1.1; \text{ observations: } 1964 \text{ to } 1984$$

These regressions will not be taken as having a structural interpretation. The coefficient of about 0.08 must represent an upward-biased estimate of the direct effect of the increases in energy prices on the GNP deflator because variables such as the level of aggregate demand or the aggressiveness of unions that affect dd also affect dp.

Conclusions: Pricing Policy

With the estimates of the effect of domestic energy prices on energy demand and on output presented here, the costs and benefits of the various paths of energy prices can be improved. As this analysis proceeds, it is important to remember that the conditions for validity of these policy analyses are more restrictive than those that lead to valid estimating equations of the form considered earlier. The reason is that here it is assumed the parameters being estimated will not change under alternative policy scenarios. This assumption is particularly problematic for the estimated responses of GNP to oil price increases because there is no complete explanation for those responses. If a better theory for these responses were available there would be greater certainty concerning how they change when policy differs. At the moment the best explanation for these responses is that firms and households act somewhat passively in the face of energy price increases. They initially pass through a large fraction of these increases onto other prices. Assuming that this passive response is independent of policy, the simulations of alternative polices are valid.

A situation in which the international price of oil doubles, as it nearly did in 1979, is considered here. Because the estimate of the long-run price elasticity of oil imports is 1.5, a policy of preventing a domestic price rise means that oil imports remain at their original value instead of falling to 0.35 of that value. In 1979, 1985 million barrels of crude oil were imported. This level of imports—instead of the long-run level of 65 million barrels— represents about \$3.7 billion of "excess" imports a year.

This finding understates the long-run costs of keeping the domestic price constant, because the increase in GNP also leads to further increases in imports. A policy of a complete pass-through would have led to imports of only 0.35 barrels for each of the extra barrels imported.

To conduct the analysis of different pricing policies in more detail, the effect of the growth of GNP on imports is ignored. Several pricing paths are considered. One is to keep oil prices and oil imports constant forever. Although the current account costs of this policy make it unfeasible, it provides a good baseline with which to compare other policies. The second path is a complete pass-through of the oil price increase. This requires that the domestic relative price of oil double.

Because any increase in the nominal price of domestic oil is associated with an increase in the price level, the domestic price of petroleum products must more than double. Given the estimate here that a 1 percent increase in the nominal price of oil is associated with a 0.08 percent increase in the price level, the domestic price of oil must increase by 109 percent. This increase, if brought about immediately, would reduce GNP by 10 percent below what it would have been the first year. The row CP:GNP of table 11-6 shows the effect in subsequent years as well—the percent reduction in GNP resulting from a policy of immediate pass-through below what it would have been if domestic petroleum prices never changed. It is worth noting that the cumulative reduction in GNP is 34.5 percent. If, instead, the one-period discount rate for reductions in GNP were 5 percent, the "present value" of the GNP loss would equal 30.9 percent.

The policy of immediate pass-through does not instantaneously reduce energy imports by 65 percent. Instead, using the estimates for d of 0.95 from table 11-2, a reduction of only 36 percent is obtained the first year. Subsequent reductions are given in row CP:e of table 11-6.

Two alternatives to the immediate pass-through can be considered now, both of which have the advantage that in the long run the current account effects disappear. The first is a policy of delaying the necessary increase in energy prices by one year—that is, the pattern of reductions in GNP is the same but is postponed for one period. These reductions are shown in row DP:GNP of table 11-6. If future declines in GNP relative to current declines are discounted, this policy might be advantageous. For instance, if the one-period discount rate is 5 percent, the benefit from postponing is 5 percent

Table 11-6. *Alternative Pricing Policies and Effects*

Policy	Year					
	0	1	2	3	4	5
CP:GNP	−10.0	−7.1	−5.1	−3.6	−2.6	−1.8
CP:e	−36.0	−50.0	−57.0	−61.0	−62.0	−63.0
DP:GNP	0.0	−10.0	−7.1	−5.1	−3.6	−2.6
DP:e	−29.0	−47.0	−57.0	−60.0	−62.0	−63.0
GP:GNP	−3.3	−5.7	−7.3	−8.5	−6.0	−4.3

Note: Figures are percentage differences relative to constant prices. Pricing policies are indicated as follows: CP, constant prices; DP, delayed pass-through; and GP, gradual pass-through.

Source: Authors' calculations.

of the 30.9 percent present value of the GNP declines, or approximately 1.5 percent of current GNP.

The current account effects (DP:*e*) of this policy are computed by applying the estimates of table 11-2 for δ equal to 0.95 in equation (11-8). The effect of this postponement is that energy demand does not respond as much the first year. Note that energy demand still falls somewhat that year because the costs of adjustment make firms and workers buy energy-using durables that are set for the future. The fall in energy imports is compared with that under the immediate pass-through policy: 7 percent less in the first year, 3 percent in the following year, and 1 percent in the subsequent two years. The present discounted value of these larger imports is about 12 percent of current oil imports, or about 22 million barrels in 1979. The value of these, at 1980 prices, was about $690 million, or about 1 percent of GNP. Of course, these larger imports cannot be viewed as a dollar loss because had they been substituted for other domestic imports, they would have had other internal and external costs. Thus, 1 percent of GNP represents a very generous upper bound of the costs (in terms of the misallocation of resources) that derive from postponing the energy price increase.

The analysis so far indicates that with a discount rate of 5 percent, postponement by one year is socially worthwhile. It is important to note that this analysis hinges on the forward-looking nature of the demand for energy. Suppose, instead, that firms and households have static expectations, so that unless energy prices increase immediately, they do not expect them ever to increase.[6] With a policy of postponement, the demand for energy does not respond at all to the increase in international prices—that is, even the first-year imports are 36 percent higher than they would have been with a policy of a complete pass-through. In the second year they are 14 percent higher, then 7 percent, and so on. This pattern leads to a present value of 61 percent more imports, with a value of nearly 6 percent of GNP at 1980 prices.

The foregoing analysis also shows that a postponement of one year is worthwhile, whereas a permanent postponement is not. The reason again is that a credible postponement of only one year leads, with forward-looking behavior, to some immediate adjustment of energy demand.

The second policy considered is one of a "gradual" pass-through. The idea is to increase domestic energy prices immediately by 20.2 percent and to continue increasing them by 20.2 percent annually for the next three years. This approach postpones the overall price increase while making it smoother. The effects on GNP (relative to never changing domestic energy prices) are given in the row GP:GNP of table 11-6. Although GNP falls less, it stays low longer, and the cumulative decline is larger because of the non-linearity discussed in the section entitled "Macroeconomic Consequences of Pricing Policies: Theory." Indeed, the cumulative drop in GNP is now 45.6 percent. Even the present discounted value of GNP losses is 38 percent, which is bigger than that for a complete pass-through. Thus, the policy of gradualism has little to recommend it, because it also results in higher energy imports along the translation path.

Korea's actual adjustment of prices to both energy shocks can be categorized as a mixture of two policies. In both 1973–74 and 1979–80, Korean energy prices rose substantially, with most of the energy price increases passed through immediately, but with some fraction postponed by one or two years. This pattern can be seen in table 11-1 in the continued rise in the ratio of domestic to international energy prices in 1974–75, 1980–81, and 1981–82. The foregoing analysis might be taken to mean that these relatively short postponements were beneficial. Because in both cases domestic energy prices adjusted significantly to the shocks, however, the non-linearities discussed in the section entitled "The Macroeconomic Consequences of Pricing" suggest that further increases in 1973–74 and 1979–80 would have had relatively minor effects on GNP.

Appendix: Demand for Energy with Costs of Adjustment

This appendix presents an alternative to the partial adjustment model of equation (11-2) that constitutes the basis for equation (11-3). The idea is to build a model in which people try to avoid both being away from (e^*) and changing their energy consumption. To this end, it is assumed that the economy acts to minimize

$$(11\text{-}10) \qquad E_0 \sum \delta^t [(e_t - e_t^*)^2 + d(e_t - e_{t-1})^2]$$

where E_0 is expectations conditioned on information available at time zero and δ is a discount factor.

The advantage of using equation (11-10) is that it explicitly takes into account that changes in energy, which are in large part brought about by changes in the stock of energy-using durable goods, are costly. Equation (11-10) also takes into account the costs of having a consumption of energy away from the long-run optimal consumption of energy (e^*). This cost captures mainly the cost of having the wrong mix and quantity of energy-using durable goods. One additional advantage of using the minimization of equation (11-10) to determine energy use is that this is a straightforward problem whose solution is described, for instance, in Sargent (1979). It is important to keep in mind, however, that while the minimization of equation (11-10) has some appealing properties, it does not completely capture the firms' or households' problem, because they must simultaneously choose energy-using durables and energy consumption.

The minimization of equation (11-10) yields the following first-order necessary condition:

$$(11\text{-}11) \qquad e_t = e_t^* - d[(e_t - e_{t-1}) - \delta E_t(e_{t+1} - e_t)]$$

where E_t is the expectation conditional on information at t.

This equation corresponds to equation (11-3) in the text. This first-order condition equates the cost of making a marginal adjustment in energy use today and postponing this marginal adjustment until the next period. Suppose that e_t is below e_t^*. Then increase e_{t-1} by a small amount while leaving e_{t+1} unchanged. This step leads to a gain insofar as the difference between e_t and e_t^* is smaller. This gain is captured by the left side of equation (11-11). This change means that some costs of adjustment must be incurred today rather than in the next period, which leads to the costs captured by the right side of equation (11-11). At an optimum the benefits of adjusting today rather than tomorrow must equal the costs. Although (11-11) is the equation that will actually be estimated, it is useful to write the solution to the minimization of equation (11-10). It is nothing more than the solution of the difference equation (11-11) subject to the transversality that requires agents to expect that, in the distant future, the change in energy will be relatively modest—that is, that e will not explode. This solution is

$$(11\text{-}12) \qquad e_t = \alpha e_{t-1} + (1 - \alpha)E_t \sum(\alpha\delta)k_{e^*t+k}$$

where α is the smallest root of the characteristic equation of the difference equation (11-10).

Equation (11-12) has the property that energy demanded at t depends on the expected future determinants of e^*. It also has the property that as long as the expected future values of e^* equal the current value of e^* (either because people have static expectations or because e^* follows a random walk), it will be identical to equation (11-2), with α equal to g.

Notes

We are grateful for the assistance of Mansoor Dailami and Mohan Munasinghe, who participated as discussants in the conference in June 1986 that led to this publication. It should also be noted that author Seok-Hyun Hong is no longer with the Korea Development Institute.

1. These numbers are proportional to the ratio of the Korean wholesale index of petroleum product prices to the Saudi Arabian price for crude oil multiplied by the exchange rate.

2. The figures are from the Korea Institute of Energy and Resources (1985).

3. For instance, in 1984 crude oil imports equaled 200 million barrels and other petroleum imports equaled 24 million barrels, while petroleum product exports (which are in essentially the same categories of fuels as petroleum imports) also equaled 24 million barrels.

4. Note that this analysis is carried out for a given money supply. A change in the money supply will obviously have additional effects.

5. This situation would happen, for example, if a geometric average of prices, in which the weight of each price is its share of GNP, were used.

6. This attitude could result from the fact that the policy of postponing price increases for one year may not be credible. After all, if that approach seems worthwhile to the government this year, will not a similar postponement seem worthwhile

the following year? The use of static expectations is equivalent to assuming that energy adjusts as in equation (11-2).

References

Ahn, Byoung-Hun, and In-Ho Lee. 1980. "Primary Energy Demand in Korea." Korea Advanced Institute for Science and Technology. Seoul. In Korean.

Ashenfelter, Orley. 1984. "Macroeconomic Analyses and Microeconomic Analyses of Labor Supply." In Carl Brunner and Allan Meltzer, eds., *The Economics of Price and Wage Controls,* Carnegie-Rochester Conference Series on Public Policy, vol. 2. New York: North-Holland.

Fischer, Stanley. 1977. "Long-Term Contracts, Rational Expectations, and the Optimal Money Supply Rule." *Journal of Political Economy* 85 (April): 191–206.

———. 1985. "Supply Shocks, Wage Stickiness, and Accommodations." *Journal of Money, Credit and Banking* 17 (February):1–15.

Hamilton, James D. 1983. "Oil and the Macroeconomy since World War II." *Journal of Money, Credit and Banking* 15 (April): 228–48.

Hausman, Jerry A. 1979. "Individual Discount Rates and the Purchase and Utilization of Energy-Using Durables." *Bell Journal of Economics* (Spring) :33–54.

Korea Institute of Energy and Resources. Various issues. *Yearbook of Energy Statistics.* Seoul.

Long, John, Jr., and Charles Plosser. 1983. "Real Business Cycles." *Journal of Political Economy* 91:39–69.

Pindyck, Robert S. 1979. *The Structure of World Energy Demand.* Cambridge, Mass.: MIT Press.

Pindyck, Robert S., and Julio J. Rotemberg. 1983. "Dynamic Factor Demands and the Effect of Energy Price Shocks." *American Economic Review* (December): 1066–79.

———. 1984. "Energy Shocks and the Macroeconomy." In Alvin Alm and Robert Weiner, eds., *Oil Shock.* Cambridge, Mass.: Ballinger.

Poterba, James, Julio J. Rotemberg, and Lawrence H. Summers. 1986. "A Tax-Based Test for Nominal Rigidities." *American Economic Review* 76 (September): 659–75.

Rotemberg, Julio J. 1983. "Supply Shocks, Sticky Prices, and Monetary Policy." *Journal of Money, Credit and Banking* 15 (November): 489–98.

Sargent, Thomas J. 1979. *Macroeconomic Theory.* New York: Academic Press.

Stoker, Thomas, M. 1986. "The Distributional Welfare Effects of Rising Prices in the United States—The 1970s Experience." *American Economic Review* 76 (June): 335–49.

World Bank. 1981. *World Development Report 1981.* New York: Oxford University Press.

12 Social Welfare during the Period of Structural Adjustment

SANG-MOK SUH, Korea Development Institute
HA-CHEONG YEON, Korea Development Institute

THE DUAL OBJECTIVES of economic development are efficiency and equity. A developing country should seek not only high economic growth, but also equitable distribution of the benefits of this growth among its citizens. A common view is that there is a tradeoff between these two goals. Some experts argue that growth must be sacrificed to achieve a better distribution of wealth, while others contend that only through increases in GNP will there be anything significant to distribute. Although the goals of equity and efficiency are not always achieved hand in hand, the experiences of some countries have shown that an appropriate policy approach can successfully raise social welfare and economic output simultaneously.

In the case of Korea, the aggressive industrialization policy of the past two decades resulted in an unprecedented record of economic growth, while until recently national social welfare reform received little attention. The 1950s were characterized by a weak government policy that had no clear objective with respect to either efficiency or welfare. Not surprisingly, that period was a time of low growth and poor distribution of income.[1] With the launching of the First Five-Year Plan in 1962, however, the Korean government began to exert tremendous influence on the economy to maximize its growth potential by pursuing an export-led development strategy. Emphasis on growth during the next two decades transformed Korea into an industrialized nation, at least by developing world standards. Between 1963 and 1980 real GNP grew at an average annual rate of 8.7 percent, with nominal values for exports and manufactured output increasing by 37.8 percent and 19.2 percent a year, respectively.

Throughout this period social welfare policy was a low priority for policymakers. Despite the lack of attention, evidence shows that initially equity improved along with growth.[2] The government's export-oriented development strategy, which focused on the promotion of highly labor-intensive industries, accelerated the rate of growth and provided a steadily expanding pool of job opportunities for the unemployed and the underemployed, as well as for the growing labor force. As a result the rate of unemployment dropped from 8.2 percent in 1963 to 4.5 percent in 1970, and underemployment was reduced from 8.0 percent to 4.7 percent; the consequent increase in the income of low-skilled labor was a positive force in income distribution.

In the early 1970s the distribution of income began to deteriorate, primarily because of a shift in government policy. In response to growing competition abroad in labor-intensive manufactures and to the perceived need to establish a domestic defense industry in light of the threatened withdrawal of U.S. troops, the Korean government promoted the development of the heavy and chemical industries through generous tax credits and preferential loans, often at negative real interest rates. This emphasis on capital- and skill-intensive industries rapidly increased the demand for highly skilled and educated manpower. The corresponding rise in the wages of skilled labor served as one force behind the worsening income distribution. The concentration of business that took place in the 1970s also contributed to urban income disparity (for details, see Lee and Lee 1985). Estimates of the Korea Development Institute (KDI) show that the share of the seventy largest *jaebul* groups (business conglomerates) in the country's GDP increased from 7.1 percent in 1973 to 17.1 percent in 1978 (Sakong 1980). The growth of these large business conglomerates gave rise not only to growing inequality in business income, but also to a widening gap in wage differentials between small and large firms.

The 1970s also witnessed adverse effects on the income distribution of the rural sector. A rice price support program introduced in 1969 widened the income gap among farm households, because large farms benefited relatively more from the high price of rice (Ban 1979). Furthermore, attempts to modernize agriculture, such as the introduction of high-yield varieties of rice and the cultivation of cash crops, may have caused even greater income disparity, because the revenue of the more innovative farmers, most of whom already belonged to an upper-income group, rose faster than that of other farmers.

In light of this growing inequality in incomes, social welfare became an increasingly important issue in the late 1970s. Motivated by social pressures such as urbanization and the raised level of education of the nation, the government took steps to improve social welfare, particularly through the implementation of programs in the areas of health and social security. The government's heightened initiative to improve social welfare in the past decade coincided closely with government measures for structural adjustment. Consequently, it is of great interest to examine the trend in social welfare during this period, as well as the relationship between structural adjustment and social welfare.

This chapter addresses the equity versus efficiency issue in policymaking, focusing on the period from the late 1970s to 1986. The chapter first reviews the social welfare policies that were implemented by the Korean government between the late 1970s and 1986. Next, it examines the trends in social welfare indicators in the first half of the 1980s. The third section analyzes the relationship between social welfare and structural adjustment. The chapter concludes with a discussion of remaining issues relating to social welfare in Korea and the lessons to be learned from the Korean experience.

Social Welfare Policies since the Late 1970s

Government expenditures on welfare showed a steadily increasing trend from the last half of the 1970s through 1986. As shown in table 12-1, the share of welfare spending in government outlays rose from 18.4 percent in 1974 to almost 30 percent in 1986. As a percentage of GNP, welfare expenditures almost doubled in the same period, rising from 2.6 percent in 1974 to 4.6 percent in 1986.

Although social development policy received increasing attention after the formulation and implementation of the Fourth (1977–81) and Fifth (1982–86) Five-Year Socioeconomic Development Plans, efficiency remained the government's primary objective. This focus was clear—government spending on welfare, whether measured by the share in total spending or in absolute levels, was still relatively low by international standards.[3] In 1986 social welfare accounted for about 40–60 percent of total government expenditures in Argentina, Chile, Sweden, and the United States but for less than 28 percent in Korea (table 12-2). In the first four countries social security represented by far the largest portion of total welfare spending.

Table 12-1. *Government Social Welfare Expenditures, Selected Years, 1974–86*

Item	1974	1978	1982	1986
Social welfare expenditures				
(billions of won)	191.4	786.4	2,494.7	3,874.7
Education	160.6	620.5	1,916.4	2,767.0
Health	10.6	51.0	110.1	279.0
Social security	15.1	70.2	262.0	456.4
Housing	1.4	22.7	133.1	197.5
Other	3.8	22.0	73.1	172.7
Share of total government				
expenditures (percent)	18.4	22.4	26.8	28.1
Education	15.5	17.6	20.5	20.1
Health	1.0	1.5	1.2	2.0
Social security	1.5	2.0	2.8	3.3
Housing	0.1	0.7	1.4	1.4
Other	0.4	0.6	0.8	1.3
Share of GNP (percent)	2.6	3.3	4.9	4.6
Education	2.1	2.6	3.8	3.3
Health	0.1	0.2	0.2	0.3
Social security	0.2	0.3	0.5	0.5
Housing	0.0	0.1	0.3	0.2
Other	0.1	0.1	0.1	0.2

Source: Budget Bureau, Economic Planning Board, Seoul.

Table 12-2. *Government Social Welfare Expenditures, Selected Countries, 1986*
(percentage of government expenditures)

Item	Argentina[a]	Chile	Sweden	United States	Korea
Education	6.04	12.53	8.89	1.74	18.12
Health	1.28	5.99	1.13	11.55	1.51
Social security	32.58	38.01	48.46	28.42	6.36
Housing	0.42	4.54	3.33	2.59	0.86
Other	0.46	0.74	0.73	0.26	1.12
Total	40.78	61.81	62.54	44.56	27.37

a. 1985 data.
Source: IMF (1985).

In its rise to power in 1981, the new Korean government had advocated the development of a welfare state following the Western model and made that its major policy slogan. After a reassessment of national priorities, however, the government adopted a strategy of pursuing social welfare policies in conjunction with stabilization, liberalization, and other structural adjustment measures that were deemed of greater short-term significance to the nation's health. Because of the emphasis on efficiency over welfare and the government's desire to avoid potentially negative incentive effects on work through an overemphasis on social welfare provisions, the "welfare state" was not pursued aggressively.

Nevertheless, the government did initiate and expand several important welfare programs. As indicated in table 12-1, social welfare expenditures as a percentage of government expenditures rose by about 10 percentage points, from 18.4 percent in 1974 to 28.1 percent in 1986. Half of this increase was the result of stronger support for education, which gained nearly 5 percentage points in its share of government expenditures. Government spending on health and social security, which may be said to represent social welfare in the narrow sense, also enjoyed more attention, with their shares going from 1.0 percent and 1.5 percent to 2.0 percent and 3.3 percent of government expenditures, respectively.

Health Programs

A number of new programs in the areas of medical assistance, medical insurance, and primary health care were initiated in the health field that formed the core of social welfare policies in the period under review.

Medical Assistance Program Government expenditures on health increased rapidly in absolute terms, rising nominally from 10.6 billion won in 1974 to 279 billion in 1986 (table 12-1). The largest single factor in this increase was the establishment of the Medical Care Assistance Program, which provided medical services for those unable to pay for them, in 1977. Dur-

Table 12-3. *Medical Care Assistance Program, 1978–86*

Year	Expenditures (millions of won)[a]	Number eligible (thousands)			Total eligible as a percentage of the population
		Total	Class I[b]	Class II[c]	
1978	5,661	2,095	440	1,655	5.7
1979	6,718	2,134	510	1,624	5.7
1980	8,171	2,142	642	1,500	5.6
1981	16,952	3,727	642	3,085	9.6
1982	24,530	3,728	642	3,086	9.5
1983	30,516	3,728	642	3,086	9.4
1984	31,862	3,259	643	2,616	8.0
1985	44,617	3,259	643	2,616	8.0
1986	56,715	4,386	643	3,743	10.5

a. Based on current prices.
b. All people below the poverty line who are unable to work.
c. All people below the poverty line who have low incomes.
Source: Ministry of Health and Social Affairs.

ing the first year the total government budget allocated for this program was 7.4 billion won, the largest appropriation ever made for a single health program. Since then, government outlays for the Medical Care Assistance Program have continued to expand rapidly, reaching 56.7 billion won in 1986, as shown in table 12-3.

In 1986 over 4 million people, or some 10.5 percent of the population, were covered by this program. Recipients of assistance were divided into those unable to work (class I) and those with low income (class II). People unable to work included those under the age of eighteen, those sixty-five or older, pregnant women, the disabled, the physically handicapped, and other recipients of relief under the Livelihood Protection Law of 1951. Low-income people included those whose income was below the minimum cost of living; they were identified annually by local government officials.

As a result of this program, people below the poverty line who were unable to work would get all their medical services free. In the case of low-income people able to work, the program paid 20 to 40 percent of hospital costs, depending on the region in which they lived, and all outpatient expenses. Moreover, the government provided interest-free loans for the remaining hospital costs. This provision of low-cost or free health services was extremely important in upgrading the status of the poor, inasmuch as high medical costs were a major reason for the perpetuation of poverty and the shift of middle-income people to the medically indigent (Kwon 1988b).

Medical Insurance Program On July 1, 1977, Korea initiated a new medical insurance program designed to improve national health and enhance social security by facilitating access to medical care in the event of illness, injury, or childbirth (for details, see Yeon 1985). Initially, the new law established a two-part program, including a requirement that employers with 500 or

Table 12-4. *Medical Insurance, 1978–86*

Year	Number eligible (thousands)	Percentage of the population
1978	3,883	10.5
1979	7,791	20.7
1980	9,113	24.0
1981	11,406	29.5
1982	13,513	34.4
1983	15,577	39.0
1984	17,050	42.1
1985	17,879	43.5
1986	19,361	46.6

Note: All figures are end-of-year totals.
Source: Ministry of Health and Social Affairs.

more workers provide specified medical insurance benefits to employees and dependents and a voluntary, community-based plan providing medical insurance for all others. Firms employing fewer than 500 workers participated on a voluntary basis. Compulsory coverage was expanded in 1979 to include firms with at least 300 workers and in 1988 to cover all firms with at least five workers. In addition, government legislation in 1979 made insurance compulsory for all government officials and schoolteachers. In 1980 further legislation extended the coverage to all military dependents and in 1981 to pensioners and their dependents.

As a result of these modifications, health insurance coverage increased dramatically in the early to mid-1980s. Although only 10.5 percent of the population had health insurance a year after the program began, by 1986 46.6 percent were covered, as shown in table 12-4. Because the medical insurance program for employees did not entail any direct government subsidies, the burden of the insurance fees was divided equally between employers and employees. The government, however, paid the expenses for administration of the medical insurance program for the self-employed. In addition, the government provided a matching fund for the regional medical insurance program equal to approximately to one-half of the total cost, including administrative expenses (for details, see Kwon 1988a).

The program grew considerably in the number of claims for cases treated. Individuals who had health insurance tended to use more medical services than did those without coverage, mainly because insurance ensured access to adequate, quality services and lowered the price of medical care at the point of purchase. For example, the number of medical cases treated per 100 covered people increased from only 76 in 1978 to 286 by 1985.

Primary Health Care The government developed a Primary Health Care Project in 1975 with the specific intent of increasing access to and use of modern health facilities. The goals of the project were to provide primary health care advice and preventive and therapeutic health services to the rural population as well as to low-income urban residents. The development of a delivery system comprehensive enough to meet these aims required the establishment of more service units, including health centers, community health centers, primary health units, and primary health posts and midwifery centers.

To provide health services to farmers, self-employed people, and others who were not covered by medical insurance programs in the 1980s, the government integrated an experimental primary health care program with the social insurance medical care schemes in six rural communities (for details, see Yeon 1981). The main features of this health program included improved coverage of basic health services, mobilization of financial resources, deployment of middle-level health workers, maximum utilization of public health centers, and improved community participation.[4]

Antipoverty Programs

The government had long provided basic assistance and income maintenance for the poor, going back to the Livelihood Protection Act of 1961. In the 1980s, however, the government's commitment to antipoverty programs increased substantially. Total government expenditures for the Livelihood Protection Program showed a rapid rise from 21.7 billion won in 1976 to 189.3 billion won in 1986 in nominal prices (table 12-5). As a consequence, the number of recipients rose from almost 2.0 million to almost 2.2 million in the same period.

This heightened attention to antipoverty programs was the result, to some extent, of a comprehensive KDI study on poverty in 1981 (Suh and others 1981). The study made the following recommendations:

- Authorities should give top priority to creating employment opportunities for the poor during an economic slowdown and to providing job training programs and job placement services, particularly in urban squatter areas.
- The transfer of poverty from parents to children must be prevented. For this purpose, middle school and vocational training should be free for low-income families, and scholarship opportunities in higher education need to be expanded.
- The government must provide essential consumption goods, or the cash to buy these goods, for those who cannot work because of a physical or mental impairment.
- Particularly in urban squatter areas, family counseling by professional social workers and day-care centers for preschool children are urgently needed.
- The physical environment of urban slums must be ameliorated. The government can assist residents' self-help efforts by supplying construction materials and tools at low cost.

Table 12-5. Government Expenditures for the Livelihood Protection Program, by Category of Recipient, 1976–86

Year	Recipients in welfare institutions		Recipients in private homes		Expenditures for those able to work		Total[a]	
	Amount[b]	Number[c]	Amount[b]	Number[c]	Amount[b]	Number[c]	Amount[b]	Number[c]
1976	1,590	96	3,210	235	15,753	1,631	21,725	1,962
1977	2,283	94	3,592	224	12,287	1,727	26,207	2,045
1978	2,530	91	4,365	198	11,227	1,655	23,783	1,944
1979	3,287	89	9,100	229	47,017	1,624	66,132	1,942
1980	4,895	47	16,782	282	43,907	1,500	73,560	1,829
1981	7,800	47	26,911	282	31,752	1,760	83,415	2,089
1982	9,411	52	29,983	282	49,106	3,080	113,030	3,420
1983	9,640	56	34,877	282	50,168	2,616	125,190	2,954
1984	10,086	60	35,731	282	49,206	2,214	126,885	2,556
1985	13,369	63	45,088	282	60,087	1,928	163,161	2,273
1986	15,758	71	51,502	284	65,359	1,819	189,334	2,174

a. The totals are greater than the sum of the columns because they include Medical Care Assistance Program expenditures.
b. Millions of won.
c. Thousands of recipients.
Source: Ministry of Health and Social Affairs.

Acting upon these recommendations, the Korean government accelerated its efforts to help the poor, as indicated by the trends in the antipoverty programs in the first half of the 1980s. For example, the government initiated programs that provided cash assistance for living expenses and tuition exemptions at middle schools and vocational training centers. These benefits were available to both categories of the poor: those who were unable to work because of age or sickness and those who were able to work but were deemed absolutely poor. In 1985, 244,675 persons received benefits under this program.

In addition, in-kind grants of cereals were given to those unable to work, while the public work program became an important means of helping the poor who could work, especially during recessionary times. Public expenditures for this program reached 55.6 billion won in 1982 but then declined steadily because of the economic recovery program. In addition, this program was estimated to have created 12 million staff-days of employment in 1982. Typical work under this program included road construction or improvement, cleaning of small rivers and streams, construction of rural irrigation facilities, and urban construction.

Korea's antipoverty program included two other important efforts. The government significantly expanded its business loan program for the poor and established an increasing number of day-care centers in squatter areas. The business loan program, which started in 1982, amounted to 5 billion won in 1985, and the number of day-care centers in squatter areas almost quadrupled between 1980 and 1985.

Public Housing Program

The rapid urbanization of the 1970s led to a great demand for housing in cities, but the recession that began in 1979 caused a drop in housing investment. In addition, the government's antispeculation laws and overall economic stabilization policy curbed the expansion of dwelling construction. These factors led to a shortage of housing: the housing supply ratio (number of housing units divided by total households) declined from 74.4 percent in 1975 to 71.6 percent in 1984. The problem was especially acute for the urban poor because of the propensity to build large housing units that were too expensive for them.

Recognizing this problem, the government adopted several measures to encourage the building of small apartments for the urban poor. First, the government increased its financing for the National Housing Fund, which offered low-interest loans to builders of low-income housing. The funding level for 1984 was 88 billion won greater than that of 1983 and almost quadruple the level of 1981 (table 12-6). Because of the increased funds, government-supported housing construction surpassed its goal in 1984, producing 119,524 units, 4,000 more than originally projected.

Table 12-6. *National Housing Funds, 1981–86*

Year	Expenditures (millions of won)	Housing units
1981	255,024	69,809
1982	465,925	50,577
1983	925,531	81,265
1984	1,013,484	119,524
1985	728,273	97,759
1986	571,245	87,456

Source: Korea Housing Bank (1986).

In addition, in 1984 the government implemented the Act for Promoting Construction of Rental Dwelling to increase the availability of rental housing for those too poor to purchase homes. The act provided low-priced land to builders of rental housing, tax incentives, and increased funding for the National Housing Fund to supply loans at a 5 percent annual interest rate, with a repayment period of twenty years and a five-year grace period for the principal. As a result the construction of rental housing also increased sharply: in 1984, 12,555 rental units were built, nearly twice the 1983 figure of 6,709.

Public Education Program

In 1972 the government repealed the financial grants for local education, which accounted for 12.98 percent of internal taxes. This measure had a large effect on educational expenditures: as a percentage of GNP they dropped from 5.5 percent in 1972 to 3.7 percent in 1974.[5] The decreased expenditures led to low salaries for teachers and deteriorating educational facilities.

In accordance with the goal of the Fifth Five-Year Plan (1982–86) of improving human capital, in 1981 the government decided to reinstitute the financial grants for local education. To raise the necessary revenues, it imposed a special education tax on interest income and on sales of liquor and cigarettes. The revenues were targeted for improving educational facilities and raising the salaries of teachers (table 12-7).

Partly because of the extra revenues from the special tax, local education expenditures as a percentage of government expenditures rose from 14.7 percent in 1981 to 17.1 percent in 1983. The emphasis on education led to many improvements, including construction of 447 elementary schools, 452 middle schools, and 200 high schools. In addition, monthly bonuses for teachers reached 105,000 won a month in 1986, up from 30,000 won a month in 1981.

Although the special education tax was scheduled to expire in 1986, it was extended to finance the continued upgrading of educational services.

Table 12-7. *Public Grants for Education, 1980–86*
(billions of won)

Year	Revenues from education tax		Public grants for education		A/B (percent)
	Amount (A)	Increase rate (percent)	Amount (B)	Increase rate (percent)	
1980	n.a.	n.a.	928	n.a.	n.a.
1981	n.a.	n.a.	1,185	27.6	n.a.
1982	198	n.a.	1,568	33.8	12.5
1983	263	32.9	1,803	13.7	14.6
1984	285	8.3	1,915	6.2	14.9
1985	321	12.8	2,124	11.9	15.1
1986	334	4.1	2,337	10.0	14.3

n.a. Not applicable.
Source: Korea, Ministry of Education (1986).

Recent Trends in Social Welfare

For a comprehensive view of social welfare trends during the period of structural adjustment, it is useful to examine movements in three areas: the macroeconomy, income distribution, and social welfare as measured by selected economic and social indicators (the trends for twenty-one indicators from 1965 to 1985 are shown in table 12-8).

Macroeconomic Indicators

Perhaps the most aggregated index used in assessing the effect of economic policy on social welfare is per capita GNP. As per capita income and real wages rise, there is generally a corresponding rise in the average quality of welfare, with the opposite holding true as well. In Korea per capita GNP fell in 1980 for the first time in twenty years, as seen in table 12-9. In addition, real wages declined in both 1980 and 1981. The negative implications of these macroeconomic trends for welfare are clear. After 1981, however, both per capita income and real wages grew steadily, with attendant positive effects on average welfare, as borne out by the microeconomic indicators of welfare.

Income Distribution Indicators

Overall income distribution is another means of determining movements in national welfare. As seen in table 12-10, Korea's income distribution pattern showed a negative trend during 1970–80, caused both by the increasing disparities in the wages of skilled and unskilled workers and by the economic recession in 1980. The Gini coefficient for all households, for example, rose from 0.3322 in 1970 to 0.3891 in 1980. Furthermore, the ratio of earnings by the bottom 40 percent of the population to the top 20

Table 12-8. Social Welfare Indexes, 1965, 1970, and 1975–85
(1975=100)

Item	1965	1970	1975	1976	1977	1978	1979	1980	1981	1982	1983	1984	1985
Total resources (GNP)	39.67	66.19	100.00	114.13	128.63	141.12	150.30	140.43	149.69	157.82	176.57	191.48	201.33
GNP per capita	48.76	71.10	100.00	112.33	124.64	134.68	141.28	129.96	136.38	141.58	156.02	166.75	173.01
Social development expenditures/total expenditures	—	100.77[a]	100.00	108.36	109.49	115.49	116.99	124.57	126.23	139.44	142.69	138.56	138.84
Health expenditures/total expenditures	—	116.50[a]	100.00	108.74	151.46	140.78	173.79	120.39	112.62	114.56	128.16	142.72	187.08
Education expenditures/total expenditures	—	106.06[a]	100.00	116.61	134.96	136.61	134.33	136.69	145.51	163.78	166.30	161.10	158.18
Social security expenditures/total expenditures	—	73.85[a]	100.00	69.61	69.96	70.32	88.69	94.70	85.51	99.29	103.18	116.25	112.05
Housing expenditures/total expenditures	—	125.58[a]	100.00	125.58	162.79	151.16	146.51	465.12	348.84	332.56	234.88	111.60	113.95
Crude death rate	79.55	77.78	100.00	100.00	98.59	98.59	101.45	104.48	106.06	107.69	111.11	111.11	112.90
Infant mortality rate	38.50	74.21	100.00	102.48	104.81	107.53	110.11	112.50	115.64	118.29	121.05	124.32	126.99

Population/physician ratio	85.97	101.58	100.00	103.98	107.39	111.59	115.89	120.63	124.98	129.85	134.70	140.26	146.42
Population/nurse ratio	19.16	34.43	100.00	111.75	119.54	131.64	148.20	164.80	179.13	188.41	209.49	223.10	249.19
Population/hospital bed ratio	64.93	85.90	100.00	103.81	118.94	127.38	143.50	166.12	169.75	186.63	241.57	277.72	295.83
Primary school enrollment ratio	94.39	96.26	100.00	100.93	100.00	101.86	101.86	99.67	100.42	101.29	100.80	99.97	97.89
Secondary school enrollment ratio	62.50	75.00	100.00	108.93	114.29	121.42	133.92	137.37	144.23	146.86	149.50	151.79	154.60
Pupil/teacher ratio (primary level)	83.01	91.04	100.00	103.19	106.15	106.58	107.69	109.05	113.85	118.00	124.22	129.82	135.25
Pupil/teacher ratio (secondary level)	106.65	104.13	100.00	98.06	97.25	95.92	95.41	94.89	95.92	98.06	100.00	101.73	104.23
Labor force participation rate	98.41	98.94	100.00	102.48	101.95	102.65	101.95	101.06	100.18	100.53	98.76	95.40	96.64
Daily calorie supply per capita	91.59	99.16	100.00	101.00	101.55	105.98	108.74	103.97	105.90	108.28	108.58	109.21	112.43
Energy consumption per capita	53.57	77.81	100.00	111.84	123.68	135.53	152.26	152.26	156.58	153.95	163.13	175.00	181.58
Rate of TV set ownership	3.04	21.31	100.00	134.75	178.03	232.13	259.67	257.70	270.49	277.38	270.49	276.39	273.50
People per passenger car	24.72	79.48	100.00	110.40	142.05	205.90	264.82	273.99	284.59	320.22	392.56	472.25	567.75

— Not available.

a. Data for 1972 are used because of differences in classification.

Source: Korea Development Institute.

Table 12-9. *Macroeconomic Indicators, 1978–86*

Year	Economic growth rate (percent)	Per capita GNP (dollars)[a]	Real wages (thousands of won)	Change in real wages (percent)
1978	11.0	1,392	169	18.0
1979	7.0	1,640	184	8.5
1980	−4.8	1,589	176	−4.1
1981	6.6	1,719	175	−0.5
1982	5.4	1,773	189	7.9
1983	11.9	1,914	203	6.3
1984	8.4	2,044	216	6.8
1985	5.4	2,047	230	6.6
1986	12.3	2,300	243	5.8

a. In nominal terms.
Source: Bank of Korea and Ministry of Labor.

percent dropped during the same period. With economic recovery, however, the income distribution figures improved somewhat, with the Gini coefficient dropping to 0.3631 in 1985. The improvement was significant for both farm and nonfarm households.

At the lower end of the income spectrum, where social welfare needs were greatest, the incidence of absolute and relative poverty in Korea conformed closely to the trend in per capita income and the pattern of income distribution (for details, see Suh 1981). In the 1960s both absolute and relative poverty declined; by 1970 only 4.8 percent of the total population was defined as relatively poor. During the 1970s, however, as seen in table 12-11, these figures rose dramatically. In 1976 12.5 percent of the population was classified as relatively poor, and in 1980 13.3 percent received this designation. With the economic recovery of the early 1980s and the favorable trend in income distribution, relative poverty again seemed to be on the decline, with the 1984 figures indicating a drop to 7.7 percent. Absolute poverty, however, saw a steady decline.

Table 12-10. *Income Distribution, Selected Years*

Household	1970	1976	1980	1984
All households				
Gini coefficient	0.3322	0.3908	0.3891	0.3567
Decimal distribution ratio	19.63/41.62	16.85/45.34	16.06/45.39	18.86/42.28
Nonfarm households				
Gini coefficient	0.3455	0.4118	0.4053	0.3655
Decimal distribution ratio	18.87/43.04	15.26/48.70	15.29/46.89	18.40/43.53
Farm households				
Gini coefficient	0.2945	0.3273	0.3555	0.2992
Decimal distribution ratio	21.24/38.64	19.45/40.62	17.48/42.19	21.36/37.92

Note: The estimates for 1970, 1976, and 1984 are based on patchwork information from various household surveys and other sources (see Choo 1980 for details). The 1980 estimates are based on a comprehensive income distribution survey undertaken by the Bureau of Statistics in early 1981.
Source: Korea Development Institute estimates.

Table 12-11. *Trends in the Incidence of Poverty, Selected Years*
(percent)

Category	1970	1976	1980	1984
Absolute poverty[a]	23.4	14.8	9.8	4.5
Urban	16.2	18.1	10.4	4.6
Rural	27.9	11.7	9.0	4.4
Relative poverty[b]	4.8	12.5	13.3	7.7
Urban	7.0	16.0	15.1	7.8
Rural	3.4	9.2	11.2	7.5

Note: The income distribution data used for calculating the poverty ratios are the same as those in table 12-10.

a. The absolute poverty line is defined as 121,000 won per month in 1981 prices for a family of five.

b. The relative poverty line is defined as one-third of the average household income in a given year.

Source: Korea Development Institute estimates.

Social Indicators

A detailed microanalysis of the social welfare implications of macro-economic performance is difficult for Korea, given the lack of adequate statistics. Within the constraints of the data, however, certain trends are apparent. In general, during the recessionary period of 1979–81 overall welfare deteriorated; over the subsequent years of economic recovery, conditions improved.

Health statistics are among the most reliable indicators of this trend. As a broad measure, average household expenditures on health increased in both absolute terms and as a percentage of total household expenditures. As late as 1974, for example, only 2.6 percent of urban household expenditures was for health services. In 1986 the figure was 7.2 percent, as seen in table 12-12.

Health expenditures in Korea grew markedly after the introduction of the new health insurance system in 1977. National health expenditures reached 3,520.5 billion won (approximately $4.044 million) in 1985, while per capita health expenditures amounted to 85,749 won (approximately $99). This increase represented a jump of 11.8 times over ten years.

As a proportion of GNP, national health expenditures grew from 3.0 percent in 1975 to 4.8 percent in 1985. If the rate of increase in health spending of the mid-1980s were to continue at approximately 28 percent a year, compared with a 22 percent growth rate for GNP in current market prices, health services will consume an increasing portion of all goods and services produced in Korea (see table 12-13).

The intake of both calories and protein has shown some improvement since the mid-1970s. Both indicators clearly suffered from the economic downturn in 1980: between 1979 and 1980, average daily calorie intake fell from 2,599 to 2,485, while protein consumption dropped from 76.2 grams

Table 12-12. *Health Expenditures, 1976–86*

	Urban households		Farm households	
Year	Yearly health expenditures (won)	Health expenditure ratio[a] (percent)	Yearly health expenditures (won)	Health expenditure ratio[a] (percent)
1976	43,692	5.0	26,841	3.6
1977	49,188	4.9	41,383	4.2
1978	70,260	5.2	60,615	4.6
1979	108,636	6.1	75,170	4.5
1980	137,016	6.3	95,895	4.5
1981	174,912	6.7	117,341	4.4
1982	210,852	7.0	166,335	5.1
1983	235,296	7.1	213,027	5.3
1984	255,996	7.1	219,271	5.1
1985	275,100	7.1	246,098	5.2
1986	307,320	7.2	267,357	5.4

a. Ratio of household health expenditures to total consumption expenditures.
Source: Korea, Economic Planning Board (1986).

daily in 1979 to 73.6 grams in 1980.[6] In the mid-1980s, as the economic recovery progressed, per capita daily calorie and protein intake gradually resumed an upward trend. In 1986 average calorie intake totaled 2,746, which was considerably higher than the 1977 level of 2,427. Table 12-14 shows that protein consumption rose to 89.4 grams in 1986, compared with 73.9 grams in 1977.

A final microindicator of social welfare worthy of consideration is infant and maternal mortality. As shown in table 12-15, from 1976 to 1985 infant mortality for each 1,000 births fell consistently from 40.4 to 32.6, a drop of 19.3 percent. In addition, maternal mortality rates dropped from 50 for each 100,000 live births in 1976 to 42 in 1979, then held constant during

Table 12-13. *National Health Expenditures (NHE), 1975–85*

		Per capita	Average annual increase (percent)		Per capita
	NHE/GNP	NHE			GNP
Year	(percent)	(won)	NHE	Per capita NHE	(dollars)
1975	3.0	8,446	—	—	590
1976	2.8	10,970	32.0	29.9	797
1977	2.9	14,321	32.6	30.5	1,008
1978	3.3	21,624	53.4	51.0	1,392
1979	3.6	29,677	39.2	37.2	1,640
1980	4.0	38,160	30.6	28.6	1,589
1981	4.0	46,944	25.0	23.0	1,719
1982	4.5	58,216	25.9	24.0	1,773
1983	4.7	68,902	20.2	18.4	1,914
1984	4.7	76,884	13.2	11.6	2,044
1985	4.8	85,749	13.0	11.5	2,047

— Not available.
Source: Kwon (n.d.), table 3.

Table 12-14. *Per Capita Daily Calorie and Protein Intake, 1977–86*

Year	Average calories	Protein (grams)
1977	2,427	73.9
1978	2,533	73.8
1979	2,599	76.2
1980	2,485	73.6
1981	2,531	76.9
1982	2,588	78.3
1983	2,622	86.6
1984	2,636	85.6
1985	2,687	86.6
1986	2,746	89.4

Source: Korea Rural Economics Institute and National Livestock Cooperatives Federation.

the 1980 recession. As the economy recovered, the maternal mortality rate declined again, falling to 34 in 1985.

Microindicators of social welfare such as those described thus far may be combined into an index to determine general movements in social welfare conditions. Two social welfare indexes were calculated for this study: the combined social welfare index (CSWI) and the combined health index (CHI).[7] As can be seen in table 12-16, both health and social welfare improved significantly from 1976–77 through 1984–85. Gains in social welfare as measured by the CSWI jumped from an index value of 8.61 for 1976–77 to 11.94 for 1984–85, but the increase was not steady. Welfare gains dropped severely following the second oil shock in 1979, as demonstrated by the low index value of 3.79.

Korea experienced an even greater rate of improvement in its health statistics. The CHI value for 1984–85 was 10.97, compared with only 5.45 in 1976–77. Again, the 1980 recession served to dampen the gains: the CHI

Table 12-15. *Infant and Maternal Mortality Rates, 1976–86*

Year	Infant mortality rate[a]	Maternal mortality rate[b]
1976	40.4	50
1977	39.5	46
1978	38.5	43
1979	37.6	42
1980	36.8	42
1981	35.8	41
1982	35.0	40
1983	34.2	38
1984	33.3	36
1985	32.6	34
1986	31.8	33

a. Number of infant deaths per 1,000 live births.
b. Number of maternal deaths per 100,000 live births.
Source: Various issues of Korea, Ministry of Health and Social Affairs, *Yearbook of Health and Social Statistics.*

Table 12-16. *Changes in Combined Social Welfare Indexes, 1976–85*

Year	Combined social welfare index	Combined health index
1976–77	8.61	5.45
1977–78	12.18	5.50
1978–79	11.48	8.48
1979–80	3.79	9.88
1980–81	4.94	5.40
1981–82	6.27	7.06
1982–83	12.18	17.41
1983–84	11.58	11.72
1984–85	11.94	10.97

Note: See note 7 at the end of this chapter for a detailed description of the indexes.
Source: Korea Development Institute estimates.

value of 5.40 for the 1980–81 period marked a fall in the health index to its 1976–77 level.

Social Welfare and Structural Adjustment

As shown in the previous section, the positive developments in social welfare and income distribution were matched by improvements in economic conditions. Indeed, concurrent with its efforts at social welfare reform, the Korean government pursued an adjustment policy that sought to achieve both stabilization, by curbing wage and price inflation, and liberalization so as to reorient the economy toward market principles.

To eliminate the hyperinflation caused by the second oil crisis, the government introduced a series of tight monetary and fiscal measures. Aggregate demand was controlled by limiting the overall rate of expansion of the money supply and by severely cutting back government spending, which throughout the 1970s had been running in deficit. The stabilization program also included an income policy, which provided government guidelines for wage increases and froze the salaries of government employees to keep nominal wage increases at reasonable levels.

In conjunction with its stabilization program, as noted, the government pursued economic liberalization to increase the autonomy of the private sector and strengthen the role of the market in the economy. Virtually all subsidized "industrial policy" loans and industrial targeting were eliminated. In addition, steps toward liberalization of the financial sector led to the denationalization of five commercial banks and lower entry barriers to both the bank and nonbank financial markets.

The most significant and controversial aspect of the liberalization program, however, was the loosening of import restrictions. The import liberalization ratio rose from 68.6 percent in 1980 to 91.5 percent in 1986. Concurrently, tariff rate and foreign investment restrictions and regulations were also reduced.

In the absence of direct evidence, it is difficult to quantify the relationship between these structural adjustment measures and social welfare. Nevertheless, the evidence so far suggests that social welfare and structural adjustment policies were complementary. Price stability and freer markets seem to have raised general welfare; conversely, improvements in social welfare contributed positively to adjustment.

It is a popular perception that structural adjustment measures have an adverse effect on social welfare. There may be some truth to this view in the short run. By restricting government spending and the growth of the money supply, stabilization policy initially places downward pressure on aggregate demand and thus on economic growth. In the case of Korea, the stabilization policy in late 1979 may have accelerated the downward trend in the business cycle initiated by the second oil shock and thus may have caused a welfare loss in the short term. The economy recovered quickly, however, and the average level of welfare improved thereafter. It is important to note that public welfare expenditures showed a steady rise during the period of fiscal restraint.

Liberalization measures increase the competition faced by previously protected industries or firms, which consequently may be forced to take lower profits or a cut in their market share. As advocates of protectionism are quick to point out, decreased demand in domestic industry hurts not only business owners, but also workers, because they may receive lower wages and have fewer opportunities for employment. The evidence so far indicates that Korea suffered little from import liberalization. Because the pace of liberalization was gradual and many Korean firms were quick to adjust to the more competitive environment, there were only a few cases of firms going bankrupt and workers being laid off because of a surge in imports.

In any case, painful adjustments in the short term can be traded off with long-term prosperity. A successful stabilization program will produce low inflation and thus improve the competitive position of a country's export industries. Liberalization of international markets can also facilitate adjustment of the economy to the changing terms of comparative advantage. Without government support, industries that no longer have a comparative advantage often decline to their demise, and resources are shifted into competitive, high-growth industries. Liberalization, especially of imports, can allow market mechanisms to elicit improvements in the quality of domestic products.

Especially important in the Korean case is the effect of the adjustment policy on income distribution. Because inflation implies a redistribution of income from those who earn a fixed income to those whose income derives from property and profit, the stabilization of the economy after 1982 favorably affected income distribution. Price stability seems to have had its most beneficial effect on urban wage and salary earners, who witnessed a steady rise in their real income. In addition, price stability bridged some of the income distribution gap by limiting the opportunities for windfall profits in real estate and other speculative ventures. Indeed, the stabilization and liberalization programs came under attack from certain quarters precisely because those activities were no longer as profitable as they were during the period of high inflation. Therefore, although it is difficult to determine the effect of stabilization on income distribution quantitatively, it is safe to hypothesize that it ameliorated income distribution, other things being held constant.

To look at the other side of the coin, social welfare spending is often perceived as an obstacle to structural adjustment. Certainly the implementation of social welfare programs can impose costs on the government. To the extent that these costs represent a sacrifice of resources that would have promoted adjustment, social welfare spending may decrease economic efficiency. In the Korean case, however, welfare expenditures were not likely to have played this role, partly because, by other nations' standards, social welfare claimed a relatively low portion of total government spending. This hypothesis is supported by Korea's healthy economic growth in recent years.

It may also be argued that social welfare gains positively support efforts to strengthen economic efficiency through structural adjustment measures, especially in the long run. Theoretically, improvements in social welfare have a positive effect on worker productivity—it is rational to assume that workers will produce more efficiently under conditions of better health, nutrition, and general well-being. In addition, social welfare measures can play a crucial role in promoting economic growth by easing social and political tensions. Structural adjustment in all sectors requires changes that are painful in the short term, but in the long run the economy is significantly better off. Social welfare policies can make the public more amenable to structural adjustment by compensating workers for the costs of economic change with immediate improvements in living conditions.

Remaining Issues in Social Welfare

From the late 1970s through 1986 the Korean government pursued a comprehensive policy designed to revitalize the economy and bolster the competitiveness of Korean industry. In addition to structural adjustment policy, the reform package included heightened government efforts in the area of social welfare.

Contrary to popular belief, social welfare and structural adjustment policy may be complementary. Although a lack of statistical data makes it difficult to quantify the exact nature of this relationship, social welfare development fits in as one of the building blocks of economic growth, as shown in the previous section. It is safe to hypothesize that positive structural adjustment, in addition to more comprehensive welfare policy measures, has contributed significantly to improvements in social welfare. As a result of a combination of these factors, the Korean experience included an upward trend in overall social welfare.

There is still much room for improvement, and as Korea progresses toward advanced industrialization it will need to address several key issues. With the continued improvements in mass communications and education, relative poverty in both urban and rural areas has become an issue of increasing concern. If left unchecked, it may become a serious source of tension. Because of the continuing—although slowing—rate of urban migration, the proportion of urban poor will increase gradually in the coming years. Consequently, the government will have to pay greater attention to providing job opportunities and training to the urban poor. In addition, the inflow of urban poor will exacerbate the squatter problem and will require renewed efforts to ameliorate their physical environment, especially with respect to housing and waste disposal.

Because of the migration to cities, the number of rural poor decreased somewhat. Helping the poor remaining in the agricultural sector poses a difficult task for the Korean government because of the shortage of land and limited scope for increasing agricultural productivity and farm income. Instead, the government may have to continue focusing on creating non-farm employment opportunities to augment agricultural income, especially through the promotion of rural industrialization.

Another significant issue accompanying Korea's rising income level is the need to foster the development of a middle class. In 1986 wage and salary earners represented one-half of the population; it is projected that this proportion will continue to rise in the future, reaching two-thirds by 2000. The challenge facing the Korean government is to help this social class become a politically stable, middle-income group.

A significant and necessary step toward this goal is an increase in home ownership. Even though the proportion of GNP invested in housing construction increased over the years, the housing supply ratio decreased steadily and will continue to drop in the future. Along with the scarcity of land for new housing, a lack of adequate financing was the major impediment to solving the housing problem. Consequently, the government may have to develop a long-term financing scheme to enhance the purchasing power of the middle class; the offer of long-term low-interest loans is especially feasible during the current period of low inflation.

Another policy area key to the development of the middle class is the minimum wage issue. While many feel that the establishment of a minimum wage is necessary for growth and social stability, the experience of several developed countries shows that this is not necessarily true, because the minimum wage decreases the employment opportunities available to the low-income group. It will be increasingly important for policymakers to decide which system is appropriate for Korea and to implement it accordingly.

Last, the expansion of the social security system in Korea is becoming a pressing issue, especially in the areas of medical insurance and pension funds. Under the current medical insurance program, the self-employed in urban areas were not served by the compulsory coverage as of 1986. Because medical fees under the insurance program were controlled by the government, the self-employed, who were mostly poor, were required to pay higher fees. In essence, those not covered by health insurance were subsidizing the workers who were.

There are, however, several limitations to extending the coverage. Compounding a poor understanding of insurance in general is the uneven income of the self-employed, which makes it difficult to determine appropriate premium payments. The lack of health facilities in rural areas also limits the utilization of health services for farmers. The government may have to focus on developing medical insurance programs that are compatible with the specific needs and resources of each region, as discussed earlier.

Despite these problems, the statistics clearly illustrate an increasing rate of coverage through 1986. By the end of that year, the number of people under the Medical Insurance Program reached 19,256,000, or 46.3 percent of the total population of Korea. When those under the Medical Aid Program are included, the figure reaches 56.9 percent. The Korean government decided to extend these programs to people in rural and fishing areas by 1988 and to the self-employed in urban areas by 1989. Thus, by July 1, 1989, everyone in Korea is to have medical insurance.

In addition, the government's social security program will have to include increased provisions for the elderly. Given the current age structure in Korea, the population of senior citizens is expected to accelerate rapidly after 2000: the proportion of the population over sixty-five years of age in 2020 is projected at 8 percent. This change, coupled with the shift in family structure toward the nuclear family, implies a rising demand for measures to supplement the income of the aged, which should be met through a pension program (for details, see Yeon 1982). To cope with this new situation the government decided to launch a national pension program in 1988.

Finally, with Korea's growing affluence, the government may have to consider implementing unemployment insurance. The main task in this area of social security is to create a system that protects the unemployed without lowering the incentive to work.

In the drive toward economic development, the major aim of the Korean government was to maximize the positive effect of the adjustment policy while minimizing its negative side effects. Social welfare measures played a significant role in attaining this goal. Indeed, the issue has not been whether the government should adopt social welfare policies, but how such policies could be implemented to complement economic growth.

In this regard, Korea has an advantage that it should continue to exploit in the future. As a latecomer to development, it can draw valuable lessons from the experiences of developed countries with social welfare programs and can profit from incorporating this knowledge into its own social welfare policy.

Notes

1. During the 1950s per capita income rose by 0.7 percent a year. Although there is no reliable estimate of the income distribution trends of the 1950s, the import-substitution policies of this period may have worsened income distribution in the nonagricultural sector.

2. This conclusion is supported by several empirical studies on income distribution in Korea. See Choo (1980), Adelman and Robinson (1978), Renaud (1976), and Adelman (1974).

3. Many welfare requirements were met by the private sector. For example, households spent a fairly large portion of their total income on children's education because scholarship opportunities were limited, and business firms very often took care of the welfare needs of their employees through severance pay schemes, medical check-ups, education subsidies, and so forth.

4. In three of the demonstration projects (Gunee, Okgu, and Hongcheon), three levels of premium, based on income and assets, were administered. At the other three demonstration projects (Kanghwa, Boun, and Mokpo), a formula was used to determine the premium rate, which included a flat sum for each household and a flat sum for each member of the family, plus additional amounts depending on income and holdings of financial and physical assets.

5. The educational expenditures referred to as a share of GNP include budgetary outlays for education provided by the central government, local autonomous bodies, and schools, as well as tuition and other sectoral expenses borne by the parents of students.

6. The impact of the 1980 economic slowdown on average nutrition intake was acute because of the bad harvest that year. For example, domestic rice production fell below an average level of about 36.3 percent.

7. All data on the economic and social indicators selected for the study were converted into indexes with 1975 as the base year because of the high availability of data for that year. The combined social welfare index (CSWI) equals the sum of the index values of sixteen social indicators divided by the number of indicators for which data were available. The sixteen indicators were life expectancy, calorie supply per day per person, energy consumption per capita, labor force participation rate, radio receivers per thousand population, rate of television set ownership, crude death rate, infant mortality rate, population per physician, population per nursing person, population per hospital bed, primary school enrollment ratio, secondary school enrollment ratio, pupil-teacher ratio at the primary level, pupil-teacher ratio at the secondary level, and adult literary rate. The combined health index (CHI) equals the sum of the index values of six health indicators divided by the number of indicators for which data were available. The six health indicators were life expectancy, crude death rate, infant mortality rate, population per physician, population per nursing person, and population per hospital bed.

References

Adelman, Irma 1974. "Redistribution with Growth: Some Country Experience." In Hollis Chenery, Montek S. Ahluwalia, C. L. G. Bell, John H. Duloy, and Richard Jolly, *Redistribution with Growth*. New York: Oxford University Press.

Adelman, I., and S. Robinson. 1978. *Income Distribution Policy in Developing Countries*. Stanford, Calif.: Stanford University Press.

Ban, Sung-Hwan. 1979. "Determining Factors of Rural Income and Income Distribution." In Hakchung Choo, ed., *Korea's Income Distribution and the Determining Factors*. Seoul: Korea Development Institute. In Korean.

Choo, Hakchung. 1980. "Economic Growth and Income Distribution." In Chong-Kee Park, ed., *Human Resources and Social Development in Korea*. Seoul: Korea Development Institute. In Korean.

IMF (International Monetary Fund). 1985. *Government Finance Statistics Yearbook*. Washington, D.C.

Korea, Economic Planning Board. 1986. *Social Indicators in Korea*. Seoul.

Korea, Ministry of Education. 1986. *Yearbook of Education Statistics*. Seoul.

Korea, Ministry of Health and Social Affairs. Various issues. *Yearbook of Health and Social Statistics*. Seoul.

Korea Housing Bank. 1986. *Statistics Yearbook of Banking Services*. Seoul.

Kwon. Soonwon. 1988a. "Major Policy Issues in Korea's Health Insurance System." A paper presented at the Korean-German Seminar on Social Security, Korea Development Institute, Seoul.

————. 1988b. "Social Insurance in Korea." Working Paper 8808. Seoul: Korea Development Institute.

————. n.d. "Trends in National Health Expenditures and Policy Issues of Cost Containment in Korea." Seoul: Korea Development Institute.

Lee, Kyu-Uck, and Seong-Soon Lee. 1985. *Business Combination and Concentration of Economic Power*. Seoul: Korea Development Institute. In Korean.

Renaud, Bertrand. 1976. *Economic Growth and Income Inequality in Korea*. World Bank Staff Working Paper 240. Washington, D.C.

Sakong, Il. 1980. "Economic Growth and Concentration of Economic Power." *Korea Development Review* (March). In Korean.

Suh, Sang-Mok. 1981. "The Patterns of Poverty." In Chong-Kee Park, ed., *Human Resources and Social Development in Korea*. Seoul: Korea Development Institute.

Suh, Sang-Mok, and others. 1981. *Patterns of Poverty and Anti-Poverty Programs*. Seoul: Korea Development Institute. In Korean.

Yeon, Ha-Cheong. 1981. *Primary Health Care in Korea: An Approach to Evaluation*. Seoul: Korea Development Institute.

————. 1982. *The Korean Economy and National Welfare Pension Program*. Seoul: Korea Development Institute. In Korean.

————. 1985. "Social Security Health Care and Its Policy Issues in Korea." Working Paper 8510. Seoul: Korea Development Institute.

13 Economic Management for Structural Adjustment in the 1980s

IN-JOUNG WHANG, Korea Development Institute

STRUCTURAL ADJUSTMENT of a national economy can take various forms, including industrial realignment, technological upgrading, curtailment of protective measures, and financial stabilization programs. In April 1979 the Korean government announced a program intended to restructure the entire economy, the Comprehensive Measures for Economic Stabilization (CMES). The CMES attempted to stabilize prices primarily by controlling monetaristic liquidity, eradicating financial and tax subsidies to particular industries and to the agricultural sector, activating the Fair Trade and Anti-Monopoly Act, and reducing investment in rural housing projects.[1]

Although the CMES would not be the only structural adjustment effort of the 1980s, it was a significant initial step toward restructuring the economy. The program embodied a radical change in the philosophy as well as the mode of government intervention in national economic management. During the 1960s and 1970s the economy had been oriented toward growth, sometimes at the cost of rising inflation. In contrast, the CMES emphasized stability as the basis for economic growth in the 1980s, because the expansionistic approach was seen as leading to a breakdown of the economy.

The effect of the CMES on the Korean economy seems to have been positive, as demonstrated by the recent price stabilization, sustained growth, recovery of international competitiveness of industrial products, and gradual improvement in the balance of payments (Aghevli and Marquez-Ruarte 1985; Kim 1984, pp. 25–27; see also chapter 3 of this volume).[2] This success indicates that the CMES deserves attention because it may offer valuable lessons in economic management. In the context of structural adjustment, economic management entails government intervention through a set of policy innovations that enable the national economy to adapt to a changing environment, both international and domestic; it also involves efficient and timely decisionmaking to cope with economic problems and effective implementation of policy decisions by mobilizing broadly based support, particularly within the business community and among the general public.[3]

This chapter presents an analytic description of Korea's recent experience with economic management of the structural adjustment of its economy. The focus is on how government decisions were made with regard to the CMES and how successfully these decisions were implemented. The study used social science research methodologies and took as its starting point data from a survey and from an analysis of literature and documents (Korea Development Institute 1981). The in-depth analysis of behavioral information was the product of extensive interviews with high-ranking officials and private citizens, particularly those who were involved in the adoption and implementation of the program.

How Decisions Were Made

How were economic decisions made in Korea to cope promptly and efficiently with changing domestic and international economic conditions? How did the government arrive at its decisions about the CMES in 1979, and how did the new government of the Fifth Republic do so in 1980? Answering these questions entails responses to additional questions: which policymakers were involved, what were their motivations, and how did they act in the decisionmaking process? Before proceeding with an in-depth analysis of the CMES, it is useful to examine the procedures for economic policymaking in Korea (the general organizational framework is described in chapter 2 of this volume).

Economic Policy Planning

The main issues in the planning and implementation of major policy packages are the interactions among policymakers and between government and the business sector, as well as the roles of the participants. Two important elements of economic planning are the five-year development plan and the Economic Planning Board (EPB). In preparing the five-year development plans, which provide the basic framework for policies over the medium term, the EPB takes the initial step of issuing preliminary guidelines for major policy targets and directions, together with macroeconomic projections for both the international and domestic economies during the plan period and beyond. At this stage the interaction between EPB technocrats and economists of the government-sponsored research institutes is crucial. Individual ministries then formulate their own sectoral plans in accordance with the guidelines. For this planning task the government makes extensive use of a number of working committees whose members are experts drawn not only from government ministries but also from industrial associations, financial institutions, universities, and research institutes.

The preliminary guidelines and individual sectoral plans are next consolidated in draft form and presented at a series of public policy forums conducted at the Korea Development Institute (KDI) and other research institutes. Many experts and representatives from business organizations, labor unions, and consumer groups are invited to express their views.

The EPB, with the help of the policy research institutes and individual ministries, formulates a consolidated draft plan for an initial series of reviews by a Plan Working Committee, which consists of the vice ministers of economic affairs, and subsequently by the Plan Deliberation Committee, which is composed of the prime minister and other cabinet members. The final step is approval by the president (Jin 1984).

To implement the medium-term plan, the government uses annual economic management plans. This system was developed for two primary purposes: to translate the policy targets and strategies embodied in the five-year development plans into specific, annual action programs and to permit revisions in policy and the list of projects to be implemented in response to unforeseen changes in the domestic and international economic environment. In addition, the system provides for a review and evaluation of performance in the preceding year and the preparation of guidelines for the government's annual budget. Finally, the annual plan contains the government's policy toward the private sector.

Every year, just before the budget cycle starts, the EPB circulates the initial draft of the economic management plan, derived from the five-year plan, to all government ministries and agencies for their use in annual policy planning and budget estimating. The EPB's annual budget guidelines are issued to the ministries and agencies immediately after circulation of the draft plan. After approval of the government budget by the National Assembly, the EPB finalizes the economic management plan, usually at the end of the current year or the beginning of the next year (Jin 1984; World Bank 1983, p. 68).

In the case of both the five-year and annual plans, the executive branch works closely with the National Assembly and the government party before the president finalizes major decisions. The individual standing committees of the National Assembly used to play an active part in shaping these plans through their reactions at hearings and policy inquiry sessions. More recently, the Party-Government Consultative Committee has met regularly to share information and build a consensus toward common courses of economic action.

Economic Policymaking

Proposals for economic policy are usually initiated by the ministries concerned with specific policy issues. Their proposals are reviewed in consultation with other relevant ministries before they are submitted to the cabinet and the president for final approval. Two institutional mechanisms are involved in the review and coordination of policy proposals: the Economic Ministers' Consultation Meeting, which is an informal or semiformal mechanism for coordination, and the Economic Ministers' Council Meeting, which is a formal setting that satisfies the legal requirements that policy proposals be submitted to the cabinet. In support of the latter mechanism, there is also an Economic Vice Ministers' Meeting.

It is noteworthy that the policy proposals of the ministries are seldom made available for public discussion. They are processed in secret or by a limited number of high-level officials. Policy proposals for emergency cases in particular tend to be prepared by small groups of the bureaucratic elite and are worked out quickly and confidentially and then presented to top policymakers for final endorsement. In other words, participation in policymaking seems to be limited; consultation with related ministries and private organizations is minimal. Even in the case of the special working committees organized by a ministry, participation by private experts and the general public in the policy debate is limited in the number of representatives and substance. In some cases the committees simply approve whatever is proposed.[4]

The lack of consensus building in policymaking reflects a "top-down" approach to government policy formulation (Kim 1983, pp. 64–68). This approach is rooted in the paternalistic tradition of Korean society as well as in the authoritarian tendencies of the government bureaucracy, both of which were particularly evident after the military coup d'état of 1961. The concentration of decisionmaking power allows the government bureaucracy to make speedy decisions and to adjust the direction of current policies once a problem arises.

These behavioral characteristics of policymaking constitute a policy planning subculture within the government bureaucracy.[5] One feature of this subculture is the dominance of the executive branch not only in policy implementation but also in decisionmaking. Although this phenomenon is common in modern states, Korea appears to be unique in that the executive dominance stems in part from the leadership's personal motivation and strong commitment to economic performance and in part from historical tradition rooted in Confucianism.

The Korean approach to policy planning is also characterized by speed and flexibility in responding to problems.[6] The government quietly prescribes a solution to a problem, constantly monitors its progress, and adjusts the policy direction as necessary. The government thus often rules through a process of trial and error, an approach that can work only when the bureaucracy is under the control of highly motivated and competent administrators.

The pragmatism of policymaking allows the government to choose, without ideological bias, among all the instruments and tools that can help achieve defined goals and solve the policy problems. Indeed, the government tends to use whatever means are suitable to the problem at hand.

Observation suggests that particularism is also prevalent in Korea's policymaking. Although this method of governing used to be seen as a behavioral characteristic of most developing countries,[7] the Korean government's approach has tended to be that of applying policy actions to a limited number of clients or particular problems in specific situations. Although the particularistic approach certainly helps in solving problems, it can fuel corruption if bureaucrats abuse individual discretion.

The top-down approach to policymaking, applied by a small group of the bureaucratic elite in a relatively confidential manner, is clearly associated with this policy planning subculture.

Decisionmaking for the CMES and the Political Environment

Which decisionmakers were involved in the policymaking that resulted in the adoption of the CMES? What were their motivations in initiating the idea of the CMES or in formulating and adopting it?

Because the substantive decisions involved in the CMES imply drastic changes in Korea's style of economic management, a conceptual framework for analysis of the policy reform can be applied. According to innovation theory, policy innovation requires a cluster of reformers as well as managers of the reform program. Reformers include the original inventors (or initiators), advocates, and adopters of the new ideas.[8] Managers solve conflicts within organizations and cope with resistance from outside. Who, then, played the roles of innovators, advocates, and adopters of policy reform in the case of the CMES? Which managers succeeded in implementing the CMES against resistance within and outside the government?

The policy reformers were those who participated in the decisionmaking that resulted in the CMES. The major decisionmakers seem to have been those with power within the political and bureaucratic institutions. Broadly speaking, these included the president, the prime minister, the deputy prime minister (concurrently the minister of economic planning), the other ministers and vice ministers involved with economic matters, leading congressmen, leaders of the business community, and high-level bureaucrats in the civil service.

Among these decisionmakers, high-level civil servants at the EPB and government economists at the KDI played a crucial role in laying the foundation for the approval of the CMES in 1979. After the KDI's study of the Korean economy over the coming fifteen years was completed in 1977 (Korea Development Institute 1977), EPB officials made a critical assessment of the actual growth potential of the economy based on the existing economic structure. The gap between the image of the Korean economy in 1991 projected by the KDI and the actual growth potential was identified as the crucial problem to be addressed by the CMES. A group of EPB technocrats led by Kyung-sik Kang and Jae-ik Kim[9] conducted a series of studies of the structural vulnerability and other weaknesses of the economy that required prompt policy action if the economy was to realize its projected development by 1991. The initial work was done in the form of an internal study, "Current Issues in the Transitional Period," and the results were presented by a group of EPB technocrats in March 1978 (Hahn 1981, p. 17).[10]

Supplementing the philosophical framework of this study were approximately thirteen staff reports on macroeconomic issues and thirty-one on sectoral issues prepared by the EPB, KDI, Bank of Korea (BOK), National Council on Economy and Science, Ministry of Trade and Industry, and other agencies. Of the forty-four reports, twenty-nine were prepared by the EPB, five by the KDI, three by the Bank of Korea, and three by the Ministry of Trade and Industry. The rest were written by other concerned parties. Three of these studies[11] represented the most significant steps toward final adoption of the structural adjustment program. Each was conducted independently by a different agency, and all were reported to the president in March 1979 for a comparison of ideas. At a briefing session President Park Chung Hee requested that the EPB prepare a policy package based on the consensus built during the discussion of the three study reports at the presidential office. According to an interview with Yi-Hyun Hahn (1986), President Park Chung Hee issued the following instructions:

> All three reports unanimously indicate that the Korean economy currently faces serious problems. Our economy is suffering from an excessive burden beyond its capacity which hinders sound economic development. Therefore, may I ask EPB to make a proposal for comprehensive measures to adjust ongoing policies where necessary. The new proposals may have to include such policies as the export drive, the heavy and chemical industry policy, and the rural housing project, although I have endorsed and strongly emphasized their current policies so far. In pursuit of this task, let me suggest that the vice minister of EPB be in charge as the team leader.

The CMES was the product of this request, produced through deliberation among EPB technocrats.

This brief history shows that the decisions leading to the CMES and eventually to the structural adjustment of the Korean economy stemmed from the initiative of highly motivated and competent technocrats and economists working with the core economic ministry. As previous research has suggested, a critical mass of competent and innovative technocrats was a prerequisite for the far-reaching policy reform.[12] In this case the strong endorsement of the technocrats' CMES proposal by newly appointed Deputy Prime Minister Hyun-Hwak Shin was also crucial in introducing these ideas into the governmental process. That reform-minded official played a decisive role in managing the internal and external resistance and resolving the conflicts that arose in the planning as well as the implementation of the CMES.[13]

The policy changes proposed through the CMES faced strong resistance from vested-interest groups, as well as from bureaucratic inertia.[14] Those who had gained special privileges under existing policies were particularly unhappy with the changes implied by the CMES. Moreover, the commitment of the top political leadership to the CMES was initially weak, primarily because President Park, overconfident about Korea's economic achievement through 1978, was not sufficiently convinced of the need for the program to support it wholeheartedly. Because the CMES was logically derived from an evaluation of the negative aspects of current policies, it seemed to be forcing President Park to admit "that there were mistakes in Korea's investment policy of the 1970s, particularly in the cases of the heavy and chemical industries" (Scitovsky 1985; and see also chapter 8 of this volume) which he had supported.

Furthermore, because of the unexpected economic difficulties in the early 1980s caused by the second oil shock, the political instability following the assassination of President Park, and a poor agricultural harvest, the CMES was not effectively implemented in its early period and did not bring about positive results. The economy suffered negative growth (Korea, Economic Planning Board 1987, p. 3). Many feel that the CMES was implemented at the wrong time—when the economy was suffering from the worldwide recession. It can also be argued, however, that the CMES deserves credit for preparing the economy to manage such economic crises as the second oil shock and the world recession. Without advance preparations such as those that occurred under the CMES, the Korean economy would have suffered an even more serious breakdown in the early 1980s (interview with Kyung-sik Kang, 1986).

Regardless, it was not possible to implement the CMES effectively during the political transition immediately following the assassination of President Park. The new government readopted the CMES as part of its political legitimization effort immediately after President Doo-Hwan Chun assumed power in September 1980. President Park had used the slogan "economic growth" to mobilize popular support in the early 1960s; following his example, President Chun proclaimed the idea of "stabilization with growth" for the same reason in the early 1980s. In fact, even before the Fifth Republic was formally established, the ideas of the CMES had been reconfirmed and endorsed by the National Guardian Council (the supreme policymaking body for national crisis management) under the leadership of (then) General Chun.

A new political leadership tends to make a strong commitment to policy shifts and innovation to demonstrate its desire for achievement and legitimization. Political leaders also tend to commit themselves to policy innovations when they face major changes in the political system and environment.[15] The quest for political legitimacy is likely to motivate a new power elite to achieve advances in relatively tangible and visible terms. Initiation of, or support for, reform from the top political leadership often determines the fate of policy innovation.

Technocrats in the government bureaucracy also tend to take advantage of political changes to introduce policy innovations. The appropriate political environment is essential to establishing the conditions that enable the political leadership and bureaucratic elite to collaborate on policy innovation and reform. In the Korean case it was fortunate that Jae-ik Kim was chairman of the Subcommittee on Economy and Science of the National Guardian Council and later became the senior economic adviser to the president. In these positions he was able to monitor the progress of the CMES and protect it from disruption. In this sense the partnership between the political leadership and reform-minded technocrats became the basis for the policy shift in economic management.[16]

In sum, the CMES was initially adopted by President Park and then more resolutely by President Chun. Government economists and technocrats were the CMES's original innovators and advocates. Deputy Prime Minister Hyun-Hwak Shin and his staff, including Jae-Duk Chung, Seok-Joon Suh, Kyung-sik Kang, and Jae-ik Kim, can be regarded as advocates of the policy reform. As the program developed, however, both technocrats and ministers consistently played a role in persuading the top political leadership to adopt innovative ideas for the structural adjustment of the economy. Furthermore, the close collaboration between ministers and EPB technocrats and between EPB officials and KDI economists with regard to policy innovation had an enormous effect on both the policy process and societal response. Indeed, the collaborative efforts of the planning minister and EPB technocrats in managing the intragovernmental conflicts and defusing the external resistance eventually made the CMES an effective program. These people fulfilled the roles of managers of policy innovation.

Technical and Behavioral Aspects of Policymaking

Systematic analysis of the adoption of the CMES may have to be based on a conceptual distinction between the policymaking process and a rational decisionmaking model (Lowi 1970). The former tends to be more circuitous and less coherent than the latter—policymaking is characteristically an iterative, somewhat haphazard, and highly political process in which the apparently logical sequence of decisionmaking may be reversed for reasons of urgency, political viability, and institutional capacity to discharge the different functions. Furthermore, in policymaking, the distinction between objectives and policy instruments is often easily confused, depending on the level of the policy decision.

In spite of such differences, systematic analysis of policymaking also requires analysis of its technical and institutional dimensions. From this perspective, the case of the CMES raises the following questions:

- To what extent was the information base suitable for policy analysis in general? An adequate information base is essential to allow more timely and accurate identification of the effects and shortcomings of current policies through the monitoring of economic performance in comparison with national economic goals and policy objectives.

- Were the problems that the CMES addressed clearly identified and clarified in terms of the legal, institutional, financial, and cultural constraints that affect policy choice?

- To what extent were technical complexity, political sensitivity, and administrative feasibility considered in designing the package of programs?

Economic policymaking involves both building a consensus in defining national economic goals and policy objectives and the sharing of reliable information among decisionmakers with respect to the monitoring of economic performance and changes in the economic environment. Technocrats and economists within and outside the Korean government seemed to share the same information base and were competent in elaborating national economic goals and objectives. As far as economic issues were concerned, these experts seemed to be able to provide the political leadership with a common conceptual framework for pending policy issues. Throughout the period covered by this study, the objectives and strategies of national economic management were "economic growth with equity, improvement in trade balance, economic stability, and promotion of technological advancement" (Kim 1984, pp. 19–20). Although actual interpretation of these objectives may have depended on the prevailing economic environment, political leaders and government economists shared these goals.

In the process of assessing economic performance and environmental conditions, government economists and technocrats again played critical roles. The technocrats had easy access to the Bureau of Statistics at the EPB, as well as to the Department of Research at BOK, and they relied heavily on administrative records and sample surveys. They supplied the top decisionmakers with relevant information, significant policy implications regarding the status of economic performance and contextual issues, their own professional interpretations of information, and recommendations for alternative courses of action. This information was processed by the technocrats through a variety of channels and mechanisms, including public forums, policy seminars, and consultative meetings on particular policy issues organized by individual ministries. The KDI played a catalytic role in interpreting the policy implications and assessing the policy directions through its long- and short-term policy studies on the economy.

Sociocultural constraints were not given much consideration in the analysis of the problems addressed by the CMES because policymakers viewed the core problem as related to purely economic issues. In actuality the CMES affected many sociocultural dimensions of economic behavior by influencing production, private consumption, and saving patterns. In contrast, from the conception of the CMES, policymakers paid close attention to the legal and institutional implications of the program. Financial costs were not an issue because the CMES mainly involved a change in the style of national economic management.

Although the EPB technocrats understood the political implications of the CMES, they tended to neglect them as they pursued economic rationality to cope with the problems that the program was to address. Both the EPB technocrats and KDI economists supported economically sensible positions, regardless of political resistance. Their deliberation of the CMES proposal seemed to reflect the extent of their commitment to structural improvement of the economy.

Because past successes made the government overly confident about its ability to implement development policies in general, the administrative feasibility of the CMES was not fully analyzed in the beginning. Although it was understood that successful implementation of this kind of policy reform required consistent support from other ministries, the business community, and the general public, policymakers did not carefully consider the need to establish support linkages. The Korean government was not accustomed to building a consensus in policymaking.

Although government officials acknowledged the merits of some degree of unanimity in policymaking, they worried that they might arouse resistance in other ministries that could impede the adoption of the original ideas. In the authoritarian subculture of policy planning, bureaucrats tended to think that conflicts and resistance to new policy decisions could be defused once decisions were made. They therefore saw attempts to build a consensus at the initial stage of policymaking as premature. Obtaining the president's approval of policy changes before worrying about building a consensus among the relevant actors was seen as the more strategic and less costly approach.

Opportunities were provided for the business elite, academicians, consumer groups, labor unions, and other social organizations to participate in the performance evaluation and monitoring of current policies, appraisal of proposed policy alternatives, and critical assessments of the international and local economic environment. These opportunities were rather formalistic, however, and outside groups were limited in their participation. Because of the authoritarianism, bureaucratism, elitism, and secretism prevailing in the Korean government, EPB technocrats and government economists were compelled to play decisive roles in the policymaking related to the CMES. Their roles included assessment of the economic situation, conceptualization of the goals and objectives of economic management, definition of problems, assessment of the environment, and development of policy alternatives.

How Decisions Were Implemented

Once decisions are made in the Korean government they are usually implemented effectively. Two features of the government facilitate implementation of new policies: the ability to use coercion to enforce the cooperation of the citizenry and the ability to direct administrative "discretion" toward desired ends (Jones and SaKong 1980, pp. 132–40). In the case of the CMES, in addition to the strong commitment of the political leadership, the government's implementing capability relied both on organizational efficiency and on mechanisms for intragovernment coordination and the mobilization of external support. Intragovernment coordination involved the establishment of institutional and organizational arrangements, devices for optimum resource use, efficient communication among implementing agencies, and mechanisms for resolving conflicts between agencies arising from policy change (Whang 1978). External support could be pursued through collaborative partnerships between the government and the business sector and the government and the general public.

Intragovernment Coordination

With regard to organizational and institutional arrangements, several points deserve attention. First, the implementing capacity of the EPB was strengthened when it absorbed the Bureau of Budget and the Bureau of Statistics. In addition, the Office of Planning and Coordination, directly under the prime minister, and the Planning and Management Units at the assistant minister level of each ministry were expected to support the EPB's implementation efforts. Furthermore, the EPB was later made responsible for price policy, administration of fair trade, and oversight and evaluation of project performance.

Second, the special effort to integrate the planning and budgeting functions under the aegis of the planning minister was noteworthy. In addition, because these two sides formerly operated in different administrative contexts with their own conceptual frameworks, a drastic measure was introduced in 1966 to improve communications and mutual understanding: the two bureaus were periodically to exchange middle-level administrators.

Third, the EPB was made a superministry through the appointment of the deputy prime minister as planning minister. This step enabled the ministry to coordinate economic policies beyond its prior capacity for coordination at the technical level through its central budgeting function (Whang 1985).

Efficient communication among economic ministries was facilitated by an informal personal network among economic bureaucrats that developed through the interministerial transfer of higher-level civil servants, primarily from the EPB to other economic ministries. The EPB became an "enclave" that produced the administrative elite for those ministries (Whang 1968, p. 97). Training programs organized by the Central Officials' Training Institute and consultative meetings among high-level officials from different ministries also contributed to the information flow at the technical level and to the formation of a communications network.

Successful implementation of major economic policies, and of the CMES in particular, required smooth coordination among ministries and agencies to bridge the gaps and eradicate the unnecessary overlaps among sectors. It also required the cooperation of the business community and the general public. The Monthly Economic Review Meeting, the Monthly Export Promotion Conference, and the Quarterly Science and Technology Promotion Meeting served as mechanisms for sharing information and enhancing coordination not only among the ministries but also between the government and the private sector. Chaired by the president, these meetings were attended by policymakers and business leaders. Furthermore, interministerial coordination was achieved through the regularly held Economic Ministers' Council, which was chaired by the deputy prime minister. The periodic Economic Vice Ministers' Meeting also served as a coordinating instrument, beyond the technical coordination achieved through the planning and budgeting functions of the EPB.

The outcome of intragovernment conflicts arising from policy shifts is often crucial to successful innovation. Explicit or implicit resistance from other sectoral ministries posed a significant obstacle to the EPB's efforts to implement the CMES. The Ministries of Agriculture, Trade and Industry, and Home Affairs were particularly difficult, resisting the eradication of preferential incentives to the agricultural sector and particular industries, the expansion of import liberalization, and the reduction of rural housing projects. In spite of its position as a superministry, the EPB was sometimes confronted with significant problems that delayed implementation of the measures in the CMES.

What specific resistance did the CMES face and from what sources? What was done to counter those difficulties? The resistance came in various forms, including vested-interest groups, bureaucratic inertia, and institutional constraints. Initially the CMES appeared to be unpopular with both the political and business elites compared with the expansionist policies that had been implemented, because the established power elite was generally satisfied with the expansionist measures (interview with Kyung-sik Kang and Yi-Hyun Hahn, 1986). Some of the business elite had made substantial fortunes from the direct and indirect subsidies available under existing policies, and some politicians and senior officials had enjoyed their political contributions and support. Predictably, these groups were reluctant to support the CMES.

Vested groups within the bureaucracy opposed the CMES for political and administrative reasons. When the process of interest articulation and aggregation through congressional politics was limited, particularly under President Park's dictatorship in the 1970s, the government bureaucracy became an arena for the confrontation and bargaining of political interests that directly reflected the social forces in policy planning. Such resistance appeared even before the adoption of the CMES. In late 1978, for example, Kyung-sik Kang of the EPB successfully obtained President Park's support for a stabilization policy that froze the existing level of investment in the heavy and chemical industries. In January 1979 the Ministry of Trade and Industry proposed ten huge projects in an attempt to gain the support or at least prior endorsement of the president (interview with You-Kwang Park, 1986).

At the administrative level it seems natural that the resistance to the CMES stemmed from tensions and conflicts between the existing bureaucratic elite responsible for current policies and the newly recruited bureaucratic elite who wanted to make a fresh start in rationalizing economic management. That conflict became apparent within two months after the CMES was adopted. In June 1979 the government took the regressive step of reviving preferential financing to support export industries. This policy measure was initiated by the Ministry of Trade and Industry in collaboration with a former minister who was then a trusted aide of President Park, and it was approved by the president in the absence of Deputy Prime Minister Shin and Kyung-sik Kang, the most dedicated reformers, who were on an overseas mission. This led some journalists to refer to an "economic coup d'état,"[17] because the export financing measure contradicted the principles of the newly adopted CMES. It had a negligible impact on the policy stance of the CMES, however, because of remedial action taken by the reformist elite.

Bureaucratic inertia was evident in the policymaking of the CMES. As discussed earlier, the process was expedited by a small number of EPB technocrats who made no serious efforts to communicate with other ministries or to build a consensus within the government prior to the actual decision. Some tension between the planning ministry and sectoral ministries may have been eased indirectly through the hidden influence of the president, who had already made a commitment to the policy change. Other difficulties were overcome through the influence exercised by the EPB through its central budgeting function and the linkages that derived from the strong political power of Deputy Prime Minister Shin.

The remaining obstacles have been managed gradually over the long term through vigorous, patient, and consistent efforts by EPB technocrats and government economists. They have instituted a series of measures to improve interministerial consultation and communications. EPB technocrats also took advantage of their linkage with World Bank expertise to overcome internal and external resistance, to the extent that the philosophy and policy direction of the CMES matched those of the structural adjustment program of the Bank (interview with Kyung-sik Kang, 1986).

The implementation of the CMES was consistently supported, explicitly and implicitly, during this period by President Chun. He proposed a nationwide campaign to exterminate the "three negative mentalities" (*Sam-*

Dae Boojung Simri), or "corruption, inflation, and disorder," which people perceived as tolerable features of daily life.[18] Moreover, his administration stressed the philosophy of the CMES and passed supportive measures. The government introduced a series of policy rationalization efforts that included the use of zero-based budgeting, a freeze of the 1983 national budget at the level of the previous year, an attempt to reduce agricultural subsidies from 1983 onward, and a gradual expansion of trade liberalization in that same year.

President Chun's commitment to the CMES was extensive. The president met with the chairmen of business conglomerates to persuade them to reduce or stabilize some consumer prices, and he personally prepared a note entitled "Things to Gain from Price Stabilization." He sometimes forced businesses to reduce prices by mentioning the possibility of import liberalization of certain items as an alternative to price stabilization. President Chun also met labor leaders and farmers to persuade them not to demand higher wages, and he increased government support prices for rice (interview with You-Kwang Park, 1986).

Efforts to defuse the resistance to the CMES included a public information, education, and communication (IEC) program that dealt with subjects related to stabilization.[19] Addressing not only the general public but also government officials of all categories to build a consensus on economic issues, the IEC program sought to resolve internal conflicts and to reinforce the policy stance the government was promoting in the CMES. The IEC programs contributed to ensuring the consistency of government action while the CMES was being successfully implemented.

Mobilization of Social Support

Successful implementation of economic policy change required close collaboration between the government bureaucracy and the business community, in addition to the political support of business. Relations between the two groups became more cooperative when business entrepreneurs were invited to participate in decisionmaking. Traditionally, the Korean economy has been fostered in part by a close partnership between government and business. When the state was providing incentives and favors to export-oriented businesses, private entrepreneurs were invited to participate in decisionmaking through such mechanisms as the Monthly Export Promotion Council meeting, policy forums, and policy deliberation working committees (Rhee 1985, pp. 186–87). The business community was able to provide information and advice on policymaking not only through such formal mechanisms but also through informal bilateral channels—the latter means seemed more powerful, whereas the former tended to be largely cosmetic. Objectively, however, informal collaboration could be viewed as a source of undesirable collusion between the government and business that is likely to bring about corruption and distortion in economic management (Kim 1986). To avert this possibility, information provided by business that influenced policymaking was appraised by professional experts as a countercheck.

On the whole, the complementary role played by government technocrats and private entrepreneurs enhanced their partnership by inducing the private sector to participate positively in economic decisionmaking and thus to commit itself to the policy decisions. The successful implementation of government development policies over the past two decades had promoted the legitimacy of government intervention in the private sector and the credibility of administrative competence. This perception had been especially true during the early stages of economic development, when the private sector was relatively weak in capital accumulation, managerial talents, and institutional infrastructure. Furthermore, Korea's traditions and Confucian social norms encouraged all sectors of society to respect the government bureaucracy, and the business community was accustomed to supporting—or at least remaining neutral toward—government policies unless it felt directly threatened by them.

Nevertheless, the business community seemed reluctant to extend its full support to the CMES, primarily because the policy shift would be detrimental to some industries that had been growing at an unprecedented rate with the expansionistic support of the government. Because the CMES involved fundamental policy shifts, obtaining social support from the business community and the general public was critical to the success of the stabilization measures.

To overcome these difficulties, the IEC program—particularly a series of *Kyung-jae Kyo-yuck* (economic education) programs—was introduced at virtually all levels of social organization, private and public. The programs explained the background, motivation, content, and expected results of the policy innovations. They also attempted to gain wider and firmer support from the audience, including government officials and the general public, for the major policy shifts and specific measures introduced by the CMES (Korea, Economic Planning Board 1982; Korea Development Institute 1981, pp. 99–104).

The basic assumption underlying this IEC program was that the intragovernmental conflicts, which were primarily the result of bureaucratic inertia and resistance from business groups, would be fragmented in nature. Therefore, government strategists believed that the resistance could be surmounted in the long run, once the government had built a critical mass of support within and outside the government (interview with Kyung-sik Kang, 1986).

Even before the CMES was adopted in April 1979 an IEC program had been initiated by EPB technocrats to advocate the idea of structural adjustment. This initial but decisive program, which took the form of a slide show, "The New Strategies for the 1980s," was presented to the president in January 1979 during his annual visit to the EPB. In essence, this presentation argued the need for a fundamental change in the philosophy underlying development policy for the 1980s, and it attempted to elicit the active support of the audience. This slide show was widely circulated to almost all government employees; to employees of business organizations such as the Korea Traders' Association, Federation of Korean Industries, and Korea Chamber of Commerce Industries; and to members of labor unions and farmers' cooperatives. It became a required course in the programs of every training institute, public and private, in the country. The slide show greatly contributed to the reorientation of government decisionmakers, businessmen, and intellectuals toward economic development policies.

The EPB prepared a series of audiovisual materials, during 1979–80 in particular, including slides and videotapes to advance the economic education of the public.[20] Some of the slide presentations were prepared for the general public, while others were aimed at specific audiences for different purposes. The common objective, however, was to enlist the cooperation and support of the audiences on various issues, including the rationalization of private consumption behavior; closer cooperation among businesses, households, and government in coping with economic difficulties; acceptance of an "equal share of pain among all sectors of society" in overcoming the difficulties of the national economy; and changes in the perceptions and attitudes of people toward the national economy and the role of government. The argument for an "equal burden of pain" was quite persuasive to people in many sectors and officials in different ministries and mobilized their support—or at least discouraged their overt resistance. In 1982 the EPB established a regular bureau to make the IEC program more extensive and professional with regard to its audience, substantive issues, and use of communications media. In addition to slide presentations, the EPB carried out a media bombardment of booklets, newspapers, television and radio programs, and public lectures designed to influence almost everyone, including housewives and military personnel.

As a result of the IEC program, businessmen, farmers, and housewives lowered their expectations of continuing support and excessive protection from the government. The program also induced people to redouble their efforts to achieve higher productivity and welfare and to cooperate with the new policies (Nam 1984, pp. 82–83). It should be noted that not only the quality of the slide presentations but also the receptivity and sensitivity of the people (a result of the high levels of education) made the IEC program a success.[21] The well-educated factory workers and farmers seemed ready to act rationally and to understand the right policy choice, within given political and structural constraints, for long-term returns to themselves and the nation.

Conclusions

Korea's recent economic performance suggests that the structural adjustment program, activated in part by the adoption of the CMES, had positive results. In this context, the whole process of economic management of structural adjustment in Korea deserves in-depth analysis. This study found that the partnership between the political leadership and reform-minded technocrats was a catalytic force that led to the policy shift required for structural adjustment. Strong political commitment to policy innovation and a cluster of dedicated technocrats came together as a powerful engine for developing the CMES into an effective program. In particular, the power elite was highly motivated to engage in policy change for its own political needs. The task of economic stabilization was taken up by the elite as a priority for attaining political stability at a time when political strife had made the economy vulnerable. Two decades earlier, immediately after taking power in 1961, President Park had enacted a special law imposing direct control over the prices of certain commodities.[22] President Chun readopted the CMES for much the same reason in 1980. The difference is that Park relied on coercive power, while Chun used a more sophisticated policy package. This difference reflects the relative levels of intellectual maturity of each administration's economic technocrats, as well as the solidity of the national economy built during the 1960s and 1970s.

Further, the orchestration of the policy innovation by EPB technocrats and KDI economists throughout the process of planning and implementation made the CMES acceptable and credible to the public. The close collaboration between the technocrats in core economic ministries and the economists working with distinguished research institutes contributed both to effective decisionmaking and to professionally legitimate and solid policy development.

The implementation capabilities of the core economic ministries for shifts in policy such as the CMES were reinforced by a well-defined administrative infrastructure. It included organizational and institutional arrangements, functional realignments, allocation of relevant authority and resources, efficient communication and coordination mechanisms, and a cluster of research institutes.

The systematic and rigorous IEC program conducted by the EPB served as a powerful instrument for overcoming both internal and external resistance to the policy changes implied in the CMES and mobilizing active societal support for policy innovation. Compared with the traditional partnership between government and business, which had developed through government favors and protective measures, the new set of relations was based on a more rational approach to economic management and seemed to be less spontaneous at the beginning of the CMES. Through the discussion generated by the IEC programs, however, the business sector regained much of its dynamism and vitality within the framework of the CMES. In addition to these directly relevant factors, other conditions were integral to the success of the CMES. The high level of education of the people made every sector of society more receptive to the policy innovations publicized through the IEC programs and paved the way for better communication between government and the people.

The CMES was implemented while the Korean economy was growing at a high rate, except during the recession of 1980. In contrast to the situation in the highly indebted Latin American countries, the nation's economic growth made the citizenry willing to share the short-term pains arising out of the CMES, because an expanding economy created new jobs and expectations of future improvements in real income.[23] Despite the common perception that the IEC program was a high price to pay for the elitist approach to speedy policymaking for the CMES, it should be stressed that the institutionalization of the IEC program seems to have been needed for the success of the policy innovation, regardless of the policymaking approach.

Because the cluster of EPB technocrats belonged to the government system as a whole, it can be inferred that the highly motivated and dedicated reformers in the core economic ministries constituted the source of the inner dynamism for the policy change. The innovative ideas developed by the team of technocrats and economists not only affected governmental decisionmaking but also played a crucial role in effecting change in the basic structure of the economy.[24]

It is difficult to carry out a scientific analysis of economic management in Korea, for it is a complex process involving political, economic, administrative, and sociocultural factors. Nevertheless, it can be concluded that successful economic management is possible only when these factors work in the *same direction*, so that they play complementary and mutually reinforcing roles in support of a common end. Economic management may be regarded, from a holistic point of view, as an art, although component parts of the process are subject to scientific inquiry within their own disciplines.[25] In the case of the CMES, the art of economic management involved technical harmony between openness and secrecy in the Korean bureaucracy and also between authoritarian bureaucratism (or elitism) and the building of a consensus in the policymaking and implementation processes.

Korea's recent experience surely demonstrates that its capacity for economic management now relies primarily on its ability to implement, as in the 1960s and 1970s, rather than on its decisionmaking capacity.[26] Regardless of the nature of a decision, the commitment to implementation is essential to the success of economic management. Total commitment at both the political and technocratic levels is the real source of the art of economic management.

The art of economic management, particularly its informal (software) aspects, which are rooted in Korea's cultural dynamism, are hardly transferable to other countries. Nevertheless, some formal institutional (hardware) components that are susceptible to scientific inquiry might be worthy of emulation by other developing countries.

Notes

This chapter is based on a paper presented at the World Bank and Korea Development Institute Working Party Meeting on Structural Adjustment in NICS: Lessons from Korea, held in Washington, D.C., June 19–20, 1986.

1. See chapter 2 for details on the CMES, as well as Korea, Economic Planning Board (1979) and Nam (1984, pp. 18–25).

2. For the effects of this program in specific terms, see Nam (1984, pp. 55–79); and chapters 3 and 5 of this volume.

3. The definition is derived from Whang (1970b), Katz and Kahn (1967, pp. 84–89), Redford (1965, pp. 63–84, 633–39), and World Bank (1983, pp. 64–73).

4. An apparent contradiction needs to be explained here. Elsewhere it is noted that the government offers the private sector numerous opportunities for involvement in decisionmaking. Its participation, however, occurs mainly with respect to medium-term policymaking (for example, the five-year development plan). At the same time, day-to-day decisions, short-term actions, and emergencies are handled by a few elite government bureaucrats.

5. For this point, the chapter relies primarily on Jones and SaKong (1980, pp. 58–66).

6. Rapidity, flexibility, and pragmatism are identified as major characteristics of policy planning in Korea by Rhee (1985, p. 184).

7. Particularism is one of five pattern variables that distinguish traditional from modern behavior. For the five pattern variables, see Parsons (1951, pp. 58–67) or Parsons and Shils (1959, pp. 80–84). For the bureaucratic implications of particularism, see Riggs (1964, pp. 22–25).

8. For theories of innovation, see LaPiere (1965, pp. 103–211), Barnett (1953), Rogers (1962), Diament (1967), and Lee (1970a).

9. Kang was assistant minister of planning from December 1977 until he became vice minister of finance in January 1982. He later served as minister of finance (September 1982–October 1983) and, finally, as chief secretary to the president (October 1983–January 1985). Kim was then director-general of the Economic Planning Bureau of the EPB under Kang, and later became senior adviser to the president on economic affairs (March 1981–October 1983). In that position, he was an effective architect of the Korean economy. He was killed by the bomb attack in Rangoon that decimated President Doo-Hwan Chun's entourage. Both Kim and Kang were the real architects of the CMES and were dedicated to policy reform throughout the planning and implementation stages of this reform program. Other members of the team included Jae-suk Chung (then vice minister), Yi-Hyun Hahn, You-Kwang Park, Jong-chan Choe, and Mahn-Je Kim (then president of the KDI)

and his staff. It should be noted that Mahn-Je Kim (and later Kihwan Kim) and the KDI staff greatly contributed to this policy reform and were the real forces behind the scenes. In addition, some university professors, including Sung Park, actively supported the ideas of the CMES (interviews with You-Kwang Park, 1986).

10. The transitional period in this case refers to the years of an upward trend in the Korean economy measured by the success of the green revolution, a current account surplus attributable to booming overseas construction, and the like. For the theoretical implications of the transitional stages in the context of the Korean economy, see Chung (1981, pp. 237–45; for a list of the various studies, see also pp. 115–23).

11. Bank of Korea (1979), Korea, National Council on Economy and Science (1979), and Korea Development Institute (1979).

12. The role of government bureaucrats in introducing policy innovations and rigorous economic development programs is fully discussed in Whang (1968, pp. 143–54).

13. Hyun-Hwak Shin served as deputy prime minister and planning minister from January to November 1979. He was dedicated to this policy reform and reported to the president daily on the progress of the EPB technocrat study team. Later, as the prime minister from November 1979 until May 1980, he contributed to the consistent implementation of this policy innovation.

14. For an example of the resistance of the Congress to the budgetary reform introduced in the Philippines, see Parson (1957, pp. 176–77). For the case of Vietnam, see Murphy (1960, pp. 148–51).

15. Examples of this behavior include President Syung-man Rhee's successful implementation of the Land Reform Program of 1949–52 (see Whang 1984) and President Park's introduction of economic planning and his vigorous implementation of five-year plans after the military coup d'état of 1961 (see Whang 1970a, pp. 19–42; Lee 1968, pp. 144–76; and Cole and Lyman 1971, pp. 78–97). Another example is President Park's rigorous drive for defense industries, which took the form of heavy and chemical industries in the 1970s.

16. For the theoretical implications, see Lee (1970b, pp. 12–13). For another specific case of a partnership between political leaders and senior administrative technocrats that made possible a major program innovation for economic development during the 1960s, see Whang (1968, pp. 127–42).

17. *Dong-A Ilbo* [Dong-A Daily News], June 26, 1979, p. 2.

18. "1982 Annual Message of President Doo Hwan Chun," *Dong-A Ilbo* [Dong-A Daily News], January 22, 1982, p. 3.

19. It is noteworthy that the government's initial attempt to use IEC activities came in the early 1960s in connection with the First Five-Year Economic Development Plan and the Ten-Year Family Planning Program, 1962–71 (see Whang 1976).

20. These audiovisual public information materials included: "The New Strategies for 1980s" (January 1979); "Economic Development and Rationalization of Consumption Patterns" (April 1979); "Shift in the Mode of Economic Management" (January 1980); "The National Economy: All of Us Should Think Together" (September 1980); and "Let Us Beat the Economic Difficulties Today" (December 1980).

21. According to the 1980 census, every Korean had received an average of twelve years of formal education (*Hankook Ilbo* [Hankook Daily News], February 12, 1984, p. 5).

22. This legislation was the Special Law for Price Control of 1961, promulgated immediately after the military coup d'état. For its administrative implications, see Whang (1985, pp. 17-19).

23. Based on comments on this manuscript made by Guy Pfeffermann during the Conference on Structural Adjustment in a Newly Industrialized Country, Washington, D.C., June 17-18, 1986. The author is grateful for his contribution.

24. An analogy was made from the theory of inner dynamics (Esman 1967, p. 275).

25. For the classic discussion of whether management is art or science, see Waldo (1955, pp. 3-7).

26. For an evaluation of the implementing capacity of the Korean government in the 1960s and 1970s, see Jones and SaKong (1980, pp. 132-33, 294-97).

References

Aghevli, B. B., and Jorge Marquez-Ruarte. 1985. *A Case of Successful Adjustment: Korea's Experience during 1980-1984.* IMF Occasional Paper no. 39. Washington, D.C.: International Monetary Fund.

Bank of Korea. 1979. *Current Issues and Policy Directions for Our Economy.* Seoul.

Barnett, H. G. 1953. *Innovation: The Basis of Cultural Change.* New York: McGraw-Hill.

Chung, Jai-Suk. 1981. *The Korean Economy in the World.* Seoul: Kwang-Myong. In Korean.

Cole, David, and Princeton Lyman. 1971. *Korean Development: The Interplay of Politics and Economics.* Cambridge, Mass.: Harvard University Press.

Diament, Alfred. 1967. "Innovation in Bureaucratic Institutions." *Public Administration Review* 27 (March): 77-87.

Esman, Milton J. 1967. "Ecological Style in Comparative Administration." *Public Administration Review* 27 (September).

Hahn, Yi-Hyun. 1981. "Process of Activating the Economic Stabilization Program." In Korea Development Institute, "Collection of Documents and Study Reports in Relation to Economic Stabilization Policies," vol. 1. Seoul. In Korean.

Jin, Nyum. 1984. "The Economic Development Plan and Economic Management System in Korea." A paper presented at the Korea Development Institute Forum on Industrialization and Trade Promotion, Seoul, May 15-24.

Jones, Leroy, and Il SaKong. 1980. *Government, Business, and Entrepreneurship in Economic Development: The Korean Case.* Cambridge, Mass.: Council on East Asian Studies. Harvard University Press.

Katz, Daniel, and Robert Kahn. 1967. *The Social Psychology of Organizations.* New York: John Wiley.

Kim, Kihwan. 1984. *The Korean Economy: Past Performance, Current Reforms and Future Prospects*. Seoul: Korea Development Institute.

Kim, Kwang-Suk. 1983. "Korea's Experience in Managing Development through Planning, Policy-Making and Budgeting." In Miyohei Shinohara, Tom Yanagihada, and Kwang Suk Kim, eds., *The Japanese and Korean Experience in Managing Development*. World Bank Staff Working Paper 574. Washington, D.C.

———. 1986. "Korean Patterns of Economic Management: Lessons from Experience in the 1960s and 1970s." Honolulu: East-West Center.

Korea, Economic Planning Board. 1979. "Comprehensive Measures for Economic Stabilization." Seoul. In Korean.

———. 1982. "1982 Economic Education Guide." Seoul. In Korean.

———. 1987. *Major Statistics of Korean Economy 1985*. Seoul.

Korea, National Council on Economy and Science. 1979. *Current Issues and Policy Measures for Our Economy*. Seoul.

Korea Development Institute. 1977. *Long-Term Prospect for Economic and Social Development (1977-1991)*. Seoul.

———. 1979. *Direction for the Economic Stabilization Policies*. Seoul.

———. 1981. "Collection of Documents and Study Reports in Relation to Economic Stabilization Policies." Seoul. In Korean.

LaPiere, Richard T. 1965. *Social Change*. New York: McGraw Hill.

Lee, Hahn-Been. 1968. *Korea: Time, Change and Administration*. Honolulu: East-West Center Press.

———. 1970a. "An Application of Innovation Theories to the Strategy of Administrative Reform in Developing Countries." *Policy Sciences* 1:177–89.

———. 1970b. "Concept, Structure and Strategy of Administrative Reform: An Introduction." In Lee Hahn-Been and Abelardo Samonte, eds., *Administrative Reform in Asia*. Manila: EROPA Press.

Lowi, Theodore. 1970. "Decision-making vs. Policy-making: Toward the Antidote for Technology." *Public Administration Review* 30 (May/June):314–25.

Murphy, Marvin. 1960. "Overcoming Resistance to Major Change: Vietnam Budget Reform." *Public Administration Review* 20 (Summer):148–51.

Nam, Sang-Woo. 1984. "Korea's Stabilization Efforts since the Late 1970s." Working Paper 8405. Seoul: Korea Development Institute.

Parson, Malcolm B. 1957. "Performance Budgeting in the Philippines." *Public Administration Review* 17 (Summer):176–77.

Parsons, Talcott. 1951. *The Social System*. Glencoe, Ill.: Free Press.

Parsons, Talcott, and Edward A. Shils, eds. 1959. *Toward General Theory of Action*. Cambridge, Mass.: Harvard University Press.

Redford, Emmette. 1965. *American Government and the Economy*. New York: Macmillan.

Rhee, Yung Whee. 1985. *Instruments for Export Policy and Administration: Lessons from the East Asian Experience*. World Bank Staff Working Paper 725. Washington, D.C.

Riggs, Fred. 1964. *Administration in Developing Countries*. Boston: Houghton Mifflin.

Rogers, Everett M. 1962. *Diffusion of Innovation*. New York: Free Press.

Scitovsky, Tibor. 1985. "Economic Development in Taiwan and South Korea: 1965–81." *Food Research Institute Studies* 19 (3):215–64.

Waldo, D. 1955. *The Study of Public Administration*. New York: Random House.

Whang, In-Joung. 1968. "Elite and Economic Programs: A Study of Changing Leadership for Economic Development in Korea, 1956–67." Ph.D. diss., University of Pittsburgh.

———. 1970a. *Public Administration and Economic Development*. Seoul: SNU Press. In Korean.

———. 1970b. "Ideological Premise of Economic Planning in Korea." *Korea Journal of Public Administration* 8 (1) (April):173–80. In Korean.

———. 1976. "Implementation of Family Planning Program in Korea, 1962–71." In Gabriel Iglesias, ed., *Implementation: The Problem of Achieving Results*. Manila: EROPA.

———. 1978. *Administrative Feasibility Analysis for Development Projects: Concept and Approach*. Kuala Lumpur: ADPAC.

———. 1984. "Administration of Land Reform in Korea, 1949–52." *Korea Journal* 24, 10 (October):4–20.

———. 1985. "Role of Government in Economic Development." A paper presented at the Korea Development Institute International Forum on Trade and Development Policies, Seoul, Korea, June 11–20.

World Bank. 1983. *World Development Report 1983*. New York: Oxford University Press.

14   Recent Experience with Growth-Oriented Adjustment Programs

VITTORIO CORBO, Catholic University of Chile

SANG-MOK SUH, Korea Development Institute

KOREA'S RECENT EXPERIENCE with structural adjustment can provide much-needed lessons for countries struggling to adjust to crisis conditions similar to those Korea faced in the late 1970s: unsustainable public sector and current account deficits, loss of international competitiveness, accelerating inflation, a trade regime with an increasing antiexport bias, a slowdown in growth, and a high debt burden. This chapter looks at elements of Korea's adjustment program that other countries might find useful in designing and implementing their own adjustment efforts. In drawing lessons from the experience of just one country and thus making inferences from a sample of one observation, it is difficult to control for factors that could make the case being studied special. An effort has therefore been made to identify the special characteristics of the Korean economy that were present when the crisis was developing and when the adjustment program was put in place and successfully implemented. Our objective is to identify the causes of the crisis, as well as the role that government policies and external factors played in dealing with it.

Many developing countries are in the middle of a protracted period of adjustment necessitated by their overall poor macroeconomic situation, which has produced unsustainable current account deficits, high inflation, and low growth. Some countries have experienced sudden and drastic reductions in net capital inflows that have forced them to make drastic reductions in their current account deficits to bring them to levels compatible with the reduced external financing. The high international rate of interest in the early 1980s and the dramatic drop in these countries' terms of trade compounded significantly their balance of payments difficulties and the need for adjustment in the external accounts. To restore growth, these countries have had to promote domestic savings as well as greater efficiency in the utilization of resources. That efficiency has often been impaired, however, by distorted factor and commodity markets and by a structure of incentives that has discriminated against export-oriented industries and encouraged inward-looking ones.

Korea did not face a drastic rationing in the external capital markets as other highly indebted countries have, although between 1981 and 1983 commercial lending to Korea was reduced by more than half. The macroeconomic imbalances that developed in the late 1970s, however, are typical of the conditions most highly indebted developing countries faced in 1982–83 and to which they are still struggling to adjust. These imbalances have included a sharp slowdown in export and output growth, accelerating inflation with increasingly restrictive price controls, appreciation of the real exchange rate, and an increasing current account deficit.

In response to its problems, in the spring of 1979 Korea initiated an adjustment program that started with stabilization but later, in the early 1980s, was extended to include many supply-friendly policies geared toward increasing output by improving the efficiency of factor use. Included in the program were policies to increase domestic competition, reduce the distortions in the intermediation of financial resources, improve the production and distribution of agricultural goods, and initiate the rationalization of the trade regime. The government supplemented these supply-friendly policies with others aimed at boosting potential output through increased public savings and better incentives for savings and investment.

It is well known that Korea's adjustment was quite successful. The current account deficit, which had reached 8.7 percent of GNP in 1980, was transformed into a surplus in 1986. Annual inflation, which was in the 25 to 40 percent range in 1980, was less than 3 percent by 1986. The growth rate of GNP, which averaged 0.5 percent annually in the 1979–80 period, reached 7.8 percent in the 1981–85 period and 12.5 percent in 1986.

To provide a context for evaluating Korea's adjustment program, we present a theoretical framework that draws on the emerging consensus on how to design an adjustment program. In the second part of this chapter we review Korea's performance prior to the crisis, focusing on the role of the policies that contributed to the crisis. Drawing on the main findings of this study, we evaluate the main elements of Korea's adjustment program. Finally, in the last section, we present lessons from Korea's adjustment programs for countries that are in the process of designing or carrying out their own adjustment programs.

A Framework for Adjustment with Growth

One of the most important initial conditions affecting the design of adjustment programs is the rate of inflation. The final objective of most structural adjustment is to improve resource allocation and to move actual output close to potential output, and changes in price incentives play a central role in improving resource allocation. Under high levels of inflation the information content of relative prices is much reduced. The emerging consensus is that in such a case, any adjustment program calling for major changes in overall economic incentives should start by controlling inflation. For countries that are also experiencing an unsustainable current account deficit, control of inflation is again a central component of overall adjustment because the rate of inflation is usually the most important source of resource misallocation and the major impediment to growth. Moreover, it is hard to achieve a sustainable reduction in the current account deficit in a growing economy suffering from a high level of inflation.

The well-documented negative side effects of inflation (Fischer 1986a, b; Yeager 1981) are of six main kinds.

- Relative prices become very volatile, which reduces their information content (because changes in the rate of inflation do not affect all prices and costs uniformly and at the same time).

- The controls over interest rates usually observed in countries with high inflation result in negative real rates that lead to credit rationing, encourage rent-seeking activities in the assets markets, distort investment decisions, and reduce the size of the formal financial system.

- The imposition of price controls is a common response that encourages black market profiteering and rent-seeking and discourages productive activities.

- Uncertainty about future inflation leads to concentration of financial transactions in instruments with short-term rather than long-term maturities, thereby reducing the availability of funds for long-term investment.

- The prices of tradables relative to nontradables change sharply and unpredictably because periodic attempts to control inflation through the exchange rate and price controls result in protracted periods of real currency appreciation. The sharp swings in the relative prices of tradables discourage tradable activities, particularly those oriented toward exports.

- The resultant periodic balance of payments crises ultimately reduce both actual and potential output.

The recommendation for an up-front stabilization program also stems from knowledge that success with an adjustment program depends on its internal consistency as well as on its credibility. High levels of inflation brought about by delayed response to these incentives make credibility difficult to attain. Not surprisingly, there are few historical examples of a simultaneous achievement of stabilization and structural adjustment. One of the most extensive studies of trade liberalization concluded that the failure of reforms has stemmed mainly from the failure of the accompanying anti-inflationary programs (Krueger 1978, 1981). At the same time, stabilization should not be achieved by means that result in wide distortions in relative prices, as will be the case if price controls are introduced for sustained periods or export taxes are levied in an economy that needs to reduce the bias against exports.

There are also macroeconomic factors that make the simultaneous implementation of stabilization and structural adjustment difficult. During the implementation of a structural adjustment program, macroeconomic policy should ensure an appropriate and stable real exchange rate, a low rate of inflation, and a sustainable balance of payments position. Countries starting to adjust under conditions of high inflation or severe real appreciation face complications. The first comes from the need for simultaneous implementation of stabilization measures and a set of structural adjustment policies that includes a real devaluation. On the one hand, successful stabilization depends on applying contractionary pressure to the economy as a whole. On the other hand, many times a structural adjustment program includes a trade liberalization component that calls for the contraction of highly protected import-competing activities and delayed expansion of export-oriented and import-competing activities with little protection. Where both programs are implemented simultaneously, the contractionary pressure on highly protected import-competing activities may be too strong to withstand.

As part of the stabilization effort a fiscal adjustment is usually needed to reduce the fiscal deficit to a level where the financing needed from the central bank is compatible with low inflation. At the macroeconomic level, absorption must be reduced to a level that is compatible with the level of output plus a sustainable current account deficit. If the reduction in absorption is not accompanied by a change in relative prices in favor of tradable goods, the demand for both tradables and nontradables will be reduced. Lower demand for tradable goods contributes directly to reductions in the current account deficit. Lower demand for nontradable goods without a change in relative prices will reduce the output of nontradable activities, which will lead to unemployment. To minimize this reduction in output, a real exchange rate depreciation is needed to change the composition of expenditures in favor of nontradable goods and the composition of output in favor of tradable goods (Corden 1977; Dornbusch 1980). In countries with high inflation, the real devaluation will be difficult to implement or will accelerate inflation.

The three main instruments of a stabilization program are monetary, fiscal, and exchange rate policies. Fiscal and monetary policies are mainly devices to reduce absorption, while exchange rate policy is primarily a mechanism for switching expenditures. Nevertheless, fiscal and monetary policies have secondary expenditure-switching effects through their influence on the composition of spending, and a devaluation policy has secondary absorption-reducing effects through its impact on real private wealth. Finally, it should be noted that policies to reduce absorption can have detrimental effects on medium-term growth if they are strongly biased against investment.

Once inflation has been controlled it is possible to concentrate on structural adjustment. The major component of an adjustment program is a set of supply-side policies aimed at improving the allocation of resources and encouraging the accumulation of further resources. Supply-side policies include reforms in the commodity and factor markets. In commodity markets, reforms include the lifting of price controls and the introduction of measures to promote domestic competition as well as to rationalize the trade regime. Rationalization of the trade regime includes lifting the quantitative restrictions on trade and reducing the variance and mean of tariff rates.

In the financial market, reforms include abolishing credit rationing and lifting the controls on interest rates, which should gradually be allowed to be determined by the market. Appropriate information systems and supervision of financial intermediaries are an integral part of financial reforms. In the labor market, reforms include measures to increase labor mobility and wage flexibility.

Economists generally agree on the fundamental principles underlying the reforms cited for structural adjustment, and these principles go a long way toward defining the final content of any reform package. Economists differ, however, on how best to implement adjustment. The suggested remedy for a highly regulated economy with widespread price controls is to lift the controls so as to improve resource allocation, while simultaneously deregulating the domestic factor markets. Governments should deregulate the financial markets (subject to appropriate banking supervision) to improve credit allocation and distribute investment more efficiently. Similarly, labor market restrictions that impede mobility should be lifted to promote a more efficient allocation of labor.

In foreign trade, the first objective of commercial policy is to replace quantitative restrictions with equivalent tariffs. Both the average level and variance of tariff rates should then be reduced, with the objective of moving toward a more uniform tariff structure. As a rule, incentives should not discriminate against export-oriented activities and should promote the development of broadly uniform across-the-board effective incentives for import-competing activities (Little, Scitovsky, and Scott 1970; Corden 1974; Balassa 1976).[1]

Although there may be a consensus on the content of a reform package, there is much disagreement over the proper order of the economic liberalization measures. Which markets should be liberalized first, and what is the best sequencing? This debate is not surprising because it involves questions about the transition to a new equilibrium, a process that requires comparing paths where many distortions are still present. Here there is no well-established theory, and only some general principles can be stated (see McKinnon 1982; Frenkel 1982, 1983, 1987; Krueger 1984; Edwards 1985; Corbo and de Melo 1987). The literature addresses three sets of issues: the speed of the reforms; the sequencing of the program, or which markets to liberalize first; and the appropriate macroeconomic policies for minimizing the difficulties likely to arise during the transition to a more liberalized economy.

At the macroeconomic level, a common problem when implementing the trade adjustment component of a structural adjustment program is downward price inflexibility. Successful trade liberalization requires a quick export response. To achieve that response, the profitability of export and import-competing activities with low levels of protection has to improve in a sustainable and credible way compared with nontradable and highly protected import-competing activities. If the prices of the latter type of activities are inflexible downward, the response of export and import-competing activities with low levels of protection will be seriously delayed, and the whole liberalization effort could be jeopardized.

To overcome this problem, trade liberalization has to be accompanied by an initial devaluation that achieves the desired improvement in relative prices (Mussa 1986). Thus, for economies with fixed or crawling-peg exchange rate regimes a devaluation should accompany the initial tariff reduction. Although this will not restore the preliberalization landed prices of imports, it will permit an improvement in the relative prices of import-competing activities and exportables with low levels of protection. For countries that have discriminated against exportables for a long time, an up-front improvement in the relevant incentives is also necessary to move resources toward exportables. A devaluation, however, will temporarily accelerate inflation or weaken the fight against it. Monetary and fiscal policies should be restrictive enough to ensure that the change in relative prices takes place.

Besides exchange rate policy, other elements of macroeconomic policy should be redesigned to support the adjustment effort. Monetary expansion should be compatible with exchange rate pegging rules to avoid a loss of confidence in the pegging arrangements that might jeopardize the success of the overall reform package. Fiscal policy should try to ensure that the fiscal deficit is compatible with the domestic credit expansion created by a stable pegging rule (Buiter 1986). In addition, the portion of the deficit financed in the domestic capital market should not crowd out the financing of sectors meant to expand. Credit policy should ensure access to credit at competitive rates for expanding sectors, while denying cheap credit to previously heavily protected import-competing activities because its availability could slow their adjustment. Finally, labor market arrangements should be flexible enough to allow for a drop in the consumption wage in previously heavily protected sectors or for the reallocation of labor toward sectors that were previously discriminated against. Otherwise, unemployment will result.

Korea's Performance up to the Late 1970s

To provide background for the study of Korea's adjustment to the crises of the late 1970s, the evolution of the Korean economy was examined in historical perspective in chapter 2. Korea is usually taken as one of the best examples of export-led growth, although some difference of opinion exists about the role of the state in promoting the expansion of exports. Some observers claim that direct state intervention in the 1960s through selective incentives for exporters had a major role in export growth (Dornbusch 1985; Sachs 1987), while others claim that the most important characteristic of Korea's trade regime in the late 1960s and early 1970s was the avoidance of an antiexport bias (Nam 1985; Bhagwati 1988; Krueger 1985; Westphal 1978). In the view of the latter group, what is important in the Korean model is that, at the margin, the incentives for sales in the protected domestic market were similar to the incentives for sales in the international markets, in spite of widespread government intervention. This pattern held true up to the eve of the first oil shock.

In the period from 1973 to 1980, Korea shifted its development strategy toward an aggressive policy of import substitution in the heavy and chemical industries. Several factors influenced this decision. First, the economic authorities had become confident because of the dramatic success of the late 1960s and wanted to duplicate Japan's development of heavy industry. Second, Korean authorities, concerned about a possible future loss of comparative advantage in light manufacturing, decided to encourage what they thought were the industries of the future. Third, the number of U.S. troops stationed in Korea was reduced by nearly a third in the early 1970s, and the government became concerned about future access to military equipment and supplies. As a consequence, it decided to promote the defense industry.

As a result of these three factors, the government fostered an enormous investment effort in the heavy and chemical industries, encouraging large-scale investment projects through special tax incentives and preferential credit allocation. In conjunction with the negative real interest rates, these measures led to major subsidies for borrowers. A side effect of these policies was that export-oriented light manufacturing was crowded out of financial markets.

When the first oil shock came in 1974, the government more than neutralized the recessionary effects of the resultant large drop in the terms of trade by expansionary demand policies financed with heavy external borrowing. Although Korea was able to achieve an average annual rate of growth of GNP of 8.7 percent in the 1973–80 period, external debt grew at an average annual rate of 28.8 percent. The expansionary aggregate demand policies also resulted in an overheated labor market, and real wages in manufacturing grew 110.2 percent between 1974–75 and 1979. As a result, in spite of a large loss in the terms of trade, a large real appreciation developed that reached close to 24 percent between 1973 and 1979. The widespread price controls in the later years of that period somehow masked the extent of the true appreciation. Export-oriented activities became much less profitable as a result, and the export growth rate became negative in 1978.

By the late 1970s Korea faced major macroeconomic imbalances similar to those faced by the highly indebted countries in the 1982–83 period. By the late 1970s growth was faltering, inflation was accelerating, a substantial real appreciation had developed (especially in comparison with Korea's major competitors in East Asia), the balance of payments was deteriorating, and the size of the external debt had increased considerably. Furthermore, the strong incentives for capacity expansion in the heavy and chemical industries created excess capacity, and the financial condition of many of the firms that had been encouraged by the promotion of the heavy and chemical industries started to deteriorate. The favorable international climate that had aided Korea's export drive in the 1960s and early 1970s began to falter as the second oil shock threatened to produce a further permanent deterioration in the terms of trade, and increased international interest rates called into question the growth strategy of heavy borrowing pursued in the second half of the 1970s.

To make matters worse, two bad harvests led to a drop in real agricultural GNP in both 1978 and 1980. The drop in 1980 was an especially severe 19.9 percent. This last development contributed significantly to the 4.8 percent drop in GNP in 1980, the worst recession in modern Korea.

The expansionary policies of the second half of the 1970s had brought an average rate of inflation during 1976–79 of 14.6 percent in the consumer price index (CPI) and 19.7 percent in the nonagricultural GNP deflator. The current account deficit as a percentage of GNP had reached 6.8 percent in 1979, a level that was even higher than the average for the 1963–70 period, when it reached only 5.0 percent of GNP. Although the level of inflation was low compared with the Latin American rates, for an economy without indexation mechanisms and as open as Korea's was in the late 1970s, even 15 to 20 percent annual inflation creates many problems. Thus, it is not surprising that public pressure was building for a reduction in inflation by 1978–79.

As inflation started to accelerate toward the end of the 1970s, a new problem emerged. The acceleration of inflation and the combination of credit rationing and negative real interest rates created a feverish demand for real estate and other nonproductive assets that led to a real estate boom. It became increasingly profitable for business firms to borrow as much as possible from banks at negative real interest rates and to invest in real assets. This trend led to an increasingly fragile financial structure. The government attempted to curb inflation through price controls, but predictably this measure produced supply shortages, black markets, and deteriorating product quality.

An Evaluation of Korea's Adjustment Program

Recognizing that a major shift in policy orientation was in order, in mid-1979 the Korean government announced a comprehensive adjustment program that included stabilization and structural adjustment elements. It was recognized from the beginning that stabilization was a precondition for eradication of structural weakness.

The stabilization program of April 1979 came into being amid a general consensus that stabilization was a requirement for sustained growth. The program included moderate fiscal and monetary policies, rationalization of heavy industry, and actions to improve the supply of daily necessities. The moderate fiscal actions included a 5 percent cut in current expenditures and deferral of some investment projects. The government raised interest rates and curtailed subsidized lines of credit. Finally, the program for daily necessities included expansion of agricultural production complexes, improvements in inventory management, a streamlined system of commodity distribution, and the elimination of most price controls.

Because of concern over a temporary increase in inflation the stabilization program did not include direct corrective actions to improve the competitiveness of tradable activities, which had deteriorated substantially in the previous five years. A real depreciation was bound to result from the moderate fiscal and monetary policies. After the sharp increase in wages of the previous five years, however, a drop in nominal wages could have required a very sharp recession. Not surprisingly, the volume of exports recorded a negative rate of growth in 1979.

In the third month of the program, Korea was hit by the second oil shock, the ensuing worldwide recession, and a disastrous crop failure, followed by social unrest and political uncertainty after the assassination of President Park Chung Hee. These external and internal conditions hampered the initial stabilization efforts.

In response, in January 1980, the government undertook a 20 percent devaluation of the won against the U.S. dollar. At the same time it announced a crawling peg system aimed at maintaining stable incentives for exporters. Because the devaluation was followed by a fairly expansionary monetary policy (bank credit grew at an average annual rate of 30.7 percent in 1976–78, 35.7 percent in 1979, and 35.8 percent in 1980–81), an acceleration of inflation followed. As a result, although the real effective exchange rate depreciated 17.2 percent between the last quarter of 1979 and the last quarter of 1980, the acceleration of domestic inflation ate up a substantial part of this real devaluation in the following quarters. In spite of a large nominal devaluation, on a yearly average the real effective exchange rate *appreciated* 4.6 percent between 1980 and 1982.

The new government that was inaugurated in September 1980 strengthened the adjustment effort by introducing a set of structural reforms aimed at dismantling the regulations that were constraining the capacity of the Korean economy to adjust to the new external and internal environments. These changes hinged on a recognition that the Korean economy had become too large and complex to depend on government planning. There was also an emerging consensus among policymakers that Korea needed increasingly to rely on stronger domestic competition to improve efficiency in resource allocation and equity in income distribution.

As part of these reforms the government introduced efforts to increase foreign competition and curtail restrictive domestic trade practices. Among the first reforms to be implemented was a preannounced program of trade liberalization: the proportion of freely importable items rose from 61 percent of all importables at the end of 1978 to 75.5 percent at the end of 1981, 81.2 percent at the end of 1983, and 85.1 at the end of 1984. The government also enacted the Fair Trade and Anti-Monopoly Act in April 1981, which eliminated cartel arrangements and price fixing and relaxed foreign investment regulations. It also initiated a move toward financial deregulation.

The economic results of Korea's adjustment program were very encouraging. In the period 1981–85 GNP growth averaged 7.8 percent a year, and wholesale price index (WPI) inflation averaged only 1.7 percent a year. In 1986 the current account moved into a substantial surplus equal to 4.9 percent of GNP.

Most of the progress toward stabilization was accomplished beginning in 1982. A drastic reduction in the rate of increase in the won price of imported raw materials contributed to a sharp decrease in inflation. The drop in the rate of inflation, a more moderate monetary policy, and a sustained tight fiscal policy contributed to a deceleration in wage increases and a further reduction in inflation. By 1983 WPI inflation was below 2 percent a year, while GNP deflator inflation was in the 3 to 4 percent range.

The chapters in this volume have explored specific aspects of the successful adjustment programs of the Korean economy. In chapter 13 Whang explored how the program for stabilization and adjustment was designed and implemented. In Whang's view, by the late 1970s a group of technocrats came to the conclusion that continuation of the expansionist and widespread government intervention policies of the 1970s was causing accelerating inflation and becoming a major obstacle to future growth. Whang believes that the announcement of the Comprehensive Measures for Economic Stabilization (CMES) program was a turning point in the direction of economic policy. The CMES included measures to control the growth in the money supply, to limit further investment in the heavy and chemical industries, to decontrol prices, and to initiate trade liberalization.

The CMES had to be drastically altered following the second oil shock and the political crisis associated with the assassination of President Park. It was left to President Doo-Hwan Chun to initiate a major stabilization and structural adjustment effort. Members of the economic team played a large role in convincing President Chun of the importance of stabilizing the economy and decreasing government intervention. The adjustment effort could not have been carried out successfully without the president's strong support. In the initial years the government played a central role in the process by reducing the public sector deficit, issuing suggested guidelines for economywide wage increases, and setting low scheduled raises for the salaries of public employees.

In chapter 2 Suh examined the evolution of Korea from a historical perspective. For this purpose, he studied four periods: the years of abundance, 1953–61; the period of trade promotion, 1962–71; the period of extensive government intervention, 1972–79; and the years of adjustment, 1980–86.

A major question taken up in chapters 3 and 4 was how Korea managed to reduce the current account deficit while achieving a substantial rate of growth in output. Corbo and Nam found, in chapter 3, that the recovery of the Korean economy in the early 1980s, with its sharp reduction in the current account deficit–GNP ratio, was made possible by appropriate macroeconomic policies and by a favorable external environment. The latter included improvements in the terms of trade, the recovery of the U.S. economy, and the decline in international interest rates. The authors emphasized how remarkable it is that, despite a high rate of productivity growth in tradables, Korea was still able to keep the real effective exchange rate fairly stable over the past fifteen years, with the exception of the years of crisis in the late 1970s.

In chapter 4, Dornbusch and Park identified four main factors as the causes of the 1979–81 crisis: a series of bad years for agriculture, the real appreciation, unforeseeable external shocks, and domestic policy mistakes and uncertainties. To explain the remarkable success of Korea's adjustment, they presented six complementary explanations: an improved external environment after 1982, inventory decumulation of imported materials and shifts in the composition of imports, a large increase in savings, favorable wage and exchange rate policies, a shift in the composition of expenditures toward domestic goods, and appropriate monetary and fiscal policies.

Dornbusch and Park also concluded (as did Corbo and Nam) that compared with other developing countries, Korea did not make major exchange rate mistakes. It could be added that it also avoided making a real interest rate mistake in the 1980s by returning to positive but moderate real rates. This stability of macroeconomic incentives in the form of real exchange rate and real interest rate stability is a principal difference between Korea's macroeconomic framework and those of the developing countries.

When examining inflation, Corbo and Nam concluded in chapter 5 that significant factors in the control of inflation were the collapse in the international price of imported raw materials and the slowdown in the rate of nominal devaluation following the change in macroeconomic stance to more moderate fiscal and monetary policies. It is important to note that while inflation was decelerating, the real effective exchange rate depreciated. Indeed, most of the real depreciation was achieved when Korea was making the most progress with its stabilization program. (The real devaluation between 1981 and 1985 was 15 percent.)

With respect to structural policies, Cho and Cole argued in chapter 6 that the financial sector played an important part in the buildup of the crisis of the late 1970s, as well as in the successful adjustment in the 1980s. In the second half of the 1970s the government used the banking system to provide direct financing at negative real interest rates and to guarantee foreign financing of investment in the heavy and chemical industries. This financial policy crowded small producers and exporters of light manufactures out of the financial market. In addition, the excessive investment in the heavy and chemical industries encouraged by the financial policy was a main factor leading to the crisis of the late 1970s.

In the first half of the 1980s the financial system grew dramatically, mainly because of the explosive expansion of nonbank financial institutions (NFBIS) such as investment and insurance companies and of the direct markets for corporate bonds and commercial paper. The NBFIS played a central role, through financial intermediation, in financing the expanding sectors that made possible the high rate of growth of the Korean economy. As a result of the deregulation of the interest rates for commercial and corporate bonds and the restraints on the growth of bank credit, the NBFIS, which had no ceilings on the mobilization of funds, were able to expand rapidly and fill the intermediate ground between the banks and unregulated financial institutions. They have been the main form of financial deregulation.

Korea proceeded slowly with the deregulation of the banking system, where the principal constraint was the weak financial position of commercial banks, which were burdened with a large share of nonperforming loans. Until that problem is solved, Korea will have to continue living with a segmented financial system that embodies a dynamic nonbanking sector and a passive banking sector. Nevertheless, a very important reform in the financial sector was instituted—the return to positive real interest rates.

With regard to the agricultural sector, Song and Ryu noted in chapter 7 that one of the major reforms was adjustment of the support prices for farms, a measure that resulted in a substantial reduction in the deficit of the Grain Management Fund. Because the deficit had been financed directly by the central bank, it had been an important source of money expansion. The government reduced the Fund's deficit by lowering the fixed price support for producers. Thus, while the purchase price of rice grew at an average annual rate of 19.1 percent in 1979–82, it rose at an average annual rate of only 3.3 percent in 1983–85.

The Korean government had traditionally provided the agricultural sector with significant protection from import competition: the effective rate of protection in 1978 was 57.0 percent, substantially above the economywide average of 43.1 percent (Nam 1985). In addition, the government had subjected a large number of agricultural commodities to nontariff import restrictions through the requirement of prior approval of import requests. From 1978 through 1985, however, the level of import liberalization increased, reaching 63.6 percent in 1985.

To minimize the distributional effects of the reduction in the subsidies for grain production, beginning in 1983 the government pursued a farm management diversification policy. The main purpose was to encourage a change in output mix from food grains to higher-value products such as livestock, fruits, and vegetables. Korea, however, needs to guard against the common mistake of pursuing import substitution policies to excess. Another more promising avenue for increasing the income of rural households is the development of off-farm sources. This approach could be an important factor in the case of Korea, where the share of off-farm income in the total income of farm households was only 35.5 percent in 1980, whereas the same ratio was 80 percent for Japan and 73.6 for Taiwan.

To promote the generation of off-farm job opportunities in rural areas, in the second half of the 1970s the Korean government initiated a set of policies to encourage rural industrialization. These programs were not very successful, however, because the development of rural industry faced the standard problems of insufficient infrastructure, limited availability of skilled labor, difficult access to capital markets, and long distances to markets. To overcome some of these shortcomings, the Farm Household Income Source Law of 1983 promoted the concept of industrial parks. It is too early to evaluate the effect of this policy.

In chapter 8 Young reviewed import liberalization policies. In the 1960s and 1970s Korea achieved a high rate of growth with a very dynamic export sector operating in close to free trade conditions and a protected import-competing sector whose growth was limited by the small domestic market. This dual industrial structure started to create difficulties for the export sector, however, as export industries became more vertically integrated.

In 1978 the government initiated an import liberalization policy. The number of items not subject to previous import approval was increased, and import tariffs were slightly reduced. Young investigated the scope and effects of this import liberalization policy and found that it did not have a major effect on industrial adjustment. Although the program liberalized discretionary import licensing of manufactures, this change took place in the presence of relatively high tariffs and was accompanied by instruments to provide contingency protection when import penetration became too high. Thus, the program retained a high level of protection and made it easy to postpone import liberalization. Not surprisingly, Young concluded that, in general, the program had limited effects, and the government needed to address the problem of the adjustment of highly protected import-competing firms. Because most of these protected sectors were producers of consumer goods, the reduction of protection would have had important favorable effects on consumers' welfare.

At the same time, Young found that the program was more successful in liberalizing upstream heavy industry products. This process improved the international competitiveness of the downstream products and promoted intraindustry international specialization in heavy industry. He also found that the gradual approach provided a credible sense of the direction of the reforms.

An important step in Korea's adjustment program was the move away from a government-led economy toward a market economy. A major reform in this direction was the Fair Trade and Anti-Monopoly Act of April 1981. In chapter 9, Lee, Urata, and Choi evaluated the change in industrial organization during Korea's adjustment. They found that when measured in shipments, the market share in manufacturing of the top 100 firms in the 1970s increased steadily to reach 46.8 percent in 1982. This increase in concentration came about despite a substantial rise in the number of firms. The authors attributed most of the increase to the government's promotion of large firms in the heavy and chemical industries.

The increasingly monopolistic and oligopolistic market structure of Korean manufacturing was even more pronounced in the case of commodities. The twenty leading business groups (*jaebuls*) increased their share of total shipments continuously from 1974 on, with an especially sharp rise between the late 1970s and early 1980s. In employment, the share of the twenty largest groups rose in a much less pronounced fashion. The authors attributed the latter result to a capital deepening that resulted from the large financial subsidies discussed in chapter 6.

The government undertook a series of piecemeal measures in 1979 and 1980 to limit further economic concentration, but it was only after the stabilization program had been in place that the government passed, in April 1981, the Fair Trade and Anti-Monopoly Act. Because the act came into being at a time when Korea was struggling to control inflation, it included a clause on undue pricing activities for market-dominating firms.

The concentration of economic power in the *jaebuls* was much discussed at the time. The heavy and chemical industries were in need of restructuring following the sharp recession of 1980, however, and the government was concerned that any regulation restricting conglomerate integration could jeopardize their survival, so it moved very slowly in trying to curtail their power.

Changes in industrial organization policy usually take a long time to have a visible effect on market structure. In the case of Korea, however, all signs indicated that the degree of concentration started to decrease. The vigorous indoctrination in fair trade principles and energetic implementation of relevant laws contributed to enhancing the degree of competition in the market. Assuming that the opening-up of the import-competing sectors continues, foreign competition will mitigate industrial concentration in many sectors.

In chapter 10, Castañeda and Park investigated the role of the labor market in the adjustment of the Korean economy. One of the most interesting aspects of the recent adjustment is that, despite the second oil shock and recession of 1980, the needed reduction in real wages was accommodated with only a small increase in unemployment and minor labor disruptions. The authors found that the sharp rise in real wages in the second half of the 1970s was largely caused by an overheating of the labor market in response to the expansionary demand policies. The adjustment program of the 1980s brought only a small increase in unemployment. The authors concluded that this was attributable to the coincidence that when growth in employment was slowing, the rate of expansion of the labor force was decreasing considerably because of a reduction in population growth and expansion of educational enrollment.

The real wage realignment in the initial years of the adjustment was facilitated by a bonus system that introduced great flexibility in nominal wages and facilitated the countercyclical wage adjustment. The lack of a major disruption while the adjustment was taking place helped to maintain the very high rate of increase in productivity during the adjustment period. The resulting slowdown in the rate of change of the unit labor cost contributed to the success of the stabilization effort.

The second oil shock came at a time when a macroeconomic crisis was unfolding in Korea. Rotemberg and Hong investigated Korea's adjustment of its energy policy to this shock and its macroeconomic effects in chapter 11. Because most of Korea's energy is imported, its principal energy policy involved pricing. The authors found that, in general, Korea made use of taxes on energy to cushion domestic energy prices against fluctuations in world prices, but that it resorted to this tax much less than the average oil-importing country. Following the first oil shock, as the foreign price quadrupled, the internal price tripled. After the second oil shock, however, both the internal and foreign prices essentially doubled.

Because both firms and households are expected to base their decisions concerning energy use on expected prices, Rotemberg and Hong argued that a policy of postponing an increase in the domestic prices of energy following an increase in international prices could be expected to have only limited effects on energy consumption. A benefit of postponing energy price increases is that the increases are associated with significant macroeconomic dislocations. A supply shock arising from an energy price increase simultaneously raises prices and slows overall economic activity. These negative effects usually result from the rigidity of other prices and wages, a factor that impedes the needed fall in real wages and in the relative price of nonenergy products. The more flexible these relative prices are, the smaller the gains from postponing the increase in domestic energy prices.

Energy policies in Korea also included promotion of alternative energy sources and a nonprice measure, energy conservation. Conservation involved government financial and educational campaigns and energy audits geared to the dissemination of information on conservation.

Rotemberg and Hong compared three pricing options: a complete pass-through of international price changes; a one-year postponement of international price changes; and a gradual increase at a constant percentage rate, with the adjustment completed in four years. Considering the effects of these alternative options on the present value of GNP and its effect on energy imports, they concluded that the policy of gradualism had little to recommend it and that adjustment should have involved a complete pass-through or only a short postponement. Given that the Korean labor market is fairly flexible, as found in chapter 10, a rapid pass-through of increases in the international price of energy was appropriate. Korea's policy was very close to a full pass-through in two years, a stance that had much to recommend it.

In chapter 12, Suh and Yeon examined social welfare during Korea's adjustment. They found evidence that the adjustment had a negative effect on social welfare in the short run but that in the medium term the average level of welfare improved. The chapter also suggested that Korea was able to sustain a steady rise in social expenditures, even during the period of fiscal restraint. Suh and Yeon attributed an important role in the improvement of social welfare to the stabilization and liberalization reforms. Price stabilization seems to have had its most beneficial effect on urban wage and salary earners, who witnessed a steady rise in their real income following the successful stabilization. Moreover, stabilization diminished the opportunities for financial and real estate speculation that usually contributes to a deterioration in the distribution of income.

Lessons from Korea's Adjustment

When the adjustment program of Korea is compared with the framework for adjustment presented earlier in this chapter, it is clear that the sequence of the adjustment effort was well designed. The macroeconomic adjustment undertaken in the 1979–82 period laid the foundation for the sharp recovery that followed. The restrictive monetary and fiscal policies of the post-1982 period, together with the flexible exchange rate policy, resulted in a reduction in the current account deficit from 8.7 percent of GNP in 1980 to only 1.1 percent in 1985 and to a surplus of 2.8 percent in 1986. At the same time Korea achieved a 15 percent real depreciation between 1981 and 1985 and a slowdown of annual inflation from 25.6 percent (for the GNP deflator) in 1980 to only 3.6 percent in 1985. A favorable external environment in the form of a sharp gain in the terms of trade, a drop in international interest rates, and the recovery in the U.S. economy also contributed to favorable macroeconomic performance. After 1982 Korea returned to the macroeconomic policies that had proved so successful in the previous two decades: a stable and competitive real effective exchange rate, a small public sector deficit, and low inflation. Stabilization as a precondition for successful structural adjustment is a recommendation that is also made by the World Bank (1990).

In structural reform, much progress was made in reducing the import restrictions and relaxing the credit rationing and price controls that had been introduced to encourage the import-competing heavy and chemical industries. As a result of the credit rationing scheme of the late 1970s, export-oriented sectors had been crowded out of the financial markets. With the reduction of this bias, access to credit was improved for other sectors of the economy, particularly export-oriented light manufacturing. Similarly, the expansion of nonbanking financial intermediaries improved the functioning of the financial markets. The government made progress in diminishing industrial concentration, reducing some of the distortions in agriculture and liberalizing both the trade regime and domestic financial markets. Progress in these areas, however, was much more modest than that achieved in the realignment of the basic macroeconomic variables.

Another area where policy actions facilitated the adjustment was the quick pass-through of the changes in international oil prices. The pricing of oil at international prices supported conservation and avoided waste.

When comparing Korea with most of the highly indebted countries that are struggling to adjust, important lessons can be found. First, Korea either avoided major disequilibrium in the most important macroeconomic variables or, where disequilibria emerged, as in the early 1980s, faced them right away. In the post-1964 period, the real effective exchange rate, with an index of 100 in 1980, fluctuated from a minimum of 93.0 in 1968 to a maximum of 127.1 in 1973. Real interest rates for the banking sector, although they fluctuated between positive and negative values, rarely reached the two-digit level. The public sector deficit was kept fairly modest. Prudent financial management resulted in low inflation. Not unrelated to long-term macroeconomic stability, capital flows were used to finance investment rather than consumption and capital flight. When Korea abandoned some of these policies in the second half of the 1970s, macroeconomic performance suffered, and a macroeconomic crisis developed that was similar to that faced by many Latin American countries today. Once the crisis emerged, however, a serious stabilization program was put in place.

Second, most of the current account adjustment in Korea came from an expansion of exports; in the highly indebted countries, the general pattern was a sharp reduction in imports and a slowdown in growth. Viewed from a different angle, the reduction in the current account deficit in Korea was accomplished with only a small reduction in the investment-GNP ratio, so that future growth was protected. This approach was possible, in part, because continuous access to international capital markets was maintained even after the international debt crisis developed. This access was facilitated by a proven export potential and the decisive actions taken to solve the macroeconomic crisis.

Third, for a long time Korea maintained a set of policies that provided incentives to make production for exports much more profitable than production for the domestic market. As the economy became more industrialized and more advanced, conflicts between the continuous protection of import-competing activities and an active export sector increased. In response, import liberalization was advanced in the early 1980s to support further expansion of the export sector.

Fourth, the labor markets in Korea were much more competitive and labor mobility much higher than in most other developing countries. In contrast, most Latin American countries are characterized by very restrictive wage and hiring practices that make any adjustment requiring labor reallocation and changes in real wages a very difficult task. In the case of Korea, after an initial drop in the first two years of adjustment (1980–81), real wages started to recover in 1982, achieving an annual growth rate of 7.6 percent during 1981–85. At the same time that real wages were growing, Korea was able to achieve a real depreciation. A large increase in productivity growth made growth in real wages possible together with a real devaluation. In the typical highly indebted country, a real depreciation has been associated with a sharp drop in real wages. The combination of real depreciation and a sharp increase in real wages was possible in Korea because of the gains in the terms of trade and the successful macroeconomic adjustment, which resulted in a large increase in labor productivity.

The most important lessons that emerge from Korea's recent experience, however, are the importance of not letting the key macroeconomic variables—the real effective exchange rate, real interest rate, public sector deficit, and real wages—get too far out of line, and the maintenance of a system of incentives that provides exporters with a competitive and stable real exchange rate that allows them to make long-term plans.

Note

1. For infant industries, a timetable for the reduction of protection over, for example, a five-year period should be adhered to (see Balassa 1976; Bell and Ross-Larson 1984). For countries with export earnings derived from products based on natural resources, it is appropriate and accepted that windfall gains be taxed during commodity booms and that rebates be offered to producers during troughs (see Davis 1983).

References

Balassa, Bela. 1976. "Reforming the System of Incentives in Developing Countries." *World Development* 3(6):365–82.

Bell, Martin, and Bruce Ross-Larson. 1984. "Assessing the Performance of Infant Industries." *Journal of Development Economics* 16:101–28.

Bhagwati, Jagdish. 1988. "Export-Promoting Trade Strategy: Issues and Evidence." *World Bank Research Observer* 3(1):27–57.

Buiter, V. W. 1986. "Macroeconomic Responses by Developing Countries to Changes in External Conditions." NBER Working Paper 1836. Cambridge, Mass.: National Bureau of Economic Research.

Corbo, Vittorio, and Jaime de Melo. 1987. "Lessons from the Southern Cone Policy Reforms." *World Bank Research Observer* 2(2):111–42.

Corden, Warner Max. 1974. *Trade Policy and Economic Welfare.* Oxford: Clarendon.

———. 1977. *Inflation, Exchange Rates, and the World Economy.* Chicago, Ill.: University of Chicago Press.

Davis, J. M. 1983. "The Economic Effects of Windfall Gains in Export Earnings, 1975–1978." *World Development* 11(2):119–39.

Dornbusch, Rudiger. 1980. *Open Economy Macroeconomics.* New York: Basic Books.

———. 1985. "External Debt, Budget Deficits and Disequilibrium Exchange Rates." In Gordon W. Smith and John T. Cuddington, eds., *International Debt and the Developing Countries.* Washington, D.C.: World Bank.

Edwards, Sebastian. 1985. "The Order of Liberalization of the External Sector: An Analysis Based on the Southern Cone Experience." Department of Economics, University of California at Los Angeles.

Fischer, Stanley. 1986a. *Indexing, Inflation, and Economic Policy.* Cambridge, Mass: MIT Press.

———. 1986b. "Issues in Medium-Term Macroeconomic Adjustment." *World Bank Research Observer* 1(2):163–82.

Frenkel, Jacob. 1982. "The Order of Economic Liberalization: Discussion." In Karl Brunner and A. H. Meltzer, eds., *Economic Policy in a World of Change.* Amsterdam: North-Holland.

———. 1983. "Panel Discussion on the Southern Cone." *IMF Staff Papers* 30(1):164–84.

———. 1987. "Discussion of Economic Growth and Economic Policy by Stanley Fischer." In Vittorio Corbo, Morris Goldstein, and Mohsin Khan, eds., *Growth-Oriented Adjustment Programs.* Washington, D.C.: International Monetary Fund and World Bank.

Krueger, A. O. 1978. *Foreign Trade Regimes and Economic Development: Liberalization Attempts and Consequences.* Cambridge, Mass.: Ballinger.

———. 1981. "Interactions between Inflation and Trade Objectives in Stabilization Programs." In W. R. Cline and Sidney Weintraub, eds., *Economic Stabilization in Developing Countries.* Washington, D.C.: Brookings Institution.

————. 1984. "Problems of Liberalization." In Arnold Harberger, ed., *World Economic Growth.* San Francisco, Calif.: Institute for Contemporary Studies.

————. 1985. "How to Liberalize a Small Open Economy." In Michael Connolly and John McDermott, eds., *The Economics of the Caribbean Basin.* New York: Praeger.

Little, Ian, Tibor Scitovsky, and Maurice Scott. 1970. *Industry and Trade in Some Developing Countries.* London: Oxford University Press.

McKinnon, R. 1982. "The Order of Economic Liberalization: Lessons from Chile and Argentina." In Karl Brunner and A. H. Meltzer, eds., *Economic Policy in a World of Change.* Amsterdam: North-Holland.

Mussa, Michael. 1986. "Macroeconomic Policy and Trade Liberalization: Some Guidelines." *World Bank Research Observer* 2(1):61–78.

Nam, C. H. 1985. "Trade Policy and Economic Development in Korea." Discussion Paper no. 9. Seoul: Korea University.

Sachs, J. D. 1987. "Trade and Exchange Rate Policies in Growth-Oriented Adjustment Programs." In Vittorio Corbo, Morris Goldstein, and Mohsin Khan, eds., *Growth-Oriented Adjustment Programs.* Washington, D.C.: International Monetary Fund and World Bank.

Westphal, Larry. 1978. "Republic of Korea's Experience with Export-Led Industrial Development." *World Development* 6(3):347–82.

World Bank. 1990. *Adjustment Lending Policies for Sustainable Growth.* Policy and Research Report 14. Washington, D.C.

Yeager, L. B. 1981. *Experiences with Stopping Inflation.* Washington, D.C.: American Enterprise Institute.

Postscript

IN THE PERIOD FROM 1986 TO 1990 Korea experienced further profound changes, both economic and political. In 1989 it was clear that the economy was again at a critical stage, and many people began to fear that Korea would be unable to sustain stable economic growth. The causes of these changes were, again, both internal and external. Although events since 1986 cannot be discussed in detail here—the cutoff for this study is 1986—it is important to take brief note of what happened in the latter half of the 1980s.

External conditions continued to be an important factor in Korea's economy in the second half of the 1980s, particularly world demand and exchange rates among the major currencies, which affect exports; oil prices, which affect imports; and world interest rates, which affect payments on foreign debt. Until 1989 external conditions were very favorable—oil prices dropped 21 percent, the yen appreciated 14 percent a year, and world interest rates were moderate. World demand for Korean exports, which are highly elastic to changes in that demand, grew rapidly and continued to be the engine of growth for the economy. The growth in exports spurred more domestic investment and consumption and thus increased imports. Korea's economy grew by over 12 percent a year, and the current account ran a surplus. By the end of 1988, Korea's external debt had fallen by $16 billion to reach $31.2 billion. The rate of saving rose substantially in 1986–87 and modestly in 1988, although only because of government saving, since private consumption outpaced private saving. By 1988 the gross domestic saving rate reached 37.7 percent of GDP.

In the face of the strong growth in GDP, labor demanded large wage increases and carried out frequent work stoppages. After 1987 wages rose at 20 percent a year. In general, the social and political reforms of the early 1980s were changing the pattern of economic development. The pledge of democratization of June 1987 exacerbated tensions among groups with conflicting interests: besides the demands of labor, farmers were opposing liberalization of the market for agricultural products, the role of large conglomerates in the economy was being criticized, and the wealthy were being questioned about the sources of their wealth.

During this period the government's macroeconomic policy emphasized a reduction in both the current account surplus and inflation, which was rising because of the strong growth of GNP and the wage increases. The government pursued a reduction in the current account surplus by increasing expenditures and by switching expenditures, with appreciation of the exchange rate and trade liberalization (opening of the domestic market) playing important roles. The significant improvement in the terms of trade left a robust current account despite the efforts to reduce it.

Beginning in 1989, the picture changed. World conditions were no longer as favorable—oil prices rose 14 percent over the previous year, while the yen depreciated against the U.S. dollar by 19 percent and the won appreciated by 5 percent over the end of 1988 (annualized rates). Exacerbating the less favorable world environment was a significant decline in Korean competitiveness caused by the higher cost of labor, a slowing in the growth of productivity, and the appreciation of the won. In the first half of 1989 the unit labor cost rose 39 percent in dollar terms in the face of a rise in nominal wages of 24 percent, a drop in the growth of productivity of 3 percent, and the appreciation of the won in relation to the dollar. Inflation also rose. Up to the third quarter of 1989, investment in machinery and equipment registered a relatively low rise of 9.7 percent. In contrast, private domestic consumption rose by 10 percent, merchandise imports by 11 percent. About the only positive note was that interest rates declined a little.

In light of these conditions, GNP growth fell to 6.5 percent, while the current account surplus shrank to 2.7 percent of GNP compared with 12 percent the previous year. The volume of exports was expected to fall 6.5 percent for the year. With the expansion in domestic demand, the current account surplus decreased substantially.

In response to these conditions, and particularly since 1988, the government adopted restrictive fiscal and monetary policies to prevent further expansion. Even with these policies, however, the volume of exports declined significantly. The business community responded to the rapid contraction in exports by complaining about the exchange rate and monetary and fiscal policies the government had adopted in response to U.S. pressure. They claimed that Korea was headed for a "hard landing." In this period the government also kept the budget deficit under control, recording a surplus of 1.3 percent of nominal GNP in 1988. This pattern was to be expected, because Korea's fiscal policy has generally been countercyclical.

The challenge for Korea now is to maintain the economic stability and high growth of the second half of the 1980s in a democratic society. The economic developments of the late 1980s indicate that the pressure to increase domestic demand will result in a smaller current account surplus and will create inflationary pressures. The large current account surplus in the period 1986–88 was, as noted, taken care of by the large expansion in domestic demand. The task for the 1990s will be to keep inflation low while accommodating that expansion in domestic demand.

Index

Adelman, Irma, 303 n2

Aghevli, B. B., 66 n2, 113 n1, 305

Agricultural sector: credit reforms and, 147–48; crop failures in, 24, 37, 41, 76, 172, 311, 335; effect of urbanization on, 148, 158; employment in, 229, 233–34, 235, 237–38; fertilizer subsidy and, 148; government intervention in, 138–58; incomes in, 146–47; investment and loans to, 17, 141, 144–45; land reform in, 10; on- and off-farm income policy for, 28, 154–58, 162–63, 167, 340; performance of, 14, 16, 41, 138, 140, 146–49, 167–68; policy reform alternatives for, 163–67; price supports and, 16, 138, 139–40, 142–43, 148–49; productivity policy for, 151–54; product price changes in, 112; protection for, 139, 159–60, 339–40; self-sufficiency policy for, 141, 149, 158–59, 163–64, 167, 168; technological change in, 7, 140, 144–45, 148; terms of trade in, 235, 237–38. *See also* Commodity market

Ahn, Byoung-Hun, 264

Ahn, Choong Young, 163–64

Ahn, In-Chan, 160, 164–65

Anderson, Kym, 139, 153–54, 159–61, 162, 163, 164–65, 166, 169 nn2–4

Antimonopoly policy, 28, 212–14, 222, 337, 341

Ashenfelter, Orley, 268

Aukrust, Odd, 100

Balance of payments: capital account in, 73, 116, 134–35; contribution of investment and savings to, 83–86; current account in, 4, 15, 20, 25, 29, 36, 38, 44, 50, 51, 73–74, 76, 79–80, 97, 168, 176, 178, 329, 348–49; effect of oil price shocks on, 69; hypotheses regarding successful adjustment in,

80–91; invisible trade account in, 72–73, 79–80

Balassa, Bela, 45, 66 n4, 88, 332, 345 n1

Ban, Sung-Hwan, 282

Banking system: deregulation of, 339; and development policy, 122–23; financial investment by, 115; partial privatization of, 24, 27, 115, 175, 212, 298

Barnett, H. G., 323 n8

Beckerman, Wilfred, 97

Bell, Martin, 345 n1

Bhagwati, Jagdish, 334

Black market, 20, 33 n20, 36

Bond market, 119, 122–24, 133

Borrowing, domestic. *See* Credit system

Borrowing, foreign, 18, 21, 22, 73, 115, 125–26, 328. *See also* Debt, external

Braverman, Avishay, 163–64

Bruno, Michael, 101

Budget deficit, 18, 26, 49–50, 90–91, 98, 99, 349

Buiter, V. W., 333

Buiter, W. H., 66 n5

Business groups (*jaebuls*): expansion of, 207–09, 224 n2, 282, 341; impact of, 223; and monopoly regulation, 212–13

Business sector: financial structure and performance of, 125–33; role in economic policy of, 318–20

Cagan-Nerlove adaptive expectations model, 65

Calmfors, Lars, 100

Capital: accumulation of, 42; cost of, 125–26; foreign, 12, 73; rate of return on, 130, 133

Capital account, 72–73, 75, 116, 134–35

Capital flight (absence of), 74–75